Nick Fowler is a child of the sixties, a lover of music, fine wine and the written word. He found himself one day running 26 miles in the New York marathon to the next being diagnosed with MS and ultimately unable to run 26 millimetres. That set him on a journey to discover the meaning of life.

Dedicated to my father, Robert Desmond Fowler, checked out of the hotel on Monday 19th May at 4 am, after 90 years, staying in the hotel, leaving my mother sitting with her suitcases in reception.

Nick Fowler

LIFE IS A HOTEL

AUSTIN MACAULEY PUBLISHERS
LONDON * CAMBRIDGE * NEW YORK * SHARJAH

Copyright © Nick Fowler 2025

The right of Nick Fowler to be identified as author of this work has been asserted by the author in accordance with sections 77 and 78 of the Copyright, Designs and Patents Act 1988.

All rights reserved. No part of this publication may be reproduced, stored in a retrieval system, or transmitted in any form or by any means, electronic, mechanical, photocopying, recording, or otherwise, without the prior permission of the publishers.

Any person who commits any unauthorised act in relation to this publication may be liable to criminal prosecution and civil claims for damages.

A CIP cataglogue record for this title is available from the British Library.

ISBN 9781035886623 (Paperback)
ISBN 9781035886630 (ePub e-book)

www.austinmacauley.com

First Published 2025
Austin Macauley Publishers Ltd®
1 Canada Square
Canary Wharf
London
E14 5AA

Table of Contents

Chapter 1: Planning Permission	9
Chapter 2: Room-Only or Self-Catering	31
Chapter 3: Dying to Leave	51
Chapter 4: Where To?	72
Chapter 5: Look at the View from the Balcony	97
Chapter 6: Arrival	123
Chapter 7: What Shall We Do in the Last Few Days?	145
Chapter 8: Which Flaw Are You On?	159
Chapter 9: Lost Property	183
Chapter 10: Changeover Day	203
Chapter 11: Housekeeping	231
Chapter 12: Have You Signed the Guestbook?	263
Chapter 13: Let's Look at the Photos!	294
Chapter 14: Would You Go There Again?	312
Chapter 15: I'll Settle the Bill!	345

Chapter 1
Planning Permission

Great to meet you, my fellow guest, it's really great to be staying here at the same time as you and, just before we start, let me say, do you realise how lucky are we, not only to be here, because the odds against us checking into the hotel individually in the first place are huge, but for you and I to be staying here at the same time? Well, the chances of that are virtually incalculable, so let us feel grateful for our good fortune; let us enjoy the experience and then discover together why life is a hotel!

I sincerely hope that you are enjoying your stay as much as I am enjoying mine and maybe we can look forward to bumping into each other around this place somewhere, in the future. In the meantime, enjoy your stay and let's share a little time together, if not in each other's company, then in thought at least.

It struck me that, seeing as I had both the time and the inclination, I would take the opportunity to consider what it's all about—the meaning of life, why are we here, what's the point, questions like that, those simple questions which, if I think about them for too long, seem impossible to answer, because there are no answers—none that are evidentially provable at least. That may see me allowing a little self-doubt to creep in, self-doubt which makes me ask myself the most obvious question—why am I writing this book? Because if there are no answers, which currently there aren't, but let's just say there are answers, then how in the world am I qualified to know what those answers are, little old me? But it is the very fact that nobody knows definitively what those answers are that emboldens me; yes, of course, there are lots of opinions, I've got a few of my own, but to this day, what remains the most amazing thing to me is that nobody, no matter how well qualified or totally unqualified, actually knows.

So here we go, for those of you who are interested is my opinion, if and whatever conclusions I do manage to come up with within these pages, there isn't a single person who can tell me, with any degree of certainty, that I am wrong. Yes, you can disagree with me all day long, indeed I would encourage debate, because that way leads to clarity and greater understanding, but to be told I am wrong is not possible. I hope in some little way to inspire you to think about things a little deeper, and by doing so, we can make some progress and come up with answers because without doubt, answers do exist, they must, so let's spend some time together considering them.

What I have always found to be baffling is that the combined brains and incredible intellect of those great thinkers who have been here before us, along with the fantastic technology that we have developed, we still cannot say with any certainty what it's all about!

When I think about it, I find it both fabulous and at the same time quite incredible to think we are all here, all sharing these times, experiencing all that our hotel has to offer, whether it be the joyous happy times that make life worth living to those unavoidable terribly sad times; we have the highs and the lows, the good as well as the bad. Although we are all currently staying in the hotel at this time, we will have very different experiences, even though we are sharing the same space. We will, of course, share many of the same experiences too, but because we are all so very different from each other, we are all individuals, that means that our interpretation of our time here and our time spent here will make it ours, a bespoke experience, one that we will own whatever we are or whatever we become; it will be our actions that will define us.

Whichever part of the hotel you are lucky enough to be staying in at the moment, I think you will agree that this place is huge, it is a rather large hotel, which in itself could be construed as being a negative; in my life, I have stayed in hotels which are too big, too impersonal, so the fact that this one is so big means it could be quite overwhelming; instead of seeing it negatively, I prefer to believe that its size is a massive positive, because that means in our lifetime we should never run out of things to do, with so many different cultures, so many different climates, diverse landscapes and incredible cuisines, there are remote places for those who prefer to spend time alone or for those who want to party every night.

There are fabulous spaces to explore, some incredible food experiences, wonderful music, beautiful art along with so many great people, so many of your fellow guests to meet and spend time with, while you are staying here. Each and every one of those people that we meet along the way will be going through exactly the same emotions as you and I and they are all striving to make their stay in the hotel as pleasurable as possible.

During your own time here, for however long it may last and not forgetting that once we have checked in, each of us will have a different length of stay, there are no guarantees; it could be longer or possibly shorter than you want or need, in order to fit everything in that you would want to, but once we have checked in at reception, we have a rough idea of how long we will be staying here. As a rough guide and in this instance for totally non-religious reasons, we have the Bible, which tells us that three score years and ten is a man's average life expectancy, which equates to a life lasting seventy years, which should be long enough to fit in all of those things that you would want to do during your stay.

While we are here, there will be times that you want to get out to explore and look around the place, seeing all that the hotel and grounds surrounding it have to offer; conversely, there may also be times that you don't want to do anything, just stay in your room and chill.

Those of you who may have been here a little bit longer than the rest of us, those who are possibly coming towards the end of their stay, people who have been staying here longer than I have myself, right through to those who may have arrived here fairly recently—we are all here at the same time and because of that, I believe we should get through our stay together and try to make our stay as enjoyable as possible, for all of us here at this time.

In the words of the fabulous Canadian rock band Trooper from their single released in 1977: *We are here for a good time (not a long time)*. I am a big music fan and although like most of you I had heard the expression, we are here for a good time, not a long time, I never realised that the band Trooper had actually encapsulated the expression into a song. The song is worth a listen, if you know the style, it is a typical 80's track, lots of rock band, big hair and dry ice going on and after discovering this song, it is now on my holiday playlist. Trooper may have sung the song in all innocence, but according to a good friend of mine and with the advent of dating websites, apparently the expression—we are here for a good time, not a long time—has taken on a whole new meaning.

For those of you intrigued enough to want to know more, apparently it refers to people who are on these websites who use the term as code for them looking for a casual sexual relationship and nothing else, so don't say I didn't tell you. However, that sounds like a whole new book to me, but that is not for now; at this time we are more concerned with us all actually being here in the same hotel at the same time, all eight billion of us, which is a lot of guests for any hotel to be catering to at any one time! Moreover, there are three hundred and eighty-five thousand new people checking in at reception every single day, which equates to one hundred and forty million people a year joining us; some you will meet and get to know really well, but the massive majority of those new arrivals you will never know or even come into contact with on any level.

To make sure the hotel doesn't get too full and to counter the vast number of new daily arrivals, there are approximately one hundred and fifty thousand people every day who check out of the hotel, vacating their rooms for the final time and sitting with their suitcases in reception, waiting for their car to arrive and to leave for good. Of that one hundred and fifty thousand, two-thirds of them, which is approximately one hundred thousand people, will leave because nature takes its course and their stay has reached its natural conclusion.

However, that leaves us with the fifty thousand people who didn't necessarily want to check out and probably thought it wasn't their time to leave. There can, of course, be many reasons for checking out early, if indeed it is early, understanding that using early as a descriptor is a purely subjective term because who knows if anything is early or late, or simply at the right time? In this case, we are using the term early because we look at life expectancy as our guide and using the biblical three score years and ten, to give us an age of seventy years the average person will live.

In relation to the hotel, this would be akin to saying that for most people, the average stay in the hotel is for two weeks, which may be true, but as we know, some people will stay for a week, whereas others will be there for a long weekend or there are those that stay for just one night, so using early in this context can be a bit of a misnomer. Among the reasons for checking out early, there is a wide range which can include serious illness, suicide or accident and we can even break down those categories; within them, the actual numbers will depend on several factors such as income level as well as location—which part of the hotel you are staying in.

Location is such an important consideration when looking at longevity and it is for that reason I believe that checking out deserves a chapter of its own, because checking out of the hotel is as important as checking in to the place. Whether we are fortunate enough to stay until the potential end of our stay, or whether we check out before we are due to, one thing is guaranteed—every single one of us, wherever we are on the hotel estate and however we choose to live our lives, we will all have our very own experience.

Our lives are a tailormade journey, different in so many ways for each of us, but one which, even though at the onset of the journey, you will have no idea of what you want to see or do along the way, but you have options; for instance, you can either plan your time in minute detail or just let things take their own course, but thankfully, there is no compulsion to say at the outset what you plan to do, or even what you would like to do before you depart, before you check out and sit in reception for the final time.

Incidentally, some of our fellow guests happen to believe that when we finally depart from the hotel, although we may no longer be staying in the building, we have actually relocated to another part of the estate, something which happens once we've checked out. Whatever happens once you have left, wherever that may be, whether you believe that there is more to life than our time on earth, we will have a look. It is because our life isn't planned and we have free will, you will find yourself in places that you never thought you would go to, you will spend times with people that you never imagined you were going to meet, people who, at the start of your stay, you were totally unaware of, oblivious to their mere existence and naturally they of yours, but paths can cross in the most innocuous of ways and friendships are created that can either be momentous and momentary or they can last a lifetime.

As long as you are getting along with those people you come into contact with, whether it be those that you see daily or you meet just once during your stay in the hotel, it is a good idea to make it as enjoyable as possible. The really good thing about staying here is that, as with most hotels, you are free to do absolutely anything you choose to do, within the law, of course, the law of whichever part of the hotel you are staying in, or indeed visiting, because there can be major differences from country to country; if you choose to visit foreign countries during your stay, then though their laws may feel a little oppressive, we need to respect them.

There is a basic code of human decency and mutual respect that should exist throughout your stay, you should not find any other person trying to tell you what you can and cannot do, but that can depend on which part of the hotel you're staying in, but overall there are global standards of acceptance and expectations that we all adhere to. What can make things a little more interesting are those cultural values in varied and different locations; in spite of the peculiarities of local law, these fabulous locations only serve to add to the richness and complexity of what our whole experience has to offer. These local variations are akin to having different house rules for different parts of the hotel complex, but then you would expect to have different rules for the guests using the gymnasium to those using the bar; think about it for a moment—you wouldn't expect to see somebody going into the swimming pool fully clothed or another going for dinner in their bathing suit.

So, across the hotel, we do have societal norms wherever we go, but if we choose to visit a place where things are done a little bit differently, then, out of decency and courtesy, we adhere to the local norms. From the outset—and let me make my own position very clear, because what I am about to say is difficult to prove either way, so it's down to my opinion—I believe that every guest is here for the first time, in fact, if I was pushed a little further, I would say that it is for the one and only time. I am fully aware that there will be some of you who will believe something totally different, I have absolutely no issue with that, I would encourage debate. No doubt some of you will tell me that they have been here before, but I choose not to believe that. I would not go as far as calling you a liar, but I do find that it stretches my own levels of comprehension, I don't think people come back for a second stay; indeed, if life was an item on a bucket list, then once you've done it, that would probably be enough for anybody!

If I look at just one of the reasons that I have decided to write this book, it is not designed to be a tour guide, it is not a contribution to the philosophical debate about the meaning of life, it is just my take on what I have concluded it is all about, a conclusion reached after spending my time so far in the hotel and despite me having no religious or cultural beliefs, I have come to the conclusion that there are a few house rules that, for me at least, lend some insight into a question that feels as though it has always resonated with me—What's the point?

By no means am I trying to make this book a definitive answer to the meaning of life, it is just my own take. For me, I have come to see this book as one of those leaflets that you find in your hotel room upon arrival, sandwiched somewhere between the trouser press and the minibar, a book that gives you a list of guest services, where to go, what to see and things available to you during your stay. This book is designed to give you a little history and background to the hotel and how it has developed into what we see today from its early beginnings four and a half billion years ago to the fabulous accommodation that it provides for its eight billion guests today; just like those informative leaflets in your room, this book aims to provide you with vital information about the facilities and fabulous opportunities available to you, now that you are here and have finally checked in.

Those leaflets in the room are either something you may pick up as a casual read between having a shower and going down for dinner, or something to carry around with you for the duration of your stay as a guide to make sure you don't miss a thing while you're here, alternatively, you may totally ignore them. If you arrived here before I did, which was back in 1960, the year that I checked in at reception, then you may have learnt a bit more about this place than I have and you may have worthwhile opinions to contribute to the debate; although there are no guarantees that you are right—as with the rest of us, they are just opinions. All that I have come to believe is that everybody's opinion is as valid as those of the greatest thinkers that our planet has ever created, because although there are over eight billion of us staying here at the moment, nobody actually knows why we are here and nobody knows what, if anything, happens next once we have checked out.

The beauty of this place is that there is so much to see and do that you will never run out of things to keep you occupied or stimulate your imagination. Like any good hotel, if you have only recently arrived here then there are many ways to get some great advice on the things to do and there are plenty of fellow guests around the place to chat with. You will no doubt be sharing your formative days with people who have been staying here considerably longer than you have; more often than not, but not necessarily, those people that you spend your early days with are family and it is to those people that you can turn to for both advice and guidance. As with any good hotel, you can always ask the concierge for advice, but be aware that the first three letters of concierge are con, and to my cost I have found that any advice given is not necessarily impartial; sometimes the concierge may have an ulterior motive. The concierge or even some fellow guests you meet along the way may try to convince you that they know a bit more about this place than they really do; you should be aware that they too exist, you can bump into these people at any time, they can appear from nowhere and it won't always be obvious to you what they want from you, that is if they do want anything or nothing more than to impart their beliefs.

I have found that most people are just decent people and have no other intention than to legitimately help you have the best time possible while you're staying here. For these people, their relationship with you is symbiotic, they get a buzz from you getting a buzz and that is what life is all about. If you are, in fact, fortunate enough to have other members of your family staying here at the same time as you are, then you will know that they can be an endless source of help and support, but be under no illusion, even in the best of families, they can sometimes be a source of frustration too.

What is important to remember is that more often than not, it is those older members of your family, those who are always there to lend you support and offer guidance, it is those people who tend to check out of the hotel before you do, simply because they have been here a lot longer than you have, inevitably they leave before you will. So although you may come to rely on them, not only for their friendship, but for both the help and inspiration that they provide, sadly you must be prepared to accept that, as nice as it would be to have them here for your whole stay and to share every moment with them, it's not really possible and sadly they will not be here for all of it.

Life doesn't work that way, in most situations it is you who will ultimately replace them in helping new arrivals when they check in, as they did for you, it is you who will find yourself showing new arrivals around the place and so life goes on, guests arriving and guests departing every single day of every single week. As well as the many guests who have been here longer than I have, there will be those who have recently arrived and are possibly feeling a little overwhelmed by the size of the place, with so much to see and do you can feel spoilt for choice, you don't want to spend time doing the things that you don't enjoy, time is short, you've got to see and do it all. Never forget those inimitable words of the Trooper classic, we are not here for a long time you don't want to waste your relatively short time doing those things that you don't really enjoy doing.

There are no shortcuts and so far we have not discovered a way to fast-forward an experience that we aren't enjoying, however there will be times that you may be invited to go somewhere new or do something different that initially you really don't feel like doing or actually don't want to do, but from experience, yes of course you may be right in your assumptions, but conversely the things that you don't want to do can also provide some of your finest moments, earning a place on what will become the *Greatest Hits* album of your life. So never dismiss anything out of hand or prejudge negatively any experience, you just never know.

I hope that this book may be of help to you at any time during your stay, I intend to consider checking in, checking out and all of those times in between, when you want to spend time alone in your room, or when you find yourself having a great night in the bar! All I can suggest is that you have a read and take from it what you can, if anything! I wouldn't be arrogant enough to suggest that I have any or all of the answers, but there are questions that need to be answered and these questions have been around since day one.

Hopefully by the end of the book, you will get an idea of what to expect while you're here and possibly look at things a little bit differently. It would be a pleasure and I invite you to come along with me as I attempt to satisfy my own personal need to answer some of those questions, it feels that many of them have been a part of my life for as long as I can remember, so I've finally decided to do something about them and search for the answers.

I am not sure where my own inquisitiveness came from, or if there was ever a trigger point in my life that made me start to think, was it a television programme that I watched, a film that I went to see, a piece of music or a place that I have visited are all possibilities for igniting the desire to know more, but when I think about it, I don't believe that there was a particular time that drove me to the point where I felt I needed to have greater knowledge than I had, or whether anybody else knew for that matter, at that point I was simply accepting that nobody knew.

I can think of two incredibly strong personal memories that thus far, have never disappeared from my memory and are from my own childhood; one was watching the film *The Graduate* in the early seventies and hearing Simon and Garfunkel's *Sound of Silence* lyrics that I adored immediately and stay with me to this day, as powerful, beautiful, clever and introspective. I read them and reread them, I learnt them parrot fashion and I love them. If you know the song, the *Sound of Silence* and you love this song as much as I do, yet like me have an aversion to cover versions of songs, allow me to suggest that you listen to a cover of the song by the American band, Disturbed; it is a thing of pure beauty, especially the studio version, which is available on YouTube, where you can see it performed on Conan, the American chat show hosted by Conan O'Brien.

The second indelible memory is one which I picked up when I was a little older, a time when I found myself working for Borders, an American bookstore. I do mention my Borders experience a little later in the book so will not go into too much detail here, but it was a story that I read and it immediately resonated with me, the story made me realise that life can be seen from many different perspectives and that unintentionally, but unavoidably, we are all limited by our experiences. So they are two events in my own life that have been impactful and made me think, I am sure there are many more but those two specifically have never left me. I have tried to consciously absorb things along the way, getting the most out of every moment, striving for a clearer understanding, greater insight and to that end, over the years, I have decided it is always best to do my own research.

Whenever and wherever I am or find myself on my travels, whether I am travelling away for long holidays or simple weekends or days away, I seem to have acquired an irritating knack of finding some people that I meet and feel a genuine affinity to; since I started this project, I tell them that I am writing a book, I explain as concisely as possible my theory that life is like a hotel, giving them a little more detail, and then see if they have any input, their own closely held beliefs or a contribution to make, a tweak to my theory. I will ask what their take is, what's it all about, is this it, or is there more; many people don't even think about it, too busy getting on with their lives, but whether they think about it or not, I feel it is the most interesting of questions and it usually goes something like, 'What do you think we are doing sitting in a bar in the Süd Tirol in Austria on a Thursday night talking rubbish, what is it all about?'

You can never assume where a conversation will lead, and you should never judge, because I have had some of the most interesting conversations over breakfast, or late nights in bad bars, on a ski lift going up a mountain or in the back of a taxi, indeed, last week I was chatting to a bloke who was begging. I was sitting outside Starbucks having been through the drive thru in Bradford, the next moment there was a knock on my window and there stood a bloke who looked to be a similar age to myself, although the years and the elements had not been kind to him, he asked me for money for a drink, but I sensed he wasn't going to buy a medium soy macchiato, preferring instead to buy a cheap bottle of wine or four couple of cans of lager. He had a nice manner in spite of his outward appearance, so we got into conversation about life, how had he found himself in his current lifestyle and what he thought life was all about, not the conversation either of us anticipated when he initially knocked on my car window.

We chatted for thirty minutes, he told me he wrote poetry and recited a couple of verses he had written, which I loved, it was a bitterly cold day and I shook his frozen hands. I gave him money, not as payment for his thoughts, but to help him immediately, yes I know it would only be a brief temporary relief from the nightmare he was currently living, but it was all I could do at that moment. I'm not sure whether it was to assuage my own guilt about giving him the money and the potential it had for adding to his misery, but I had the conversation with Ian and told him I had a dilemma, do I give you £20 knowing you will buy alcohol, which may give him a couple of hours respite but ultimately perpetuating his misery; or do I give him nothing, forcing him to seek relief either unsuccessfully or worse, criminally? It was a dilemma for me but I succumbed, I capitulated and gave him £20, he was happy, even if for a brief moment, we parted as temporary lifelong best friends, I will never forget him.

As I have grown older, I have come to understand that there is no definitive answer to the meaning of life and so opinions are all that count, whether it is Ian or Aristotle, all opinions are valid and so this book, for what it's worth is mine. Fashioned by extensive reading of books by other people, which always gave me other people's opinions, looking at the numerous different religious views available throughout the hotel, I would read anything and everything that I could find, all of them written by individuals, all with different life experiences and telling me what they thought. Anything that I could find to help me investigate or learn along the way was consumed, all in an attempt to discover the point of it all.

There are currently over eight billion of us, all staying here in this hotel and yes, I know it is not the simplest question to answer but it is one that does niggle away at me and I, like so many of us, would love to know the answer, because there will be one. As I have mentioned earlier and something that I do find amazing, is that there is no definitive answer, which in is incredible, if not simply because, when you consider the intelligence of those incredible brains who are currently staying here but combine them with the global intellects of those who have stayed here before us and we are talking of some supremely talented individuals, those great brains combined with the rest of us mere mortals, who may have our own thoughts, understandings or beliefs, in spite of all of these people, we still haven't stumbled over the answer, an answer that has to exist, it's just that we still haven't found it.

Of course, not everybody is concerned and understandably so, there are some people who just couldn't care less, it's sufficient for them to be getting on with the trials and tribulations of their daily lives, who needs to waste time and energy considering, how we got here, what we are doing here or what it is or is all about. At the other extreme, there are those amongst us who have made it their life's work, indeed they devote their lives trying to solve the conundrum, whether it is through their culture or religion, they are focused on greater understanding.

Given that these two extremes exist, the 'couldn't-care-less' and the 'I know the truth' are equally as valid, because who amongst us knows and can say so with any degree of certainty?

The answer, of course, is nobody, not one person can say within any degree of conviction that they know, that they have the answer, because thus far we haven't found an answer.

Although we are all on the same planet, we are staying in the same hotel, all of us experiencing the same things in our everyday lives as everybody else. Life can be incredibly difficult for some, it can be absolutely intolerable for others, pleasantly bearable for the majority and to those sybarites amongst us, the search for pleasure can be an end in itself. It is absolutely because we are all going through the process, that there is one simple question that presents itself and for me it needs to be addressed, not only addressed but answered to the satisfaction of those of us who, just like me, would like an answer, because there has to be one! Why are we all staying in the same hotel at the same time, with guests checking in and checking out and others just getting on with living their lives, is there a plan, is there a reason, is there a point?

There must be answers to these straightforward questions and it baffles me that we still haven't figured it out. Of course, there can be many different opinions to the answer, all of which tend to stay within the same constraints, we are limited by what we know and have no way of knowing what we don't know, how could we? If there is a definitive answer or maybe a simple explanation, one that is so obvious that we are all just missing it and never think that we could be missing what is right in front of very our eyes, alternatively there could be nothing, no point at all, to any of this, we are all here without consequence. Whatever you choose to believe, I thought there was an opportunity for me to write down my own thoughts, things which, despite my extensive reading, I have never read or heard from any other guest, past or present, so I am not plagiarising the thoughts of others, this is all my own work.

When I started writing and began explaining my understanding for the first time to other people, I was pleasantly surprised to be met with a lot of nodding and incredible positivity, this affirmation along with the reciprocal enthusiasm, has led me to having the confidence and requisite patience to write this book.

As I have grown older and now find myself in my sixtieth year in the hotel, my search for greater understanding and a desire and equally as important a need to know or at least search for the answer to the simplest of questions, what is the point, I feel it resonates more than ever. As I have already mentioned I have no idea what is driving this desire or need to know, I am not a great philosopher, I don't have firmly held religious beliefs, but what I do find incredible is that, we the guests as mere human beings, all of us going through this same process, of being born, where we check into the hotel at reception, live our individual lives and once our stay is over, death becomes each and every one of us, we check out, we vacate our rooms readying them for the new arrivals checking in, to repeat the process. To me the question that seems so simple, if not just an obvious one, appears to be so very hard to answer and answer definitively.

Throughout my stay here, I have been fortunate to travel extensively and once I've settled into a place, wherever that may be, once I have found myself on nodding terms with a few of the locals or fellow travellers, or even the person sitting next to me on the plane, all are fair game, let the inquisition begin, so however meandering the conversation may be I tend to find myself directing the conversation into asking the question that I want answering. Don't get me wrong I am not asking in some performative way, because I am genuinely interested in what other people think we are all doing here.

I am sure my wife can see me as a bar-room bore as she can probably sense when I am preparing to challenge my next victim, sorry, acquaintance with the eternal question, what's the point! But she has stuck with me and luckily for me we find ourselves in many obscure locations and more often than not we have a great time and some fabulous conversations, with a smattering of twaddle. I am not and am far from being a scientist, but when you consider that the earth itself is 4.5 billion years old, I find that thought staggering and virtually impossible to comprehend.

Four and a half billion is too big to contemplate and makes me feel even more insignificant than I already am. 4.5 billion years ago, what do you think the hotel was like at that time, who were the first guests, what were they like and who was it who started to build the place? Obviously, there is nobody around today who was here when the hotel opened for business, so that gives us two options when looking for answers, we can either believe the science or believe in a religion and if we do choose religion, then which one should we choose, there are many, at the last calculation and yes somebody has taken the time to calculate a definitive number and that number is currently 4,300, so with so many different beliefs, it is impossible for them all be right, so which one should you choose? If we look at what the science says, it will tell us that the earth was formed 4.5 billion years ago and that is approximately one-third of the age of the universe.

Who is calculating these numbers, they are mind bending and therefore I find them impossible to comprehend and because of that they are impossible to challenge, why not 4.4 billion or 4.6 billion years old, I realise there's a degree of approximation, but who decides? As the galaxy is older than this planet, does that mean that we are in our fabulous hotel but there are hotels around the galaxy created before this planet.

Is our hotel a part of a chain of hotels, like Holiday Inn or Malmaison, with others dotted around the universe, similar to our own and if that is the case are those other hotels that are part of the chain throughout the universe, full of other guests all having similar experiences being enjoyed by people just like us, or by possibly by different types of beings or maybe the company that owns the business, has sold up, the other hotels no longer exist and ours is the last property in the portfolio? So between twelve and fourteen billion years ago, yes that's billion, the prevailing opinion amongst a majority of scientists, not all by any means, so it is not an absolute opinion, but certainly a significant majority, tell us that there was a Big Bang, like me you will have heard the expression many times, but what does it mean.

Without trying to sound too scientific, there was a time after the Big Bang had occurred, that masses of gas and dust were thrown around in space. This was an unimaginable scale and remnants of the explosion combined with other clouds of gas and together they combined to create the galaxy. Yes, I know that is incredibly simple, but basically that's what has happened, subsequently, massive amounts of energy combined with the gas and dust, making them very hot, as they swirled about they then began to compress into small clusters, which in turn clung to other small clusters to make bigger and bigger lumps of matter. Simply calling them lumps of matter sounds a bit bonkers to me and probably adds to my lack of understanding, so in the absence of a better word, or probably a better vocabulary, I will continue with the L word. These lumps simply got larger and then began to pull themselves together, this was the effect of what we now understand as gravity.

Briefly, for those interested, although I do think it's relevant, gravity is something that still has scientists baffled. Two guests who stayed in the hotel many years ago Albert Einstein and Sir Issac Newton, two eminent scientists that even I have heard of, well they have both studied gravity and would you believe it, they came up with different theories! However after all of the theorising, nobody knows exactly how it works. Basically gravity is an invisible force, that keeps the moon in orbit around the earth and holds the planets, or as I like to see them, the other hotels in the group, orbiting around the sun, stretching the metaphor, the sun can be called head office! More importantly to the guests in the hotel it is gravity that keeps our feet firmly on the ground, something which we take for granted, but it exists and helps to make our lives possible.

Back to the lumps swirling around the galaxy, the largest of them became so dense and so hot that it became the sun! Then other lumps started to form around the sun and as they got bigger, eventually they had their own gravitational pull and became the planets as we know them today. The Earth was one of those newly formed planets and was created this way, an amalgamation of smaller lumps, all of this happening 4.5 billion years ago and then, another amazing event occurred, apparently, a planet the size of Mars bumped into the Earth, knocking a huge chunk off and that chunk would you believe, became the moon.

As we've mentioned, nobody who was around at the time is still a guest at this hotel, but it is believed that in its earliest stages the earth looked nothing like it does today, which may be stating the obvious, but all it was, was simply a big and I mean big ball of rock. There were no oceans, there wasn't an atmosphere and masses of land, joined together that looked nothing like we know the place today. It took millions of years for the earth to cool and in doing so it started to become a little bit more like we see it today, although it was far from being the finished article. Then, the earth experienced a bit of volcanic activity and along with meteors hitting the earth, piercing the surface and releasing various gases and water, which had been below the surface, this saw the oceans form and an atmosphere being created.

I did say earlier that if you wanted to look at the early stages of the hotel how it was created and what it looked like then we had two options in order for us to get a little insight, we could look at either science or religion, to consider their opinions. I don't want to make this a book about science and neither do I want it to be a book about religion. Either of the subjects can be written about by people far more qualified than I to do so and those people tend to be much more invested in those subjects and have a greater passion for them than I have ever will have. Not because I don't have an interest in either topic, but they are both so vast, that they demand years of study and understanding and even then, you can never know it all and I don't know how much nearer in either subject you would be towards reaching a greater understanding.

The simple aim of this book is to give you the reader evidence to my theory that life is a hotel. I have spent a lot of my time researching and it was while doing so that I have found that there is one common element in both, something that straddles both science and religion and it is with the help of the research that I have discovered the importance of the greatest star of all, the sun which is crucial to both. Really, the sun being such an important feature in our lives shouldn't have come as a major surprise, I should have known, off the top of my head I can remember staying in the Hotel Sonne while skiing in Austria, the Hotel Sol when visiting Spain and I have definitely walked past but never stayed in the Hotel Helios in Greece!

The sun, which I believe most of us take for granted simply because it is usually just there it is a part of our daily lives, although saying that and as I sit here writing this in Haworth, commonly known as Bronte country in West Yorkshire, hopefully getting subliminal inspiration from the great authors who were guests in this part of the hotel nearly two hundred years before I checked in, today the sun is conspicuous by its absence and apart from the odd intermittent and unreliable appearance, it won't be seen in all its glory until March later in the year and that is if we're lucky, it's certainly not a given.

As I say, I am in Haworth writing this book, as was Emily Bronte who wrote her one and only completed work, *Wuthering Heights*, in the same location, if *Life is a Hotel* is as successful as that classic then success is assured, although the purpose of writing this work is for neither money or fame, it is my attempt to leave my mark, a legacy, to amuse future guests, when finally the answer to the question reveals itself. You can imagine subsequent generations of guests laughing at the naivety of current guests, asking how come we didn't know what the purpose of our stay is. I would imagine it's akin to those of us here currently who would choose to ponder how earlier guests had seriously believed that the earth was flat, but knowledge grows and I believe one day we will have worked out the conundrum of life's purpose.

I believe there are fellow guests staying in the hotel at the same time as we are, with whom this book may resonate and who will appreciate the time that I've taken to write this, a book that is a little bit more than an in-depth TripAdvisor type review of my own stay. Anyway, for now let's back up a little and turn our attention to the Sun. First I think it is important to give a few basic facts about the sun, these are designed to inform and possibly educate, without sounding too pompous, but I think seeing as it plays such a major role in hotel life, then not only should we acknowledge it, but also to know more about it. Through research for this book, I have certainly enhanced my own knowledge of the sun and now see the sun in a totally different light, no pun intended!

Without the intense energy provided by the sun, ultimately there would be no life on earth. The sun is the largest object in our solar system; it is at the centre and our little hotel here on Earth is ninety-three million miles away from it. The sun, unbelievably is a ball of gas and it is gravity that thankfully stops any bits of it flying off all over the place and holds it together. The connection and interactions between the sun and Earth are many and they are fundamental to our existence, their relationship drives the seasons of the year, the weather, the ocean currents and of course climate. It is incredible to think that the sun is 109 times bigger than the earth, not 110 but 109 and if you wanted to fill the sun up with planet Earth by volume, it would take 1.3 billion planet Earths, not only fascinating but mind-blowing.

Although we consider it to be special to us, which of course it is, there are billions of stars like our sun scattered across the Milky Way! I know, I know please stop, my brain has started to hurt writing this stuff and I imagine that you were looking for something a little less taxing when you picked this book up, the title made it sounded like an untaxing read by somebody attempting to write a book about the meaning of life. Hopefully, it is all of those things too, but I'm afraid that we need a few technical and big numbers because they are vital to reinforce the theory, so I will try to keep it as simple as possible. That's the big numbers done, at least for the time being, all we need to know is that we are in a hotel which, in the great scheme of things and in comparison to other planets, is minute, but because we are here and it is all we have, it feels to us as though it is huge.

The earth is 100% of what we know and it is ours, and yet in order to look at our standing in the great scheme of things, we need to have a little understanding of what else is out there, what other hotels if any, there are or there could be in the solar system. So far what I have given is a brief outline of the science and the relevant facts, but as I mentioned earlier, the sun is incredible in that it straddles both science and religion. So I think it would be worthwhile to look at the sun and check a few relevant facts about the role it plays in religion, because the celestial body is a powerful feature in many of them. The sun helps us all to live and thrive, it is probably the most vital thing that we have and is second only to water in order for us to sustain our existence in the hotel.

The ancient religion of the sun has been one of the greatest influences on human history and understandably so, we know it was worshipped by an ancient lost civilisation, tens of thousands of years ago and subsequently these beliefs were then passed on to other major civilisations of the ancient world, civilisations that also venerated the sun. These ancient peoples created and gave rise to many of the worlds sites that we know that sun worship took place, it was here that the worship became combined with some of the worlds most revered wisdom and traditions. These sites are found all over the hotel estate and necessarily they are discovered in suitable locations, it is because there are so many of them, that it shows us the extent to which the sun influenced those guests that were staying here at that time and latterly, those who were to follow.

On a personal note, I have been known to watch the sun going down any evening I find myself in Port d'Andratx in Majorca, I wouldn't say I was there to worship El Sol, but I would certainly toast its repose every evening with a chilled bottle of Ruinart Rosé, sitting outside Cappuccino watching it set behind the distant mountains before heading off to a restaurant for dinner. That doesn't constitute worship, but it is something that I like to do, an acknowledgment of the sun's existence and its vital contribution to another fabulous day in Majorca or whichever coastal location I find myself, for me it has become a little tradition that has certainly become embedded in my own personal culture. We have Stonehenge in this country, the pyramids in Egypt and Mexico, the world-famous temples of Machu Picchu in Peru which are associated with the Incan religious cult dedicated to the worship of the sun. There are so many gods dedicated to the sun and its worship, too many to name, but through my own research, I have to conclude that my own favourites are the Egyptian sun gods of Horus, the rising sun, Ra the noon sun and finally Osiris, the god of the dead, manifested by the setting or dying sun.

Ancient civilisations across many parts of the world marvelled at the sun, moon and stars, and I believe, rightly so, who amongst us hasn't gazed at any one of these celestial superstars and not be in awe, whether it's because of their distance, their power and the regularity of their cycles, giving life to us and the earth that we depend on and therefore we should not be surprised that worshipping of the sun followed. The sun and its role in their lives, specifically for the first guests to stay here, was understandably both vital and intriguing, they would not have any way of knowing the vital role that the sun was playing in their emerging world, only aware of its daily appearance which would surely have had them wondering not only what it was, but where it went every night and was it the same one that came back the next morning.

So many questions that those first guests must have had, can you imagine what it must have been like and it is for that reason that I felt we needed to look at a few of the facts attributed to the sun in order to give a little context to the building of the hotel before the first guests arrived, putting in the foundations if you will. So for us to be here today, with all of the advancements that we have made as a society and as successfully as we currently see ourselves the progress we have made within the hotel, looking at our emergence from the Big Bang and its subsequent creation of our universe in which the sun for us is vital, we have managed to put ourselves in a position to look at a time when and how the hotel opened for business and those first guests arrived!

So when did those first guests arrive you may ask, which is a reasonable question, because it was these people who were staying in our rooms before we got here, so it would be nice to know when these first guests checked in. Once again we are taking in terms of billions of years, which I have already told you, for me is mind blowing but as it's all we have, so we need to take a look. The earth is approximately 4.5 billion years old, so those guests must have started arriving soon after, we have discovered a set of rocks that have been approximated as being four billion years old and it is these rocks that we find evidence of life emerging, it is primitive life I grant you, but life is life! Don't ask me how they work out the four billion number, but they have and these are the experts, so who are we to challenge them? These oldest of old rocks were found in the Jack Hills of Western Australia and upon analysis it is these rocks that have revealed their hidden treasure, because they house filament like fossils that might have been extracting energy from sunlight 3.5 billion years ago!

There are also fragments of rock that have been found on earth that were not of the earth, they never originated here which is not uncommon, as they are just lumps of detached rock that found themselves flying through the atmosphere and happened to attach themselves to our hotel. One piece of rock found on earth was seven billion years old, it is thought to be a meteorite from another planetary system and we have named it, the Murchison meteorite. To counter the Murchison meteorite, the Apollo 14 crew found a piece of earth rock on the surface of the moon, which when brought back to earth, an analysis of the rock found it to contain minerals not found on the moon but common on earth, so that gives you an idea of the celestial chaos all of those billions of years ago as the galaxy was a constant pin ball game of rocks and gases. I mention these examples not to intellectualise things too much, but to simply demonstrate that analysis of rocks and planets and dating is a little like putting a jigsaw together, all of the pieces are in the same box, but it's a very big box and there are trillions of pieces but when you initially open the box it all appears to be so random.

Currently, we believe that we are staying in the only hotel in the universe, sharing our experience with every other guest who has ever stayed or are also lucky enough to be staying here at the same time as we are. The scientists amongst us would express our hotel, sorry, earth as the only part of the known universe that harbours life. Until I started writing this book, I was totally unaware of the size of the universe, yes, I realised it was massive and as incomprehensible to me as the number four billion and on the incomprehensible chart, they were neck and neck, so suffice to say, when you consider the size of the universe and every other planet and star that float around in it, it is amazing that given the size of the place, it is you and I that find ourselves here in the hotel that is the Earth and earth is the only place with human or indeed alien life on it.

To make sure that we both understand what the universe is, the definition goes something like this, it is the totality of known or supposed objects and phenomena throughout space, it is everything, all of the space, all of the matter and all of the energy, oh and all of those lumps of rock irrespective of their size that find themselves floating around in that space. Earth, our fabulous hotel and the moon are obviously a part of the universe as are the other planets and their many dozens of moons, there are asteroids and comets, along with the planets that orbit the sun.

The sun is just one among hundreds of billions of stars in what we in the United Kingdom call the Milky Way galaxy, a galaxy which is 13.6 billion years old; incidentally, the name Milky Way I find to be a rather lovely way to describe the appearance of the galaxy from earth, which is a white band filled with indistinguishable stars, dust and gases, but interestingly, the white band according to Greek mythology, was created by the goddess Hera, who sprayed milk across the sky. Just as interestingly and maybe handy if you are on a quiz team or just love a bit of trivia, what we call the Milky Way is also called the Silver River by the Chinese and the Backbone of the Night in South Africa.

Whatever we call it, this is our galaxy, and in terms of the universe, we could call it our neighbourhood and as our hotel circles the sun, so the solar system orbits the Milky Way, which is all interesting stuff, but to go on just a little further, the Milky Way is just one of billions of galaxies in the observable universe. All the stars in all the galaxies and all of the other stuff that astronomers can't even observe are all part of the universe and hopefully that's it, everything, that's the universe, 100% of the whole kibosh!

No doubt you can gather that I find it all a little overwhelming, but that doesn't help any of us, so let's plough on! The Plough, if you didn't know, is the most recognisable collection of stars in the night sky, so that was quite witty, even if I do say so myself. Between five and seven million years ago, the first guests arrived in the hotel, guests who are best described as human beings in their earliest form and they started to inhabit this planet. I'm not sure we can consider them as guests, not as we understand them, especially when we compare their lifestyle to our own, but I fundamentally believe that life in whatever form being housed here is a guest.

For us, it is quite hard to think of a time when humans didn't inhabit the earth, but of course there was such a time. The early humans and the society that they unknowingly were starting to form was totally different to our current understanding of what society means. Physically the early human form was far different than we are today, language hadn't evolved, probably a series of grunts and groans made communication a little easier, their days to day lives consisted of hunting, gathering food and finding shelter from extreme environments, all of which would have been dependent on their location in the hotel and it was their location that determined how extreme conditions would have been and how much harder their lives would be according to those extremities.

Don't forget that the world was a very different place, it was undeveloped, plenty of vegetation and wildlife and inhospitable in most areas, therefore simply surviving was an achievement, it was key and although those first guests were unaware of it, they were at the start of a process, they were an integral part of our own evolution, those first guests became as much as a part of the process as we are, helping mankind not only to evolve to the complex people we are today and to who knows what in the future, wherever it leads. As we too are the product of that evolution, that suggests to me that there is a process that we are a part of but we don't know why and if evolution is a thing, which unquestionably it is, then why, where is it headed, what is the point of the process, indeed is there a point?

It is obvious that we are evolving and we will no doubt continue to do so, but who is monitoring our progress, who or what if anything is watching over this experiment, is there an endgame? If any athlete trains hard to improve their performance, there is an end goal, or if an academic reads vociferously to accumulate knowledge and improve themselves, there is a point a duet here we are, getting better and better as human life, learning more making society a better place and we have come a long way from those first guests, but to what end, who is controlling the experiment, are we just a stepping stone to achieving perfection and once we have achieved perfection, what happens next, is a perfect life an eternal life, will the perfect human have a perfect life and life forever? Questions, questions, with no answers.

In my quest for a meaning or a purpose to life, I have read many books and articles, absorbing any written works that were all striving to provide the answers that I am looking for, there have been hundreds, if not more. One such work, which helps us to understand our societal development, is Maslow's Hierarchy of Needs, by Abraham Maslow. This work has no scientific basis and is more an emotional observation of the universal needs of society, a bit like I am attempting to do by writing this book, if I do flatter myself with a Maslow comparison. As you will have no doubt gathered, it is my contention that our life here equates to a stay in a hotel and we are simply guests who check in for temporary residence and all that entails.

Unintentionally, Maslow has described in his hierarchy many of the features provided by a hotel. Yes, there are major differences, otherwise I may simply construct a pamphlet for publication and call it Maslow and Nick's Hierarchy of Hotels, or something similar. However, I believe that there is enough of a difference for me to describe my belief that *Life is a Hotel* and therefore write this book. As I say, Maslow described needs in the hierarchy which are provided by a hotel, but the hotel provides a more complete experience of life and it is this that I intend to explore and hopefully leave you feeling that the hierarchy and the hotel complement each other perfectly.

Chapter 2
Room-Only or Self-Catering

We all have needs in life all of which are designed to enable our basic human survival, these needs are universal and irrespective of colour or creed, they are as they describe, they are basin, which means that they are the simplest demands needed by us as human beings in order for us to function, to live our lives on a daily basis and to thrive during our stay in the hotel. Basic needs are never changing demands that are required for the most basic of human life to exist, therefore crucial to our existence and the survival of mankind, this may all sound melodramatic but these needs are fundamental to us all, if you think about it, there aren't many things in the world that apply to every single one of us, but these do and it is for that reason that I believe we need to acknowledge them and understand how they apply to us all throughout our stay.

Indeed, if these needs are not met, any individual person could feel an incredible sense of unhappiness, displeasure and insecurity, leading them to feeling vulnerable, an unnecessary susceptibility to their mere existence. It is with this in mind that this chapter is called self-catering, which in full alignment with my *Life is a Hotel* theory tells us that as we have basic needs, then the hotel also has its most primitive form of residence, colloquially known as room-only or self-catering. Of course, in this scenario, you are still treated as a guest in the hotel, but you will not be in receipt of all that hospitality or fabulous guest services that the hotel has to offer.

So, as guests staying in the hotel, we need to establish what those basic needs are and once we have established them and equally as important, how to source them it then becomes possible for us not only to exist and thrive but to achieve bigger and better things, having a better stay, even changing rooms, moving to a suite or moving to a nicer hotel, going from a one-star hotel to a two-, three-, four- or even a five-star hotel.

It's a metaphor for life, some of us are staying in one-star accommodation just getting by and having a no-frills existence, others are living the dream, staying in five-star accommodation, pink champagne on tap, enjoying every sandwich.

When you check in at reception and you are enjoying the first few days in the hotel, your demands are very different from your expectations in your later years and the quality of accommodation that you are prepared to accept when you are young is very different to that you would hope to have in later years. I remember when, as a 17-year-old, I went to a hotel in Lloret de Mar with two of my very good friends, we stayed at what you would consider to be a fairly basic hotel, we were young and that was all we needed at that time in our lives, somewhere to leave our clothes, somewhere to sleep and three dodgy meals a day.

However, although the memories have faded, I sense that if I revisited it today, it would stand comparison to the residences of those early cave dwellers with hieroglyphics on the walls; the hotel was, to say the least, basic. I remember fondly that first holiday abroad with my mates, we were brave young men, conquering Europe, we were pioneers, we thought we knew it all, we were heading to Spain for two weeks—Jules Verne, eat your heart out. Sadly, I have forgotten the name of our hotel, what I do remember is that it wasn't the best that our Thompson Holidays brochure had to offer, but as a 17-year-old, opulence isn't high on the agenda, Egyptian cotton sheets, wine tasting on Thursdays and a flamenco night on Sunday were not our major consideration at the time of booking, it was purely down to price.

Thinking back, I do recall that our hotel selection was more down to affordability than a discerning taste for the decor, as I mentioned we needed a place to crash as we stumbled in each morning before the sun rose and our hotel was perfect, we were as near to the action as we needed to be and close enough to all that Lloret de Mar had to offer, which seemed like a lot to us naive fools!

We weren't treated like royalty, so much so that during our stay, the cleaners and catering staff went on strike and the three of us, who were sharing one room, had to make our own beds and keep our bathroom clean; can you imagine the state of the place? Three 17-year-old lads sharing a bedroom and bathroom and nobody apart from us to keep the place looking good, trust me it didn't, but then again, we were young, so it didn't matter.

Food in the hotel was very basic and a buffet every evening provided a limited selection of decidedly uninspiring foods which served merely as an appetiser before the three of us headed into town to buy a dodgy burger before our nights on the town began! I fondly remember the three of us, after a late breakfast, during which we would recount tales of our exploits and sometimes conquests of the previous evening, stories that contained embroidery that would stand comparison with the Bayeux tapestry, but we laughed all day and legends were created. Breakfast was followed by a day on the beach, we would go back to our palace and graze at the hotel buffet, then we would head into town and grab a burger.

We would then head to a bar called the Duke of York, an intimate little place with a great bar which was populated by four or five British bar staff, who were all great lads. There was a tiny stage in the corner, where for a couple of hours every night, an acoustic guitarist would get up and play two sets of incredible music lasting approximately an hour each session, after which he would take requests from the crowd. The atmosphere was fantastic and we loved the place, during the two weeks that Lloret was our home, we got to know the lads behind the bar on first-name terms and they became our best friends forever, I think these days that translates as BFFs; of course, we were never to see any of them ever again, but we didn't know that at the time and so the friendships, though brief, were intense.

One of the reasons that the bar was so special was the acoustic guitarist, who would, at the end of each set, take requests from the sweaty, tightly packed crowd. I think his name was Steve, but can't be sure, it doesn't really matter, the memories are enough for me. It was around this time in my life and after seeing the band on tour at the Liverpool Empire, that I had become a big fan of Santana, the American rock band, in fact, to this day I still love the band and have seen them many times since that very first time in Liverpool. Carlos has given me many happy memories and the albums are part of the soundtrack of my life.

Another of my theories of life can be introduced at this stage, one that relates perfectly to the Duke of York and our time in Lloret de Mar; it was there that, apart from Santana, three other songs became a part of that holiday and stay with me to this day—*Do Anything You Wanna Do* by Eddie and the Hot Rods, *Give a Little Bit* by Supertramp and *Highway Star* by Deep Purple. Even today, over forty years later, these songs are still played in my car, at home, on holiday or wherever I am.

Now, this isn't an original thought, but I believe that as you go through life and during your stay in the hotel, music evokes powerful memories, not all happy, some sad, incidentally. *Labelled with Love* by Squeeze is a song that I love but was in my life at a particularly sad time and whenever I hear that song, it takes me straight back to those days. I simply offer that as a balance, that not all songs remind you of the good times, even though you love the song, the memories aren't always good but the song is beautiful and as we can all agree, life isn't all fine wine and roses.

We accumulate memories daily but some become far more significant than others, inevitably there are highlights, often these memories are triggered by music and it is these songs that appear on the Greatest Hits album of your life. Friendships, places, moments all appear on your Greatest Hits; indeed, lately it has become popular to play a couple of your Greatest Hits as you check out of the hotel, as your friends and family share a couple of songs from your album that have resonated so powerfully with you during your stay.

Hopefully, I still have a little time to go and a couple of tracks to add to the Greatest Hits album before I need to contemplate my coup de grace tracks so let's just finish off in the Duke of York before we go any further. As I was saying, the guitarist, let's stick with Steve, would take requests at the end of each set and therefore when he shouted 'any requests', we replied with the obligatory, 'get off', which wasn't a request for a song but an instruction to Steve, it made us laugh every time. Any requests Steve shouted, I would be there as a Santana fan and would ask him to play *Samba Pa Ti*, which is an instrumental track from the band's 1970 album *Abraxas*, a song that I loved but not the easiest in the world to play and one that Steve struggled with, so never accepted the request; however, once I realised he couldn't play it, I would request it every night, going as far as taking my Duke of York T-shirt, costing 250 pesetas, emblazoned with the words, *Play Samba Pa Ti* across the back of the shirt, and instead of having to shout it out, I stood in front of Steve and turned around!

Lloret de Mar and a cast of thousands made it a holiday to remember and highlights my point that in those days we put up with things that we wouldn't imagine being acceptable today, but we were young.

When you are young, this is the time when you have just checked into the hotel, you have been to reception and your bags have been taken to your room, things are happening around you and to some degree, although you are mentally unaware of it, the perspective of time and longevity are totally irrelevant, time doesn't matter, life is lived in the moment, there is too much going on, most of your experiences are new, so obviously you tend not to consider your long-term future in those early days and why would you, there will be sufficient time for contemplation in the future.

These are your formative days and it is you that is being formed, shaped, you are developing a personality an identity and developing the traits that will invariably stay with you for the rest of your time in the hotel. Living in the moment is easy in those first few days in the hotel, unknown to you, other guests will be looking after you, looking over you, protecting you from any potential dangers, having learnt from their own sometimes painful experiences, collected having checked in long before you arrived, unknown to you they are serendipitously making your stay as pleasant as possible, with no pressure on you to do anything but discover and grow.

One of my favourite ancient Greeks, Euripides, spoke one of the greatest truths when he said, 'no one can confidently say that he will still be living tomorrow'. Imagine the prospect of a teenager having a fascination with their own retirement, that would be a little bit too weird, so our minds don't work that way, today and possibly tomorrow are all we have and they are sufficient to consume our thinking. In your earliest years, you are going through the initial phase of checking into the hotel during which time and with any hotel, you are both learning about and finding your way around the place. Indeed, with any hotel you go to, whether it be in a resort or any city centre, you very rarely go to every part of the locale, instead you tend to find places that make you feel happy and make you feel comfortable; and then for the rest of your holiday, similar to our love for the Duke of York in Lloret, you will more often than not revisit these favourites throughout the duration of your stay, because we are all creatures of habit.

I imagine psychologically we are replacing our comfort blankets with things that we both trust and know by being in places that make us feel warm inside. It is in these early days that you are getting to know some of the places available to you and that you are able to discover and explore, you will be enthralled by some places and totally disinterested in others. You will discover new foods, drinks, restaurants and people, making friends along the way, friends some of whom will stay with you for life or others who are just acquaintances, intense but brief relationships, these people are simply interlopers in our lives, temporary companions along the way. As with any stay in a hotel, it is not an obvious consideration and may sound counter intuitive, but you can only get to know the people who are staying in the hotel who are staying there at the same time as you are!

Recently, my Aunty Shelagh died, which for our family was an extremely sad thing to happen, we dutifully attended her funeral in Liverpool; my cousin Angela, her daughter, gave a really nice eulogy and a couple of Shelagh's Greatest Hits were played as the curtains at the crematorium closed and that was it, Shelagh had gone, she had checked out of the hotel.

Continuing with this thought process, let us not forget that as Shelagh was checking out, there were new arrivals checking into the hotel and so the process begins. Those guests arriving today, checking in and any guests that check in at any time in the future, unless they are part of my own family, they will never know that my Aunty Shelagh ever stayed in the hotel, although she had checked in, spent a relatively large amount of time here, don't forget she was in her eighties, she got to know those guests who were staying in the hotel at the same time as she was, she had met and spent time with many people who had checked in long before she had and also with those who have arrived long after her own check in until the day that she finally checked out.

Yes, she met a lot of other guests and touched many lives, but she never painted any great works of art, never wrote an international bestseller or performed in front of the president of America at Carnegie Hall, therefore to the massive majority of guests, they will be unaware of her existence.

At this moment in time, it is currently impossible to meet those people who were guests in the hotel before you arrived here and your stay began and similarly, it is currently impossible to meet those guests that will arrive once you have departed. This may sound rather obvious, but note that I say currently, because who knows what the future holds, will there ever be a time when we can meet those who have stayed here long before we have, maybe meet our ancestors, will we ever find a way to communicate with previous guests or even more thought provoking, will we ever find a way somehow to meet those who are to follow us, people who haven't checked in yet.

These are huge questions, that are currently unanswered, but I imagine that eventually things may be a little different than they are today, who knows where we are headed, but that's not for now. So let's have a look at the way that some guests believe that we can get in touch with those earlier guests, people who have checked out, people who are no longer here but believed by some to still be accessible, all it takes is a little belief and faith in the process, all you have to do is do what these people tell you. Firstly let's consider the word of spiritualism, who are those amongst us that believe that we can make contact with previous guests and the way they do so is through the medium of a spiritualist.

A spiritualist will tell us that individuals survive their bodies in death and it is their spirit that survives and manifests as the individual, the spirit then ascends into a spirit existence, these spirits are called discarnate humans and their condition after death is directly related to their moral existence, while they were here on earth and while they are in human form, a spiritualist will tell you that contact with these spirits is totally possible and all it takes for us to get in touch is belief and faith in spiritualism.

So, as long as you are a good person while you are here on earth, then your spirit will live on in peace and harmony and you, through your spirit, will be able to contact your earthly friends, what a lovely thought! Next let's take a look at reincarnation, which is also called transmigration or rebirth; reincarnation is the philosophical or religious belief that the non-physical essence of a living being, again this could be a spirit or similar, this essence of the person begins a new life in a different physical form or a different body after their biological death.

Resurrection differs from reincarnation, it is a belief commonly held in some of the religions and that belief is that you come back to life not only in spirit but also in the same body. Some religions, in this case mainly the Indian religions, believe in resurrection but there are some elements of those religions that instead of resurrection believe that there is an afterlife, which offers a subtle difference between reincarnation and resurrection; complicated yes, but not too difficult to comprehend, especially if you are looking for a meaning or purpose of life.

Throughout your stay, you will make friendships and build relationships, with the other guests and it is these relationships which can help to not only contribute to determining the quality of your stay, but also to the quality of your afterlife. Relationships are irrational, friendships can present themselves anytime and anywhere, of all of the people that you meet, who are those that you get close to, of the current over eight billion guests, who do you get to know, inevitably your close family, but what about the rest of the huge cast of billions, given the potential number you could meet, there are in reality very few that you will get really close to and build friendships with, while the overwhelming majority we will have absolutely no contact with, zero, let alone speak to them, it is all so random.

Randomness is an intriguing proposition and as we are still at this early stage of the book, I believe it deserves a little consideration. In order to discern whether your stay would be better, worse or exactly the same whether you met those staying at the same time as you, or not, how different could our lives be if we hadn't have met some people of the people that we had, or if we had met others that we hadn't. We can all think of important people in our own lives, people outside of your immediate family that you have met along the way and have had a powerful influence on us and our stay here. If you look at it quite simply, those people that we meet here during our time here do influence our stay and can either affect us positively or negatively and it is difficult, if not impossible, to know how each relationship will result, so let's take a look at the randomness of it all and start by looking at a definition of the term.

Randomness is in essence unpredictability, it is the quality or state of lacking a pattern or predictability in events. A random sequence of events is exactly what it says, it has no order and does not follow an intellectual pattern, life has many and various outcomes, but there are limits, there are extremes to those outcomes and because there are limits, we need to look at probability, or the probability of potential outcomes. Probability is simply defined for example when rolling two dice, the outcome of one particular role is totally unpredictable but it is known that a combined total of seven will occur twice as often as four, if the dice are rolled in a sequence.

This tells us that given certain parameters and limitations that randomness is not as haphazard as it may initially appear to be, it is simply a measure of uncertainty of the outcome.

That example of using two dice is a simple one and offers a maximum number of six on each dice and a minimum number of one on each, this exposes limitations on the outcome when rolling two dice. What I mean by this is, the maximum combined number possible when two dice are thrown is twelve and a minimum number when both are thrown is two, with every combination of one and six in between.

We can apply this simple logic to our own stay in the hotel once we have arrived in reception and have checked in, however, the biggest difference between life and a pair of dice is that the combination of two dice is limited to any number from two until twelve, which isn't a huge spread. But life is very different, the number of outcomes for any one person staying in the hotel of life are virtually incalculable because there are so many variables, far greater than any two dice can ever offer and therefore the outcomes are so much harder to predict, although predictions can be made.

This does not negate the possibility of numerous outcomes and the reality that no two people will ever share the exact same experience. We will revisit this point later, but in essence, not only will two people share the exact same experience of life, but two people staying in the same place at the same time, sharing the same experience at the same time in the same hotel, will come through it with totally different feelings of their stay.

How many times have you been to a restaurant for dinner and had a fabulous evening, while other people in your party, who have dined at the same table and shared the same experience, get home and declare that they will never go back to that place again? Two people having the same experience but having very different outcomes, this all adds to the intrigue of everything life has to offer and making our individuality the thing that defines us. 'You can please some of the people all of the time, you can please all of the people some of the time, but you can't please all of the people all of the time,' wrote John Lydgate, the monk and poet, observing this as early as the fourteenth century.

We are all different but we have commonality, which is a bit of an oxymoron, the commonality are the traits that we all share, yes all to varying degrees but traits nonetheless and those traits can lead us into the probability that we as guests can share amongst ourselves, our expectations, our demands and our dreams while we are staying here. Interestingly and to reinforce this commonality we can look at something that both attracts us as individuals and allows us to share our experiences and this was the creation of TripAdvisor, which was launched in 2000 and it can be argued that its emergence has changed the face of travel forever. As most of you fellow travellers will know, TripAdvisor is a review platform and as such it aggregates reviews and opinions of its members from all over the planet, of destinations accommodations, restaurants and activities throughout the world.

Some people I have met now use TripAdvisor as a starting point when researching destinations for holidays or even going to a restaurant, happy to accept the experiences of others, people that they have never met before; they are allowing the opinions of these random people to become a guide to their own future choices. There are those who will only choose to use TripAdvisor as a place to report their findings, be they positive or negative, never seeking to use it as a platform on which to base their own decisions, but rather to use their experiences to advise others, vainglorious maybe, slightly pompous I agree, but of course, nobody is compelled to use TripAdvisor, therefore you do so at your own peril. The advent of the review platform is a recent phenomenon and it has become a game changer for both hotel and restaurant businesses and it is not unusual for those businesses to actively encourage their patrons, especially those that they sense have fully enjoyed their experiences to contribute a positive review to their hotel or restaurant TripAdvisor page, why wouldn't they, these reviews have become a popular way for potential new visitors to check out, if they are looking for new places to visit, so it becomes a powerful marketing tool.

Who better to advertise on behalf of your hotel or restaurant than a satisfied customer; it works perfectly, but don't forget, not everybody enjoys their experience and those who have been disappointed can be equally as active on TripAdvisor and therefore can possibly be a little more caustic when offering their opinions, some revelling in the opportunity to display their lexicon of words and their tributes or condemnations can take on a poetic artistry comparable with the great writers.

I have a very good friend, the wonderful Dulce Bergantiños, who I originally met when she was managing one of my favourite hotels on the island of Majorca; my wife and I are regular visitors to the hotel and we got to know her well and naturally, she has become a good friend. Dulce always looks sharp when she is front of house at work, floating around the hotel in her inimitable stylish way, because of her effortless style and a reluctance to call her Dulce, I nicknamed her Gucci, which has stuck and I think she likes it; however, she took her revenge by nicknaming me Elton, after Elton John, which isn't as flattering, but I'll take it.

Anyway, Gucci is currently managing a really cool hotel in Madrid and has a wealth of experience in the hotel industry. I told her about writing this book and she kindly offered to give me as much help as she could and to this end, we discussed how the hotel business had changed, even during the relatively short time that she had spent in it. We discussed many areas of the business and naturally we discussed the future, which is when the influence of TripAdvisor and then more recently Google as a comparison site or a travel opinion aggregator, their role becomes more difficult to describe as their remit expands and the ambition of their business changes, which inevitably it will due to its success and its rapidly expanding database.

My friend Dulce, which is the Spanish word for sweet, has been helpful with my research into the ever-expanding role that these sites have in her industry. However, the arrival of these platforms is not all good news; firstly, there is a potential for manipulation of the reviews that are submitted and therefore it is possible for those who may be inclined to post an unfavourable, if not an absolutely dreadful, review of a business, giving those with a vested interest, should they choose, to post totally unfair criticisms of the business in order to damage the competition and therefore ruin its reputation and give themselves an advantage.

It wouldn't be difficult to imagine a competing hotel or restaurant, writing a poor review and posting it using a pseudonym or even using a compliant author who was happy to write the review in receipt of remuneration from the devious competitor. Speaking to Dulce she told me about a case when she was working in Majorca where a disgruntled local taxi company saw guests at a neighbouring hotel using Uber taxis instead of the local service on offer, which was a long-established Majorcan family business, who didn't like the idea of competition from Uber. Accordingly, numerous unsubstantiated bad reviews of the Uber-using hotel appeared on TripAdvisor, and the hotel suffered dreadfully.

Fortunately, there is an appeals system within TripAdvisor, which allows any offended party who has received a negative review to challenge said review, or in this case, reviews. In this instance, the management team of the hotel contacted TripAdvisor and requested an investigation into their numerous recent negative reviews as they seemed suspicious in their volume and the fact that they had never experienced such negativity before combined with the fact that the hotel staff had not received complaints that mirrored the negative reviews.

So, TripAdvisor investigated the hotel's objection and it was discovered that the drivers of the irate local taxi company had submitted reviews independently, each of them criticising it for a multitude of reasons, all simply because their own taxi business was losing out on fares due to the arrival of Uber. What is also problematic is that there is no burden of proof on the reviewer and therefore once a bad review is published on the site, it is difficult to have it removed if it is unfair, or in this case, malicious fantasy!

Dulce told me that the introduction of TripAdvisor and similar platforms has seen the advent of the savvy customer, a new generation of customer fully aware of their newfound power that these new sites have given to them, the once muted customer who will now happily negotiate with the front desk as they check in, looking to receive free services as soon as they have arrived and in return for these add-ons they will not be posting a negative review, but a glowing report, which has now become such vital currency in the world of hospitality.

We spoke in-depth over many hours, but it was Dulce's final words of our conversation that would stay with me the longest, and indeed those words contained a metaphor for our experiences in life itself—it takes many happy customers to write a good review but just one to write a bad one. That says it all for me, it is the bad one that gets noticed in a sea of positivity, some of us choose to focus on the one poor review, in spite of many being complimentary and indeed that applies to many other experiences in life and not just the evolving world of TripAdvisor reviews. Therefore, it is those who do accept a TripAdvisor review in good that faith may be guided by another person's views, without ever knowing anything about that person, their values or their preferences and whether, if they ever met that person in the real world, would they consider that persons opinion sufficiently worthy in order for it to allow them to have so much influence on their own destiny.

We can treat TripAdvisor as one of the contributors to the randomness of our lifestyle choices or we can choose to totally ignore it, either way, consciously making any decision has an impact on your future and so unknowingly and minute by minute we are subconsciously steering our future, our destiny in everything we do.

There are so many things can determine your enjoyment of any experience, I have found that it doesn't really matter which stage of life that you are at when you have the experience, the pleasure derived is as powerful and enjoyable whether it happens in your teens or your sixties, as you age, the norms change and your perspective is different. It is your age and your maturity or indeed immaturity that appears to be a major contributing factor to this, if you think about it, there are reasons that you won't find many old-age pensioners at the numerous summer music festivals around the country, festivals such as Glastonbury, which is the biggest in the UK, but it is just one of many more events all over the country; similarly you won't find hordes of teenagers at the Chelsea flower show, unless they are dragged along by their parents.

Yes, I know that there are some ageing hippies, midlife crisis contenders or simply those who wish to grow old disgracefully and will find themselves stumbling around at Glastonbury or Creamfields and, by the same token, there will be the odd young horticulture enthusiast spotted among the flora and fauna of the Chelsea or Southport flower show. But these are the exceptions and not the norm, and that is my point.

Do you think if I asked a random group of cool kids who frequent night clubs if they had ever fancied playing crown green bowls or popping out on a Saturday afternoon for a game of bingo, again understanding that some will, just to be contrary but the vast majority would simply laugh at the thought.

So, how is it that forty years later, some of these once 'cool kids' find themselves with a large heavy black ball in one hand, standing on a manicured square of grass, smoking a pipe, or equally, sitting in a bingo hall with an oversized felt tip pen in hand, waiting for one number to be called. It is maturity, which is something that plays a crucial role in the hotel of life, but we shouldn't confuse maturity with being old; all maturity means is that you have reached a stage of development in your life, you are in the latter days of your stay in the hotel—there is a time for going to a nightclub and similarly there is a time for going to a bingo hall.

In terms of the ageing process that each of us go through, it starts with us being cared for by parents or similar guardianship were we are the responsibility of an appropriate adult who are in control of and making the decisions that control our lives, until we become mature enough to decide for ourselves and ultimately taking personal responsibility for our own welfare.

Maturity has different definitions across society, in legal, social, sexual, political, emotional, intellectual and religious contexts.

The age of maturity or qualities assigned to each of these contexts are tied to culturally significant indicators which can be different and will vary from country to country, or culture to culture, but all culminating in our independence which can vary as a result of social sentiments. It is because of these very sentiments that the notion of maturity and immaturity are somewhat subjective. It was the American psychologist Joseph Bruner who told us that the purpose of the initial period of immaturity was to allow us to have time in our lives for experimental play without having major consequences.

Think about it, that is exactly what immaturity gives us, it allows us all a period of our lives when we could play all day without consequence, with no money in our pockets but imagination in our heads and the only thing that we had to remember was what time we had to be home for tea. It would be like arriving at a hotel, it could be any hotel, anywhere in the world, but you are there for the very first time, you don't know your way around and within the first few days, you have found yourself in the wrong part of town, you could be in the wrong bar, the wrong restaurant or down a dimly lit back alley that you didn't intend to be in, you can even find yourself becoming friendly with people who, up you think are friends but by the end of your stay, you positively avoid making contact with these people at all costs, they don't enrich your life, but have a negative impact on your stay.

But these mistakes are often made early on, a time as I said, when you don't really know what you're doing, whereas, by the time your half way through your stay, you are a bit wiser and know what to look for and so aren't as gullible as you were in those first few days. I have been made aware of Burners theory, which I love, but which is a generous one, insomuch as it allows us to make silly mistakes in our lives, mistakes that we can put down to our own naivety, or as a symptom of our age, or we can simply put them down to experience. We can have experiences during our childhood, which are simple mistakes, but mistakes that can have massive consequences for the rest of our lives, mistakes which certainly effect the rest of our stay in the hotel, a night spent in the wrong place at the wrong time or maybe meeting the wrong person at the wrong time, moments like these can actually become a life or death decision.

This challenges the Joseph Bruner theory that experimental play without consequences is a reality; instead, it is reasonable to believe that potentially, play isn't necessarily as secure as it sounds. As with every stay in any hotel, our first days after our arrival at reception and checking in, become no more than distant memories by the end of our stay, from a time of not knowing, a time of not understanding and a time of knowing nothing about anything, we spend our time during our stay, collecting memories along the way, every single day presents us with an opportunity to make an emotional investment, both good and bad and it is these moments which create those memories that our stay gives to us and that we choose to protect, that ultimately define us.

Which brings us back to the hotel and staying on a room-only or self-catering basis, it is those things that subliminally toughen you up, the difficult times, the hard times when trouble presents itself, when life is a little bit harder than it could be or should be, life at its most basic, no frills, but plenty of spills, which are a lot rarer when staying in a superior hotel, but room-only and self-catering means you fend for yourself. However, some people prefer the opportunity a basic existence, they would rather stay in a self-catering hotel or have a room-only experience. Preferring what they would consider to be a more real experience, resisting having every extravagance being indulged, avoiding the pampered environment that a five-star hotel offers. From the very basics of going out and buying your own food and drinks, bringing them back and preparing them for you and your family, to then making sure your environment is decent, doing your own cleaning, making your own beds and keeping the place as tidy, or untidy as you wish.

If you want to have your breakfast at midday, then that is no problem, if your kids like to eat at five while you prefer to eat at seven, then that is okay, maybe you prefer to take a long time to eat your meal and indulge yourselves by sharing a bottle of wine or two, that's your call. Self-catering or taking a room-only offers you total flexibility, allows you to come and go as you please and effectively lets you set your own timetable, with nobody telling you what you can and what you can't do. If you choose either of these options, you as a guest are given an opportunity to be a little more adventurous in the way that you come to terms in discovering and getting to know your new surroundings you no longer need to feel obliged to take part in compulsory hotel activities, you won't be compelled to meet the hotel rep over a warm Prosecco in reception on day two, as invariably you are obliged to when staying in a large hotel.

Of course, those hotel-based activities are often attractive and complete the package in offering many things that compliment your stay, from the obvious such as breakfast and dinner to the indulgent but available spa and gym which are included in your five-star lifestyle. The flexibility offered by either room-only or self-catering can also help you to budget, if you so wish, for example if you are out exploring in and around the locale during the daytime you can pop back to the hotel and grab a snack or plan your day and make a packed lunch before you set off.

You would wonder why anybody would ever choose the self-catering option when a hotel where all of your needs are catered for is an alternative and price isn't necessarily a determining factor in your choice of hotel. People are very different, one person's five-star luxury can be another person's five-star misery, we don't all like the same things in life and therefore variety is there to service the demand and why there just as many people who get pleasure from doing their own thing by self-catering or just taking a room as those guests who prefer to luxuriate in five-star opulence.

From self-catering to five-star and every gradation in between, it is easy to perceive the alternative as a little more restrictive, with times for meals, classes and tastings all working within a fairly rigid timetable, but as a trade-off for those restrictions, the freedoms you have doing your own thing appeals more than any restrictive practices ever do. Preferring a life lived with basic amenities and less demands on formality and a more easy going life to the grandeur of the five-star option and all of the demands that can put on a person with greater conformity required. So we can see that life is not simply a progression through the hotel star ratings that see us experience the gamut of what life has to offer, it is not self-catering in your teens, three-star in your thirties, four-star in your forties and so on, but we somehow manage to find our level, the star rating that suits who we are and the status that helps us to enjoy our experience more and is therefore conducive to a life well-lived.

We can be in self-catering and loving every minute while there will be others amongst us who can't bear it and desire instead to be pampered and inevitably progress through the star ratings. I say progress, not as a pejorative or to denigrate either option, indeed some would pay more to be in self-catering than to be in a five-star hotel, so it's not always about money and aspiration, it is more to do with mental well-being, with what suits you and which environment is the most suitable for you!

However, it would be commonly accepted that a five-star hotel is better simply by the amount of money it would cost to stay there and the quality of the services provided. The idea of a self-catering, room-only option lends itself perfectly to our hotel theory, with the emphasis in that descriptor on the word *self*.

After all, self is all we have, each of us is an individual and your sense of self is who you are, the you deep down and within, it is your identity, fundamental to your existence and I believe that we should explore this a little further to give us an understanding of ourselves, as an individual or part of a greater society. The study of Self is a whole area of research that has been undertaken by academics throughout the ages and conclusions have been reached and fundamental understanding of ourselves and our time here as guests in the hotel are now universally accepted. Again, I believe it is important to acknowledge the self because to a certain degree this simple word is the basis of all that we are throughout our stay here, I don't want to complicate the book by over analysing psychological theory, but I believe that a simple understanding will help guide us through the rest of the book.

The most basic form of self has been described as the Existential Self; this is you and the sense that you are an individual and of being separate and distinct from other people. That is quite straightforward, next we have the Categorical Self, this gives us a realisation that we exist as an object of the world and we are one of the many.

It was Carl Rogers, a humanistic psychologist, who broadly agreed with Maslow in 1959 that there are three components to the Categorical Self. Although I believe it is important that we don't get to entrenched in these works as they are not at the core of my basic belief that *Life is a Hotel*, however I do believe that for those of us who find this topic interesting and that a little bit of further reading if you choose to, could be both beneficial and informative. So with that in mind, in the short term, I will give the briefest of outlines of Rogers assertions as I believe they are helpful in order to further explore the role of self in self-catering! Self-image, self-esteem and the ideal self are the three components of the Categorical Self.

Self-image is quite a bizarre phenomenon, in no way does it have to reflect reality, I am sure we all know people who are delusional about their own importance; however, self-image can be broken down into four distinct areas— Physical Description, Social Roles, Personal Traits and Existential Statements. Quite obviously, physical description describes height, weight, hair colour, immutable traits that do not change and are fundamentally you.

Social roles is your job, or clubs that you may be a member of or possibly the church you attend, or religion you follow, your football team, you get the idea, we are talking about those things that help to make up your character. Personal traits such as, I'm nervous, I'm a ditherer or I'm impulsive, I'm strong, I'm determined or I am focused, these are traits that are used more often than not by you to describe yourself and therefore they are usually positive, because that is how the majority of us want to see ourselves. Finally, Existential statements, these are a bit more defined, for instance I am spiritual, I am religious or I am eclectic, again these are similar to personal traits but sounding a little more worthy, a little more aspirational, how we would like ourselves to be defined for our humanity, if that doesn't sound too self-obsessed.

These four areas combine for us to define the self, that give us a worldview of ourselves and how we wish to present ourselves and possibly more importantly, how we wish to present ourselves for others to see us. Interestingly we find through extensive research that younger people tend to describe themselves in terms of personal traits, whereas older people amongst us would choose social roles to define themselves. It is interesting to acknowledge the difference and our change in perception of ourselves as we get older for it is these changes and our personal development that is at the core of life in the hotel and sees us change from the day we check in, to the day that we finally check out, we are a work in progress, or as Heraclitus said, we are always becoming, never being.

From appearing to being an obscure factor in our stay, the self is indeed interesting in its relevance and along with other factors that contribute to our stay, they change over time, daily in fact, we are a work in progress and each of us changing second by second. TripAdvisor or Google, despite both becoming a vital tool for many, are totally ignored by the vast majority, so not everybody is allowing their decisions to be influenced by the thoughts of others. But as we know, change is a constant and is always on the horizon, so as demographics mature and the users of those platforms start to get older, the use of these review platforms is surely inevitable and will grow as non-users depart from the hotel at the end of their stay and new arrivals will simply accept them as the norm and will get involved.

What these many new platforms are doing is harnessing and collecting data which makes their potential for future growth incredible.

We mustn't forget that neither TripAdvisor nor Google existed fifty years ago so they may not exist in fifty years' time, but within the next fifty years, a new incarnation will have emerged and whatever form it may take, it has become obvious that collection of data has become currency and however the data is collected and whatever the vehicle for collection is called, it is important to the development of a future society, although privacy is an inevitable trade-off. Whether people are accepting of this or not, will continue to be debatable but the benefits of accumulation do exist and these must be stressed to endear a sceptical public to it being necessary.

Wherever the future takes us, those basic demands of every human remain and it is only once we feel we have achieved them that the pursuance of our other needs can be built on those foundation stones. The pursuance of safety is crucial to us all it is fundamental to our mental and physical health, so we acknowledge it as such. Belongingness similarly is important to us, apart from the role we play in wider society we have relationships with people and institutions that need care and constant monitoring as they mature and grow stronger or wither and die, for it is these relationships that will ultimately define us, however we shape them.

Of course, we all know people who live an insular life and don't go out of their way to make friends or build relationships, we may call them a loner, which is a negative connotation because as a society we are encouraged to embrace society, for all of the right reasons, but we know that amongst us, people are very different and so we shouldn't be surprised that we don't all want the same thing! Esteem, or rather self-esteem is vital in our lives and how we establish esteem comes from within and is pursuant to belongingness, it is how you feel about yourself and see yourself as deserving the respect of others, conversely when your self-esteem is low, you put little value on your thoughts, your ideas and the value of your opinions, you become a punchbag and the knocks can become part of everyday life.

So, it is easy to see why esteem and self-esteem play a vital role in us becoming 'everything you are capable of becoming', which is another line from our old friend Abraham Maslow. This was Maslow describing self-actualisation within the hierarchy of needs, where personal potential is fully realised after basic bodily and ego needs have been fulfilled. Life is an evolving process for us as all as individuals and society in general evolves too and as we evolve, our understanding of our society hangs on to those old theories that are still relevant but they have become adapted for the age. For example, Maslow's Hierarchy of Needs and its description of self-actualisation is still totally relevant today, but these days self-actualised people are focused on health, growth, wholeness and humanitarian purpose and the real problems of life. Currently, as I write this, one real problem of life is the war in Ukraine which is creating real problems in a world where Will Smith slapping a comedian at the Oscars can consume our mainstream media for weeks, when in reality it is fluff and inconsequential.

Real-life problems can either be our own personal issues—being overweight, disliking our place of work, or biting our nails—or global issues that resonate with us and allow us to put everything else into perspective, justifying any shortcomings that may exist in our own world because things could be so much bleaker, look at that war over there, the famine over here, so many distractions around the world, which are now part of our lives within moments of happening because communication is immediate and rolling news is everywhere. If we compare our situations to the worst things happening around the planet then the majority of us will believe that we are lucky, fortunate or both.

We will discuss later how the part of the hotel we live in can determine the quality of our lives, which I believe to be true, but having looked at the self-catering option, then for all of us it is not a bad place to start our stay in the hotel—at least we have somewhere to sleep.

Chapter 3
Dying to Leave

Every single one of us is checking out of the hotel at some unknown point in the future and although at this moment in time we as a society are only aware of one way of checking into the hotel, which, at the time of writing, is when the mature biological female of the species, commonly known as a woman, although even these terms are currently the topic of hot debate on the fringes of society, so if you're reading this and the term woman is even more confused than it is today, then I apologise, so let's look at where we are today and work with what we think we know now.

Currently, a woman has the option of either being artificially or physically inseminated by a medical procedure or alternatively a physically able male of the species and after impregnation by a biological, currently not a transgender male, then following an approximate nine month gestation period, the female gives birth to a baby, This is currently the only way we know of for a new guest to present themselves at reception and check in to the hotel. Conversely when it comes to leaving the hotel, when you finally check out of this place for the final time, there are numerous ways of checking out, possibly too many to list, however, suffice it to say they are abundant and varied and on a scale of preference they range from the acceptable inevitability of death to the downright scary and potentially horrible exits that nobody would choose, given the opportunity.

Depending on which part of the hotel complex you are staying in, there will be factors that can influence how long you stay for, that is because there are massive regional variations on causes of death and I believe it behoves us to take a closer look at those, as they will give us a clearer understanding of our stay here and as importantly our departure.

It is not for any morbid fascination but simply because it concludes our stay in the hotel and it would be remiss of me as the author to ignore such a vital part of the journey simply because it was a little too sensitive to discuss and it may offend you the reader, hopefully we can handle these conversations.

This may be an uncomfortable discourse, but they present themselves at every turn and there is no point hiding from them, because each of us will face them at some stage, so let's take a closer look at the part of the whole experience that every single one of us is guaranteed to face, although we know not when. This reminds me of the old joke, one man says to his friend, 'if you could have one wish, what would you wish for?'

'I wish I knew where I was going to die,' replies the friend.

'Why is that?' the questioner asks.

'Because I wouldn't go there,' the friend replies.

There is a certain logic to that joke, because none of us has the privilege of knowing, where, how or when we will go to reception and check out for the last time, but if it was in our gift, then what would we choose? I suppose if you think about it, it is probably a good thing that we live our lives in complete ignorance, if you imagine that we did know the hows, whys and wherefores, of our demise, then that would inhibit the rest of our stay and inevitably our experience would be lessened, with death being at the very least a distraction, if not for worse for those who are inclined, for whom it would become the focus of our stay. To highlight my point, I needed to draw a parallel with another sentient guest that we are sharing the hotel with, but this is not another human being, it is an animal, yet in spite of this, I consider the comparison to be suitable and it works for me.

Having become a vegetarian four years ago, which initially started as a new year's resolution but now years later, I know I will never go back to eating meat and a major part of the reason for this is the example of the life of a lamb. Is there a single person on the planet, is there anybody that you have ever met who doesn't look at a newborn lamb either in real life or a photograph and not be taken by its innocence, its beauty, the pure life-affirming loveliness of all that it is? But wait, I have heard that people eat these little beauties, who have been on the planet, staying here as guests, just like you and I, in the hotel for anywhere between just four and twelve months. Four and twelve months of life, which ends not only prematurely but brutally by a gunshot to the head or worse by having its throat cut; either way, it is being slaughtered, which for any of us, man or animal, is not the nicest of outcomes. I'm not trying to make a political point or comment on eating meat or not eating meat as a principle, I am not on a personal crusade to change the world about meat eating, for me it is a sense of not feeling that another's life has not been traded in order to provide me with fifteen minutes of pleasure, a temporary taste sensation, an aural pleasure that is as relatively fleeting as the life that has provided it, it feels as simple as that for me.

Combined with the fact that if I had to kill the animal, any animal, in order to eat it, I guess that like most of us, I simply couldn't do it, but of course the whole industry is sanitised for the carnivores amongst us, to that end we have people to do the dirty work for us, so that we do not have to. So far removed has meat become as a product, that it is no longer to be confused with having anything to do with an animal, so much so, that in a recent survey of children aged between four and seven years old, they believed that meat was made in supermarkets and bacon came from plants, with the perennial kiddies favourite, chicken nuggets which were also believed by a majority in the survey, to be grown in fields.

The survey found that the children thought it was not ok to eat chicken, pigs and cows, yet so successfully have they been manipulated to believe that the food that they eat has nothing to do with their lovable farmyard chums, that they see no correlation with their beef burger and a moo cow! These kids don't see any problem with the meat they consume, which of course is totally acceptable, because to them it isn't animal related, but I do sense a mood change and this change is coming from with Gen Z kids, indeed it would not surprise me to learn that sometime in the future we will look back at a world in which animals were farmed for their meat, as fondly as those days when children used to be sent up chimneys. I'm not sure how far away that day is, but I sense that the way society is changing, that there will be a day when we will despise those people who rear animals, encouraging them to bring new life into the world simply to profit from those lives and indeed their deaths, which when you actually say it out loud, sounds totally abhorrent.

For now, animal farming is totally acceptable, so let's accept that we are where we are, which is not necessarily where some of us we would like to be. I have wandered a long way from the point that I was making about knowing how and when you are going to check out of the hotel, but I believe this brief sojourn was worthwhile, however we get back there, let's just reinforce the sentiment. The whole point of introducing lambs into the conversation was to ascertain that whether knowing that they would enjoy only four to twelve months of life and acknowledging the barbaric cruelty of their departure, if they had the choice, would they still choose life or would they choose not to experience it. These beautiful creatures gambol through fields in blissful ignorance of what their future holds, but aren't we all, aren't we also, gambolling through our own lives, totally unaware of what lies ahead of us!

We live unaware day to day, not knowing what our own future has in store for us, of course most of us will die of natural causes and live full lives with no hint of regret that we have stayed in the hotel, but there may on the other hand, be some guests who, as with any hotel, have reservations about their time there. If, like those beautiful lambs our destiny was to reach an ugly conclusion, would we choose never to have checked in in the first place, or does being unaware of our ultimate demise make every preceding day a thing of pure beauty? If we had to choose the best way to check out of the hotel, then I would imagine the ideal way to leave is by natural causes, but what exactly do we mean when we say natural causes? The simplest explanation of natural causes is an illness or internal malfunction of the body an event that is not directly impacted by external forces, or more likely an event which could be considered to be an accident.

Society has come to use the expression 'death by natural causes' as a euphemism for dying of old age and as we will discover, old age is subjective depending on whichever part of the hotel you are staying in, for example old age in Hong Kong, the average person has a life expectancy of 85, while those in Chad have an average life expectancy of 55, so location becomes crucial, but we will delve a little further into that up ahead. We begin the ageing process on the very first day that we arrive in the resort and check in at reception, it will then continue until your final day and the moment that you check out.

Ageing is in effect deterioration, a deterioration of all of your vital organs which will at some point start to lose some function, until worn-out completely. Ageing changes occur in all of the body's cells, tissues and organs and inevitably these changes affect all of our body systems, none of us has the privilege of stopping these pernicious effects as the body deteriorates.

Living tissue is made up of cells of which there are many different types but all of them have the same basic structure. Tissues are layers of similar cells that perform a basic function, the different kinds of tissues group together to form organs. Cells are the basic building blocks of tissues, but as they age they become larger and less able to divide and multiply, which means that they find it harder to renew themselves.

Many cells as they age start to lose their function or if not that, they start to function abnormally, which can be equally as disastrous. Because of cell and tissue changes your organs will also change as you age, inevitably our ageing organs slowly lose function, which means that we start to slow down but of course, because the majority of us rarely use these organs to their optimum level, you hardly notice the loss of function immediately and so although we are gradually deteriorating we are not so finely tuned that we notice.

Unfortunately, you have no choice in whether or not you leave the hotel, because that decision has already been made at a higher level, although what remains debatable, is by whom and when, but it means that there is one thing that we can all agree on and that is that it is completely out of our own hands.

Your interpretation of how that decision has been arrived at is completely subjective, you may or may not have an opinion either way, you may have religious beliefs or none at all, you may believe in a scientific explanation, whatever your understanding is, we can agree that none of us factually knows the answer, in spite of it being such a big question! So if we can acknowledge that one day we will all have to get out of this place, check out of our room and take our luggage down to reception then the next consideration becomes the method of departure or of checking out. Ideally, I would imagine that death by natural causes has to be the best option, after that there is a hierarchy of dread, where the options are unattractive to say the lest and frightening at worst.

Depending on which part of the hotel you are staying in, then there can be huge variations in causes of premature deaths by types of illness that are most common in the part of the hotel that you reside in, but initially it is important to look at the process of administering a death, I am currently a guest, staying in the United Kingdom which has created its own customs and culture system, so I will run you through the process after death occurs, in this part of the hotel. In the United Kingdom when the tragic event of a resident passing occurs and one of the guests dies, one of two things will happen, either a doctor writes a death certificate giving an acceptable natural cause of death or if the cause of death doesn't appear to be natural, then a coroner will investigate the death.

Coroners are independent judicial officers who investigate deaths which have been reported to them and their work will entail them initiating enquiries necessary to discover the cause of death, there are several methods of further investigation, including ordering a post-mortem examination, obtaining witness statements and medical records of the guest or holding an inquest.

However, in spite of all of these, the majority of deaths in the United Kingdom are certified by doctors without autopsy or coroner involvement. For our own understanding, it is nice to know the categories for verdicts in the United Kingdom which are fairly self-explanatory and are as follows:

Homicide
Suicide
Attempted or self-induced abortion
Lack of care or self-neglect
Dependence on drugs
Non-dependent abuse of drugs
Want of attention at birth
Death from industrial diseases
Death by accident or misadventure
Stillborn
Death from natural causes
Open verdict disaster

If you think about it, there isn't a method of leaving anything in life and that includes you leaving any event or a special occasion prematurely, as being a happy one, because an early departure usually signifies that something untoward has happened and that our plans have been thrown into turmoil, to a greater or lesser degree, but with the finality of death, that really means it's the end of the journey, our stay is over and our time in the hotel has come to an end.

If we are fortunate enough, we get the time to bid farewell to some of those people who are close to us, those that we have met along the way and shared our time here, if we are lucky enough to have that luxury of saying farewell before we go, then that is all we can ask, however the stark alternative to that is the grim prospect of dying alone.

When we check out, we must relinquish those worldly goods that we have accumulated along the way, we are taking none of them with us, so they all become inconsequential, from treasured items that we have had for years that remind us of others to the new car sitting on the drive which meant so much when we picked it up, but now is just a collection of metal and plastic.

I would like to look at the list of options available to all guests on checking out and as we scan through the alternatives, there is one that stands out as being dreadfully sad, while simultaneously remaining an incredibly sensitive area in comparison to the others.

Suicide is without doubt one of the most controversial discussions to be had when dealing with premature death.

There are polar opinions to be heard and these are equally as valid to those who hold them.

If you are in a hotel and you are not enjoying your stay, taking the decision to leave early could be seen as being a decisive personal decision, because the other alternative could be to stay an endure an experience that, to put it mildly, you are not finding pleasurable.

Now that is a very simplistic view in relation to the fascinating subject of suicide, but one that explains it beautifully.

The word suicide comes from the Latin word *suicidium*, which literally means the taking of one's own life. The decision to take your own life is inevitably a complex one, because there are so many factors which can influence the chances or risk of suicide in a person.

It is believed that mental illness is present in 27% to 90% of those who commit suicide, with up to half of those committing suicide having a personality disorder. There are a number of psychological conditions which can increase the risks of suicide, amongst them are, depression, poor coping skills or even a lack of pleasure in life.

The lack of pleasure in life is the one that interests me most, especially amongst those guests who are staying at the hotel at the same time as ourselves. Finding a lack of pleasure in life is a recognised condition and you will not be in the least surprised to learn that there is even a word for this state, the word is anhedonia, which interestingly, we can see is derived from anti-hedonism, hedonism being the pursuit of pleasure, so anhedonia is the antithesis of this.

Anhedonia is not only the lack of experiencing pleasure but also the lack of seeking it. Anhedonia can be a sexual condition as well as a social condition and if it were concerned with any other subject, we would simply define it as boredom, but is it possible to become bored with life, maybe so, if things aren't working out and life is tougher than we expected. The experts would determine that as a Rational Suicide, where the perpetrator makes an informed decision on their life.

But there will be those who consider that suicide, however justified it is in the mind of the perpetrator, can never be a rational decision, surely that ultimate decision is only ever to be made by one person and that is the person who owns the life.

We also, of course, have euthanasia or assisted suicide, which has become an acceptable practice in several countries, it is intended for those who have a poor quality of life, without the possibility of that life improving or getting any better.

The countries that accept assisted suicide are supportive of the arguments for a right to die, which in itself is another topic that divides opinion. When you consider that assisted suicide is often completed with the assistance of a health service provider, it sounds counter intuitive, because surely a health provider is there to improve or at least sustain your life and not to terminate it.

But that is the issue, when your health is so poor or your condition has deteriorated to a point when you feel you should be checking out of the hotel, a decision freely made while you are still in a position to make it, then some believe that decision is totally within your gift, whereas others, for various reasons believe it to be totally unacceptable to do so.

You will have your own opinion either way, but suffice to say that as a society we have not developed a maturity that allows people to totally control their lives, allowing them to make the ultimate decision.

There are certain countries that have legislated for assisted suicide, many in Europe and the West and in those countries, certain criteria exist in order for a patient to qualify for legal assistance.

The criteria can include the patient having a terminal illness, being of sound mind and taking the decision voluntarily, not all countries demand all of the criteria to approve the final decision and this adds to the sense that there is no societal or cultural consensus or a single view in this tricky area.

The terminology increases sensitivity, indeed those who don't support it will call it assisted suicide, making it sound as unpalatable as possible whereas those who do support it will call it assisted dying, desperate to avoid the negative connotation imposed on the debate by the word suicide and the 'usual' methods of death associated with that word.

Whatever you believe, I sense its use, for those in desperate need for relief from illness desire, is surely an acceptable reason to offer the service.

You often hear, 'they wouldn't treat a dog like this' offered as a comparison for a terminally ill pet at the vets compared to a much loved relative struggling with the end of life in hospital and the options available to both.

In 2019, we saw the creation of the Assisted Dying Coalition, which is exactly what it says, and its aim is to unite organisations working in favour of legal recognition for the right to die and bring about international acceptance. As well as the contentious issue of assisted dying, there is the equally controversial area of the suicide debate, which is another form of suicide, that is equally as polarising and that is, the fascinating area of the suicide debate which is altruistic suicide. Altruistic suicide is where one gives their own life in order to benefit others, for the good of the group, or even in order to preserve the honour of that society, that the life is given for.

Whatever your opinion, the thought of giving your life for the greater good of the society in which you live is indeed the ultimate sacrifice for a perceived, greater good and it takes some mental gymnastics from those who are detached from the situation, in understanding anybody who is prepared to do so.

In order to understand it further, I believe it would be helpful to look at two very distinct types of altruistic society, but two examples which differ, one where the suicide enables the society to be the beneficiary by taking reducing the donors demand of it, whereas the other is giving your life in an aggressive statement to further the political success of a society. Both are altruistic in their purpose but equally different in their nature.

Firstly, I have chosen to look at the prevalence of altruistic suicide amongst the Inuit people of Canada and secondly its use by the kamikaze pilots of Japan, two totally different perspectives, I hope you agree.

The Inuit people are the culturally similar indigenous people living across the Arctic regions of Greenland, Canada and Alaska. The Inuit people are descendants of what we would call the Thule people, who emerged from Western Alaska, they have their own language with many dialects and whose people are diverse, living within their own communities.

Those of us south of the regions of their homelands used the generic name Eskimo for these people, but this name is despised by the Inuit people, as it ignores the subtleties of the people and their heritage. Eskimo literally means eater of raw meat, and obviously there is a lot more to these people than simply eating raw meat.

Because of where they live, the Inuit people have an incredibly hard life, they are a spiritual people with no conventional religion, but where healers mediate with spirits, they are niche, these people perfectly exemplify a boutique hotel or a floor in a major complex, they are outliers, but still accommodate a person's stay in the hotel. Their lives are lived in a splendid isolation, independent of our western idealism and identity although efforts to help assimilation into a global world through coercion rather than willing integration and it is an ongoing affair, but there is a reluctance to accept full integration, with a desperation to retain their cultural identity.

It is understood that the Inuit, who regularly experience desperate winters across their lands, would commit the act of senicide on the elderly members of the community. Senicide is the harsh act of killing the elderly or unproductive people in the Inuit communities, the thinking being that those members of the community could only be a drain on the society and be unable to contribute to it, especially when resources are scarce, as they are during those desperate winters, this inevitably can only be a hindrance to the success of the society.

When food was scarce and hunters were needed to get food for the group, it was thought that the elderly could be the biggest burden to the group, both needing food and yet, physically unable to hunt.

Old people having outlived their usefulness and had become a burden not only to themselves, due to illness and lack of mobility but also to their relatives, so the answer is that they are put to death by stabbing or strangulation.

I sense that we would perceive these callous actions as understandable but also extreme, but when there is no health service, there isn't a welfare system to provide financial benefits, then the stark reality of survival of society, then anything that contributes to the greater good is justified.

The whole scenario is unattractive, surely it can't get any worse you may think, but as if senicide, wasn't bad enough, the Inuit also practice infanticide, it seems unimaginable to us in our cosseted world, where yes things can be tough, but to actually consider killing the old and the young of our society would be unthinkable.

Sadly, the Inuit people don't have the luxury of choice and sadly yes, infanticide, the killing of babies in the group is also practiced, merely as a response to the dreadfully difficult conditions.

It is not easy to calculate the numbers on either of senicide or infanticide as these two dreadful methods as a cause of death as not only are they unpalatable and inevitably getting people to acknowledge them is understandably difficult, because they appear in nature to be such savage acts, yet the contradiction is that to the Inuit people themselves they are both obviously necessary for the good of their society.

Whenever you stay in any hotel, and the bigger the hotel the more relevant this example is, each floor or in some cases each building in the complex tends to develop its own culture.

There are small and intimate boutique hotels with only a small number of bedrooms, which tend to create their own micro environment, most people know each other whether it is guests or the staff, because there aren't a large number of faces to get to know, you tend to bump into the same people every day and this can be either, exactly what you want, or it can feel a little claustrophobic, whereas at the opposite end of the scale, there are some hotels which are virtual cities in their own right.

I am thinking of hotels that I have seen in Las Vegas or Dubai and these places are so vast that even some members of staff don't know each other. Of course, there is no science to it, it is purely about feelings and your preference, alternatively, the intimate boutique hotel would be perfect for a romantic weekend away, while the Las Vegas convention hotel would be ideal for a stag night or bachelor party.

My point is that when you stay in one of the super-size hotels that it is virtually impossible to be on first-name terms with anybody apart from the person that you are sharing your room with. Out of interest, the largest hotel in the world is currently to be found in Malaysia, the First World Hotel in Genting, which has an incredible 7,351 bedrooms, mall shops and many restaurants; it is an economic entity in its own right, but totally impersonal.

In these hotels, because they are so vast, they tend to create micro communities, smaller communities which develop on your own corridor, the favourite bar that you have discovered and frequent, or the swimming pool area you use daily. We are all creatures of habit, we have our favourite seats in the restaurant, we know where we like to sit by the pool and it is in these spaces that we tend to meet the same people daily and the community tends to grow and thrive, within a community.

Within either example of the hotel being small or large, community develops and this is mirrored in society; the Inuit community can be seen as a small boutique hotel, an entity in their own right, or as part of a super complex, which has developed a sub culture.

If ever there was an example that highlights the disparities that exist, then the need to cull surely serves to do just that, which is determined by the part of the hotel in which you are staying, then surely this is one of the most extreme!

There is another form of altruistic death that we can consider, although this one gives a totally different perspective to how the giving of one's own life for the greater good of society can be justified by the giver, who in this second example, is not doing so because of their own deteriorating health or physical weakness, indeed those 'donating' to the cause in this case are supremely fit individuals who strive for what they perceive as a higher cause or superior ideology.

I want to look at the altruism of the kamikaze pilot, now your first reaction may be the same as mine, in thinking that anybody prepared to give their life in order to fulfil the ambitions of any political regime, whether outside or inside the theatre of war is not worth considering, but in order to establish how we feel, we need to be armed with the facts.

When we are considering an altruistic suicide for the good of others by any person, then the kamikaze pilot must be acknowledged for their commitment to the cause that they are giving their lives for, no matter how misguided we believe them to be, their total commitment is there for all to see.

Death instead of defeat, instead of capture and instead of shame was entrenched into the Japanese army and has been its mantra throughout the country's military culture. The word Kamikaze means 'Divine Wind', Kami, being the Japanese word for god or in this case divinity and Kazi the word for wind.

The very first kamikaze pilots were not experienced pilots but were passionate young men who were aged between just 17 and 30 years of age, they were the best available to the Japanese Air Force and many volunteered from the navy and from universities to be kamikaze pilots. These young men usually had between 24 and 40 hours flying time and training before they were allocated their final missions.

Many of these pilots willingly participated in their acts, dressing in ceremonial uniform, including a white scarf and a headband, many carried a samurai sword along with a picture of the emperor in the cockpit and in those early days it was not hard to find volunteers for the role, but latterly they became a little more difficult to find and young men had to be conscripted to find suitable candidates.

The Japanese used in total approximately 6000 pilots most of them flew in 1944, the majority of their targets were United States naval ships during World War 2, following the Japanese attack on US naval base in Pearl Harbour,

Honolulu! Until that time the USA had been a neutral country in WW2, but that attack brought America into the war.

Once again, there are too many historians and written historical records for me to attempt to make my contribution to the voluminous content accumulated, so it would be rather pointless for me to add my ill-informed opinion.

But as a contribution to life being a hotel and to see these young pilots checking out early simply for the good of their country, I find it interesting to understand how and why they found themselves in a situation where giving their lives for the benefit of their country became not only laudable and acceptable it was considered to be an honour.

The Yasukuni shrine in Tokyo was built to commemorate the kamikaze pilots, at the shrine there is a plaque which honours these men and reads as follows, the suicide operators, incomparable in their tragic bravery, struck terror in their foes and engulfed the entire country in tears of gratitude for their outstanding loyalty and selfless service.

These men were driven by nothing more than self-sacrifice, however there are at least two perspectives that we can consider when looking at their decision to pay the ultimate price for and on behalf of others.

Initially, the kamikaze units were oversubscribed with the pilots seeing it as an honour to die for their country and the emperor, but as we know, this changed a little as time went on. No doubt their perspective would be reflected in the patriotic death poem by Motoori Norinaga; loosely translated, it reads:

Asked about the soul of Japan
I would say
That it is
Like wild cherry blossoms
Glowing in the morning sun

This beautiful verse sanitises what was, ultimately, death by suicide, so in order to compensate for this and dispel the glamour, the pilots manual took the romance out of the act and brought the pilots mission back into sharp focus, saying, 'When you eliminate all thoughts about life and death, you will be able to totally disregard your earthly life.'

These two contributions can be seen as a positive reason to die for the cause, but as we have discovered, the romanticism of the act and those pilots doing it, were not felt throughout the country, not everybody in Japan observed their acts with affection and as time progressed, those who didn't see them as noble soldiers, felt compelled to say as much.

There is a well-known Japanese journalist and businessman, his business and work interests include Japan's largest selling daily newspaper, *Yomiuri Shinbun,* and the country's largest commercial television station, Nippon Television Network and his contribution to all things media in Japan is significant. His name is Tsuneo Watanabe and as recently as 2006, he said:

It's all a lie that they left filed with braveness and joy, crying 'long live the emperor'.
They were sheep at a slaughterhouse.

Tsuneo certainly offers a controversial opinion and he may find many who agree with his position, however, you can't question, that willing or not, these young men gave their lives for their country, in doing so they effectively checked out of the hotel early and therefore they were no longer staying here as guests. Those altruistic suicides, because of their historical nature and because we as a society have had time to dwell on their impact and form an opinion have subsequently become well documented as ways of checking out of the hotel, now that they are historically well established.

One more recent development in the field of altruistic suicide is the suicide bomber, although if we consider it, those kamikaze pilots would by today's standards be considered to be suicide bombers too, although they were operating as instruments of the state. This has become to be known as state sponsored terrorism, whereas the suicide bombers that have become all too familiar these days tend to be non-state actors and are usually associated with terrorism because more often than not and rather disappointingly, they tend to target civilians.

The modern suicide bombing era began in the Lebanon in the 80s, in fact it was in Beirut on October the 23rd 1983, when two truck bombs struck buildings containing American and French servicemen who were part of the multinational peace keeping forces operating there during the Lebanese civil war. This attack was claimed by Islamic Jihad who wanted the multinational peace force out of Lebanon and they eventually got their way as the peace force withdrew.

Since 1983 there have been many suicide bombings around the world for varied and different causes, from Sri Lanka to Palestine to Chechnya where one group who became known as the Black Widows, a female group who used suicide bombings in their fight for Chechnyan independence.

It is believed these women had come together because they had lost their husbands and brothers to the conflict and because of their gender, they attract less suspicion than their male counterparts. Latterly, Boko Haram, the Islamist group based in Nigeria, have used female suicide bombers for similar reasons.

But surely, in the minds of any of us that were staying in the hotel at the time, one of the most memorable events of recent times for all of the wrong reasons was what I would dare to suggest has become the ultimate suicide bombing in the history of the hotel.

It's not difficult to recall the dreadful incident of the attack on the Twin Towers in New York in 2001. The terrorist group Al Qaeda attacked four sites in the USA on 9th September 2001, resulting in 2,977 fatalities, the deadliest terrorist attack in human history and known forever by 9/11.

Four passenger airliners which had departed airports in the North Eastern part of the country and bound for California were hijacked by 19 Al Qaeda terrorists. Two of the planes flew into the North and South towers of the World Trade Centre, a third plane flew into the Pentagon and a fourth flew into a field in Pennsylvania after passengers thwarted the terrorists.

It is difficult to establish a definitive reason for the attacks, however they were initiated under the authorisation of Osama bin Laden the leader of Al Qaeda and he claimed that Al Qaeda was solely responsible for the attack.

This was one of those moments in time when you remember where you were and what you were doing when you first heard or saw the news, this was after all in the early days of rolling 24 hour news and for the record I was staying with my wife and friends in Cala Llamp in Majorca and had just returned to our villa after a fabulous lunch in Port d'Andratx.

I put Sky News on and the four of us couldn't believe what we were watching, we sat around the TV watching for the next couple of hours, realising that our world had changed forever, although we weren't sure how, but we knew it would change irrevocably and I also believe that the unspoken consensus amongst the four of us was that things certainly weren't changing for the better.

The 9/11 attacks were possibly the most extreme example of global terrorism that the world had ever seen, watching as young men committed suicide for their cause, so what could be the motivation for those 19 men who were aboard the four aeroplanes doing the work of Al Qaeda.

In fact, before we look at their reasons or justifications for committing the horrendous attack, I am going to mention something that although a little incongruous, does provide a tenuous link with 9/11 that affected not only those poor souls who perished and their families, but the ripple effect reaches as far Stoke-on-Trent, nearly 3,500 miles away.

I did not intend to discuss this story at this stage of the book, but bear with me, because it is relevant not only to the attack on the Twin Towers, but also how fate can and does play an incredible part in all of our lives during our stay in the hotel. If it wasn't for Osama Bin Laden, my cousin Mick would never have met Jayne, who he has subsequently married.

Let me explain a little further, as I have already mentioned, I was in Majorca when 9/11 changed the world forever and as a consequence our flight home three days after the terrorist attack was grounded because there was a fear that many commercial flights didn't have the appropriate insurance cover to fly as they had prior to the attack.

We, as the rest of the world's tourists, were unaware of the turmoil that was effecting the travel industry and duly arrived at Palma airport at the appropriate time for our flight back to the UK. The airport was overcrowded and we were fortunate to have found two seats in the departure lounge.

Flight information was scarce and we were all sitting around with very few flights departing, the atmosphere was frazzled with none of us having a clue what was going on, don't forget, this was in the days before the mobile phone and its many travel apps had become mandatory if not essential for the global traveller.

I popped to the toilets in the airport departure lounge, there was a bloke in there stripped down to his underpants using a washbasin and was virtually having a bath in, the minuscule porcelain sink.

Desperate men take desperate measures, I thought, it was pretty fraught out there in the departure lounge and for some bizarre reason, maybe it was his attitude or appearance, I had convinced myself that this man was from Germany. I went back to where I had left my wife and suitcases, she was talking to another lady, who I subsequently discovered was on our flight, back to the UK.

I told my wife about the German guy in the toilets having a shower in the washbasin, we laughed at his desperation as we sat unaware of our own departure time. As we continued chatting with the lady that my wife had started talking to, our conversation naturally turned to what we were doing and where we were when we saw 9/11 happening.

It was at that moment that the German from the gents toilets came over to us and sat next to his wife, who happened to be the lady we were chatting to, he wasn't from downtown Hamburg, but was flying back to England on our flight and then heading home to Stoke-on-Trent, we were in the foothills of a new friendship, let me introduce you to Trevor and Rosa.

That day at Palma airport, we had the luck or good fortune to be sitting next to a couple from Stoke-on-Trent who were on the same flight as us back home, but after several hours of our flight being delayed, it was finally cancelled and we were told to collect our cases and get onto the waiting coach outside which was to take us to the nearby resort of Cala Viñas, where we checked into a nice hotel just in time for dinner.

We sat in the hotel restaurant with English Trevor and his wife, Italian Rosa; dinner was fabulous, we had a few drinks and after an impromptu bingo and karaoke night, laid on for us by our tour operator, yes I know, it sounds a bit cheesy, but we totally threw ourselves into it and on a night that we were due to be back home, sifting through the accumulated two weeks' post, going to a late-night supermarket for bread, milk and beans and collecting Kookie from the cattery, instead we found ourselves playing bingo in Majorca.

We had an early pick up the next morning, the hotel wanted us out and taken to Palma airport who desperately wanted to shift the backlog caused by mounting delays. We flew home, having swapped the obligatory phone numbers and promised Trevor and Rosa we would see each other again and be best friends forever.

I did call Trevor a couple of times once we had returned home in the weeks that followed and our lives were back to normality. Trevor, who happened to be a twin, was due to celebrate his 40th birthday within a couple of months of our return and obviously he invited us to the party at his local pub in Stoke-on-Trent.

Stoke isn't a place that I know very well, having been there four or five times before, of which at least two of those occasions were for Liverpool matches, neither Diane or I had any other reason to visit prior to meeting Trevor and Rosa.

That was all about to change, I have a cousin who lives in Stoke, having only just moved there, he had recently divorced and was currently single, although he did have an on and off relationship with a mad woman, who he had met subsequent to leaving the RAF several years earlier, I felt it may be a nice night out for my cousin Mick and an opportunity for me to catch up with him, so I asked Trevor if he minded me inviting him to the party, 'no problem' said Trevor, so I called Mick, told him we were coming to Stoke for a night and that it would be great to see him there.

The night of the party, my wife and I drove down to Stoke approximately forty miles away and found our way to a pub on the outskirts of town, Trevor and his brother and their joint 40th birthday party was in full swing, we were introduced to their friends and were soon joined by my cousin Mick who lived in the area and not a million miles from the pub.

As I mentioned, Mick had divorced a couple of years earlier and so he brought his current girlfriend to the party, we hadn't met her before, so we were introduced and we were having a good night.

At some point a little later in the evening, I sensed that things between Mick and his girlfriend weren't going well and she left the party early to go home alone. Mick stayed and he appeared to be enjoying himself, in spite of or maybe because of his girlfriend's departure.

To cut a very long story short, it was while at the party that my cousin would meet the girl of his dreams, well, at least the girl that was to become his future wife, a person that at the start of the evening he didn't even know existed. Mick met Jayne, who was a long-time friend of Trevor and Rosa at the birthday party and for the next five years they grew closer until finally getting married in 2015.

The whole point of the brief interlude in this chapter is to highlight how your stay in the hotel can change, even when the ultimate cause, in this case 9/11, was to create the circumstances that would initiate global change and had absolutely nothing to do with Mick and Jayne indeed it was totally out of their control, yet it changed their lives forever.

When this happens, you can call it fate, luck or just life, were Mick and Jayne always destined to meet, after all they both lived in Stoke, or would they simply have coexisted passing each other in the queue in Starbucks in town totally unaware of each other's existence, but when given the opportunity to meet, they can become so entrenched in each other's worlds that they can commit to each other for the rest of their lives.

That then begs the question, how many people do we never meet during our stay, that we could share our lives in the hotel with and moreover, if Osama bin Laden hadn't have ordered the destruction of the Twin Towers, would Mick be married to Jayne?

I hope you feel that was worth the interruption, however we need to get back on track and discuss the reasons the suicide bombers of 9/11 felt compelled to do what they did.

As we now know, what they chose to do changed our world, they took the most dramatic actions the world has ever seen, taking not just their own lives in the attacks but those of the innocent victims, numbering 2,977, along with over 6,000 who were injured.

For most of us, the mentality of those prepared to sacrifice themselves to kill others is virtually impossible to understand. It was assumed that they were committing suicide in the name of their religion, that they weren't necessarily doing it for altruistic reasons, but were possibly being selfish, because in their religion they are known as jihadists or an Islamic militant.

Jihadists extol the virtue and they actually honour martyrdom as a solemn declaration of faith, it is the noblest deed a Muslim can perform, so however misguided non-believers may think they are, these people could actually be the most selfish amongst us.

These believers understand, believe and are therefore convinced that there is a greater value on death than on life. They are convinced that they are bringing victory against their perceived oppressors but they also believe that their actions give them the assurance of eternal life in paradise with all of the fabulous rewards that it offers.

There are many terrorist organisations throughout the world, throughout the hotel, so let us take a closer look at their understanding of the world.

Hamas is a Palestinian nationalist movement and one of the areas two leading political parties in the region, it governs more than two million Palestinians in the Gaza Strip, it is best known for its armed resistance to Israel and it is dedicated to the establishment of an independent Islamic state in Palestine. Hamas also has a terrorist division who strive to achieve their clearly defined political goals through terrorism, so much so that they have written:

Allah builds good and pleasant dwellings in heaven. The inhabitants receive rooms under which flow rivers. There are also tents in heaven each one made of pearl sixty miles high and sixty miles wide. Each mile contains a special corner for family members of the believer. In paradise Allah provides the inhabitants with rivers of water, milk, honey and wine. The shahid (martyr) for Allah receives immediate atonement of all his sins with the first drop of his blood being shed...and he weds seventy-two virgins, the shahid receives the potency of seventy men.

That is quite a lengthy contribution to use in a book that is about *Life is a Hotel*, but as this chapter is about checking out, I believe that this contribution is rather interesting and leads inevitably to one of the later chapters in the book being, 'Where To?' The suicide bomber through his death has somewhere to go, so it's not so much that they see themselves as checking out of the hotel, but as the first part of a two-centre holiday, with the first part of their time being spent in the hotel, that we are all staying in before they move on to the next part of the trip, spent who knows where.

So it could be a little difficult to suggest that this is an altruistic suicide, moreover it is, indeed they are, incredibly selfish.

Of all of the people all over the world that I have ever discussed the point of life with and there has been many, there has only really ever been one person who had any conviction in their answer and their belief and that they were convinced that they knew what would happen next and assured that this life, where all of us spend our time in the hotel, wasn't the important part of our existence, as there was much more to come.

I speak of a good friend of mine called Usman, a Muslim who had the firm belief that there is life after death, Usman told me it is called Akhirah. In Islam it is Allah that decides when a person dies, he believed that Muslims, once dead, remain in their graves until the judgment day. On that day they will be brought before Allah and judged on how they have lived their lives.

Those who have performed more good deeds throughout their lives than bad enter Jannah, effectively this is a paradise, a garden of eternal bliss and a home of peace. There is of course an alternative, not every Muslim can lead a perfect life adhering to their religious principles and demands, so those that do primarily bad deeds will enter Jahannam or as non-Muslims may call it, hell.

Having a belief in life after death is central to the meaning and purpose of most Muslims' lives. Many Muslims believe that they are on this earth for a relatively short period of time and they are preparing for eternal life after death.

They view their time spent in this hotel, as opposed to the next hotel, or whatever manifestation their new accommodation takes, as simply being a test in order to try to do as many good deeds while they are here as is possible in order to get Jannah.

Irrespective of whether you believe what Usman believes, it gives a sense of purpose or structure to our stay and the promise that a life well-lived will get to enjoy a permanent extended stay, what's not to like?

We are all going to check out at some time or other and therefore why not make the prospect of our departure more attractive by the promise of an even better future. What we do know is that nobody knows for sure what happens once we leave and in the words of Benjamin Franklin, 'but in this world, nothing can be said to be as certain apart from death and taxes', I think you'll find it hard to disagree.

Chapter 4
Where To?

So that is it, it's over, your time here is coming to an end, you knew it was going to happen at some time, it was inevitable and hopefully barring accidents or serious misfortune, you knew or at least had some idea that this would be it, not the precise time exactly but given your age and the state of your health you knew approximately that this would be the length of your stay.

As with all departures, whether it's getting ready to go for an evening at the theatre, or checking out of your hotel room for the final time, they all take some degree of planning before you finally leave, so you make plans in advance, several people that I have met have this down to a fine art, starting the process a few days before the end of their departure, they will start begin packing in readiness for the off, whereas other friends I know leave everything to the last possible minute, these friends are famous for their disorganised, haphazard attitude.

For those who like to plan their departure from the hotel way in advance and are prepared to go when the time comes, they will get their suitcase out, start filling them with those clothes that they wore in the first few days of their stay, that are now either too dirty to wear again or have been discarded in favour of different items of clothing still waiting to be worn and hanging in the wardrobes, they can be put into the suitcase, safe in the knowledge that they will never be needed again.

If they have any of the local currency left, especially coins, followed by notes, they will start using them instead of putting things on their hotel bill, usually the incidental purchases that tend to crop up while you are mooching around the hotel for their few remaining days.

But I have friends who are not that way inclined, have no interest in tidying up the loose ends before their stay is over, none of that is important to them, choosing instead to optimise every single minute of their stay, believing that there is plenty of time for things like that when they are no longer in residence as a guest, once they have checked out and are no longer here.

While you are still in the hotel, all time is precious and can be better used positively, enjoying your limited allocation in the hotel for as long as possible and any time spent on packing or doing the necessary administrative duties could be construed as wasting some of that valuable time allotted to them, understanding that their departure is inevitable, so those things can take care of themselves once they've gone. Once it's over, depending on your understanding or your beliefs, that's if you have any, that relate to the 'Where To' or even 'What's Next', debate and if indeed anything does happen next, you will presumably have all the time in the world to dwell on the thoughts prior to your departure, so let's not waste any time by thinking about it while we are here.

However, even if you have packed your cases and you are anything like my wife, in spite of believing that you have packed everything, you still can't resist having a last look around the room to make sure that you haven't left anything behind, but even after all of those precautions, I have known her to get home and then find out, she has left clothes in the wardrobe, cosmetics in the bathroom or gym kit in a gym locker.

Of course, there are always the items of clothing that you have left out to wear, there could be items of jewellery, your watch or currency or those other items that you have put into the safe in the room, to keep them safe, they indeed are so safe, that you forget all about them.

If you are lucky enough to have ever been on a skiing holiday, you will know that more often than not your skis, sticks and boots are usually kept somewhere else in the hotel, usually in a remote part of the building, the boot room can be found in the basement of the hotel and it is very easy, especially if the last day of the holiday has ended up with an extended après-ski party, then it is all too easy to totally forget to collect your equipment before leaving.

As your stay comes to an end and whether you start packing early or leave it until the last minute, you always find and pardon me, but this is probably an obvious thing to say, you appear to have accumulated a significant amount of excess baggage during your stay, certainly enough to fill your case with a lot more ephemera than when you first arrived and it is a lot harder to cram all of those things into your case, rather than having the luxury of the extra space that you had in there when you first arrived, so full is your case as you ready yourself for departure that you can have trouble actually zipping the thing and you will sometimes need a willing relative, or the nearest member of hotel staff to sit on the lid while you desperately try and zip the thing up and finally lock it.

Then there is Sod's Law, which invariably means that you will have to go through the whole process once again as you find a pair of swimming trunks that you left drying out on the balcony, or the anti-perspirant you left until the last minute in the bathroom, before once again cramming them into your suitcase, but this time you refuse to open the whole case, instead like a senior surgeon practicing keyhole surgery, you open the zips with just enough of a hole to squeeze the potential escapee through, zipping the case up immediately once the offending article is securely encased. I believe that this whole process can be seen as simply a metaphor for the end of your life, your packing up, it's time to go and whether it's planned or last minute, that's the only input you have into its inevitability.

The day that you check in, you arrive with absolutely nothing, you check in at reception with a lifetime in front of you and although when you finally leave you also leave with nothing, there are a lifetime of memories that you have collected, but it is only memories, of course you also have all of those physical items that once upon a time seemed to be so important to you, to your everyday life and possibly they were, but ultimately they are as transient as the case you carry them in.

Once you've packed, you do your final look around before you head down to reception where you ask for your bill, simultaneously you may also ask for a porter or the concierge to help you to bring your luggage down from your room.

At reception you are presented with an itemised bill, a list of everything that you have consumed during your stay, starting on the day you arrived and added to every day that you stayed, you then take the opportunity to scan through your bill and it is at this time that you are reminded of those nights at the start of your stay, the nights that had become a distant memory and seem like a lifetime ago, there are those drinks that you've had in the bar before dinner, the wine you've had with your meals and even the expensive nights when you had a late night and extra drinks with the new friends that you made in those delirious, heady first few days of your stay.

Great memories come flooding back, but they aren't all adrenaline filled, crazy nights, because as well as the nights you let it rip, there are those quiet nights, the nights when you didn't fancy getting dressed up and going down to dinner, when all you wanted was to get into your PJs and instead of the nightly glamour of getting dolled up and heading for the a la carte dining room, all you wanted to do was switch the TV on and choose instead to order from the well-thumbed room service menu.

As you scan your bill, your eyes are drawn to an item that reminds you of that afternoon that wasn't so great, you ordered lunch that day and unfortunately you didn't particularly enjoy it, it wasn't the best, either the quality of the food, poor service or it was pouring with rain, whatever it was, it was a disappointing experience, but it was just a small part of the whole stay, you don't dwell on it and you won't let it spoil the rest of your stay, in fact, if it wasn't for the record of it on your final bill, you would have forgotten all about it.

As you approach the final few days of your stay, it is inevitable that you have at least one eye on your departure, whether you decide to do anything about it or not is up to you, but as we know, many of us do and so it is those people, the ones that start to plan for it, anticipating their last day when they will finally check out at reception!

I have come to believe that there are two ways of playing this, you can either cram in as much as possible in order to squeeze as much into every remaining moment out of your stay, or conversely you can start taking things a little easier, safe in the knowledge that you have got the more adventurous things out of the way earlier in the stay and now is the time to relax, slow it down, take it easy and let those who have recently checked in, the new arrivals get on with discovering, what the hotel and its surroundings have to offer.

But as you look back over your time spent in the hotel, the memories remain, the good and the bad, the highs and the lows, the happy and the sad, all come flooding back at the most random moments, in spite of these, it is hard for your focus not to change and it is at this time that we start to concentrate on where we are going to next.

Having checked out and sat with your suitcases in reception before the taxi arrives to take you to the airport, in between walking up and down, or looking out of the window, possibly with a couple of friends that you have met during your stay, who, unlike you are not leaving today but have simply come to say goodbye and then the time arrives, the taxi is here, you walk outside, a few final farewells, hugs and kisses and maybe a few tears before you walk outside, you jump into your taxi and the driver utters the immortal words, where too?

Usually, you have a destination in mind and you may believe that you know exactly where you are heading, it could possibly the airport, or maybe the ferry, or the station or depending on your location the taxi could be heading straight home.

If you're not heading straight home, you may be facing a far longer journey, you may be travelling by aeroplane, you may be heading to the ferry terminal to head home by ship and this is only the first leg of your journey, it may be long, it may be traumatic so you mentally prepare yourself for the long day ahead, for what can be a draining experience but it is all part of the sacrifice necessary to get back to the place you call home.

Looking forward to getting back to your house, your home, your place of sanctuary, where everything gives a sense of familiarity where you can look forward to spending your time surrounded by your stuff, making a cup of tea with your kettle and of course, sleeping in your own bed.

As you sit in the taxi, you head towards your final destination and you have time to think back over your time in the hotel, from the moment you arrived and the first impressions that you had, Impressions, some of which turned out to be exactly what you thought they would be and inevitably those others that were incorrect and which during your stay meant that you changed your mind.

There may have been the barman, the guy who at first you felt was stand offish or a little austere, but as time went in, they became somebody who you would actually look forward to seeing and equally they would look forward to seeing you, indeed in many cases they will have become a firm friend, no matter how temporarily, but certainly for the time you are there.

You travel with your memories, they are your companions for it is they that are all that is left at the end of the whole experience, stories of great days, great nights and great friends you have met along the way, obviously it will not all have been fun and games, like for everybody, there will have been trials and tribulations along the way.

It is very interesting, when you try to consider what it is that determines a happy and successful life, but it's not as simple as that, it doesn't work that way, we are all very different, we all have different aspirations and it is for that reason that satisfaction can present itself in the most unlikely ways.

Life is a process in which there will be highs and lows, in order to have highs, you must have lows, in order for us to understand good, you have to know and understand what bad means.

It is these basics that allow us to understand life, there is no silver bullet, there is no panacea, there is no perfect life, I think we all know that such a thing does not exist, the older you get, the more you realise, there is no such thing as perfection.

Yes, it exists in the moment, in isolation you will find utter contentment and if you do, grab it, because these are times precious and you don't know when they are coming around again.

However, if perfection could exist with longevity and in order to establish the possibility of it, you had a survey, let's say you chose to ask one hundred individual people to name the one thing that they believe would guarantee a good life, then I feel confident that you may get a hundred different answers, but if there was one common denominator amongst those answers, something that all of those questioned felt may help in your search for perfection, then I would imagine that the one single thing they might observe as a major contributor to the perfect state, that would make for a happy life for everybody, then that thing would be money!

So I think it is worthwhile for us to take a moment and use it as an opportunity to analyse this, is money the one single item that would guarantee happiness, let us take a look at people or indeed families who have had more than the requisite amount of money to provide happiness, but find that in reality, having this privilege hasn't quite worked out that way we would imagine and wealth isn't quite the universal remedy it may appear to be. For those of us who are lucky enough to be living here in the UK, we have the perfect example of absolute wealth and how it absolutely is a quick fix for happiness and a fulfilled life.

In the United Kingdom, we have what is known as a monarchy, this is a form of government in which a single person, known as the monarch is head of state for life or until abdication.

Monarchy does exist in other forms all around the world, but it takes different forms and although the purpose of this section is not to discuss the types of monarchy available it certainly allows us an insight into the benefits of being the monarch.

There are a plethora of titles available to the monarch and they are different throughout the world. Once again, for our purposes, these are not of importance, it just happens that at this moment in our history we in the United Kingdom are enjoying the reign of King Charles the third having exceeded to the throne following the death of his mother Queen Elizabeth the second who died on the

8th of September 1992 aged 96, as I write, the relatively new king is learning to live with his loyal subjects, for that is what we are, having celebrated the queen's platinum jubilee, on the 6th February 2022, that is seventy years of service that our queen had given to us her people and to her country.

The king as our country's current head of the monarchy, the monarchy being the rest of his family who are known collectively by that title, that is his immediate family and relatives, a system often criticised for its indulgence of lesser royals and affording them a lifestyle fit for a king or queen, without the responsibility and demands of either.

One crucial factor in this whole equation is that in the United Kingdom the monarchy is hereditary and therefore as long as the government continues to be a monarchy and not a republic, which is the political alternative, then the kings family will remain as the head of state.

Within this system, there is obviously great responsibility required and with it a dedication and service to the country, but as a result of that, the position provides great wealth, a lot of it as a custodian, but inevitably an incredible income is afforded to the monarch.

If we look to evaluate the wealth of our recently deceased queen, the research tells us that and this is for the most recent numbers available; in 2020, Queen Elizabeth was personally worth £350 million and the monarchy in its entirety was worth £72 billion. So, if we go back to our mythical survey asking 100 people the simplest of questions, which is, 'what is needed for a happy life', it would seem that as the queen and her family have such incredible personal wealth, it would naturally suggest that as an individual and within her own family, Queen Elizabeth should arguably be one of the happiest people and her direct family one of the most content families on the planet, or rather staying in the hotel.

But wait, because when we actually look at the lives of those family members that make up the British royal family, the monarchy and their sense of individual fulfilment, although we have no direct access to their inner thoughts, we can certainly imagine what their answers would be.

In order to do this, we need to look at their current situations and demonstrably we can see that from the relationships both successful and failed amongst the queen and her deceased husband Prince Phillips' direct family, that it would appear that vast wealth is absolutely no guarantee whatsoever of a perfect fulfilled life.

They have four children all of whom have independent wealth, this is probably as a by-product of their royal status, but nonetheless they are extremely wealthy, but that wealth appears to have brought with it, its own problems with three of the four children, Charles, Anne and Andrew, all having marriages that ended in divorce, while Edward, the youngest of the four children remains happily married to this day, having married in 1999.

The Queen and Prince Philip were married in 1947 so they are a fabulous example to their children of how to make a marriage work, but wait, their longevity could possibly be because they came from a different generation a cohort were divorce wasn't as easy as it is today and staying together was also a sense of duty especially as the reigning monarch whose own marital strength was necessary to provide stability and inspiration to the rest of the country, their lead seen as being crucially important to their subjects.

Incidentally, between the 1970s and 2020, the divorce rate in the United Kingdom has doubled and societally there is a different perspective on failed marriages and it has become a little more acceptable, so as well as being a generational thing, the failed marriages of her children reflect the fact that her children have grown up in this changing world.

The Queen and Prince Phillip married in 1947, but the years after their wedding, looking at the 1960s, divorces were far from the norm, in fact In those days, Britain was still operating under the 1937 Matrimonial Causes Act, an Act which to us looking at it through today's values would appear to be unacceptable.

The Matrimonial Causes Act demanded that in order to divorce, one partner had to prove against the other, that a commission of a matrimonial offence had occurred, there were several options available and they consisted of, cruelty, desertion, adultery or incurable insanity.

It see incredible to us today and equally unbelievable is the fact that no divorce was allowed within the first three years of marriage.

So, as we can see, the world was a very, very different place, but irrespective of the changes in society, over 70 years of marriage suggests that our queen and her husband are the perfect example of how to make a marriage work, of course they have experienced difficult times but they have held it together.

But if you look at the next generation, the queen's children, being brought up in an existence of both wealth and privilege, having the benefit of virtual unlimited wealth has not provided a happy, untroubled existence for at least 75% of them, indeed their wealth may have added to the complexities of their lives.

So the assumption that money will give you a perfect existence while staying in one of the nicest parts of the hotel doesn't naturally follow; indeed, we could go as far as to say it is a myth.

Although one memorable quote that sticks in my mind and related to this topic was from the American actress Bo Derek, a stunning woman most famous for her role in the 1979 film 10. The well-known actress said, 'Whoever said that money can't buy happiness, simply don't know where to go shopping'.

So it appears that there is no definitive answer and as with everything, life is about opinions and Bo Derek certainly knew hers.

As we near our ultimate destination, reflection of our time spent in the hotel is all that we have left and I believe that this is as an important part of the whole equation, as important as life itself, if we are fortunate enough, we allow ourselves a mental TripAdvisor review of what our stay at the hotel has been like, from start to finish.

There will be those things that we have loved and we rejoice in their memories, conversely there will be the things that we would rather not contaminate our thinking with as our final destination nears.

Reflections are an important and a beautiful part of life and are the primary function of the *Where To* chapter.

In one of our earlier chapters, *Planning Permission*, we looked at how the views into the creation of the Earth falls roughly into two offerings, religion or science and when we are deciding our own opinion of how the hotel was created and how those earliest days of our hotel, shaped and gave us the planet that we know today.

Unless you are aware of a third option, you have these two options, they fall into the choice between either a reliance on your faith, your religion of choice or maybe it's the science that guides you and informs your position on creation and those same two guiding lights are there beckoning us as we end our journey.

Where To is just one of the questions of life that of the eight billion staying here today and all of those who have ever stayed here as guests before us have in common, when faced with that question and it is their commonality of view, a consensus that we can all agree which is that none of them know the definitive answer.

Does that mean because there isn't a definitive answer or is it just that we still haven't found it yet? What are the options? Well, I would prefer to consider views of the afterlife by looking at three potential answers, just to see if we can get an insight into us forming an answer or at least starting to form an answer.

Firstly, let's look at religion because there are so many followers of different religions across the world, in many guises and offers diverse opinions to the question of *Where To?*

The other two areas that I have looked at are esotericism and metaphysics so maybe they can offer an opinion where the afterlife is concerned.

Esotericism is a wide range of loosely associated ideas which have developed in western society, as a collective they can be seen as a part of a wider culture and its traditions although they that may not necessarily be aligned to any single culture, inevitably as a matter of course there will be a lot of common ground and crossover with various religions.

That being the case, there is no definitive 'Where To', answer, at least from an esoteric perspective, but it is felt that to believe in a 'Where To' option then you necessarily have to have a religious commitment, a belief in god, a god that leads us to an afterlife a where to go to.

It is difficult to find cultural references outside of religious beliefs that lead to a belief in life after death, it appears that in order to believe in an afterlife that it comes with a religious belief in order to validate it, otherwise, it appears that once you've checked out, that's it, there is nothing else.

Finally, there is metaphysics, which if you don't know, is a branch of philosophy where the fundamental nature of reality is examined. The relationship between mind and matter, between potentiality and actuality and finally between substance and attribute. Metaphysics studies to understand what it actually means for something to exist and once that is established, it studies what types of existence there are.

For metaphysics to decide on Where To, it needs to establish whether the person is a complete entity or whether there is more than the available evidence of life, more than we actually know or understand that actually influences our progress. Metaphysics is a minefield and the complexities of the subject make a straightforward answer to the 'Where To' question incredibly difficult to decide upon.

Intellectually, it boils down to a conversation about surviving physical death if that is possible and once that is accepted, then what form does the inevitable demise of the physical body result in and what is the legacy of what was us, what happens to the person that we were or possibly still are.

In ancient Greece, Plato, a student of Socrates, suggested that there was not only an afterlife but a pre-natal life, a life consisting of the soul and suggesting that it is the soul continuing to live after the death of the physical body.

Indeed, it was Socrates who suggested that death may be welcome because it was simply a part of the process that led to our soul enjoying a fantastic afterlife having lived a good life in the world as we know it, the soul continues beyond physical death.

To me, that actually sounds quite plausible. Providing a juxtaposition in those ancient times was Epictetus, who conceived a person's death as a person ceasing to be, that was it, it's over, there is no more. We should not fear death, Epictetus ventured, because we will not exist after death.

Two completely contrasting opinions from a time when even as today, that the truth continues to remain unknown to us, though the debate continues from all those years ago.

What I find more incredible is that today, in 2022, nobody knows the definitive answer to the question 'Where To' and that my opinion, your opinion or the next barman you discuss it with over late-night drinks, is equally as valid as that of the greatest thinkers that have ever stayed in the hotel, whether it be Socrates or Epictetus! Having given the briefest of nods to the existence of esotericism and metaphysics and looking at their understanding of any of us extending our stay here, we are left with the difficult subject of religion! I describe it as difficult because with so many believers in different religions, it is often a balancing act, that when discussing or analysing any religion then trying to navigate the sensitivities that each bring with them can be challenging. Obviously I would never intentionally insult or undermine anybody's conviction or truly held beliefs in their religion of choice, but it is the nature of the beast that whatever you write or verbally opine, you will be challenged by an advocate of that belief system.

So, hard hats on and reiterating my desire not to make this book a theological classic but I believe, in the absence of any cultural opinions, because as we have discovered, 'Where To' is not a cultural thing but driven by religion.

So as religions are driving our understanding of the subject, it would be not only important but helpful to take a brief look at what the world's major religions have to offer from a 'Where To' perspective.

Firstly, what is a religion, how is it defined? Well, a religion is a belief in and worship of a superhuman controlling power, a personal god or gods.

Moreover, it is a collection of cultural systems, belief systems and worldwide views that encompass all things from humanity to spirituality. Religions often have narratives, traditions, symbols and sacred histories that are intended to give meaning to life, or to help to explain the origins of life and the universe and in some religions but not all, to create an understanding of what purpose our lives have and whether there is a life in any form after death.

Of the different religions in the world, Christianity with 2.4 billion followers who are currently staying in the hotel, makes it the world's biggest religion. Christianity is based on the life and teachings of Jesus of Nazareth, a man born in Bethlehem and brought up in Nazareth as a Jew. Believed by Christians to be the Son of God, miraculously conceived by the Virgin Mary, wife of Joseph.

Jesus, along with twelve disciples, undertook two missionary journeys through Galilee, performing miracles, teaching and proclaiming the coming of the Kingdom of God. There are different denominations of Christianity throughout the world and even amongst those denominations there are differences that exist especially and particularly for our interest, we can look at those differences regarding their views of the afterlife, or in our case, their views on *Where To*, if you will.

Most of the denominations of Christianity believe that your life on earth, which is all of us currently staying in the hotel and based on the assumption that you accept Jesus Christ as the Lord, then they believe that at the end of your human life you end up in either heaven or hell.

That is the equation in its simplest form, we have heaven for those who have lived good lives while they have been staying here and there is the dreadful alternative of hell, for those who have chosen a different, but more troublesome path during their stay.

Catholicism has the Pope as its head, regarded by followers as God's representative on earth, or without being too flippant, the holiday rep of the travel company that you booked with who often visits the hotel to stay in touch with guests and is available regularly for advice while staying here in the hotel! What is interest about Catholicism is that as well as believing in heaven and hell, Catholicism also provides a holding place which is called purgatory, this is an in between stopping off point, a place to reside while you are absolved of sin.

Sin, if you don't know, but I'm sure you do, is best defined as any immoral act or transgression against divine law while staying in the hotel.

Purgatory is a state for those who die in god's friendship, who are assured of their eternal salvation, but who still have need of purification in order for them to enter into the happiness of heaven, what that means to you and I is that they will get into heaven, but there are a few points to clarify before they are allowed to proceed through the pearly gates!

Purgatory is often thought by some, not to be a physical place, but rather it is a state of transition, where those who have committed venial sins and not mortal sins are held, it is not however a last chance for the unrepentant to avoid hell, but more a last stop for purification before going to heaven.

Interestingly one point about purgatory from a Catholic's point of view, is that they can still help those souls, most often their friends or family who have recently deceased and who are considered to be in this transitory state by offering prayers to them.

Fundamentally, the understanding of those Christians is that there is an afterlife; Christian eschatology is the all-encompassing description for the afterlife and literally means the study of the end of things. The Christian belief is that there is an afterlife it is in a heaven, where we imagine chubby cherubs strumming harps, to an audience of angels resting on clouds, but in reality, the Bible tells us, heaven is where good people will spend eternity.

Conversely, there is hell, as we have acknowledged, this is where eternal damnation, being a place of conscious, eternal separation from the blessings of god, the antithesis of an eternity spent in heaven is an eternity spent in hell.

Those briefly are the *Where To* beliefs of Christianity, fairly straightforward and probably an inspiration and helpful guide to living a good life and being rewarded once your time on earth is over and also providing a, what happens next solution, for those who need one.

Secondly, I would like to look at Islam, the second largest religion in the hotel with approximately 1.9 billion followers and within that number, there are different sects of which the two largest by far are Sunni with 85% of followers and Shia who make up 15%? The number of global followers means that Islam has nearly 25% of the world's population, of those guests currently staying here in the hotel, conscientiously hanging on to every word.

Islam and its followers, who are called Muslims, believe that life after death, is not an idea that should surprise anybody, death and the afterlife are as integral to the process as life and it is central to the meaning and purpose of most Muslims lives.

Many Muslims believe that they are on this earth, or should I say, staying in the hotel for a relatively short time and it is during that brief time here that they are preparing for the eternal life which comes after death.

Life for a Muslim is viewed as a test and ideally, a good Muslim will try to do as many good deeds as they can while on earth as possible and in doing so they will achieve Jannah, which is known to them as the eternal life.

Jannah being the Muslims equivalent of what is known to Christians as heaven, conversely they too have a version of hell, this is the alternative to Jannah and it is called Jahannam.

For Muslims, a well-lived life is one spent fulfilling Islamic obligations and will see that on the day of judgement the good will receive reward and the bad will receive punishment. Akhirah is what Muslims know to mean life after death and crucially they believe that it is Allah who decides when a person dies, it is Allah who determines when their stay in the hotel comes to an end.

Once they have died, they will stay in their graves until the day of judgement, which is known to believers as Yawm Al din. On the day of judgement, Muslims are raised from their graves, brought before Allah and it is then that they are judged on how they have lived their earthly lives, this is known as the resurrection of the body. It is then that they are directed to either Jannah or Jahannam—heaven or hell.

In order to achieve Jannah, there is a clear path for Muslims to follow while they are staying in the hotel, these are five basic duties and collectively known as the Five Pillars of Islam. I thought it might be interesting for us to know what they are, for it is these five pillars that guarantee followers who adhere to them, eternity in heaven, what a prize, who wouldn't want to go? The five pillars are Shahadah, the basis of Islam, the declaration that you have a faith and belief in one god and that is Allah.

Salah, committing to pray five times a day at specific times, which is a constant reminder of the importance of Allah in the life of a Muslim. Zakah, considered as an act of worship, this is donating a percentage of your wealth to charity, usually once a year, designed to create a bond between rich and poor Muslims, while simultaneously, purifying wealth and avoiding greed.

Sawm, by fasting during the month of Ramadan, Muslims connect with Allah and those less fortunate than themselves. Hajj is a special pilgrimage to Mecca, a good Muslim is expected to undertake this at least once in their lifetime, that is assuming that they are physically fit and can afford it.

Many Muslims believe that adhering to these five pillars will help them get their place in paradise, even if the rewards are not obvious in life. Isn't that fantastic, as long as you stick to these rules, be a good person and live a good life, having enjoyed your stay in the hotel, you can be assured that once you have checked out then for eternity you are guaranteed to be in paradise!

The word paradise is emotive in itself, I sense we will all have an idea in our mind's eye of what that beautiful word conjures up when we try to our hardest to imagine what it means. Paradise is subjective and what would be a perfect existence for some, will not be perfect for others.

Therefore, we will all have different ideas of our own version of the final abode of the righteous, indeed in order to understand what paradise means, it is best described as, somewhere unable to be understood until you actually see it.

So from the point of view of *Where To*, the parameters are clear, although the definition of the reward is a little vague, it instils into the believer that a lifetime commitment to the faith is demanded but the rewards are eternal, thus negating the *Where To* question for followers of Islam, that must be incredibly comforting.

Hang on, I've just realised that I don't expect to see many purchases of this book across the Muslim world. What have I done, I've just lost 1.9 billion potential sales!

I'll have to write a book that is only applicable for Muslim readers. I've got it, I'll call it life is a two-centre holiday, this life and the afterlife. But seriously if you are born into a religion that has such a rigid framework for your time spent in the hotel does that either inhibit your life or enhance it, that is a difficult question to answer, but for those of us non-Muslims, those without the rigid framework for life that it provides, it could actually give us a few points to consider.

So with Islam providing all the answers and virtually nullifying the need for this book, let's check out some other belief systems, but these are ones don't necessarily have all of the answers.

So to that end, let us have a look at Buddhism, which some of you will not consider to be a religion, more a philosophy, but whether you consider it to be a philosophy or a religion is not really up for debate at this point, that is not for our consideration, but seeing as it has over 500 million followers worldwide, it certainly justifies consideration and for the Buddhist, reincarnation is fundamental to life, its purpose is to achieve the ultimate state of nirvana which is the state that the Buddhist believes is the liberation from suffering.

Suffering, now that may seem like an extreme word to choose, because all life is not spent suffering but any suffering that is endured while going through the life process, which is known to Buddhists as Samsara, or the endless cycle of life, death and rebirth all striving for one final, splendid state, which we now know is nirvana. Interestingly, Samsara is the concept of rebirth and is a fundamental belief of most Indian religions, it is the endless cycle of life, death and rebirth, it is without beginning or end and is frequently referred to as the wheel of existence.

Buddhists believe that everything has a soul which they call an Atman and it is that soul that moves on into a new body after death.

It is here that we introduce karma, for it is karma that will sustain the endless samsara until the person becomes sufficiently good to find nirvana and break the wheel.

With each rebirth, the persons karma, short of reaching enlightenment, will determine their status of rebirth, in which their past life determines their next incarnation, all in an attempt to achieve the state of perfect quietude which, as we know, is nirvana, the attainment of nirvana is the final destination and the most important purpose of Buddhism.

There are various interpretations of Buddhism, but the attainment of nirvana as the ultimate state, or as the final destination is unanimous, however, though nirvana itself is universally acknowledged, there are varying opinions from it being a state of existence, they range from it being objectless, infinite, unsupported, beyond time and without spatial location, to it being a physical place, a place of perfect peace and happiness, something a bit like heaven.

So there we have a brief, potted look at Buddhism and how it contributes to the *Where To* discussion. Buddhists belief that nirvana remains the goal and purpose of our lives. A never-ending, repetitive cycle of birth and death, wandering from one life to another with no particular direction or purpose apart from liberation, the ultimate spiritual goal, nirvana, finally escaping reincarnation and finding eternal peace.

Hinduism is believed to be the world's oldest religion according to many scholars, with its roots and its customs going back nearly 4,000 years. Today, Hinduism has approximately one billion followers and is therefore the third largest religion in the world behind Christianity and Islam. Roughly 95% of the worlds Hindus live in India.

Hindus believe that all living creatures have a soul and this soul is the true self of every person and that soul is eternal! The goal of life amongst many Hindu thinkers is that your soul is identical to the supreme soul, the supreme soul is omnipotent, present in everything and everyone, all life is interconnected and there is a oneness in all life. Hinduism preaches that the soul gets reincarnated into a new life form, depending on your actions in a previous life.

Hindus believe that depending on how you choose to live your life, then your actions and the choices that you make during your stay in the hotel, all of these things lead to a new existence after death, a reincarnation, but that reincarnation is not simply limited to returning as a person coming back in human form, far more exciting than that, Buddhists believe that you can be reincarnated in your next life as either an animal, a plant or insect so not necessarily a human being, your life choices will determine your return.

Similar to Buddhism, the ultimate goal of the Hindu is to escape the cycle which Hindus also call samsara and instead of achieving nirvana, the ultimate goal is achieving moksha. Moksha is a state of being that can be defined as having achieved insight and the extinguishing of craving. Hinduism is a diverse religion that has a range of philosophies and concepts in which there are four aims of human life.

To make sure you're well informed, I will give you their Hindu names and their purpose, because if somebody tells me they have a code for life and how it should be lived, then I want to know all about it, I hope you find them as fascinating as I do. It tells me that there is a lot of thought going into the living of life and the process that we are all experiencing, inevitably they will have a *Where To* part of the equation, so let's take a look.

The four aims are encompassed in one word, the Purusarthas, meaning an object of human pursuit:

Dharma, righteousness and moral values
Artha, prosperity and moral values
Kama, pleasure, love and psychological values
Moksha, liberation, spiritual values and self-actualisation

Of these, moksha is considered to be the ultimate ideal of human life, it is a freedom from the cycle of death and rebirth and this all comes from the most intimate knowledge imaginable, which is that of knowing your true self, seeing life as more important than simple material 'things' and values, moreover it is an understanding of you and your role in the universe.

Moksha is a release from craving and clinging to passions and the mundane mind, because it is believed that all of these trinkets are unnecessary, in an eternal existence free from the trappings, the glitz and the glamour that a human existence entices, a life that encourages people to crave, those bright shiny and new consumables, but ultimately all this does is to enable a vacuous existence of never ending dissatisfaction and ensuring a life unfulfilled, moksha is the answer!

From a *Where To* perspective, it means that your human form is relinquished, just the soul is left and it is the soul that spends a life beyond conventional life and inevitable physical death, once any soul attains moksha it never again enters the human realm.

I think we need to clarify, that is for you as well as me, we need to know what a soul is, for it appears as a factor in most religions, philosophies and mythological traditions, it is a ubiquitous feature in the realm of any good conversation about the afterlife.

Although I feel that the word is bandied around often in conversation amongst those both with and without religious conviction, the word transcends religion, but the assumption that we all know what it is, is acknowledged, but we do use it, often without a clear definition of exactly what it is.

The soul is best described as the incorporeal essence of the living person, meaning it exists as a fundamental part of each living person but it is not composed of matter and has no material existence. I know, it's a difficult concept to grasp, something that has no matter and does not materially exist, yet it is so powerful and all-encompassing, but that is exactly what religion, any religion is, it depends on its believers and followers having faith in its teachings and completely buying into it.

The soul is eternal and whether its final resting place is moksha, nirvana or heaven, then so what, what has been the point of it all, so after everything you have gone through, the good and the bad, you end up with your soul in a resting place, somewhere, forever, so what?

It's not you resting there in eternal peace, or is it? This is why I'm struggling, yes I fully understand that there is a reward for a life well-lived, a prize for navigating and surviving the obstacle course, but so what, the irrelevance of one in a population of eight billion is not lost on me, yet religion will have each of us believe that our individuality is everything. As I said, religion, all religion depends on faith and I don't mean this in a nasty way, but I obviously don't have any.

Judaism is the tenth largest religion in the world and it has between 15 million and 18 million followers. A little contrary to the religions we have looked at so far, Judaism concentrates on life in the here and now and although it has long taught that there is life after death, the details are unclear and are long debated. This is because Judaism puts far greater focus on people's actions and their purpose in their earthly life.

For many Jews thinking about whether there is a reward, punishment or any sort of afterlife at all, is not important, indeed the teachings suggest that although there is an afterlife, it is important how a person lives their life and what happens after death should be left to god.

Good deeds in life should be done for their own sake and not to ingratiate yourself with god looking for a favour after death. *Be not like servants serving their master for the sake of receiving a reward.* That is written in the Ethics of the Fathers and is a fabulous line, one of many fabulous contributions that all religions offer and that resonate with any of us whose minds feed on that sort of thing.

So, Judaism confers the time spent in the hotel as the single most important part of the equation and though there are opinions on Where To amongst the followers, there is no agreed definition that is acknowledged by the faith, which amongst other religions, singles Judaism out as rather unusual amongst its peers.

Many Jews believe in Olam Ha-Ba, which strictly interpreted means the world to come. This is a perfect version of the world that will exist at the end of days, similar to heaven, nirvana or moksha, after the messiah has come and god has judged the living and the dead.

One great quote I found in the Mishnah, which is an early written book of Jewish tradition, tells followers that, This world is like a lobby before the Olam Ba Ha, prepare yourself in the lobby so that you may enter the banqueting hall I do like that and as I mentioned earlier, world religions are littered with powerful lines of text that can make sense of any situation whether you are committed to a religion or not.

But back to Judaism specifically, in order to have a good afterlife, many Jews believe that all efforts should be made to repair the world around them, while most Orthodox Jews believe that those who follow the laws given by god, will be sent to heaven when their body dies.

Yet in Jewish scripture, there is no description of what heaven looks like. Similar to other religions, heaven is thought to be similar to the Garden of Eden, a place of sunshine and happiness, however there are differences in understanding of the Garden of Eden being a physical place or simply a state of consciousness where the soul feels closer to god.

Jews similarly believe either there is a state of existence prior to the Garden of Eden where sinners can be cleansed before spending time with god, but those who have committed serious sin may spend a time in eternal punishment as they cannot be changed for the better.

Jews ultimately believe that there will come a time when God will rise along with all souls returning to their physical bodies! This is one of the reasons that Jews never cremate their dead, preferring to keep them in tact for the resurrection.

This makes perfect sense to me, in fact let me interject here with a little bit of an insight into my own way of thinking, long before I had researched for this book and discovered, the Jewish predilection for burial, which as I say, has in no way informed my own thinking and neither have I been influenced by any other religious belief or culture, but a thought process which is purely my own creation, from my imagination and thinking, which in some way, along with many other things which have combined for me to feel it necessary to write this book about the hotel.

The Judaism belief of burial and not cremation fits perfectly with me, I am getting buried, just in case you do come back, then cremation would make it an impossibility.

Yes, I know it's a long shot, but sometimes long shots win, so I'm just erring on the side of caution. I have long thought that life is like having a relatively brief stay in a hotel and indeed that is the title of the book and therefore it is the theme running throughout the book, but as with every stay in any hotel, there is always a time to leave, to check out as new guests arrive.

Therefore, as well as my stay in the hotel, I have always considered the *Where To* factor, what happens next, if anything and if there is nothing, then what was the point of the whole thing, in many ways I consider it as being nearly as important as our actual stay.

As I have already mentioned, what I find incredible is that of the eight billion people currently staying in the hotel and every single one of the millions of previous guests who have stayed here, not a single one of them has a clue as to what happens next.

Many can hazard a guess at what may happen and some have credible arguments and scarily, utter conviction that they do know, but nobody actually knows, so my guess, my theory is equally as valid as that of the greatest philosophers, theologians, men of god, or my next-door neighbour, all of whom, like me, haven't got a clue!

There aren't many things in life that you can make that bold but irrevocable statement about, in fact, I can't think of any as I write this passage, but feel free to get in contact and give me your thoughts.

What has always baffled me is that each one of us is staying in the hotel going through our lives to a greater or lesser degree of success, meandering our way through the daily grind not one of us knows what the point of it is and none of us have an idea of what if anything happens next.

So to this end I have always thought that when I finally check out, however, wherever and whenever that may be, as I have said, I would always choose to be buried and not cremated, oh and by the way, I would refuse to donate any of my organs.

Yes, I know, that sounds incredibly selfish and doesn't reflect well on me and I know all of the arguments for organ donation, which are difficult to oppose, but I have come to my position, not for selfish reasons, I actually like to think of myself as a generous, giving person, yes I understand that legislation has recently been introduced into the United Kingdom that will change our country forever, but in spite of all of that, you never know if you will need them again.

Here in the United Kingdom the government changed the law on compulsory donation on the 20th May 2020, meaning that it was assumed that every adult in the country would donate their organs unless they had recorded a decision not to donate or they were in an excluded group.

I have decided to opt out, recording a decision not to donate, now that may not be the most heartwarming or charitable line that you have ever, but indulge me and think about it, if nobody knows the answer and let's just say that we are all reincarnated at some time after our physical death, I would rather be walking around the planet with my eyes and lungs perfectly intact and in the places where I last left them.

Yes I know, I could be wrong and if I'm wrong, I'm wrong; however, I'd rather not take the chance. Who would want to walk around the planet, not able to see the beauty of the Lake District in spring, or breathe the freshest of fresh air at the top of an Austrian mountain? So I've made my choice; for me it's a burial and no organs donated, just in case.

Anyway, forgetting my desperation to remain intact, ready and waiting for what, if anything happens next, let's just go back to the *Where To* question and look at the remaining religious or cultural beliefs held here by many of us in the hotel.

We have considered the religions of Christianity, Hinduism and Judaism as well as Buddhism, which can be classed as either a religion or philosophy; next, we will consider spiritualism. Spiritualism is a religious movement, it is based on the belief that the spirits of the dead exist, not only that, but they have both the ability and inclination to contact the living.

Spiritualists once again believe that there is a soul and that the soul lives on and they take their consciousness with them. In the spirit world, the afterlife is seen as a place where spirits evolve and the contact between the human world and the spirit world is a reality.

Spiritualists believe that spirits are more advanced than humans and it is because of this, that they are able to offer an insight into life, from both a moral and an ethical perspective.

It is those options looked at from the point of view of religion that I would briefly like to consider because as with any believer in the soul existing beyond our ultimate departure from the hotel must also have an opinion on Where To.

In the spirit world, the spiritualist believes that the spirit continues to evolve, grow and can achieve perfection, progressing through higher planes because of the nature of the environment.

Not only does spiritualism offer the soul a future spent commensurate with your life led on earth, or as they put it, compensation and retribution hereafter, for all the good and evil deeds done on earth. Combine that with the understanding that because of the belief in an afterlife, that for those left in the hotel and suffering from grief after the death of a loved one, are now offered the possibility of communicating with them.

So an afterlife, an eternal resting place for any soul irrespective of their religious denomination while here on earth and an opportunity to get in touch with those in the hotel who still hadn't checked out—what's not to love?

Before I leave the section of our friends with religious conviction, I would like to lighten the mood a little and to that end, offer you my favourite jokes regarding the afterlife. That may seem a little perverse but because I do canvass opinion on the subject, I have a couple of jokes on the same theme which I find incredibly funny and love to use them at every opportunity.

If somebody asks me if I believe in reincarnation, I will say either one of two things which are both quite humorous, believe me, my reply to the do you believe in reincarnation question will either be, no, I don't believe in reincarnation and I didn't in my last life, or yes I do believe in reincarnation and I have left everything in my will to myself.

I told you they were good, what a couple of crackers, please feel free to use them at any opportunity that presents itself.

However, I digress, let us finally look at those who have no god.

When I was growing up I was never sure of the difference between an atheist and agnostic and although the names themselves at least are quite similar it is important to understand the difference.

Firstly, an atheist does not believe in god or in any other divine being, put simply, atheism is a doctrine or a simple belief that there is no god.

The main arguments put forward by atheists to expose the non-existence of a god are many, but a few examples could be, the lack of empirical evidence, they could offer the inconsistencies in revelations and the mere existence of evil, all as the most obvious contradictions of an all-seeing and all-knowing being.

There are nevertheless subtleties in defining the existence of a god or deities, different religions, see their gods indifferent ways, but regardless of definition the atheist is unaccepting of the existence of any of them.

Atheists are hard to define or categorise with common traits, they are a diverse group as there is not one single belief system to adhere to, the only commonality they have is their total lack of a belief.

It is difficult to apportion general views to the group, however they see life as the main event, their see their stay in the hotel as everything and so the maxim, you must make the most of it, appears to be the consensus.

Atheists see death, or as I would prefer, checking out of the hotel, as part of the circle of life and therefore they are accepting of it as part of the process, in fact it is thought that religions were created in order to satiate a need created by death and as we know, most religions do provide a solution to death and call it the afterlife.

One of the most famous atheists, Professor Stephen Hawking, said of his impending death, 'I regard the brain as a computer, which will stop working when its components fail, there is no afterlife for broken-down computers, that is a fairy story people afraid of the dark.'

Brave words from such an incredible man. As an alternative to atheism, let us look at what agnostics believe, or rather what they do not believe. Agnostics believe that the existence of god or deities is unknown or unknowable, arguing that human reasoning is incapable of providing sufficient rational grounds to justify the belief that either god does exist or god does not exist.

It seems counterintuitive to then question what an agnostic may believe with regards to our *Where To* question, because if a person believes the existence of god is unknown or unknowable then surely their view on *Where To* must be exactly the same. So we can canvass opinions but there is no structure and depending upon the persons commitment to agnosticism the answers will vary.

One final consideration for *Where To*, or at least one that I believe is worthy of consideration is the Clockwork Universe, a theory given to us based on the works of Isaac Newton. Newton's body of work laid the foundations for the Clockwork Universe theory, which tells us that the universe like a clock has been wound up and set in motion by god, but is governed by the laws of science!

When Isaac Newton gave us the laws of motion, he also showed us that combined with the laws of universal gravitation, then these laws showed us that we could predict the behaviour of both terrestrial objects and the solar system.

That's all quite wordy and a little bit techy, but when Newton opines on anything, especially the earth and its functionality then I would suggest that his thoughts merit further consideration and maybe a little further research.

Given that Newton's thoughts on this subject aren't globally accepted, I mention them for no other reason than his own standing as an eminent scientist and given that he has made a contribution to the debate, that contribution may assist with our cause.

Interestingly, and if you ever find yourself in Canberra, Australia, the National Science and Technology Institute has an instillation by the renowned artist Tim Wetherell; the piece represents the Clockwork Universe, contains moving gears and a working clock and perfectly encapsulates Newton's theory, making its understanding easily accessible.

So *Where To* is the question and it appears that depending on your religious beliefs or your lack of them that ultimately determines your opinion on the matter. There are many opinions ranging from a bleak, nothingness to eternal privilege and in between those two is everything you can think of, but only you, during your stay in the hotel can decide what to believe or hope for.

As our destination nears and we start packing our cases readying ourselves for checking out of the hotel we may on what might have been and what might be, it's all part of life in the hotel, an adventure as individual as you are.

What is not in question is that nobody actually knows the definitive answer to one of life's biggest questions; is there an answer and we just haven't figured it out yet, or will it remain as life's eternal mystery?

Chapter 5
Look at the View from the Balcony

Fifteen years or so ago, I had the pleasure of being part of a 'Get In' team for a company called Borders, a really cool bookshop, when they were opening a new store in the North of England.

I say it was cool, obviously that's only my opinion, but what I did like about it was the fact that not only was it a really great bookshop, but it also had a really extensive music section and not just that, there was also a Starbucks coffee shop on site, three of my favourite things on the planet—what a lethal combination!

Sadly for me and any other fellow Borders aficionados out there, the fabulous trinity was not a triumph, so successful was this magical formula, that the Borders group closed all of its UK stores in 2009.

I still miss it to this day, but the world has moved on and as we watch the high street evolve in this post-Amazon world of price, determining the future of most of our retailers futures, we are left to lament as we bask in the memories of our customer experiences that include being able to touch, smell or hear the product in an often pleasant environment whose expense, unfortunately, didn't justify its existence!

So, as I rekindle fond memories of Borders bookstore, re-Kindle, that's a really nice word to use when you're having a conversation about books! Purely because this was a time in my life when I found myself exposed to reading material that I would not normally have found myself reading, or even considering doing so, but when you're spending days filling the shelves of a brand-new bookstore with the works of Jacqueline Wilson, or solemnly giving the world religions your full attention, you tend to look beyond the oh so important ISBN number and browse through what is actually inside the dust cover.

For those of you that don't know, a 'Get In' is the period when a brand-new store is opening and there is not a single book on the shelves, a term which is also shared with a travelling theatre production when it arrives at a new venue and the set and the props are relocated from the previous venue to their new temporary home.

I say that the purpose of the 'Get In' was to put the books on the shelves but in this instance when I first joined the team there weren't any shelves in the store for the books to go on.

The shop was a brand-new building and it was getting kitted out in the Borders corporate colours and was starting to take shape and looked really good.

Once the carpets were down and the shelves were up, I watched as truck after truck arrived full of pallets of books in all shapes and sizes and every subject on the planet, or rather in my case, every subject in the hotel.

It was a great thing to be a part of, watching an empty space become a place where you could learn about anything and everything, the things that you were interested in, things that you weren't interested in and things that you didn't yet know that you would be interested in.

Today, you can access the contents of the whole store from your mobile phone, anything and everything is on that piece of tech, but whether this means the end of the bookshop or worse, the end of books, who knows?

What it does mean is that opportunities present themselves for an innovative new retailer or e-tailer to take advantage of this changing world.

I sense that books will always exist in a physical form which may lead to a proliferation of smaller, more niche, specialist shops, which to some extent already exist and they can be fabulous places to lose an hour or so on any day of the week.

There is a parallel here, which can be drawn with record shops, which like booksellers, such as Borders and W H Smiths, record shops had in recent years been ubiquitous in most major UK towns and cities, you would always find a Virgin or HMV in most places, but as the world continues to turn and with rapidly changing technology, most recently seeing the advent of downloads and the demise of the previous most popular incarnation of music purveying, the compact disc, global sales of which had peaked in the year 2000, sadly record stores have dwindled, of course, nothing is forever and sales of CDs had in turn virtually replaced the demand for vinyl records but as we know, evolution continues and revolution takes over.

Times may change, but bizarrely, over the last ten years or so, vinyl records have actually made a comeback, they have become popular with the younger generation and to those hard core collectors who had never deserted them, feeling that the physical record or LP, short for Long Player as they became known, are a piece of art in themselves, from the cover of the album, to the feel and ultimately the sound, they all combine to make vinyl a more satisfying and complete experience than, the soulless, intangible download could ever be! In 2020, vinyl sales were once again greater than the sales of CDs, although both had been majorly eclipsed by downloads, but this highlights how things change and change is the only constant.

Similarly to record sales and record shops, I think the book sales may replicate or at least be very similar to that experienced by the musical industry, in the world of the written word, we have seen the advent of Kindle and Audio Books, yet there is still a massive demand for a physical book, which still remains by far the popular way of consuming the written word.

Millennials are sometimes blamed for an industry being killed off and with the availability of a tech book version, being the downloaded audio book, you would have imagined that the younger generations would have gone for these options.

However, it appears that younger people are actually popularising print, currently 63% of physical book sales in the UK are to those under the age of 45, while 52% of those buying eBooks are over 45.

The numbers are similar in the USA where recent figures taken from 2017 tell us that 75% of people between 18 and 30 have read a hard copy of a book in the last 12 months.

Inevitably, technology will develop within the sector and we can expect further change, but while the appetite is strong and demand is high, let's all rejoice.

Back to the Borders, Get In, where the crew, as we were funkily described, consisted of all types of people and personalities, describing us as a crew made us sound cool, but don't forget, when the Marie Celeste had left New York heading for Genoa on November 7th in 1872 it too had a crew.

But I do us a disservice, for inevitably there became a team ethos about the whole experience, all of us having a shared love of the written word in common and many with their favourite section of the shop in which they wanted to work on while in the store, I had no such demands and was happy to be enjoying the experience.

What I soon realised was that there was or what appeared to be a hierarchy of the genres amongst the old hands, those who had worked on the 'Get In' at other new stores within the company's portfolio, with what they deemed to be the elite genres to be working with, the kudos that went with the section lending its identity to the crew member installing it.

That may sound a little contrived, but in the same way that a dog's owner tends to develop and grow to look like their pet, then so to the culture and values of the relevant book section seemed to reflect upon those filling its shelves.

Believe it or not, I was working on the children's fiction section, which surprisingly was at the bottom of the pecking order, or certainly the lowest of the Hierarchy of Reads, as we would expect Maslow to say. My hierarchical observations didn't appear to resonate with the old hands, the elites if you will, me hardly registering in the pecking order at all and if I was registering, then doing so in last place, a mere blip on the reader scale! But as I said, this wasn't of any consequence to me, I was enjoying the experience and had no need for my self-importance to be observed, or my ego to be stroked, I didn't have to be putting the science-fiction books in the correct order on shelves in order to feel fulfilled!

I must have been doing a great job amongst the Gruffalos, Big Friendly Giants and the Lions, Witches and Wardrobes, as my talent for filling shelves with books was spotted by one of the elites and I was moved upstairs, a promotion of you will, I was privileged to be trusted to install the section that held the written works of the world religions, believe me, it was heaven.

I wasn't to know it at the time, but this move was to be a revelation for me, it would prove to be an enlightenment for more reasons than one, so let me elaborate.

It is true that I was to learn many lessons throughout my brief time with Borders and as with many experiences in life, they didn't all appear obvious to me at the time, often, it is only when you reflect and evaluate what has just happened, that you realise the impact anything has had on you during your time here.

Indeed as your life progresses and you enjoy your stay in the hotel, many things that you experience along the way, whether they appear to be good or bad can always be used during the rest of your stay, experience, whether it be good or bad is invaluable.

So I would possibly argue that, whatever happens to you along the way, it can and will more than likely be used constructively at some point in the future.

If an experience is good then the gratification is more often than not immediate, however the expression, 'If it doesn't kill you it makes you stronger' exists for a reason, some experiences that aren't necessarily beneficial to you in the short term, will make you more resilient in the long run, they toughen you up, not necessarily pleasant at the time, but part of the mental growing pains of life.

It was my promotion from children's books to world religions that provided one of my most pleasant experiences while at Borders and actually gave me a small insight into the world of religion and although religion per se wasn't a massive part of my life, either then, or as we speak today, I was however always intrigued by world religions and the people who were totally committed to them and had the faith to commit themselves and live their lives to a set of rules laid down by their religion, whichever religion it may be.

Even in those times and I would think it must be at least twenty or so years ago, I was thinking about a meaning of life, yes I know it sounds a bit pompous but it was of genuine interest.

I had even painted, what I felt was a tremendous work of art, if as it was, a little abstract, the piece was titled, 'What's the Point'; a question that remains with me to this very day, still unanswered satisfactorily by anybody that I have met while staying in the hotel.

The painting was framed and proudly hung on a wall in the kitchen for all to see, but after a couple of house moves, it has gone, missing in action, I haven't seen it for ages, but I did love it.

However, a painter I'm not, so let's head back to my burgeoning bookshelf-filler career, back to Borders. I was asked to start on their world religions section of the store, a fascinating department to be involved with, I was looking forward to taking on the challenge.

World religions was, believe it or not, a lot less politically challenging than the children's fiction department, which itself was a hotbed of political activism, with the likes of the non-PC and now cancelled Dr Seuss and his back catalogue of racist works adorning the shelves.

What ethical challenges would or could the world religions offer to compete with the world of children's literature, surely none, with peace and spirituality at the heart of every belief system, but little did I know.

On my first day in the department I was given a list of books to put out on the appropriate shelves in the fabulous new store and as a person with genuine interest in the genre, purely from a 'What's the Point' position, I was genuinely interested in what gems, if any, I may discover in what was to become, my temporary sanctuary of religious readings.

I was happily putting the many religious texts on shelves and of course there were many editions of each text, however it gave me an opportunity to browse through the various texts at different breaks throughout the day, taking care of course to treat the books with great reverence and keeping them in the pristine condition that any purchaser would expect, is there anything worse than purchasing a new book only to get home and find it to have been well thumbed during its shelf life, only for you to receive it in a state of distress.

It's akin to buying a pair of socks from your favourite clothing store only to get them home to wear them for the first time and finding a broken toenail in there, obviously somebody else had purchased them in untarnished condition, tried them on, or bought them and returned them to the store, soiled and ready for you to stumble over them.

Is there anything nicer than opening a brand-new book in pristine condition, I don't believe that there is, so treating each book with reverence was crucial.

As the shop was brand-new, there weren't the traditional gaps on the shelves that you would usually find in a long-established, well-used bookstore, spaces created by either, customers simply buying copies of books, or alternatively having picked a book up, intent on buying it, subsequently walked around the shop with it for fifteen minutes only to put it back on the nearest shelf, before leaving the shop empty handed, deciding against a purchase, but nevertheless leaving spaces to be filled with either a replacement or replaced copy.

As the shop was so full, space on the shelves was at a premium and often when filling a section the desperation for space necessitated my use of not only the appropriate shelf but also continuing to use the row below, which in this instance were for several copies of the Koran which I was putting on the shelves and making a fabulous display of, doing a really nice job, even though I do say so myself.

Suffice to say, I found sufficient space for the Koran on both the appropriate top shelf location and the second shelf down, then as the end of my shift drew close, I stood back and admired my work, calculating the shelf space and the remaining titles that I had to fill that space the next morning, there was still work to do, boxes to be emptied and shelves to be filled, but it was all going well.

Having enjoyed my day with the crew I said good night to my new friends in the shop as I wandered through the various sections on the way out of the store.

One guy, Craig, who became a good friend was working in the romance section and in spite of a disparity in our ages, he was a lot younger than me and at the time was studying literature at the local sixth form college, but in spite of this, we were both on the same wavelength where our sense of humour was concerned, we discovered this in the first couple of days of the get in and the laughs continued until our final shift.

What we discovered, and it was quite by chance, but Craig was working in the romantic fiction section, hardly the ideal genre for a slightly overweight, male, sixth form student, but that's where he had been allocated, so he was making the most of his brief liaison with fictional romance. I think he discovered it first and naturally the subject came up in one of our regular conversations over lunch and what he had discovered, merely by browsing through the covers of each, book he was putting into its allocated space on the shelves, was that there is a genre of romantic novel that has as either its title character, or certainly the hero of the book, a kilt wearing Scotsman, invariably with an unbuttoned dress shirt, a chiselled jaw, showing an incredible physique, all of these things were combined with a suitably tough-sounding name.

Craig, who spent his days with his head filled with romance in that section, would scan the titles and the dust covers of the books, for the names of the heroes that featured inside and would reveal the names of the new contenders to me at either the days first coffee break or at lunch time, at which point we decided that it would be our goal to compile a Top Ten list of those fabulous names and trust me, this provided the two of us with hours of fun, okay, maybe I'm exaggerating ever so slightly, minutes of fun.

There were many names, all sufficiently bizarre to be ridiculed during a rainy lunchtime, but the one that stuck with me and to this day still amuses me is Jancken MacNachton, don't ask me why, but we both found it so amusing, but the genre, combined with the stereotypical description of the romantic lead, was to us incongruous, especially in today's society!

I find it hard to believe that the feminists of the northwest weren't on permanent protest outside the store, protesting the misogynistic, squash-buckling, macho male lead, but luckily they weren't, because they were either oblivious to the existence of the super masculine Jancken MacNachton and his swarthy lothario chums, or they were secretly reading these fabulous works of fiction and loving every word.

Romantic fiction and its fabulously named characters were a lovely distraction after days spent packing the shelves full of world religions; however, there was one unforgettable morning that I came in early to start the day and my empyrean peace was shattered and I was brought down to earth with a bang.

Each morning the Borders gang started with a typical sales rev-up session of the crew standing around in a circle at the front of the shop and all sharing details of their current reading material, their latest book of choice, or whatever else that they were reading, details of which would be shared with the rest of the group, all with maximum enthusiasm, often irrespective to the quality of their reading matter.

This mutual sharing of our reading dependency, a Bookworms Anonymous if you will, admitting to the group that our lives would be unimaginable if we never had our daily book fix.

This was followed by joke of the day, which invariably wasn't necessarily as funny as its title suggests; once we stopped laughing uncontrollably, we had a final chest-beating speech to get us into the right frame of mind to fill those shelves; we would then disperse throughout the store with a smile on our faces.

Suitably positive, I sprinted back to the world religion section, where store manager Andrew was standing looking very solemn, maybe it was a reverential observance of the world religions section that he was stood smack in the middle of, maybe he didn't enjoy the joke of the day, or worse, maybe something was wrong.

"Nick," said Andrew, the head of the crew, who was responsible for executing the Get In and as I was to discover, a man with a tremendous eye for detail, "Nick, you have made a dreadful mistake." I couldn't begin to think what I had done, as I am a bit of a perfectionist myself and thought I was doing a great job. "You have quite rightly put the Koran on the top shelf in the section," he said, "however, you have then gone on to put the remaining copies onto the next row down, which is below the top shelf."

He was right, I had three copies that wouldn't quite fit onto the shelf, instead of taking them back into the vast stockroom, I put them at the end of the next row down.

This was totally unacceptable apparently and unfortunately, unknown to me, because the Koran in Islam is not allowed to be below any other book as it is considered by Muslims to be the all-important word of god and accordingly to be put above common place things, or other books in this case, effectively, the Muslim community were demanding that their book be placed above all others.

In my total lack of understanding of religious etiquette, by putting the three copies that I couldn't fit onto the top shelf onto the shelf below, I could effectively have started an international incident! So in the world religions section in every bookstore, you will find what I like to call a Hierarchy of Reads, a hierarchy which must always have the Koran at the very top!

Since those days, things have changed a little, subsequently and understandably the other major religions have requested that their books, which of course are equally as venerated to their followers as the Koran is to its Muslim followers, must also to be kept on the top shelves, parity has broken out.

So in future, no offence will be caused to any religion as the scriptures of all of the major faiths are given equal respect and kept alongside each other on the top shelf. I'm not sure whether this change is a comment on the insecurity of the different religious beliefs or speaks to the insecurities of their followers, or maybe this was just acknowledging the importance of their individual books to them and the decent thing to do.

What was certainly interesting was that critics of the practice of top shelving and the demands that religions were putting on bookshops and libraries meant that by accommodating their demands, the shops and libraries were treating the books as objects of veneration and not simply books to be read.

Was there a debate to be had? Libraries and bookshops are not places of worship and should not be run in a accordance with religious beliefs, or compelled to do so, some may argue, however bookshops are there to make money and what the customer wants the customer gets, you want your book on the top shelf, you have it.

The only danger I can foresee is that bookshops and libraries in the future will have only one shelf in the world religions section, but it is extremely long and goes right around the store as a huge continuous shelf, with nothing below it apart from the floor and definitely nothing above it, only then will everybody will be happy.

Andrew soon realised that my indiscretion was totally unintentional and I soon got over my gaucherie regarding the positioning of the Koran, subsequently I would spend several enjoyable days filling the world religions shelves and it was there that I read one of the most powerful pieces that would stay with me for the rest of my life and would influence me in many ways, it was partly responsible for concentrating my thoughts sufficiently enough to consider writing this book and searching for my own theory which has culminated in my belief that *Life is a Hotel*.

As was my wont, and constantly aware of the time constraints of the Get In, we had a time deadline to achieve our goal by, I would scan the covers of the majority of the books, speed-reading their covers before putting them onto the shelves, especially in the world religions section, where I had a genuine interest and it was there that one afternoon I picked up a book about Sufism, a religion which I had heard of but never really knew much about, less could I give you a pithy explanation of what it was, that was until my time at Borders.

On this particularly wet afternoon in the North of England, having spent a lunchtime in the staff canteen with Craig and his latest list of kilted heroes, sufficiently satiated I went back to the world religions department and was finishing off putting the books about Rastafarianism onto the shelves, as I did and in the distance, I could hear *One Love* by Bob Marley which appropriately was emanating from the music department, easing the staff into an afternoon of shelf filling, while maintaining a chilled vibe, the mood was good.

The R's finished, I went back to the stockroom, where boxes awaited my arrival, full of books focussing on religions beginning with letter S, little did I know that opening those boxes would have such an impact on me, as I proceeded to look through them, loving the smell of brand-new books and the size and feel of what the boxes contained, I was indulging myself with the S's.

It was inside one of those boxes that I would find *The Principles of Sufism* by A'ishah al-Ba'uniyyah.

Interested by the title, I started browsing through and it was there that I discovered not only the basics of the religion, which in their own right were captivating, I also discovered a fascinating parable about blind men and the elephant!

The parable of the Blind Men and the Elephant originated in the ancient Indian sub-continent from where it has been widely diffused and now finds itself reinterpreted in many religions and cultures across the region.

It is a story of a group of blind men none of whom have ever come across an elephant before, so have absolutely no idea of its size, colour, physique, absolutely no idea, their mission is to learn and then conceptualise what the elephant is like, simply by touching it.

Each of the blind men is given one part and one part only of the elephants body to touch, ranging from the trunk through to the ear, leg tail and so forth.

Remembering that these men are blind, they then describe the elephant based on their limited experiences and their descriptions of the elephant are vastly different from each other.

I have read several versions of the story and in a couple of them, the men come to blows, believing that the others are being dishonest about both their interpretation of and descriptions of the beast!

The moral of the story is that human beings claim absolute truth based on their limited and subjective experiences while tending to ignore other peoples limited subjective experiences which may be equally true.

Further research amongst the world religions section showed me that the parable was shared across religions, the earliest versions are found in Buddhist, Hindu and Jain texts, approximately 500 BC These different versions of the same tale passed have indeed been around and reinterpreted through various religions and cultures, all of which are to be found after that original text emerged.

It is a wonderful and powerful piece of imagery, which immediately resonated with me for some reason, I love its clarity and how simply it explains an understanding of what I have come to believe to be one of the basic truths of life.

The truth that I believe it explains for me at least is this, in life you are limited by your experiences and it is those experiences that determine the way you approach life and how you handle virtually everything that you are confronted with throughout your stay in the hotel.

It is those experiences that condition your attitude to life and as a result, it is your attitude that determines your whole stay in the hotel, I believe it is that fundamental, that important.

Now this may be just me, especially me when I was a young child, but once my mum and dad had checked the three of us in to our hotel, I could not wait to get up to our new room and enter the place that was to be our home for the next however many days of our lives we were staying for. This would be the place that was our temporary home and the first thing I wanted to do once inside the room, was to throw the curtains back, often with the help of my dad, those Spanish hotel curtains tend to be really heavy, and once pulled apart, I was desperate to get out onto the balcony and check out the view.

Whether it is up in the mountains for a skiing trip or on a sunshine island surrounded by the sea, I do believe it is preferable to discover that your balcony has the privilege and luxury of either looking directly at the imperious slopes or with a view of the beguiling, twinkling lights of the bay, both equally as satisfying and often a perfect location to round off an evening off with a nightcap as you retell the heroics off the day and contemplate the magic that the next day's morning will bring.

I definitely think that your state of mind, your mental wellbeing, or your personal feelgood factor, however you wish to describe it, are all improved for having an awe inspiring, mind blowing, inspirational vista of the locale, it has a really positive effect on your mental wellbeing.

So inevitably it follows that, if it is really nice and a positive thing when you are given a fabulous view from your balcony, then the opposite must be true. If you are situated at the back of the hotel, overlooking the bins.

So what if you are not fortunate enough to have the spectacular vista available at the mere tug of a curtain and instead of looking at the village, you find yourself looking at the car park, or worse, looking over the hotel's waste management facility? Does it then naturally follow that if you are mentally stimulated by the beauty of the vista, then the hideousness of the antithesis, in this case, the dreadful view must surely numb the senses or at least dull the imagination, and therefore devaluing your stay.

That presents us with a real chicken and egg situation, does our environment determine our attitude to life or does our attitude to life determine our enjoyment or quality of life.

I have always maintained that I could have a party in a phone box, it is always sunny in my world, irrespective of the weather, I am always positive, yes I have lows, yes bad things happen, but I refuse to accept them, I refuse to allow them to determine my mindset.

I am not naive enough to believe that everybody's mood or wellbeing would be improved by a beautiful view, but, speaking for myself, the beautiful view isn't crucial in order for me to enjoy my stay in the hotel, but given the choice, it's the twinkling lights every time.

When you have a beach holiday whether at home or abroad and your hotel has a coastal location, you arrive at the hotel, immediately you look around, your first impressions are crucial, whether they are of the building, the location, or even the other guests and the hotel staff as you walk in.

Arriving at reception, you are allocated your room, your private space for the duration of your stay, where you will live your life for the duration of that stay, it is one of the most exciting parts of any holiday, especially as I mentioned earlier when you are younger to get into your room moments after you have arrived and rush over to the balcony, to see what you can see from your balcony, somewhere that is your own personal space, if only temporarily. It is the contrast that you can feel, when you get onto your balcony for the first time to discover a stunning view over the bay, on your beach holiday or the slopes if you find yourself up in the mountains on a skiing holiday.

Conversely, is there anything worse than finding yourself at the back of the hotel, where you are fortunate enough to have been allocated an incredible view of the bins by moonlight, or backing on to the staff quarters! The dilemma is what do you do if you find yourself in a room that you don't feel good in, whether because of the view or the location, you can hear the banging of doors, or the elevator going until after midnight, ferrying late-night revellers back to their rooms in the early hours.

Do you make the best of a bad situation, or do you go straight down to reception and ask for another room, or do you go to the extreme and check out of the hotel altogether. In life itself it is important to establish what you believe you are deserving of as you live your life day to day, how you feel that life should treat you and if and when you feel let down, you change the narrative, you take control and demand better.

There are things that you would tolerate in your youth that wouldn't even enter the equation of possibilities as your stay in the hotel goes on, whether it is because of age, possibly a little maturity and even an appreciation of the better things in life as you get older, things which hopefully becoming a little more affordable as you age, not necessarily gracefully, but certainly more enlightened.

One of the major benefits of getting older, not for everyone, I do realise, as life can be both kind and cruel, but as you grow older, you tend to be able to afford those things that you could not afford in your younger days, yes of course it isn't a fact, more as a rule of thumb it is a fair guide to how we navigate our way and life progresses.

There is a trade-off, there always is and in this case it is that your health, looks and longevity all change as you get older and not necessarily for the better, they're all going one way.

Health, of course, can be maintained, you can work at it, but in my experience, the miracle that is the human body which is a complex machine and has many things that can go wrong with it and they do. I believe that health is a lottery, you can go to the gym every day and then succumb to the most innocuous of health issues that can have major implications; conversely, you can make no investment in your physical health and just cruise through life in great shape.

Throughout life, we will all have bumps, scrapes and falls, skiing holidays, summer holidays, nights out all types of events can contribute to the slight knocks and general wear and tear, which have all occurred during your stay, gradually they take effect on you, both mentally and physically, they have a cumulative effect on each of us as individuals as we navigate our way through life, I've often looked at it as to be reminiscent of a canoe slalom race, in the rapids, struggling against powerful waters, battling the forces of nature, a gruelling test of endurance that test you at every turn, that's a lovely metaphor for life.

It is not only sad but inevitably true, that your looks don't usually improve as you get older, probably because your skin tends to deteriorate and as you age, while wrinkles and grey hair can sometimes offer a degree of dashing good looks that are not available to our younger selves, but as a trade-off to the inevitable decline, they offer us a chance to retain some semblance of looking good in old age and indeed this can be a welcome bonus.

Longevity is totally random, it was Euripides, my favourite tragedian of classical Athens, who profoundly told us that 'nobody can confidently say that he will be living tomorrow.' I do like Euripides and would go as far as to say that he is my personal favourite ancient Greek, if that doesn't sound too pompous!

However, I am a big fan of language and more specifically words and how great thinkers can interpret their thoughts into the written word for our consideration.

Euripides was a poet, a playwright and a tragedian and he has written some of the most incisive words that I have ever read and the most incredible thing, for me at least is the fact that he wrote these words in 480-406 BC, when the hotel was a very different place to the hotel we are all staying in today, even though it is the same hotel, in spite of this the words resonate as powerfully as I assume they did on the day he first conceived of them.

I wonder how the regular ancient Greek public viewed Euripides and his chums?

We look back at them with reverence today, but were they held in high regard by their own generation or looked upon as a collection of odd balls and weirdos, it would be fascinating to know.

Speaking many years later, I realise, but another of the hotels great thinkers, Benjamin Franklin told us that 'in this life nothing is certain apart from death and taxes'. Benjamin was talking about the certainty of death, something that is common to all and that no man can avoid and as we know our time in the hotel is limited and as our departure nears and you start to pack your bags, the way in which you optimise your experiences during your stay while realising that it is likely through health and wellbeing that there will be limits out upon your options as your departure nears.

Attitude to life varies differently for every person and many factors can go into determining an individual's handling of those circumstances, be they positive or negative. Attitude determines altitude, I remember being told as a young salesperson in Liverpool in the early eighties, in what was a very salesy environment with attitudes that could never exist in today's politically correct world, it was a moment in time, but we all bought into the culture in our desire to 'live the dream', although for some of us it was more a case of 'living the nightmare'.

These were the days of Gordon Gekko, a salesman's dream and a character played by Michael Douglas in the 1987 film Wall Street for us go getters, us aspiring multimillionaires, Gordon Gekko was the ultimate role model. He was a hero to us all, a character who advocated unrestrained greed with his, Greed is Good mantra, and in our world of hard sell financial services he became our style icon and business guru, sharp suits, bright ties and opulence, we loved it all.

We knew his catchphrases and repeated them verbatim, anybody that dared pop out of the office at midday for a sandwich and a bag of crisps would be told that lunch is for wimps, one of Gekko's classic lines.

It was the attitude that Gordon Gekko had to business that determined his success and we all thought we had a little bit of him in ourselves, desperate to replicate his success, he embodied all we wanted to be.

It didn't all end well for Gordon Gekko and the stock market crash of 1987 and subsequent crisis in 2007 saw the temporary demise of the attitude that saw him achieve his success. This fictional character and those who maintained his couldn't-care-less attitudes have subsequently become synonymous with crises in the financial markets and the greed displayed by marketeers pushing for growth based on flimsy foundations, striving for profit at all costs.

Gekko was mentioned in several speeches by world leaders and eminent bankers when justifying market collapses. For us, as salespeople his emergence was symbolic of the world we existed in which we found it difficult to separate fact from fiction, we all believed it to be realistic and achievable, even though the character was flawed and was desperate for even greater success, so much so that he even resorted to illegal means to achieve his goals.

Should we have been surprised, possibly not, it's all been done before and in the words of French novelist and playwright, Honore de Balzac who told us that 'behind every great fortune, lies a great crime'.

We were totally unaware of Balzac's thoughts two hundred years earlier, we followed Gordon and his attitude which may I suggest, irrespective of our sales abilities, his existence played a part in pushing all of us on to greater achievements!

I fundamentally believe that a positive attitude to life is crucial, are you a glass half full or glass half empty, type of person you will hear asked, some of the people that I have met in my life haven't even got a glass.

I don't know what has made me so resilient but having experienced several negative occasions in my own life I have always felt mentally strong and remained very positive in spite of any adversity that I have ever encountered.

Even today as I live with primary progressive multiple sclerosis and life is challenging every single day, I refuse to feel negatively about the reality of my own situation, yes of course I acknowledge the disability, but I refuse to allow it to define me.

I don't believe that any of the current over 8 billion guests has a perfect life and in the simplest of terms, I have worked it out thus, there are three categories in everybody's life and they are health, wealth and relationships all of which have to be managed on a daily basis throughout our stay in the hotel.

I do not believe that of this triumvirate, that anybody who is staying here in the hotel at the moment or any of the millions of previous guests who have been fortunate enough to stay here before us has a perfect score, a ten out of ten in each of the three categories.

You could be in a public place and with my condition you can see that physically I am not great, although I use the gym every day, my mobility and balance are poor so it means that I need to use a wheelchair or electric scooter.

Indeed, as we speak, having been out for breakfast at the Cow Shed at Fraisthorpe, which is near to the beach my wife Diane and I, with long-time friends Jimmy and Fiona and their daughters Maddy and Emily, are lucky to be walking along at this very moment, the beach looks gorgeous, it is a sunny, windswept, but bracing Saturday morning on the east coast, my scooter obviously wouldn't work on the beach, so I am sitting in the car writing as they walk a breakfast off, of course I would prefer to be with them, but I can't.

So do I sit here feeling sorry for myself that I'm not there to walk with them, do I ask them not to go because I can't go with them, or do I simply watch and value their friendship, a gorgeous breakfast and embrace the views of the beach, the rolling sea and kite flyers, wind surfers and the numerous beach activities surrounding me.

I value it all, embrace the good, ignore the bad and love life, playing the cards you've been dealt to the best of your ability, so that's what I choose to do. So physically, with me, you can see that all is not great and more often than not, people are genuinely decent and help as much as possible, so it is easy to be aware of physical issues, but what if we look at another of the big three.

Relationships, indeed I believe that good relationships are a vital to a happy life, If I had a terrible relationship, my marriage was rocky or if I had no long-term relationships and I was lonely, then simply by looking at me it would be hard to know this.

The third of the three crucial ingredients is money, you can have little or none, but it can be hard to discern this by looks alone, yes you may be a little unkempt, your clothes may not be the best, you may not have money to spend on frivolities and by simply looking at a person it can, more often than not be hard to discern this.

At least in my case you can see what is wrong with me, therefore when strangers see my situation, as I have said, they are more than happy to lend a helping hand.

I have a very positive attitude, naturally and this too has made life a little easier, when it would be very easy to feel sorry for myself, focussing on the things that I can no longer do, when instead, I choose to look at what I can do and maximise my efforts to enjoy them as much as possible.

In fact writing this book could fall into the category of using my talent and or enthusiasm into focussing on what I can do.

I am writing this because I do have a genuine interest in wondering what it's all about and am determined to have a more informed opinion by researching the alternative opinions that are out there and also, contributing my own thoughts to the debate.

I also see this as being a part of my positive attitude, an attempt to write a book, which I have never done before and which, it is very easy to say the words, I am going to write a book and the reality of actually doing it and having it being a part of your life on a daily basis is a totally different proposition. However as I write this, I have worked on it every day since the first of January 2021 and what started as a New Years resolution, will, I believe will become a fulfilled goal.

Your attitude to life can influence your enjoyment of your life, it is not the hotel, or the room that you are allocated by reception upon your arrival that should determine the quality of your stay but what you make of your stay while in that room that is the determining factor, you determine the outcome, not the room.

Of course, there will always be a better quality of room, there will always be a better hotel that you could have stayed in, but if you think about it, what is it that determines whether they are better or not!

Ultimately, you have to make the decision to commit to making your stay as enjoyable as possible, expecting the inevitable setbacks along the way, because they are all part of the game and as we know, nobody has a perfect life, we are all dealing with issues in our own way, some of us successfully, some others are struggling.

A positive attitude is not all about wearing a smile on your face every day, it's more about having a positive mindset, even when things are going supremely well or are a little chaotic.

Treat those two imposters just the same, Kipling told us, but more of that later. I realise that it's sometimes easier said than done but I do believe that if you start to feed your mind with positive thoughts then you will see amazing change.

If you start thinking optimistically then your mind becomes clear of negative thoughts and you see not only the world but yourself in a different light, you will become happier, feel more self-confident and become more focused!

Happiness comes from within and is a state of mind, it is not dependent on external factors, but it is certainly effected by them. Self-confidence comes from having a positive attitude and feeling better about yourself, enabling you to push yourself and believing that success is assured in the face of positive challenge or adversity. As a byproduct of happiness and a growing self-confidence then a more focused self emerges, which gives you emotional balance. It is vital that you don't kid yourself about being positive, don't try telling the world you feel invincible when in reality you feel invisible, when you feel incredibly negative, because that is self-defeating, and will only compound the grief when the inevitability of failure occurs, there is only one person that you can't get away with deceiving in life and that person is yourself.

Without conviction or being committed to a positive attitude, it is impossible to fake a positive attitude, you may be able to get away with it to others but not to yourself and in this equation, you are the only person that matters.

If you are not convinced that your positive attitude is genuinely improving your sense of purpose and wellbeing then, as good as they are, any amount of *Chicken Soup for the Soul* type books will be worthless apart from satiating the odd ten minutes of downtime with a witty tale or a new throwaway life-affirming bumper sticker.

You cannot lie to yourself and that is why the desire must come from within in order to correct any of our weaknesses or if not weaknesses, certainly the areas of our lives which we feel we could improve.

There are numerous self-help books on the market all designed at self-improvement for the reader and it was calculated that by 2022 the self-help market alone would be worth over $13 billion, and by 2022 the market for all genres of self-improvement books, life coaching and workshops will be worth $40 billion.

So this is a massive and a growing market and it is easy to see why, the world of the media has changed so much, in order to feed our insatiable appetite for self-improvement and the elusive perfection of airbrushing and of celebrity.

With 24-hour rolling news, the internet, the advent of the gossip magazine, combined with the established lifestyle glossy magazines that emerged in the 50s, 60s and 70s, it is easy to see how those who previously felt inadequate or lacking in self-confidence can, in these days of wall to wall Z list adulation of non-entities, who have as many, if not more insecurities as the reader does, you can feel even further diminished and search for an answer in the nearest self-improvement or life coaching book! But who are these gurus, those who are happy to give us advice and in return are remunerated sufficiently to achieve the lifestyle which they are trying to convince us that we can achieve.

They happen to be staying in the hotel at the very same time, they are simply guests, just like we are, and for whatever reason they have come to prominence, they have achieved great things and actually deserve recognition for those achievements, whereas in other cases they are simply famous for being famous, we can all think of useless 'celebrities', who in spite of achieving nothing, are happy to advise others on improving their situation.

Those that have achieved great things can be respected and their words can be sufficient enough for us to respect their opinions and their points of view sufficiently to allow them to influence our own lives and taking their advice on achieving whichever goal we are looking to achieve.

But never forget, theirs is only another opinion in the global collection of opinions and given that nobody on the planet has a greater insight into the reason for us being here and how to make a success of it, than you or I, it's an opinion which may or may not help you, however their take on life may resonate with your own views, so never forget that.

So although you can feel isolated with your issues, whatever they are, it is exactly the same for every other person staying in the hotel, searching for the way to achieve a state of well-being in life, the trick, if there is one, is to find a way that enables you to do whatever it takes for you to enjoy your stay to the optimum.

Before starting this journey, I have discussed my writing of this book with many friends who work in, manage or own hotels all over the world in order to consolidate my thinking of the hotel metaphor and maybe to allow them to either dispel my thinking or alternatively if they felt it had credence then to add to my thinking or even improve the analogy.

When I originally had the idea of committing my thoughts to paper, I needed a little direction, so I put a list together of those friends that are in the industry, employed in many and various aspects of the trade in so many wonderful locations all over the planet! From an historic family-owned castle in this country to a snow-wrapped mountain winter retreat or those sun-bathed, sea-splashed locations all over the world I collected their thoughts about my proposition and my theory, I will happily assure each of them that their feedback was incredibly helpful, positive and constructive, providing the direction that I had craved and amongst their contributions were thoughts that I hadn't possibly had or originally even considered.

Amongst many questions, all in the cause of research and specifically pertinent to this chapter, I specifically wanted to know how they saw those clients who wanted to change rooms once they had arrived at the hotel, those guests who were not happy with the room allocated to them at reception.

Their feedback was interesting and varied, especially as I was already contemplating this chapter and how a view from the balcony, for some guests can be vital to an enjoyable stay.

In my own mind, I had anticipated that they would have taken an instant dislike to any guest who inferred that their hotel or at least their allotted room wasn't good enough for them, somebody who was not prepared to accept the accommodation that the hotel had deemed suitable for their new guest, but interestingly I was wide of the mark, the consensus was to be understanding and compassionate and accommodate the wishes of the errant guest in more ways than one.

There are always different versions of living your best life, but we as humans tend to be creatures of habit, anything for a quiet life, we tend to follow the path of least resistance, not wanting to make a fuss and ultimately not asking for a different room, instead choosing to stay in the one that we were given on arrival.

This is an incredible thought process if you dare explore it further, instead of choosing the security of the cocoon we inhabit, we could trade the silence and look at the other opportunities that may exist outside of our safe space, what would we become, what could we become of us if we dared to step into the world of the unknown?

Instead of having the temerity to want a different room to stay in, imagine if we challenged everything in our lives, accepting nothing but the values that we believe in.

We can inhibit our personal growth by opting to play it safe throughout our stay, choosing not to push ourselves to our unknown limits or finding out what we are capable of. To some extent we live our lives playing the hand that we have been dealt and for whatever reason, we choose to make the most of our situation, but maybe we need to look at potential alternatives.

The alternative is invariably a little more difficult, of course it is easier to do nothing and so much easier to stay in the room allocated to you on the day that you first arrive in the hotel, when the alternative is to go down to reception, cause a stink and tell them of your dissatisfaction and your need for a change of room.

One of my favourite films, the terrific 1998 classic, Sliding Doors, it dealt with how one person's life and how if they had followed two different paths when taking one single decision on one day that they decided to go left instead of going right, although in this case, the film documents and contrasts the two very different life choices, focussing on whether they were on time for their train and actually caught it, or alternatively they were late and missed it, plotting the alternative outcomes of both and how different their life could be by going one way instead of another, but showing the outcomes for both.

The film, although manifesting as a fairly lightweight romantic comedy, is actually based on the earlier 1982 film called *Blind Chance*. What is fascinating about the film is that it gives us a tremendous insight into the potential life-changing decisions that are made if we ever choose to break from the routine, a routine that we all develop and maintain at various stages of our lives, if we break the routine and adopt a different pattern then outcomes can and more often than not, will inevitably be different.

Fate can and does play a major part in the lives of each of us, sometimes we are aware of when we have made either a positive or a negative choice in our lives.

If it is positive we can be pleased with the result of our choices because it manifests into something rather nice, buying a winning lottery ticket, making a new friendship by being in the right place at the right time, there are many positive examples of good luck, the results are not always immediate and there can often be a delayed gratification.

Conversely, if we make a mistake it is often obvious immediately, as soon as we have made an error, dropping an expensive plate in the kitchen, tripping over a rogue child's toy in the bedroom and many more are immediate, but what intrigues me are those things that we don't know, we don't know.

What we never know are the times that we have made a decision and it has turned out to be for the best, because by making the choice that we have made, we have avoided something catastrophic, instead of a disastrous decision, we have made a good call.

Had we have chosen an alternative course, it could have ended badly, or worse, in tragedy, but because we went a different way we have totally missed what could have had a very different outcome.

In spite of this, having avoided calamity, the outcome may still have been unsatisfactory, but not realising how fortunate we have been because things could have been far worse, I think they call it dodging a bullet.

We must be aware that these times inevitably exist for all of us and appreciate that because everything goes smoothly, we don't question anything, we only challenge our decisions when we experience negativity, why didn't I do X when I could have done Y, we tend to beat ourselves up.

In my own life, I have a couple of examples that I can think of, but let me refer to one example of good fortune that I have had. It was an innocuous moment in my life when things could have ended disastrously had they had worked out as I had planned. I was 18 at the time and early on a Sunday morning in Chester with two friends, we found ourselves near the racecourse at the top of a leafy lane which led down to the low wall surrounding the course.

I was a good sprint runner in my youth and challenged my two friends to a race down the lane to the course, the first to touch the low wall being the winner, hardly the stuff of great Olympians, but it entertained us, no matter how briefly. Challenge accepted, we started down the 200 metre sprint course, as I was leading quite easily, my two friends' appetite for competition rapidly and literally came to a standstill. I coasted up to the wall a long way clear of the non-existent opposition.

The ancient Roman walls of Chester witnessing yet another gladiatorial victory, as I won the race. Had the competition been a little fiercer, I had intended to celebrate victory by jumping the two-foot-high wall as part of my extravagant celebration; however, because of the nature of the win, I had no need to exploit my excessive conquest and took pity on the deflated combatants.

As I stood at the wall celebrating the win, looking at my disconsolate friends walking towards me, I had the opportunity to look at the majesty of the racecourse on a beautiful, English summer Sunday morning it was manicured to within an inch of perfection, as I looked on the other side of the low wall, I was horrified to see a 100-foot drop, a drop which I had intended to jump.

Had the race been closer, it could literally have been my finishing line, but it wasn't, I had just had a lucky escape, a near miss and I knew it. So luck can and does play a part in our lives, even when we are unaware of its appearance l it is said that, if you believe in good luck, you must also believe in bad luck. Luck itself is the phenomenon that defines the experience of positive, negative or improbable events. The nature of things tells us that positive and negative events happen all the time due to random and non-random, natural and artificial processes and even the most improbable of events can happen by chance.

In this view the epithet of lucky or unlucky is a descriptive label that refers to an events positivity, negativity or improbability. The 'lucky' label can also be applied to a person, I have always sensed that I am a lucky person, I seem to get more than my fair share of random good fortune. Conversely, my wife and I have a very good friend who we have known for over thirty years, Carol; we called her Lucky, yes, to her face, but not for the right reasons; sadly for her, we use this name ironically, but she allows us to and nods along every time she recounts the latest in her procession of bad luck stories!

Carol is the unluckiest person we have ever known, whether it was with houses that she has owned, incidents she has experienced while driving or relationships with men she had known over the years.

She is the loveliest of people, which made it even more bizarre that her run of bad luck should continue unabated for as long as we have known her, she doesn't deserve any of it.

In Carol's case is it bad luck, is it that she has made poor choices, was it her own incompetence or maybe, it's simply random? A supernatural view of the unfortunate Carol could be that she was unlucky because she was seen unfavourably by a deity and its influence over her life. But in that world view she could counteract the stream of misfortune by carrying a lucky charm, a rabbits foot, a horseshoe or even partake in some obscure, contrived and often nonsensical routine that may bring the person good luck, standing on one leg while sniffing a four leafed clover, avoiding walking under ladders, there are many superstitions, indeed they exist in most cultures.

How many of us carry a good luck charm or maybe a memento of a loved one, no longer with us, believing they will help bring us good fortune or maybe a little spiritual guidance from our departed guest, who we expect is looking down favourably on our every move.

As most cultures often have their inherent superstitions, these rituals or items tend to live alongside the culture that observes them and over time they increasingly become ingrained in the culture that adopts them, becoming a normalised part of that culture.

There are so many fabulous examples of this, one such is the number 8 in Chinese influenced cultures, where it is seen as incredibly lucky, then we have the ladybird, this is often seen as lucky, indeed the Serbians even have an old children's song about them and their talent as bringers of good luck.

From four-leaf clovers, chimneysweeps and dreamcatchers, all are seen as good luck charms in different cultures for reasons uniquely their own, while conversely there are objects that are signs of bad luck and every culture has them, examples are numerous and various, but popular examples are, the number 4 in Chinese culture, putting a pair of shoes on a table, or saying the word Macbeth in a theatre and there are many more examples.

Good luck, bad luck or do we make our own luck, who knows but many of the guests in the hotel hold these beliefs close, believing them to be true, whether they work or not, we will never know, but I believe if it works for the individual, then it works, that's all we need to know.

While looking at luck and superstition, there is another example that I feel falls into this category and we need to acknowledge and that is astrology, which is a virtual industry in itself. Astrology is a pseudoscience that claims to have incisive information on a person's future based purely on, terrestrial events by studying the movements and relative positions of celestial objects and can trace its origins as early as 25,000 years ago.

Throughout most of its history, astrology was considered a scholarly tradition in the same mould as astronomy, meteorology and medicine, it was well respected.

In earlier days, it was present in political circles and was even written about in the works of the great authors—Chaucer, Shakespeare and Dante, for example. However, from the end of the 19th century, researchers successfully challenged astrology on theoretical and experimental grounds and found that it had no scientific validity or explanatory power and thus astrology lost its academic and theoretical standing and common belief in it largely declined.

I am an Aquarian and don't really believe in astrology, which isn't surprising as apparently, all Aquarians think the same, that being the case, I will for my own personal amusement, from time to time, like many of us, read my stars. I won't go out of my way to do it, but if I'm on holiday or find myself somewhere where I find a newspaper lying around, maybe the barbers, the airport or in a bar, I will flick through the paper and invariably check out my stars. If they are positive I believe them, if they are negative I disbelieve them, but as an astrological guide to life, that's about it for me.

The view from the balcony depends on whose eyes you are looking through, but ultimately, you only have your own eyes, your own vision. It is preferable to look at beauty and not the beast, but both coexist in the hotel in various guises during our stay, we must realise that whether it's King Kong or Fay Wray, we must be at ease with both, accepting the inevitably of either, grateful for the beauty, accepting of the beastly—that's life during your stay in the hotel.

Chapter 6
Arrival

Arrival, as those of us of a certain age will know, is the hugely successful ABBA album, which was released in 1976 but more importantly and certainly for the purposes of this book, arrival is taken to refer to our own arrival here in the hotel.

In order for us to leave, then you have to arrive, so arriving becomes the one of the most important parts to the equation of our time spent in the hotel, as with any visit to a hotel, your personal experience starts the moment you check in at reception, as soon as you walk through those doors and present yourself at reception, then the whole experience is underway.

I think it would be nice to get a definition of the word so will consult the esteemed Cambridge dictionary to provide their interpretation of the word *Arrival*, which is written thus, 'the act of someone or something that reaches a place or comes into existence or a person or thing that reaches a place.' We need to step back a little, for in order for each of us to arrive at the hotel reception in the first place, an incredible number of fortunate coincidences must align, for you the reader and I the writer to be sitting here doing what we are doing.

As with most of my musings in this book, I believe that there are several thought processes that we can have in order for us to process the information, the information of what we do know in order to establish what we believe to have happened for us to be here and for us to have the opportunity to stay in the hotel.

Without doubt our arrival in reception is a gift, an offering to all of us, one that we have been presented with, an opportunity to experience all that the world or the hotel has to offer and therefore I believe it is only right that we consider the forces that, against all odds, have conspired to come together in order for us to be here today.

Maybe we can also consider that if our stay here is a gift, then who is it or what is it that has gifted it to us, these are big questions I know, in fact questions don't get much bigger, but in spite of their size and ambiguity, it would be nice to know.

We must hark back to the olden days, these were the days of the milkman, those hardworking, mainly men and the odd woman, who would deliver milk in all weathers—hail, rain, snow or sun—straight to your front doorstep. In those days, people would leave their empty milk bottles on their doorstep the night before an early morning delivery the next day, when bottles of fresh milk would replace the empties!

My friend, David's mother, called Nancy, who is in her nineties, and I caught up as recently as three months ago. On the night before this particular April 1st, David and I had been out for a night at the pub, we had a few drinks and were quite merry, that pleasant juncture, just before you're drunk, when you are still fully in control of your faculties, but find most things amusing.

Instead of heading straight home from the pub, I called in at David's for a coffee and to listen to a few album tracks by Santana, finally leaving his house at around 11.45pm, it was at that moment in my diminishing state of inebriation that I remember the date, it was the 31st of March, the night before April Fool's day, of course I could start a little early, yippee! As I left the house, I once again glanced at my watch and it was indeed approaching midnight, five to twelve to be precise, I've always been a bit of a rascal and that combined with having enjoyed a couple of drinks earlier and the fact that April Fool's day was imminent, I felt a prank coming on.

I spied David's mum's empty milk bottles on the step outside the front door; there were four bottles on the step as David shared the house with his two sisters, his mum and dad and the consumption of milk in their house was in copious amounts!

I waited for the family to go back inside the house, after they had waved me off in their usual way, it was like saying goodnight to the Waltons as one and all stood at the door and waved me off, as I meandered down the drive and into the distance. But not this night, this night I bided my time, letting them all get back into the house, giving them time to believe I was long gone and well on my way for the two-mile walk that lay in front of me that would take me home.

Once the coast was clear and the family was happily ensconced in their luxurious abode for the evening, I crept back and put a note for the milkman inside one of the bottles—this was quite a regular occurrence in the 'old days', don't forget, this was a long time before mobile phones, so communication with your milkman was often via a note left in the bottle, increasing or decreasing your order, adding a yoghurt or half a dozen eggs here or there was commonplace.

The note that I left however was a little out of the ordinary and if truth be told, I didn't think the milkman would fall for it, after all, it was April Fool's day and the request was quite unusual, it read, fourteen extra pints today please, which Nancy's milkman duly left and they were standing proudly on the step the next morning, when Nancy came downstairs in her dressing gown to get the milk in!

All of these years later and whenever I see her, Nancy reminds me of it and it has become a happy memory for us both, there was no malice intended and to this day, I blame the milkman! So that's my own favourite April Fool memory, which has absolutely nothing to do with our arrival in the hotel but everything to do with one of my favourite tricks and it is April the first as I write this, so please indulge me for a couple of paragraphs. So let us look at the options for our arrival and our chances of being on the planet in the first place; what are the odds of you or I or the rest of the eight billion of us, currently staying here as guests and actually having the opportunity to stay in the hotel?

Well, apparently, talking about the odds of this happening, somebody a bit cleverer than I has actually taken the time and the odds have been calculated and in order to do be given the opportunity for either of us to be here, it has been calculated and there are several factors that have to be considered when looking at this equation.

Firstly and most obviously, your parents had to meet and given the fact that there are approximately eight billion people on the planet, the chances of that are incredible in themselves, but take a step back and combine this with looking at the chances of your ancestors, or even just your grandparents getting together before your parents themselves created you, those odds calculated separately are massive, especially when you consider that they were totally unaware of each other's existence before they stayed in the hotel.

Luckily for us, Dr Ali Binazir, who works at Harvard college in the United States, has calculated the odds of this incredible journey, taking into account all of the relationships that need to happen in order to result in you arriving at the hotel reception and the odds that he calculated are a ridiculous four hundred trillion to one.

Four hundred trillion to one, the number is mind-boggling and too big for us to comprehend, but what it does mean is that effectively, I am a miracle and you are a miracle, we are all miracles, or are we? In common parlance, we would consider ourselves to be such, but in order to do so, we need to consider what a miracle is, in order to establish whether or not we can legitimately categorise ourselves as such. A miracle is defined as an event that appears to be inexplicable by natural or scientific laws, which we can all understand, but the word has been hijacked by religion and for most of us, the word miracle has become synonymous with a religious act, an improbable occurrence in the name of your chosen deity!

So, if that is the case, let us look at religion, where it is described as an event or happening that has been performed by a god, a saint or a religious leader! Informally and without the religious interpretation, the word is characterised as and has come to mean a beneficial event, a nice thing to happen.

Because it is not totally contrary to the laws of nature, therefore it is not an impossibility, but by all serious consideration, it is deemed to be improbable or virtually impossible! So what we have to be wary of is not confusing what is actually a marvellous coincidence with something that actually is miraculous.

Surviving a natural disaster may not be against the laws of nature but may simply be a fortunate occurrence, irrespective of the calculated odds of it happening or even being possible, it happens.

What does that even mean? Well, let us consider for a moment a recent example of a natural disaster that not only had an incredible global impact when it happened, but this was prolonged for several months afterwards, I will use this in an attempt to highlight the point that I am trying to establish, when referencing a miracle.

Let us take ourselves back to the 26th of December 2004, one of the biggest days of the year, it was Boxing Day and for many of us in the Christian world, just as we in the United Kingdom are slowly recovering from the overindulgences of the previous day; we awoke to the dreadful news and accordingly the rolling news coverage of a tsunami off the coast of Sumatra Island in Indonesia.

A powerful earthquake of 9.1 magnitude ruptured a 900-mile stretch of a fault line where the Indian and Australian tectonic plates meet, causing the ocean floor to rise by up to 40 metres, triggering a massive tsunami. It was 7.58.53 local time, when the earthquake occurred, the third largest that the earth, our hotel, has ever seen and it is the largest in the 21st century, causing a series of massive tsunami waves up to 100 feet high, heading inland having been created by the underwater seismic activity offshore.

Communities along the surrounding Indian Ocean coastline were devastated, with an estimated 227,898 People in 14 countries being killed, once again, making it one of the deadliest natural disasters in the recorded history of the hotel.

The Boxing Day tsunami was a disaster in every sense of the word, with so many tragic deaths, but in spite of those tremendously sad cases, there were survivors and we began to hear their stories.

As we have acknowledged, the death toll was enormous, so in line with the theme of this chapter being how fortunate coincidences and other contributing factors combine to create the odds of us ever actually arriving in reception, it is with those odds in mind, that we look at those who survived the tsunami of which there are many, so it helps to take a look at a specific example of how fortune can play a hand in all of our lives.

Aceh province is situated on the northern end of the Indonesian island of Sumatra, it was hit the hardest, more than 160,000 people died in the area, which represents approximately 5% of the population, with those in the worst hit areas either, being killed, or with survivors losing their homes and livelihoods, with their communities reduced to rubble.

In the immediate aftermath of a disaster such as the Boxing Day tsunami, the way forward is unclear, lives are thrown into disarray, they are changed forever, not only the lives of those who are fortunate enough to still be alive, but for those who are yet to arrive in the hotel, those who are yet to be born, those who will now never check in at reception, fate has denied their opportunity.

Having researched survivors stories, of which there are many and in order to provide us with a greater understanding, I have chosen to look at just one example of a survivor whose life has changed forever and therefore, on a micro level, will change the course of life in the hotel forever, not only for him, but also for all of those people in his sphere of influence.

It is fascinating that through the example of the tsunami helping to give us a greater understanding of how random events can and do determine the course of lives forever, then we can understand that even the most basic of our life choices or our daily actions those things, no matter how small, apparently inconsequential, the actions that see us navigating the slalom course of life in our single seat canoe, every moment of every day ultimately leads you to the conclusion that life itself is a series of fortunate or unfortunate events.

So the example that I have chosen to look at is one of a single survivor, at the time of the tsunami he was a young man, who not only lost his wife, which in itself is incredibly sad, but he also lost his child and an incredible twenty-seven family members in the disaster, horrific we can all agree.

However, since then, he has moved on and remarried, creating relationships, friendships and life, that would not have existed, had the tsunami never happened.

Think for one moment about the implications on all of those lives involved in this story, not just those that were lost, but those that will be created by these new relationships and any children that are born subsequently, who, more than likely, would not have existed had it not been for a disaster, a freak occurrence.

In the face of disaster, any disaster, there is new life created that would never have been created, what a mind-boggling thought and my own contention is, that these life-changing events are just part of our daily lives, obviously in the vast majority of instances they appear to be totally insignificant, indeed often they are subconscious choices and totally innocuous, when compared to the example, scale and size offered by the tsunami, but they are life-changing all the same.

I don't know if you know this piece but it is a personal favourite poem of mine, *To a Mouse*, written by Robert Burns in 1785. The beauty and understanding of life that Burns displays through his words lead me to believe that life really hasn't changed that much in nearly two hundred and fifty years.

I could be true to the work by quoting it in its original form, which was in the Scottish language and for those of us who don't speak the language fluently, the work is too good to misunderstand a single word.

I need to quote the complete work here, I could offer you a couple of really nice lines that I feel are perfect in providing an analysis of the fragility of existence and how fate or randomness can influence all of our lives, whether they be human or that of the mouse, but it is the whole observation that makes it such a joy.

It is the appreciation that Burns has for all life, no matter how small and without hierarchy, that I absolutely adore, what a guy, but enough of that, instead let me set the scene.

Legend has it that Burns was ploughing in the fields and accidentally destroyed a mouse's nest, which it needed to survive the winter, so distraught was Burns that his brother tells us that he wrote the poem while still holding the plough:

Little, cunning, cowering, timorous beast,
Oh, what a panic is in your breast!
You need not start away so hasty
With bickering prattle!
I would be loath to run and chase you,
With murdering paddle.

I'm truly sorry man's dominion
Has broken nature's social union,
And justifies that ill opinion
Which makes you startle
At me, your poor, earth-born companion
And fellow mortal!

I doubt not, sometimes, you may thieve;
What then? Poor beast, you must live!
An odd ear in twenty-four sheaves
Is a small request;
I will get a blessing with what is left,
And never miss it.

Your small house, too, in ruin!
It's feeble walls the winds are scattering!
And nothing now, to build a new one,
Of coarse green foliage!
And bleak December's wind ensuing,
Both bitter and piercing!

You saw the fields laid bare and empty,
And weary winter coming fast,
And cosy here, beneath the blast,
You thought to dwell,
Till crash! The cruel coulter passed,
Out through your cell.

That small *heap of leaves and stubble,*
Has cost you many a weary nibble!
Now you are turned out, for all your trouble,
Without house or holding,
To endure the winter's sleety dribble,
And hoarfrost cold.

But mouse, you are not alone,
In proving foresight may be in vain:
The best laid schemes of mice and men
Go oft awry,
And leave us nothing but grief and pain,
For promised joy!

Still you are blessed, compare with me!
The present only touches you:
But oh! I backward cast my eye,
On prospects dreary!
And forward, though I cannot see,
I guess and fear!

I do enjoy that poem and don't want to analyse it too deeply, but for me it shows how life in the hotel, in whichever part you live during your stay and whether you are a man or a mouse, your plans can be thrown into turmoil, literally so in the case of the mouse, who has his world, with his family, turned upside down and thus Burns gave us that beautiful line, 'the best laid schemes of mice and men, go aft awry'; yes, we can all make plans, but we can take nothing for granted.

Personally, I believe that as you get older and the longer you have stayed in the hotel, those words ring even truer, I think it comes with the realisation that nobody stays here forever, even the greatest of us, check out when their stay is over and every day that you are here as a guest is a step towards your last, it should not be surprising to any of us that it is inevitable that your thinking changes, you start thinking about your own mortality and you maybe savour each memorable moment as they present themselves.

We see that in Burns' work, he emphasises the bond between mouse and human, the fragility of each, in spite of their differences and the uncertainty that each faces in their respective futures and although there is a degree of pessimism in his words, there is a sense that life is worthwhile.

You may or may not know *To a Mouse* by Burns, but I do hope you feel that was a worthwhile segue, because what have we, if not an ability to appreciate the contributions of those who have stayed here before us, especially when we realise that they have exactly the same concerns that we do today, nearly 250 years later, that said, let's bring things back to today and have a look at events that can determine whether we are here as guests or not.

To remind you, if you had forgotten, this chapter is concentrating on our arrival at the hotel and to that end, it is beholden upon us to consider the extremes that influence our chances of being here and in doing so, we must consider those life-changing events that are either man made, such as a war, or those that occur naturally, often disastrously such as an earthquake.

So let us look at the way people currently staying in the hotel that have religious inclinations, to whichever faith, account for those events that we describe as being miraculous, or simply a miracle.

Religions all have names for miracles and for each, the miracle has a different perspective in their religious thinking, from Christians seeing god intervening in some elements of human activity to Muslims seeing Allah as the direct cause of all events, making gods eternal presence as the reason for anything being miraculous in their world.

But what about those of us who have no religion, could this allow them to believe against all of their better judgement that a superior being is at work, or could it simply be the theory of Occam's Razor?

What is Occam's Razor, you may ask; well, Occam's Razor, otherwise known as the Principle of Parsimony, is attributed to the 14th century logician and Franciscan friar, William of Ockham. Ockham is a village in Surrey, England, where William was born.

The principle itself sounds simple but it is quite powerful in its thinking and it is this simplicity that accounts for its longevity: 'Entities should not be multiplied unnecessarily'; brilliant, but what does that mean?

I think the simplest yet most understandable interpretation of the statement is, 'when you have two competing theories that make exactly the same predictions, the simpler one is the better.'

Even Isaac Newton chipped in giving his opinion to the debate, 'We are to admit no more causes of natural things than such as are both true and sufficient to explain their appearances.'

The reason that Occam's Razor has presented itself to us in this chapter is because it brings the opportunity for those people without religion to look for a reason for our arrival in reception. I imagine those who are not religious look to the Big Bang theory for their inspiration, certainly as a starting point for life and thus leading ultimately, though millions of years later, to their own arrival in the hotel reception, checking in for their own stay here.

There are many creation narratives around the world and as we discovered earlier they tend to be culture based and don't necessarily lean on a religion to provide the answers. Often they are cosmological myths or theories, that describe the ordering of the cosmos from a state of chaos and amorphousness, into what we have today. As with any theory, including religious theory it is easy to pick holes in or challenge their understanding of how we got here, speaking personally, I do not believe I have found one explanation that manages to answer the starting point conundrum, which put simply, is the what came first, the chicken or the egg?

Until that can be answered, I think we are all struggling, whatever our conviction or belief, however I do believe there is an answer, there must be, the only problem we have is that we just haven't worked it out, yet.

Maybe that's part of the game, it's the ultimate whodunnit! Using the Occam's Razor principle, does it give us an insight into the creation of the hotel, the world as we know it, do we have an accepted hierarchy of non-religious views, that lead us to believing in the science?

Richard Dawkins in his book, *The God Delusion*, claimed that: 'Historically religion aspired to explain our own existence and the nature of the universe in which we find ourselves, in this role it has now been totally superseded by science'; the inference is that as science explains more and more about the world, there is less and less need for god.

In order for us to evaluate Dawkins' input into this subject, we must know that he is a noted academic but is an atheist and well known for his criticism of creationism. Two thousand years ago, it was quite acceptable to invoke god as an explanation for natural phenomena, but here we are, in a place where over the last five hundred years, the progress that science has made has started to strip away gods role in the building of the hotel. So if we apply Occam's Razor to science and God, the implication is that if science can explain the world around us, then there is no need for both science and god.

Yes, of course, they can coexist, but religion becomes folly as there is no need for two explanations when one will do. For many non-believers, that will suffice but then we are not allowing the watchmaker's analogy to have any credence.

Hang on a minute, you may be thinking to yourself, what is the watchmaker's analogy? Well, it is known as a teleological argument, which advocates for the existence of god, and this particular analogy was given to us by William Paley in his book, *Natural Theology or Evidences of the Existence and Attributes of the Deity*, which he wrote as far back as 1802. Paley progressed the watchmaker's analogy, indeed before him we had both, Sir Isaac Newton and Descartes both who both chose to take a similar view, accepting that the workings of the universe were akin to a watch, wherein the watchmaker is god.

So let us briefly consider Paley's watchmaker analogy, it is interesting because in this analogy, the implication is that any design has a designer, which makes sense, especially an intelligent design which is how I would describe our fabulous hotel, which like any other fabulous hotel on the planet, has an intelligent designer, a creator, an architect, an originator if you will and in the case of the universe, due to its size and complexity, it is possibly the work of a deity? So popular has the analogy proven to be, that it is used to support the existence of god and his, or her, intelligent design of the universe, it is recognised in both Christianity and Deism.

Deism is a philosophy that takes the position that reason and observation of the natural world are sufficient to establish the existence of a supreme being or creator of the universe. As I mentioned, Sir Isaac Newton offered this thought, 'the physical laws that he had uncovered revealed the mechanical perfection of the universe to be akin to a watch, wherein the watchmaker is god.'

Can you imagine if the watchmaker analogy were to be written today, for the younger generation, we would see the watchmaker and the watch replaced with Apple and their iPhone, justifying the existence of a god and the intricacies and evolution of the mobile phone, comparing it to our hotel, this would support the argument of the existence of a deity but atheists may then argue that it is man who has speeded up the design and development of the iPhone which would then take us on a little further in support of Charles Darwin's theory of natural selection as our guide to evolution.

Arriving in reception in order to spend our very own time in the hotel has been analysed by many and throughout the history of the hotel, it is worth reminding ourselves, that of the eight billion guests currently staying in the hotel, nobody holds a more valid opinion or actual understanding than you or I as to the answers to those big questions such as, who built the hotel, how we got here, what the purpose of our stay is, or where if anywhere we go to, once we have checked out and left the hotel forever.

From the great philosophers of ancient Greece to the great thinkers and philosophers of the modern day, who despite having access to all of the very latest technology to assist in their findings, there remains an unlimited number of theories that attempt to guess at our reason for being, but incredibly, those guesses remain just as plausible, although they are possibly a bit more informed, they are still as accurate as the guesses that either you or I may have.

It is this fact that fascinates me, we are all going through the same experiences, having varying levels of success, however success is perceived, is success making lots of money, a fabulous career, is it having a large family, lots of friends, or are we successful if we simply survive, however it is manifested, we are all striving to achieve our chosen understanding of the goal, all without fully understanding why!

Epistemology is an area that we must consider in order to assist us with our thinking, it is a branch of philosophy that provides us with an undiluted view of our lives without looking for a religious intervention and using only stark reality as a guide!

Epistemology is quite simply a branch of philosophy concerned with knowledge, studying the nature, origin and scope of knowledge, which ultimately provides epistemic justification, the rationality of belief and various related issues.

The word epistemology is derived from the ancient Greek word episteme which means knowledge and it is our understanding and definition of the word knowledge that helps with our interpretation of exactly what it means.

Of course, our language is crucial in constructing and setting self-imposed limits on what we are allowed to think and say, for without the vocabulary to define a thought, feeling or emotion, then it is difficult to observe our thoughts, feelings or emotions.

Linguistic determinism is the theory that language and its structures limit and determine human knowledge or thought, as well as our thought processes.

German philosopher Friedrich Nietzsche even went so far as to say that language is a prison, which is incredibly powerful imagery and the proposition is as equally compelling and adding to this argument is the brilliantly incisive and prophetic novel, *Nineteen Eighty-Four* by George Orwell in 1949.

Nineteen Eighty-Four tells us of the fictional region of Oceania, which is a dystopian super state with a language called Newspeak, designed to meet the ideological requirements of the political party running Oceania, thus limiting personal expression; it provides for the reader a powerful example of linguistic determination. The point is that Newspeak with its restricted vocabulary and grammar makes it impossible to speak or even think of rebelling against the totalitarian government.

In this instance, Newspeak highlights the determination proposition that if a language does not contain the words to express certain ideas, its speakers cannot conceptualise them. As I mentioned, it is remarkable to think that *Nineteen Eighty-Four* was first published in 1949; it makes you think how prescient the words of Orwell were, his vision has to be applauded and his novel, inevitably, would add to British culture, the likes of those ubiquitous terms, Big Brother, Room 101, Orwellian and even CCTV, all spawned by the writer's apocalyptic words.

As this chapter is titled *Arrival*, it would be remiss of me to ignore the 2016 film of the same name, not one of the classics I agree, but notable no less. *Arrival* is based on the short story, *Story of Your Life*, by Ted Chiang; it is a science-fiction film and at its core is the notion of linguistic determinism, which is the concept that language limits human knowledge or thought.

Before I tell you about *Story of Your Life*, let me give you my own working example of linguistic determinism. I have two examples, the first is from when I initially started learning the Spanish language, which was purely for tourism purposes and was simply to enhance my pleasure when visiting that fabulous country and its islands, one of the first phrases I learnt was *dos cerveza por favor*, which many of you will know is two beers please; perfect tourist fodder, but absolutely useless if you are touring the ancient Alhambra Palace in Granada, Spain, one of the most famous examples of Islamic architecture in the world, but not a great place to go if you're looking for a bar to grab a couple of cold beers.

The second example is a phrase that I like to use a lot when at home, that I thought would be lovely to use when abroad, the phrase that I like to use as a term of endearment is, you are a fruitcake, which translates to *eres un pastella de frutas*, which once I had learnt verbatim, used several times in bars and restaurants, proud to show off my linguistic abilities, only to be confronted by looks of bemusement.

Apparently, the expression, you are a fruitcake, doesn't travel well and when I asked a Spanish friend of mine why nobody in Spain was falling about laughing at my use of the expression, especially as I was using it in their native tongue and all I was met with was a perplexed waiter or bartender, my friend told me the expression was meaningless in the Spanish language.

So despite having the vocabulary, it proved to be useless when those words have no meaning, et voila, my own example of linguistic determinism, right there. My travails around the ancient history spots of Spain were initially constrained due to my sparse Spanish language skills, luckily, my Spanish vocabulary has improved greatly since those days, spurred on by willingness to learn and my desperation to please my hosts, but I digress.

Let's go back to the Ted Chiang classic, *Story of Your Life*; in the book the story follows a linguist who is recruited to decipher the messages of extra-terrestrial visitors to Earth. The linguist, Louise Banks, spends her time learning their language which consists of complex circular symbols while simultaneously experiencing flashes of her own daughter's life and death. It is later that it becomes apparent that these flashes are a glimpse into her future and it is by acquiring an understanding of the language of the extra-terrestrials that she is able to see both past and future.

This award-winning film shows us that if we acknowledge the concept that language determines thought, that when Banks learns this new 'language' and a new way of thinking, she totally transforms her worldview and is able to drastically transform her perception of time, all because she now has the tools to understand and provide another level of understanding.

This is all a very long way from us signing in at reception, when we first arrive, but we must always bear in mind that it is not just you and I that are looking for answers but many of the earlier guests as well as those current residents, who are all striving for a greater understanding.

Language therefore is an important factor in contributing to us understanding our purpose, but nevertheless I feel it is an important one, however, having acknowledged the spoken word, I would like to return to the philosophy which took us there, which is the world of epistemology.

The reason epistemology is important to us is that it is the study of acquiring knowledge and knowledge is the assembling of and understanding the facts, which give us reality.

So, effectively, epistemology should provide a solution to our understanding of the hotel, our arrival, stay and departure because if you deal only with the facts then by analysing what we know, then our purpose may become more apparent!

Religious epistemology is a broad church and considers epistemology from a religious perspective, which may appear to be an oxymoron, but don't lose faith, it is an attempt to understand epistemological issues that come from a religious belief!

The questions that epistemologists ask about religious beliefs apply to each and every religion, are they rational, justified, warranted and reasonable based on evidence!

Some arguing that evolutionary explanations of religious belief undermine its rationality, indeed I have always felt that all religions, no matter which one, they all require a massive leap of faith in order to believe in them and take them seriously and have faith in them.

For some people this does not present an issue, having faith is easy and it is often reassuring, comforting, but for others, having faith, can be a difficult proposition, especially when it is presented without evidence.

Faith and rationality exist in varying degrees in both conflict and compatibility, yet they address issues of religious beliefs from very different positions. Rationality is based on reasoning or facts, whereas faith comes from inspiration or revelation. Faith refers to a belief that is sometimes held in spite of there being a lack of reason or evidence, alternatively a belief can be held in spite of or against reason and evidence or possibly held with just the smallest degree of evidence.

The relationship between faith and reason has been debated since the days in ancient Greece when the great philosophers would argue how knowledge was arrived at and that knowledge existed because of faith, effectively meaning that the knowledge we have has been passed down to us and our faith in those predecessors means that those things we believe that we know is because of the faith that we have in previous generations and our complete trust in them, those guests who stayed here long before we arrived in reception.

As society progresses, future generations will be in no doubt about the lives that we currently enjoy and that is because they are so well documented and in so many different forms, where once we relied on hieroglyphics to decipher what our ancestors knew, our descendants will not have to work too hard to uncover the reality of our lives.

The deliberate assimilation of faith and reason to become one certainly confuses the issue and when you are looking to simplify our experience as I am attempting to do, then the intricacies of the calculations of thought of our great thinkers, cloud the issues that we are looking at and hinder more than help in our quest for understanding.

'I think therefore I am,' said René Descartes, which, when I was younger, I was aware of that line's existence purely because it was quoted in a Monty Python sketch, it appeared in a song that if truth be told, I never really understood what it meant. In those days, I probably just thought it was a comical observation based on classical philosophy that the Oxford university-educated members of the Pythons crafted into one of their funny songs.

All of which happens to be true, but as I have grown older and have read more than I did in the days of my irresponsible youth, I have come to understand the profundity of the line.

'Cogito ergo sum', is the philosophical statement made by René Descartes, a Latin expression that translated into English becomes, I think therefore I am. Descartes statement provides a foundation for knowledge and became a fundamental element of western philosophy, in fact it is thought to be what is known as, an absolute truth, of which there can't really be that many of in life.

As an absolute truth this statement and all other rationalisations are built outwards from this single realisation and are therefore subject to change at any time with the arrival of new truths as and when they are established. If this statement is so powerful in establishing in our own minds our existence, our mortality, our fallibility, indeed our relatively short stay in the hotel, it helps by giving clarity to understanding that we are staying in the hotel and should we embrace our search for greater understanding of our stay, then we have the mind that allows it to do so. We can only ever live in our own minds and in that respect we can only ever truly know our own minds and it matters not, how long you spend with another person, or no matter how close you can be with a person, then there is only one mind you truly know and that is your own.

I am not sure if that is a good thing or a bad thing, but I do know it is true. This may all sound rather deep, even a little irrelevant, when we are looking to establish the question of our arrival in the hotel, however I really do believe that it is better to have too much information rather than not having enough, working on the principle, that it's better to have and not need, than to need and not have. Towards that end, let us look at two points of view which take different positions but will give us not only a different perspective but also give us an opportunity to consider a position that we may not have considered.

The rationalist point of view would tell us that you cannot prove that anything we see is real, but you can prove that you as a person are real and rationalist belief then is maintained until something inconsistent happens, this differs from a faith based belief where your belief is consistent irrespective of any inconsistencies that the world may have with your belief, it is a faith that cannot be shaken.

In relation to our hotel, it is possible that we can get through our stay in the hotel by living with the understanding that what we see with our own eyes, we trust.

It is because we have seen it with our own eyes and felt it with our own experiences that allow us to trust, while other guests similarly will enjoy their time in the hotel totally trusting to faith along with their own experiences and the experiences of others to guide them.

It is possible to get bogged down in analysis and theories of where we are, why we are here and what happens next and all of those types of existential questions, because no matter how fascinating they are, unfortunately, there are no definitive answers and that means that everybody who is contributing to the debate is guessing.

Nobody has a definitive answer to any of the big questions, so although of itself it is not a pointless exercise, it will inevitably be fruitless and that is because nobody knows.

Analysis equals paralysis, I have heard said, looking for meaning where none exists is a futile pursuit for any person, but a desire for greater understanding in itself is no bad thing.

What if we are searching for impossible answers and if they are impossible, why would that be? Are we as individuals or man in general, limited by our own capacity to understand, are the answers too complex for mere mortals like you and I to comprehend, or do we find ourselves in that peculiar situation of the hamster on its wheel, with no ending or beginning, the only cessation coming from an accidental occurrence bringing a premature conclusion or a natural end and death providing an exit strategy.

What is the point of life is a question that many people will have asked themselves during their lifetimes, because for many of us, it is possible to discover that at times, our time in the hotel can seem so futile, whereas at other times it can be incredibly fulfilling, so finding meaning can be the key to providing meaning for your mere existence.

There comes a time in our lives when no matter how successful we believe we are, we have a need to question why we are here and what is the purpose of our being, what are we doing, indeed where are we going.

Eight billion guests in the hotel, all currently experiencing everything that this place has to offer, but while some of us are staying in the presidential suite, there will be others who will have a bunk bed in the basement, that doesn't seem fair, so how has that happened and who is it that decides?

Sometimes posing these questions can help us to evaluate our own lives, the way we live, our lifestyle, our goals our physical and mental health, but when we can't find the answers we can feel even more vulnerable, wondering what the point of life is and those thoughts can amplify feelings, which can lead to depression, anxiety and an emptiness that ultimately can take us to a dark place.

As humans we believe that we are unique in the animal kingdom and not least because of our quest to find both happiness and fulfilment in our lives, this can be seen as just one of the many reasons that we as humans, believe ourselves to have a sense of superiority to our fellow guests, those in the animal kingdom.

Although this opinion may be given common consent in the world of ecology and zoology, I do feel we take things for granted at our peril especially by pushing a narrative of human superiority. Even by using my own casual observations of the animal world, I honestly believe it is impossible for us flawed individuals to judge the achievements or shortcomings of those that inhabit the animal kingdom by the achievements and shortcomings of us as humans.

To plagiarise the feminist Gloria Steinem, 'The animal world needs man like a fish needs a bicycle', her quote originally a feminist trope, telling the world that, 'A woman needs a man like a fish needs a bicycle'—how we laughed.

It would not surprise me if Steinem plagiarised the quote from a very similar quote often credited to Einstein, in which he tells us, 'Everyone is a genius, but if you judge a fish by its ability to climb a tree, it will live its whole life believing it is stupid'.

This is a fabulous observation which tells us that if we judge animals by human values then we make a spurious comparison, something like comparing apples and oranges.

Should an eagle ridicule humans for their inability to fly and maybe they do anyway, but if they do, then we as humans would be on a very sticky wicket. The human condition means that we are looking for more than, eating, sleeping, reproducing and finding somewhere safe to stay, although if we remember Maslow's Hierarchy of Needs mentioned earlier in the book, then these needs, those which we consider to be the basic requirements for a good life are also basic requirements for those who inhabit the animal kingdom, so when you consider it, they are not a million miles from our own demands for life.

So it is the quest for meaning that makes us different and has characterised humans since the beginning of times and it has become a central question in every culture and throughout the hotel. Scientists have given extensive research and found that the man's search for meaning appears to be coded into our nature, our brains are large and with this comes the ability to appreciate things beyond meeting our basic needs, we have intellectual capacity, allowing us to explore all of those things that we have created, those things that are beyond life's basic demands.

Science and philosophy, art and music, theatre and religion, the list is endless, but all of those things that we have created and that we continue to develop, meanwhile we do not stop looking beyond our achievements, we want more, we are looking for a greater understanding of our world and to suck as much pleasure from our stay as is humanly possible.

Individually, we have choice, we have preference, what may be good for you, may not be good for me, we are lucky, we have the fortune to explore our own lives, push them to the limit and should we choose to, over our own mortality, but whatever you do, whether you are ultra cautious or reckless, you are going to die, you should reconcile to the fact and somehow make it part of your world view. That acceptance may lead us to ask, what is the purpose of life, well maybe there is no single reason, maybe it is our journey, the time we spend in the hotel once we have checked in at reception is the whole, maybe that is the point.

When we talk about the journey, we are talking about all of our experiences, the good and the bad, the memories that linger, from the fabulous days out spent with friends, to the sadness experienced when a loved one dies and checks out of the hotel forever, we find ourselves taking pleasure from things we've got right and learning from the mistakes we made and those things we have got wrong.

For the journey or your stay in the hotel to be meaningful, your life has to be lived through your own choices, you can look for meaning or fulfilment in wealth and fame, but those imposters are simply a byproduct of decisions that you have made, as a living being, or as I would prefer to identify each of us, a guest in the hotel.

It is your call, you have the unique opportunity to decide what your purpose should be. It was John Lennon in his fantastic song, *Mother*, who wrote the immortal line, 'Mother, you had me, but I never had you'; a great line that describes what was a troubled relationship with his own mother in the early years of his life, so much so that he ended up being brought up by his Aunt Mimi, his mother's sister, because his mother Julia had been accused of neglecting him. It is the actual line from the song that we are considering when we are talking about a unique opportunity to devise our own purpose.

Although these words are personal to Lennon, the line is actually relevant to every single person in the hotel today, every person is created as a byproduct of another person's dream, another person's ambition or expectation, of what they want from their lives.

The ultimate control over your own destiny must lie in the fact that you have the opportunity should you choose, to create another life, a life that more often than not, will be staying in the hotel long after you have checked out and left for the airport.

You are leaving your legacy behind, evidence that, if it matters to you, the proof is there for all to see, that you once stayed in the hotel and therefore fulfilling what many people believe including most that I have spoken to during my own research, to be the reason for our existence.

With one voice they will tell me that the point of life is procreation, it's as simple as that. Procreation entered our vocabulary in the late fourteenth century, a combination of an old French word derived from Latin we had procreation, which simply means, the process by which an organism reproduces others of its biological kind, the sexual activity of conceiving and bearing biological offspring.

As I discussed mentioned earlier, having been to different parts of the hotel, you find that different cultures have different values for living life, however the most popular answer when I have asked people that simple question, why are we here, the answer procreation is the one that most people have come back with, across language and cultures, I believe it is the single most popular belief.

I have come to feel that although we don't have a definitive answer, so that makes any answer correct, to simply trot out procreation as a one word answer feels not only lazy but fundamentally lacks intellect, it may be unfair but I have always wanted more from those I have asked.

Procreation in some cases is said almost without thinking, it's too easy, there has to be more, or maybe I was expecting too much from my interviewees, or maybe those providing me with the answer were contemptuous of me and my interrogation of them. Whether it is relaxing on a Sunbed by a swimming pool, sat in a dimly lit bar, or in a restaurant, I was asking them a question to which I did not know the answer and could neither give an informed opinion on whether their answer was right or wrong, even if they offered an in-depth justification for their opinion!

The eternal quest in searching for a meaning of life can be so overwhelming that the very thought of getting started can intimidate you to virtual stagnation, trying to discover what the actual point, if there is one, is something that it is a lifelong journey and the various steps and stages along the way, including the length of the journey, will be different for everybody.

There is no doubt however that if you do find a purpose in life then it can bring you closer to happiness, but if you don't find a point, a purpose, then you shouldn't torture yourself.

If you are rushing into finding an answer, this can cause undue stress and anxiety which can disturb your thinking and ultimately be incredibly unhelpful, it becomes more destructive than constructive. You can find yourself looking at other people for inspiration or find yourself simply comparing their lives to yours and all that you believe to be true, believing that they have it all worked out, especially compared to you, but even this is unhelpful.

I believe that the point is to live life on your own terms and live it at your own pace, it isn't a race there is no finishing line, the only conclusion is one that you don't want to reach too soon.

So if there is a point then without sounding sybaritic, then it is to live life to its fullest, however that is for you to interpret there is no definitive answer, you can't be wrong.

Find joy in what you have, value what you have, not what you don't have, but strive, with ambition, try to live in the present, at some point you will find your answers, in the meantime simply enjoy your stay in the hotel, you're here for a good time, not a long time.

Chapter 7
What Shall We Do in the Last Few Days?

We are all creatures of habit, we are merely flesh and blood, though our brains are incredibly complex, we are evolved machines, we are able to govern the basic processes needed to sustain life, such as food intake and breathing, to the extravagances of pleasure, such as appreciating the works of Shakespeare or a night at the opera! As we have discussed earlier, we have basic needs in our lives, needs which must be satiated in order for us to survive and thrive whether it be individually or collectively as a society.

We believe we have free will, which sets us apart from other animals that we share the hotel with; set apart primarily by our capacity for reasoning, yet if you actually watch people closely, you will find that we are more instinctual and a lot more like other creatures than we would care to think.

I read a recent study that ninety per cent of what people do in any one day follows routines so complete that their behaviour can be predicted with a few simple mathematical equations. This tells us that most of everyday life is determined not by our conscious intentions and our deliberate choices, rather we are going through actions determined by mental processes put into motion by our environment, we are creatures of habit.

There is a wonderful line by the ancient Greek philosopher Aristotle, 'We are what we repeatedly do.' It is often said that familiarity breeds contempt but apparently and to the contrary, the human psyche connects positive feelings with familiarity, meaning that when we form routines and rituals, they make us feel better about our lives, reinforcing a feel good factor, as though we are on the right track and ultimately this is beneficial for human development and the evolutionary process.

There is a downside to routine and this is where the line about contempt is relevant, when we become complacent with routine and rituals we resent them, because in some ways we can become dependent upon them for getting us through the day, making us stagnate, stifling our personal growth and development.

But as we go through our lives our habits and rituals do play an important role as they provide us with a much needed structure, which while still enabling us to enjoy random acts of pleasure or pain while having a foundation of what we feel works for us, which is always there as a back stop.

Look at your own life, from time to time we may go to a different restaurant, go out with those occasional friends that we rarely see, we may listen to a different radio station just for a change or, if we're feeling really intrepid, order something totally different off the takeaway menu.

We allow ourselves these experiences safe in the knowledge that our favourite restaurant is still there, our best friends, those who get us, are on speed dial our usual radio station is still there in your 'favourites' section, or if the worst happens and we make a catastrophic mistake, we can go to our comfort food and order the same takeaway dish that we always order.

It is not by accident that if you do your supermarket shopping online, then there is a favourites section where you can speed up the ordering process by ordering the same things as you usually order every week.

It is incredible that with the unbelievable variety that our society offers us, we prefer to stick with what we know and trust. This has massive implications for our life in the hotel, meaning that from our earliest days of our stay we are constantly learning to be ourselves and about what we like and what we don't like, what we value and what we don't care for. Those early days in the hotel as with life itself, are a period of rapid personal development as we experience major life transitions and it is those changes that will influence our later lives as we go forward.

Our propensity for change diminishes the longer we stay in the hotel, therefore the majority of change is experienced in the early years as you become you. There are so many changes in those early years which occur right through to adulthood and it is these modifications or alterations that will determine how we spend the rest of our time in the hotel, we go through education, we seek employment, followed by cohabitation and then possibly, but not guaranteed, followed by parenthood.

Current analysis suggests that numbers hovering either side of 40% of the population are parents, which I find to be a surprisingly low number, but obviously parenthood is not for everybody and given that there are global issues that will affect the future of our world, then some people may see it as a responsible position to consciously choose not to bring a child into this world.

In a 2020 survey, a study of 600 people aged 27 to 45 were factoring climate change concern into their reproductive choices, concerned about the well-being for any future, the children they may have, living in a world experiencing the vagaries of climate change. This sort of opinion given by those surveyed, believing that in good faith, they would be unwilling to bring a child into this world, only for them to try and survive what may be apocalyptic conditions in the near future would be unconscionable on their part.

These views were based on those who had a pessimistic assessment of the impact of global warming, carbon footprints and food poverty, but whatever was driving them it certainly showed us that today's society had presented current hotel residents with problems that earlier guests had never considered, or felt the need to consider.

The importance of those early days on a baby and into early childhood can't be stressed enough, researchers tell us that exposure to stress and trauma can have long-term negative influences for a child's brain, whereas talking, reading and playing will stimulate brain growth. None of this will come as an earth-shattering revelation to any of you, it all seems rather obvious, but what it does tell us is how important those early days really are, once we've checked in at reception and taken our bags to our rooms.

There is a theory offered to us by the 'Zero to Three Movement', an American organisation born out of the National Centre for Clinical Infant Programs, whose mission is to ensure that all babies and toddlers have a strong start in life, they believe that it is those first three years of a baby's life that are the critical period for a child's brain development and persistent deficits in those years of any of either, cognitive, emotional or even physical health will result in lifelong effects, the magnitude of which will only expose themselves as the life of the child progresses into youth, adulthood and eventually old age.

It is incredible that we accept every day of our lives as something that is expected, a given, that we are here at all, when in reality it is much more than that and having looked at the chances of our being here, then really, nothing should ever be taken for granted, but instead we maybe should acknowledge the privilege that we all. We can be aware of our good fortune and acknowledge how lucky we are to have the chance of life, but to dwell on it hourly or by acknowledging our gratitude for every minute, then our stay in the hotel we would be wasted and just too intense.

So how do we make the most of our shared experiences in this place together, when ultimately we are just one person, an individual, doing our utmost to optimise what we want to get out of our stay? And once we have checked out, believing we have made the most of all that we have been given.

Over recent years, we have seen the development of a modern phenomenon, the bucket list. I seem to recall that I first became aware of the bucket list in or around the turn of the millennium, when I believe if I remember correctly, it being something that was mainly created for or by people with a terminal illness, a list of favourite things or a list of things that they had done before and enjoyed so much that they wanted to do it one more time, or additionally, things which they hadn't yet experienced but it would be their dream to do so.

Because it was originally synonymous with a premature death, some people chose not to use the term 'bucket list' and instead chose something that didn't have connotations of an early demise, opting instead for something like, 'life to-do list', 'dream list' or even 'life plan', something a little more ambiguous but still powerful enough to state its intent! It is import to do things that you enjoy in your life, doing things that will make you happy, while you can still enjoy them can energise you and ultimately serve in making you more relaxed and even fulfilled.

Depending on the type of goal on your bucket list, the sense of achievement and self-esteem can be immeasurable, a bungee jump as a opposed to reading a book, climbing Everest as opposed to knitting a scarf, although they are all achievements in their own way, there is inevitably a hierarchy accomplishment.

There is a conversation to be had about relative achievement and its place in the greater scheme of things, but any success has to be seen as a success and the discussion about magnitude should it be needed, can be discussed, but ultimately the feeling comes from within, the person achieving their bucket list goal is the only person that needs to be satisfied that an achievement has been made to their own satisfaction.

A fabulous example of this was seen in the UK last year when Captain Sir Tom Moore, who was born on 30 April 1920, set himself the goal of walking one hundred lengths of his garden at the ripe old age of 99; not the most spectacular achievement of all time, but with everything taken into consideration, it became one of the greatest achievements of all time.

On the 6th of April 2020, at the age of 99, Captain Tom Moore began walking with the aid of his walking frame, one hundred lengths of his garden in order to raise £1,000 for NHS Charities. But he exceeded everybody's expectations achieving his goal of 100 laps of the garden, while simultaneously raising an incredible £39 million for charity and by the time of his 100th birthday on 30th April, we as a nation were all lucky enough to know of Tom; because of the publicity that surrounded his fundraising achievements, he enjoyed many TV appearances, he recorded a number one hit record, the oldest person ever to do so, and also had trains, monuments, buses and even police dogs named after him.

I wouldn't have imagined that Tom would have even considered doing 100 laps of his garden or even raising a magnificent £39 million for charity, neither would have been on his bucket list, but as life changes, our priorities and values change too along with new physical limitations that can come along when we are least expecting them; so, a big well-done to Tom, he certainly signed the guest book before he left. When we come to spending our own last few days in the hotel, we will think differently to the way we are thinking at the moment, perspective changes and demands can become acceptance of an inevitability that we will all face.

Life can change in a moment and life-changing events can alter our lives forever, depending on the magnitude of the change we experience, it is how we come to terms with the change and learn to adapt to a different way of living, if that is how the change presents itself, I believe this to be true of both sudden change or of progressive deterioration.

As we enter the last few days of our stay in the hotel, the likelihood for change becomes virtually inevitable, if not guaranteed, it may be our perspective on life-changing and even our expectations and needs too, but physically change is bound to happen, the unfortunate thing is that as we age, we deteriorate not only physically, eyesight, heart, hearing, strength and other major organs combined with the more visible aspects of our visible appearance, our hair, skin, teeth and even our weight can increase as part of the ageing process, sounds fabulous, what's not to love? We need to come to terms with these changes and as we do, we need to find a way of accepting the inevitability of change, which can sometimes be both dramatic and permanent, and this is not only in ourselves, but also those loved ones that have enjoyed our stay in the hotel with us, this is not always easy to do, but acceptance is vital. The driving emotion behind many of our decisions as we get older can be memories of good times we have from an earlier time in our life when our physical and mental self were very different, we have to accept the person although still the same, that we become in old age and because deterioration is inevitable, then this can lead to disappointment when revisiting places we once loved, whatever the reason may be because as we are now different people.

Let's make this make sense and look at an example from my own recollection. I used to enjoy going to the Tuxedo Princess in Newcastle-upon-Tyne in the early eighties, it was a floating nightclub and I loved every minute spent there; although the ship is no longer there, let's just assume for the purposes of the example that it is. I doubt that if I put on my disco gear and go there tonight, I would have as much fun today as I did in those fabulous days when I was in my twenties! The people in there would have changed, the music would be different, the drinks would be different, my fashion sense would look ridiculous and I would stick out like a sore thumb!

At the time it was incredible and the memories are mine forever; I am lucky to have those, but that's all they are and all they ever will ever be, those who were in the hotel at the same time and were staying in Newcastle in those heady days may have equally fond recollections.

What is hard for me to equate is how every moment or period of time in our lives, be they good or bad is simply a snapshot or possibly a video or a short film, that builds up in our mental library and remains with us until we check out at reception or, in some cases is cruelly stolen from us by dementia.

I often wonder whether we become so fond of our precious memories of our past, just because our present is so disappointing, thus intensifying the warmth we get from those times that we experienced great pleasure and convincing ourselves they were even better than they really were. Because we can be so invested in a monogamous relationship for our adult lives sharing them with just one other person, then when tragedy strikes and that other person is no longer with around, we can experience incredible sadness and as if it could get any worse than the sadness culminated in loneliness, once the grief has lost its intensity, that is if it chooses to do so.

If we are fortunate enough to navigate the pitfalls or bunkers of life, then we can spend our last few days in the hotel with those that we love, if not, then we will enjoy our last few days alone and contemplating what might have been. That sounds incredibly bleak, but I believe it is true, for while researching for this book, it is those of the older generation who have contributed by indulging me and my inane questions by offering me their thoughts and opinions on life as a hotel, and what they were experiencing and indeed expecting from the latter days of their stay.

It is difficult not to generalise and obviously I am reluctant to compromise any one individual by revealing their identity, but it is true that loneliness is not a friend to those who are left to check out of the hotel after their life partner, be they husband, wife, girlfriend or boyfriend or simply a true friend who has shared our stay with us, has left before they have. Loneliness can be with us at any age, it is not exclusive to old age, but the later in life it happens, the more set in our ways we are, we are more comfortable with the routines of life which we discussed earlier and therefore our opportunities for making new friends and relationships become increasingly limited.

Loneliness is best described as a state of mind, more than simply an absence of a physical partner, loneliness causes people to feel empty, alone and unwanted, craving companionship or friendship, but their mental state can work against them, it can prohibit them developing new relationships and worse than that there is the possibility that even maintaining existing relationships can be difficult.

According to many experts in this field, loneliness is not necessarily about being alone, it is about how you feel, if you feel alone and isolated, then that is how loneliness plays into your state of mind. Thinking of spending your remaining days in the hotel without the person who has been in the same room as you for a big part of your stay can be difficult and that can be one of several contributing factors to loneliness. The symptoms for loneliness like the symptoms for most things in life tend to exist in a spiral which is either positive or negative, the spiral I always live my own life by with regards to my own personal fitness has always driven me, to maintain my own commitment to my own goals.

Simply put, and looking at fitness negatively, you see it as a chore or an imposition, then the less you do, the worse you feel, the more unfit you become, so you do less exercise and once again you feel worse and so it goes, until nothing is achieved and you are physically unfit. The flipside of the negative position is that you exercise, which makes you feel better, you feel better and are encouraged, because you see signs of improvement, you keep exercising, you get better, stronger, fitter and so it becomes a habit, a positive contribution to your wellbeing.

I believe that with anything in life that improves you as a person, or even your quality of life, the starting point for this self-improvement is irrelevant, I don't believe it matters where you start. You can always come from a very low base as your starting point, but if you are committed and disciplined enough to stay with your chosen regime, then I honestly believe that success is guaranteed. Applying this mantra to loneliness is exactly the same principle, if you find yourself no longer with a loved one, for whatever reason, then you must keep in contact with friends and family, you need to demand their time and engage in new environments, in spite of any natural resistance that you may have, you need to break out of your comfort zone, if not for your own sanity, you must keep going and thereby create a new normal. Of course, it will always be easier not to interact and become withdrawn but this can be fatal, literally fatal in some cases, because depression is a symptom of loneliness that nobody should endure.

Depression is a low mood that can last for a long time, if you experience it in its mildest form, it can just mean that you are in extremely low spirits, it does not stop you leading a normal life but it can make everyday life a lot harder and even make things seem less worthwhile. At its extreme, depression as I mentioned earlier can be a killer, but luckily we are in an age when mental health issues are discussed more openly than ever before, the stigma is lifting gradually and what once was a taboo subject now is encouraged to be discussed and then supported if a person is looking for help.

There are many changes in our lives that we can experience as we enter our last few days in the hotel, many negative but also there are positives, you know more about yourself, you are better equipped to know what you like and dislike, places, people, food and drinks, you are aware of the things that you still want to do, places that you still want to see and those things that you have absolutely no interest in seeing or doing. As we briefly discussed earlier, the bucket list originally appeared to be a wish list for those unfortunate to be living with a terminal illness, but it has morphed into a to-do list for anybody who chooses to have one.

Incredibly subjective, they can be tailored to fulfil the demands of the most demanding thrill seeker, whether it is for those of us looking for an extreme experience to others who are a little more conservative in their aspirations. Crossing items off a bucket list is one of those things that those in the last few days of their stay in the hotel can look forward to most, a period in your life when hopefully you have navigated the working years and now see the demands and intensity, winding down a little, as you find yourself in retirement.

If you have dreams of climbing Mount Kilimanjaro or sipping your way through the vineyards of Napa Valley, or have an interminable list of those things that you have never done but have always dreamed of doing but never got around to for whatever reason, whether it is time, money, family or work commitments or any of those reasons that stop us leading the life of a sybarite, then here is your chance. However, the bucket list can simply consist of doing those things again that you know have given you so much pleasure in the preceding years, things that you know are guaranteed to be exactly what you expect them to be.

How often in life does that happen, when you go back to a place that you have really enjoyed whether it is a restaurant, a bar or back to a holiday location, this can go one of two ways, you can either have an equally good time as when you first had the experience, if not possibly improving on the first occasion, this time feeling more comfortable and knowing what was so good the first time, or conversely you may feel totally let down. It is difficult to know what makes for a perfect night or that memorable holiday, there are so many factors that are brought into the equation that need to pull together in order for the magic to happen, not least of all is your own mental preparedness and being ready for the time of your life.

I feel it is important to mention the times when going back can never be as good as that first time, it is impossible to recreate what made it so good, there is a parallel to be drawn here with our stay in the hotel. Everything has its time and as we come to the end of our stay at the hotel, it is impossible not to notice those who have just checked in or have recently arrived, doing all of those things that you did years before and talking enthusiastically about their new found pleasure, happy to share it with other guests, just like you did and those that have long ago checked out have and those yet to arrive will.

When you go back, do you see the ghosts of those earlier days when life was very different, our memories are what stay with us and are a powerful part of our lives or do you see things through the eyes of the you of today, as if seeing things for the first time.

Memories are incredible, the emphasis as we go through life is always on the experience itself, but as we know, the experience only lasts for a certain amount of time. We do spend a lot of our lives and a lot of our money engineering the pleasant experiences that create good memories, booking airline tickets to visit, beaches, skiing chalets or glaciers, when in all of this the emphasis is always in the experience itself, which only lasts for a certain amount of time and once it is over and we have enjoyed the experience, it is consigned to our personal dustbin of history!

The dustbin where we keep all of those things we have collected during our stay. I suppose for some it will be a dustbin for others it may be a wicker hamper tied with an oversized bow depending on our fondness for the recollection concerned, not all memories are good, not all will be bad but they are ours and they make us what we are, some will be scars and run deep, others will be the tattoo picked up on a beach in Mexico! Apart from those permanent reminders that we may carry on our person, either the scar or the tattoo, most of our memories, which are voluminous, for we create them every day, tend to stay in the earlier mentioned dustbin and can resurface at the most innocuous times.

We can be sitting at our desk at work, or walking around the supermarket aisles, when the most random of things can trigger a memory of something totally unrelated, can have us sitting back on that Caribbean beach or skiing into an apres-ski bar as dusk arrives, just in time for the first schnapps of the early evening.

Memories are a vital part of our stay in the hotel and while discussing our memories, this could be an appropriate time to mention Deja vu.

Have you ever experienced Deja Vu?

Have you ever experienced Deja Vu?

Sorry, I couldn't resist that, it has always been one of my favourite jokes, but it is a valid question.

Deja vu is the feeling that you have lived through the present situation before, the French phrase literally translated means 'already seen' and by some is interpreted as a paranormal experience, but this is rejected by mainstream science. It is generally thought that up to two-thirds of people have experienced a Deja vu moment, but these are simply put down to being prevalent in those who are frequent travellers or those who tend to watch a lot of films. I think I prefer the simplicity of that explanation to one explanation that I discovered in my research for this book—cryptomnesia, where information learnt is stored in our memory but has been forgotten, then similar occurrences invoke the retained knowledge, leading to a feeling of familiarity and Deja vu.

So that is Deja vu, all part of the memory puzzle and its role in our lives, but it is our memories that we were considering in relation to the last few days. Those memories need nothing to be rckindled other than ourselves, nothing more technical than that, no extra apparatus is needed to be able to access our past.

We don't even need to carry a camera with us, we are the camera if you will, a camera that is constantly snapping, it is always on and incessantly taking photographs or recording videos, of everything we ever see.

All of our time in the hotel is recorded, not all of it is recalled constantly, in fact large chunks of it are never accessed at all, but those memories remain, some a little more blurred than others, but they are vivid and intact, just waiting for us to recall them on demand by asking a leading question that will take us right to them and just like a reference library we can take out the information and browse the subject further.

How many times have you been discussing a shared memory with a loved one or a good friend and simply by recalling one event, you will both continue to remember extra details and from being a simple memory of say, what had started as a civilised night out together, you find yourselves laughing at your physical state after arriving home at some unearthly time the next morning.

These memories are all just sitting there in the reference library waiting to be accessed, how incredible and how very lucky. It is this reference library that will give us not only an enormous amount of pleasure, but also guidance for our last few days in the hotel, remembering what was good and maybe choosing to replicate those times.

We often talk about virtual reality and yet we are our very own virtual reality machines stored in our own heads, as I mentioned earlier, we can access an on-demand collection of our Greatest Hits; if you shut your eyes right now, you can travel back and stay a while amongst those most happy, life-affirming, funny, or whatever emotion you desire, moments of our lives, brought back from the past.

It is believed that explicit memory starts around the age of three years of age, and before that we have what you call implicit memory, there is a difference between the two which I feel is nicely explained by the example of getting on and riding a bicycle. When you jump onto a bike and proceed to ride off you are using your implicit memory, your actions are as if you were on autopilot, but if you think of an actual bike ride that you have been on and enjoyed, you are using your explicit memory.

Our explicit memories are those specific to our own world which serve us throughout our lives but possibly more importantly in our latter years, while our implicit memories are those that keep us on track as we meander our way across the planet.

As we ramble through our lives and approach the last few days in the hotel, we will utilise our memory banks to help us fill those days and if we go back to our bucket list we will look to revisit some of those places, or try to relive once more those experiences that have made our stay such fun. I must just mention before I go back to the bucket list, an experience this morning which totally encapsulates the role of our memories in our lives. Every Wednesday morning I visit my local hairdresser for a quick trim, a coffee and a chat with Tina and have done for the last six years, as usual we catch up with what has been happening in and around the village and what we have been up to, of course I have been keeping her up to date with my progress writing my book.

Currently, they are filming *Railway Children Two* at our village railway station, so we are all keeping our eyes open for a glimpse of Jenny Agutter; we are still in a state of semi-lockdown for the Coronavirus and I am currently writing about memories in my book.

As we were talking, Tina spontaneously told me a story from when she was an eighteen-year-old and worked in a pub at weekends before getting a lift over to Wakefield, some thirty miles away, to go to a nightclub.

The memory was so powerful that she remembered what she was wearing as well as being searched by a bouncer before going into the club. I asked her when she last discussed that memory and how incredibly vivid it is thirty-two years later, she told me that she had never discussed it since it happened. My point, if it needed reinforcing is that we have thousands of memories dormant or oft revisited that are stored waiting to be accessed at any time and as long as we are of sound mind and in good mental health, time cannot diminish our recollections of those earlier days and maybe, just maybe their recollection will bring a smile to our face.

The memories serve to take us to our bucket list in the last few days in the hotel, taking us to those memories that we would like to enjoy at least one more time before we check out at reception. Interestingly, I have also discovered a moral bucket list, a list that contemplates the ways we achieve self-fulfilment or purpose in our lives, examining our achievements or successes at a more fundamental level, rather than where we have visited during our stay, but more what we are as a person and the character that we have created for ourselves during our stay.

Self-reflection, examining ourselves and actually looking for a deeper meaning in life can be incredibly rewarding and possibly provide a purpose. Armed with a list of characteristics that would be perceived as being virtuous, we can tick off what we consider that those who know us well would consider us to be. There are many traits that we can consider to be attractive for the person who has enjoyed a full and decent life, so let us consider several of these, including humility, dependency, love, conscience and many others.

If life is about self-improvement as a gradual process, seeking to improve and striving for decency, compassion and ultimately acceptance then turning these things into a list of those things we feel progress us to the point of contentment then that surely is a good thing. Life goes through many stages as our characters develop throughout our stay in the hotel and a major part of our development is the value we place on our development both in terms of our physical experiences and our development of ourselves as a valuable member of society.

Maturity is one ingredient that has a profound effect on our lives as we progress through our stay and because it doesn't happen at any set rate and its effects happen to us as individuals at a different speed and in some maturity doesn't happen at all.

This is a category which I can often stray into, or so my wife tells me, then maturity becomes one of those factors which we must consider for our overall reflections on our time in the hotel.

We learn many things during our stay, one of which is that it won't last forever and the profound impact of the realisation that, as with everything, nothing lasts forever can be disturbing. There is a limit on your stay because of course there are more people waiting to check in and if those before you hadn't checked out then you wouldn't have had your opportunity to stay.

So it is with this understanding that we live our lives, living according to the way the society that we live in has dictated we do, wherever that may be, from the western society that I have been brought up in, to the uncontacted Indian people of Brazil.

However diverse they are, they are both manmade cultures and will necessarily have developed a structure for the people that inhabit them.

As I've never been to the Amazon or met those people in Brazil, those who we would once describe sneeringly as tribes, we now realise they have parity with ourselves and as much right to coexist in the hotel as we do. The way you interpret your stay is up to you, nobody is right and nobody is wrong, it's your stay, you enjoy it as much as you can. I believe that we can all learn from each other, those staying in the hotel today and those guests who checked out before we arrived.

Chapter 8
Which Flaw Are You On?

When I was a lot younger, mum, dad and I were looking forward to going off on our summer holidays, which in those days meant either a trip abroad if I was very, very lucky, or maybe a caravan at the fabulous Kiln Park in Tenby, or something a little nearer to home, possibly a hotel on the North Wales coast, any of which sent my excitement levels sky-high, times of uncomplicated fun, the three of us together; it was hard to contain myself at the prospect of the impending adventures with my mother and father, would we would meet new friends, discover new places, possibly taste unusual foods for the first time.

This was a time when affordable travel for the masses was in its infancy and although these days, flying as a part of your holiday regime has become a bit of an irritant, in those days it was very different and was seen as a far more exciting prospect; we were pioneering buccaneers, seeking new worlds overseas. Phileas Fogg had nothing on us; indeed, when my mother, father and I flew from Speke airport in Liverpool in 1972 to Ibiza for our first continental holiday, my grandmother, aunties, uncles and cousins came to wave us off—I remember it vividly.

You would have thought we were never coming home, or we were flying to the deepest, darkest jungle, with no idea of when we would return, when in reality, we were off to San Antonio for a fortnight and would be back in Liverpool two weeks later. Having enjoyed every minute of the build-up to our holiday, going to Boots, buying suntan lotion, rolls of film for the photographs, even a new toothbrush and flannel which were essential purchases for the trip and once bought were suitably placed in my suitcase a fortnight prior to flying, but the anticipation was part of the fun and I loved it all.

Then came the big day, we were off, saying our fond farewells to the assembled members of the family at the airport, we boarded the aeroplane, it was a Cambrian Airways, BAC 1-11, I remember boarding it as if I was Neil Armstrong boarding Apollo 11, on the 16th of July 1969, although it was one small step for me, it was a giant leap for our family and one that I will never forget.

We landed at Ibiza airport and the three of us, along with the rest of the passengers, walked down the steps at the back of the aeroplane, my father wearing a three-piece suit, a collar and tie, he certainly wasn't prepared for the incredible blast of heat of Spanish sun that was about to hit our English skin, for the first but fortunately not the last time in our lives.

It was a very different heat although it felt a little unnatural to our sensitivities, we were used to a British climate of wind and rain in the summer we were about to be exposed to the fabulous Mediterranean sunshine every day for the next two weeks, I don't think we saw my dad's three-piece suit for the rest of the holiday as t-shirts and shorts became the order of the day for both of us and mum bought some summer dresses in Ibiza Town, it was a memorable holiday our first sojourn to foreign lands.

The highlight of our stay was arriving at our hotel, my parents had chosen the Hotel Riviera in San Antonio, a place which in 1972 was very different from the San Antonio of today, in the seventies it was a quaint fishing village which was just starting to realise the potential of tourism, that tranquil idyll was a million miles and a lifetime away from the cool clubbing capital of the world that it is today, where it is seen as a mecca for the trendies, clubbers and the beautiful people.

Thankfully, they weren't the criteria when we were there, otherwise we wouldn't have got in, but get in we did and we arrived at the Hotel Riviera and as my parents checked in, I stood guarding our suitcases with my life until dad approached with the key to our room, which was attached to a key ring that I was to discover was like a shotput ball, with a size and weight that would have tested the Olympian skills of former British Commonwealth champion, Geoff Capes.

Impatiently, I asked my dad which floor we were on; I was twelve years old, so it was the higher the better for me, thinking of the view that would greet me every morning as soon as I got out of bed and last thing at night as I reluctantly returned to my bed to dream of the days to come, we were on the sixth floor, which was the top floor of the hotel, I couldn't have been happier! However, we managed to assemble in the lift with our cases and door key and I can remember as the lift made its way to the sixth floor, I had a sense of anticipation as we entered our room and I was desperate to see the view from our balcony.

It was early evening and we'd had a long day, Liverpool seemed a million miles away, as we entered our room the anticipation heightened but I had to wait a little longer as the room was darkened by the fully drawn curtains, I ignored everything else and drew them back as quickly as I could to be presented with an incredible view of the distant mountains and immediately in front of me sprawled the bay of San Antonio, it was a beautiful sight and completed a perfect day.

As darkness fell on our first evening in Ibiza, I sat mesmerised on our balcony watching tiny boats ferry people from one side of the bay to the other with their lights being orchestrated by each rippling wave that challenged them. My parents literally had to drag me down to dinner, so reluctant was I to miss any of the nautical delights that had me fixated since drawing back those heavy curtains.

My first precious memories of our hotel and travelling abroad, magical in every sense. I say our hotel and most of us do, whenever we take ownership, however temporary our custodianship of our room wherever and whenever we have an opportunity to reside in one.

I felt so lucky to be on the sixth floor overlooking the bay but in this case, the floor although not crucial to my enjoyment certainly enhanced the experience, after all, we could have been in a room at the side of the hotel overlooking the local tienda, or worse, at the back of the hotel, overlooking the bins and the staff car park.

There are so many things that can influence our stay here, so many outside influences can affect our daily lives, either bringing us pleasure or causing us pain, but I don't want to focus on those things that we allow to determine our enjoyment, but instead, look at how we as individuals can influence our stay. As we have acknowledged, none of us is perfect and nobody has a perfect life, we all have issues of one sort or another to deal with every day of our lives, but we also have our individuality which can either help or indeed hinder us when faced with any given situation.

Our individuality can be the cause of problems that we may have or situations that we find ourselves in. We start our lives as a blank canvas, a lump of clay, there to be shaped and moulded, it is our personalities that define us and of course we are all very different yet it is our individuality that allows us to express ourselves, to live by the values that we want to live by. We have a self-image, a view of how we both see ourselves and how we would like others to see us, but ultimately, in spite of our best efforts, we are all flawed individuals. But never forget, as a famous person once said, perfection only comes from imperfection and it is important to consider that sentiment during our stay in the hotel.

Although personally, we may strive for perfection, however and whatever that means, to either us as individuals or the culture of the places that we live in as a greater whole perceive it, because it is hard to define perfection, so we could be striving to achieve the unattainable.

That probably means that in spite of our efforts to achieve a flawless existence, each of us is flawed and the only option we have is to determine whether it is to a greater or lesser degree. Thinking about it, maybe it is in this chapter that we stumble on one of the reasons for our stay in the hotel, could it be that we are here simply to make the best of ourselves, which may initially sound a little narcissistic, but after all, we are just an individual, one person and ultimately, we are the only thing that we can have control over.

So if the purpose of our lives is to fashion ourselves to become what our society or culture believes to be a decent, honourable member of that society, then that should be regarded as a success, the only success, be the best you can be.

As I write and the more I think about it, I do believe that if this is our purpose and that being a decent, honest and a good member of society, then this presents us with a bigger question, if we are all striving for decency while simultaneously busying ourselves with populating the hotel during the time that we have been given to us and procreation is a vital element too, then what is the point of that? It strikes me that if we are simply being nice individuals, replacing ourselves constantly, we are simply perpetuating the hotel's existence, which is great, but that just becomes an infinite game.

This is the issue that I am struggling with, so let me explain that in a little more depth because I believe it is worth understanding, an infinite game will have very different rules to a finite game and you would play each game very differently.

Of course, both can coexist but in order for us to understand which one we are playing and which rules we are adhering to, then that can mean that our lives are a little aimless. If we acknowledge that there are two options, then let us take a closer look at both, firstly let us look at a finite game, which is one which is one that has fixed rules, the players are easily identified and they have clear goals to strive for and hopefully achieve during the fixed period of time. There is a beginning, a middle and an end, in these games, the competition between individuals or teams is often to finish first and this inevitably means that there are winners and losers.

Winning and losing are often symptoms of human behaviour, exposing human strengths and human frailties, winning is often highlighted by things such as competitiveness, creativity, enthusiasm and an obsession to overcome the competition. Losing similarly has its own defining traits, often the direct inverse of or an absence of those winning habits, as well as possibly a lack of self-confidence and maybe a decline in confidence in others, those negative things that often conclude with defeat in a finite game. An infinite game however is a rather different proposition, there are no strict rules, but general frameworks, participants can innovate and conduct themselves determined by their own principles, or lack of them.

With no time horizons, there is no end game, there is no concept of winning, but the only goal is perpetuating itself, which in this case, it would appear is keeping the species going and promoting it indefinitely.

Applying these two principles to our own world, I would suggest, we have a hybrid of both, which is unhelpful in itself because a hybrid can lead us to different conclusions about our purpose and that is due to the ambiguity of our purpose and a complete lack of clarity. I see it as a hybrid because for each of us life is a finite game and that is because, as far as we know, our time here is limited and yet the framework that we work within is dictated by societal and cultural values, all leading to an inevitable conclusion of our own short stay here, whereas the infinite game is the world outside ourselves, there was the time before we arrived in the hotel and what remains long after we have checked out.

If you think of a football match between two teams, this has a finite time, usually ninety minutes, where two teams face each other and attempt to score more goals than each other, all played within an acknowledged and universally understood set of rules.

Each team will have tactics for the game, attack early, get a lead and defend it, or tire the other team out and then score late on when they are tired, there are many ways to win, using defenders and attackers at appropriate times and using substitutes to bolster each area at appropriate times, all in a bid to win a match at the end of the ninety minutes.

But what if football was an infinite game, how would it be played, would you start really slowly and let your opposition run around and tire themselves out, would you take a long time to substitute players, not knowing how long there was to go, yet wanting to keep the team fresh, you wouldn't know how to play the game and there is the dilemma that you don't have in a finite game. Life is, I believe a hybrid of our understanding of the words finite and infinite, yes our time is limited, but potentially we have a long time, which starts once we have checked in, it is enough time indeed to plan, to have life goals, to build a career and even the opportunity to bring children into this world if we wish to do so, but there are no guarantees of either longevity or health, of happiness or sadness.

So although our stay here is finite, the length of stay in the hotel, is guaranteed for nobody. It is the simplicity of this, that I love, it explains things in a way that we can identify with, but the downside is that it can leave many unanswered questions, especially for the enquiring mind. So it's a game with no guarantees and other than the opportunity of replacing ourselves as residents in the hotel, is there any point in simply keeping the world populated, surely there must be, or maybe there isn't, maybe this is it, so what's the point? We know that there are 8 billion people staying here in the hotel at the moment, all trying to be their best, doing all that they can to get by, making their stay at worst bearable, at best pleasurable, which is great but if that's all we have, then what is the point of that? If we do all end up being lovely, warm, decent people, so what, so what, what is the consequence of that, apart from short term personal hardship while we are here, is there a longer term consequence for making a success or indeed failure of your time here?

Alternatively, what if we create an absolutely dreadful society, one in which we are all narcissists and care about nobody else apart from ourselves, then apart from life being more difficult for all concerned, then what would the outcome be? Some may suggest that we as a society are on the way to the latter, certainly in the western world, where we have a culture which is currently populated by selfies, celebrity magazines and newspapers filled with stories about people who are famous simply for being famous, with zero observable talent, other than their love of self-promotion.

Are they vacuous or are they successful, the older guests amongst us will see them as tawdry, whereas the TikTok generation will love them and aspire to be them, it's a generational thing, but who really knows, who judges them, there are so many unanswered questions, we can only answer to ourselves, judge ourselves, that's if we can be bothered to and if we have the honesty to confront our flaws.

Whatever society we create for ourselves, then I assume that the Earth will keep on spinning and life will continue to flourish, we are in the hotel for a relatively brief stay, we are just an incredibly small part of that process. Unknowingly, I may have fallen into a trap here and that is because there is a theory called the Naturalistic Fallacy given to us by acclaimed British philosopher, G E Moore, that everything we define as good isn't necessarily so and that those values which we believe are decent is done by basing our opinions merely on certain objective facts.

Moore objected to the use of the word good as a descriptor, rendering it near to useless because good was too ambiguous, impossible to define as a quality or a value. The inference is that when we describe anything, instead of using the word good, it is more useful to use more extreme words, either fabulous in the case of a positive outcome or disastrous if a negative conclusion was reached, leaving the reader or listener in absolutely no doubt whatsoever as to your level of appreciation of that being described. So it may be a valid position, Moore may be correct, because good in itself may be impossible to define but I think the common consensus of any society will understand the meaning of good to infer something to be fair, decent and honest, so although debating the semantics can be incredibly fulfilling for those black belt philosophers amongst us who rejoice in the dark arts of interpretation, actually understanding what we are striving for makes our goal a little clearer if it is a lot easier to define.

This type of thinking is certainly challenging and possibly counter intuitive, yet this is the basis of Moore's theory of acceptance and challenging that which we as a society consider to be good. It is easy to get bogged down in this or similar areas, debating language and yet we must consider what those who have stayed in the hotel before our arrival, our forebears thought about the time that they had spent here, learning from them but acknowledging the fact that no person has ever provided us with a definitive answer to the meaning of life.

On the understanding that we are all flawed, it is possible for us to gauge our progress to our ultimate goal of eradicating those flaws or weaknesses, striving for perfection and given that we can create a list to check off our successes, our self-improvement, then quite legitimately a close friend or family member could look at our very personal list of foibles and ask us that very personal question, which flaw you are on. Which of those negative character traits of yours that you have, that we all have, are you looking to improve upon or ignore and totally disregard have you managed to change.

Being flawed means being human and of course we all have our flaws, to a greater or lesser degree, this is because we our all complex individuals and so therefore the issues that we face, both personally and culturally and as a symptom of just being here, require complex change, should we choose to address them. In order for us to address our flaws, we first have to admit to ourselves that we are flawed, which isn't necessarily the easiest of things to do.

Once we have acknowledged the flaws, we must never beat ourselves up for having them, but grasp the nettle, own them, confront them and if at all possible, try to change them. In our daily lives we are trapped in an endless cycle of push-push, yet never wanting to look overwhelmed, struggling or worse, defeated, the desire is to appear to be cruising through life, being successful, but making it all look as effortless as possible. I am reminded of the phrase, 'Be like a swan, paddling madly underneath the water, but appearing to be graceful and elegant on the surface. Do not let things get to you and find a place of peace.'

These words are a little too simplistic for me, because the swan is still working hard to retain its beauty and dignity, it may appear to be effortless but the hard work, stresses and strains are still happening, just out of sight. That makes more sense to me, because as we know, we all have issues, we are all flawed, none of us has a perfect life, so it is how you handle the adversity that is important.

So, if it is how you handle, or indeed how you appear to the problems that you face is important to you, then it would be looked upon as being weak to show that we are not in control, handling our issues badly, showing strain and we cannot be seen as being weak, we must appear to be strong, remain positive and stay in control.

We currently live in a post-Covid world, which has given us greater uncertainty than in recent times, it has created a dramatically different place for those staying in the hotel at this time, different than we have ever known. Possibly because Covid is a global issue whose ripples have been felt throughout our world and affecting every guest who is staying here currently, which in itself is highly unusual, means that there is greater sympathy and understanding of its effects. Outside of Covid, possibly in spite of it, there remains so much pressure on people to be as perfect as possible and to succeed, that subliminally it puts even more stress and anxiousness on individuals, conspiring to make those individuals even more unhappy.

Perfection, if it is that for which we are striving, is defined in any decent dictionary as 'the condition, state or quality of being free or as free as possible of all flaws', so there is no pressure there then! Well, guess what, we all have flaws, in fact it is those flaws that make us all unique, so in fact in spite of us seeing them as a negative, they are actually a positive thing and it is our flaws that give us our individuality, making us all just that little bit different from the rest of those people staying in the hotel currently.

So, if we understand that having flaws is not something that should necessarily disappoint us about ourselves, and of course about others, then our acceptance of them and even rejoicing in them, coming to terms with them, means that we shouldn't feel so bad about them.

If we have a friend or family member who is a workaholic, or a family member who is rather lazy or a friend we regard as a cleanliness freak, then we shouldn't really care, because that is who they are, embrace their quirks and try not to be judgemental about them.

Life is about being happy and finding joy, however and wherever you may find it! If you want to have a lazy day or a duvet day as they have become known colloquially, just sitting in front of the television, drinking beer, eating fast food and being busy doing nothing, instead of getting on with that piece of work that needs to be completed by the end of next week, or cutting the grass that has needed cutting for a month and is looking more untidy by the day, then you have your lazy day, recharge the batteries, enjoy the feeling of release, with no pressure to do anything.

Although that type of thing doesn't sit comfortably with me and I rarely find myself having this sort of day, I do believe that it is fine as a one-off. I imagine that it can actually be fun, but this behaviour can become an issue when it becomes a regular occurrence and it is the norm rather than the exception.

As people we are all individuals, we are all very different, thankfully and to that end we all have different values, embodying perfection in very different ways, which ultimately is what is so magnificent about being human.

There is no definitive answer, no ideal, no perfect person that we are all striving to become, all we can do is be the best version of ourselves that we can, there is not much more that we can do.

To that end and because we are not all the same, you will find that people do things at a different speeds to each other, whatever that task may be and added to that, the quality of completing the task in hand will vary from person to person, at one extreme you will find those who are happy to do a slap dash job, just to say the job is done, whereas others are perfectionists and like to approach and complete each challenge to the very best of their abilities.

I have known people of both types and each can be as frustrating as the other, I have met people who have OCD and I have known and know those who have absolutely NoCD, those with OCD are compulsive about their mission, whereas those with NoCD have a couldn't-care-less attitude; if I think of my own attitude, I tend to err towards the top end of the OCD scale, my wife, has NoCD and I always tell her that I follow her around finishing off the jobs she has started, how we laugh!

It can only be a good thing that we are not all the same and it can make for a more varied life presenting quite amusing situations, often unintentionally. There are certain occupations that demand a level of competence or attention to detail when completing a task, some of which if not done properly can have serious consequences of sloppy work, they demand attention to detail.

I am thinking specifically of mechanics on aircraft or motor vehicles who, if they are not meticulous in their work ethic, lives could be endangered, changed forever or at worse ended.

In our personal lives, we can find that we surround ourselves with those people whose values or standards are identical or at the least, very similar to our own, indeed, we have maxims that express this type of attraction, how often have you heard the expression, like attracts like, but as if to totally contradict this popular saying, we also use the expression, opposites attract, to observe human behaviour, both are in common usage but individually taking very different positions, both equally valid and will resonate with many of us, you decide which one fits into your world.

Like attracts like is a basic principle of the law of attraction, where as individuals we are attracted to certain types of people, those people in which we see similarities to ourselves, which in turn is often reciprocated by similar types of people being attracted to us. In simple terms, like attracts like is best explained by people with similar energy levels being drawn together, it is understood by many that we as individuals give out a frequency of our energy levels and it is believed that those we do attract are functioning on similar frequencies.

Hence, two people operating on the same frequency feel an intuitive pull and attraction to each other, that seems to make a deal of sense. Our frequency is determined by our environment, our thoughts, feelings, talk and our actions. Similarly it is thought that this can also happen in reverse, those people that don't get us or are on a different wavelength or frequency can be alienated from us simply by not feeling us, but hey, you can't please all of the people all of the time.

Of course, it is totally possible that you can consciously change your frequency in order to attract people, but what would be the point of that, you would not be being true to yourself and worse, you would be attracting the type of people whose wavelength you are not on, meaning you would not be meeting those people that would be the ideal people to be a part of your stay in the hotel, which would be a loss to all concerned.

You have to be true to yourself, some people will get you, some people won't, that's just the way life is, it is impossible to like everybody and for everybody to like you, that's the way it is, don't beat yourself up for the realities of life, neither you or I will ever be able to change centuries of human nature.

To counter the 'like attracts like' maxim and to utterly contradict that thought, we give you 'opposites attract', even though it would be a lot easier and potentially a lot less messy if we were attracted to those personalities who were exactly like us and not polar opposites.

Although those differences on face value may appear to be problematic and only serve to hinder not help a relationship to thrive, but it is these differences that can actually make a relationship thrive, by adding a little extra spice to our relationship.

Amongst the obvious considerations of attraction, we are drawn to another person by their ability to satiate needs and desires that remain unfulfilled in our own lives or security, love, support and comfort.

Depending on which stage in your life you are going through, your demands and needs from a relationship or another person can be vastly different. In your earlier years the younger version of today's you would have had vastly different dreams goals and aspirations than you do today and therefore as we all evolve constantly throughout our stay in the hotel, we will find that there are times when, like a perfectly ripened fruit, we are ready for picking. If you think about it, if we don't meet the right person at the right time, our lives could be totally different than they are today, that is such a powerful thought.

There is an incredibly incisive quote from Heraclitus the Greek philosopher, who is considered to be one of the most important thinkers in the history of our hotel. Heraclitus stayed in Greece from 530 to 470 BC, gave some incredible thoughts to ponder and debate amongst ourselves and it was the subject of change, which was one of the areas that he tended to focus upon. So thoughtful and incisive is his work that it is believed to be a perfect starting point for those who are considering change at any stage in their lives.

Let's take a brief insight into the world of Heraclitus; he was born into a wealthy family but renounced his fortune and chose instead to live in the mountains, where he observed nature and its constant state of change. My personal favourite from the words of Heraclitus is translated from his Greek words, 'We both step and do not step in the same rivers, we are and are not.'

There isn't a strict interpretation of those words as we aren't lucky enough to have their author still staying with us in the hotel, he is long departed, so all that we can do is have them interpreted by a modern-day philosopher, somebody who is staying here currently. It appears that Heraclitus is saying that you can't step into the same river twice, this is because the river is constantly changing! So should I one day decide to get the famous, ferry across the River Mersey in Liverpool, the city of my birth, then the water beneath that boat is not the same water from moment to moment, especially in the case of the Mersey, as it is a tidal river, created by three tributaries, which are streams that lead to another body of water. Mersey has the second highest tidal range in the UK, going from a low of four metres on a neap tide to a ten-metre peak at its highest on a spring tide.

The river itself is still a working river and inevitably because of the amount of industrial traffic that uses it daily, either entering the port at Liverpool and travelling to Eastham to collect oil refined at Stanlow or taking goods to Manchester, it tends not to be the cleanest river on the planet. The heavy traffic on the river, although being excellent for the local economy of the major northwest towns and cities, unfortunately has the effect of making the River Mersey rather polluted, but remarkably, there has been a successful campaign and a concerted effort to clean the river, so much so that in 2009 it was announced that the Mersey was cleaner than any time since the industrial revolution and is now considered to be one of the cleanest rivers in the UK, which shows what can be done when minds are focused.

The River Mersey is considered sacred to Merseyside's Hindu community and worshipped in a similar way to the river Ganges, with immersion ceremonies now being held annually, where clay figures of Lord Ganesha, the elephant deity riding a mouse, are submerged from a ferry boat as flowers, coins and pictures are thrown into the river. The Hindu followers treat many rivers as deities, due to their belief that the river has such significance in so many people's lives, this may seem to be a rather extreme move to treat a river as a god, but more often a goddess, but think about it, how important a role rivers play in our world, depending upon their location, they are vital to sustain life and the economy, thus demanding a symbiotic relationship, where we both love and respect them, and indeed deify them, why not?

So, it should come as no surprise that the Ganges, India's most important river, is the most sacred, a goddess who can cleanse the sins of those bathing in her waters and carry a Hindu to moksha, a vital part of the Hindu belief system.

The Mersey, as well as the local Hindus having respect and understanding for it, itself is vital to the region of Merseyside and beyond; it has become a living heartbeat and inevitably with all of the activity, from the changing tides to its tributaries means that the river is constantly changing, the water ebbing and flowing, an amorphous mass with a composition that changes from second to second and because it is constantly replacing itself, Heraclitus would tell us that were we to walk in the water more than once, then because it is different every time we do, then we never step into the same river twice, who can argue with the man?

Not only is the river changing from second to second but we as individuals are replicating this, experiencing a metamorphosis of ourselves; if you consider that we are ageing second by second then although the change is so small as to be unnoticeable, if we actually scrutinise it very closely, then it is easy to see how massive change only takes a moment.

We had an example of this just last weekend, on Saturday 11th of June 2021, forty-two minutes into a football match at Euro 2020, the Denmark player Christian Eriksen—a footballer at the top of his game, representing his country at international level in a competitive match against Finland—had been playing well up until the forty-first minute; Eriksen collapsed in full view of the watching crowd; the match was live on television, being shown throughout the world. Thankfully, urgent medical assistance was on hand and attended the player moments after the incident occurred and gave him CPR and defibrillation, before taking him to hospital.

One day later, Eriksen posted a picture of himself on social media with his thumbs up. Here is a 29-year-old man with incredible fitness levels who one minute literally has the world at his feet, the next, who knows; I am neither qualified or wish to speculate on his future, but life will be different than he had planned and it all changed in that one moment and without notice. This is a simple but current example, just one of many which I could have chosen, but this parallel shows in graphic terms that a person's life mirrors the ever-changing river, the only constant in both being *change*.

So, when Heraclitus gave us his incisive observation, it could be considered that as the human body changes, that change is ultimately heading towards absolute deterioration and sadly for you and I, this means death, whereas for the river change is but a snapshot in time of something with greater permanence than humans will ever have; people check in and out of the hotel every single day, however, barring natural disaster, the river is here forever.

As we head on our journey through life, it is likely that those things we perceive as flaws within ourselves are picked up along the way, so let us go with that thought.

We could be born flawed and simply be here to fulfil our destiny as we get older, becoming the inevitable, flawed individual we were always going to be from day one, we had no option because the flaws were in-built and we had no free will. If we are lucky, we are born in perfect condition, with every part of our body functioning as it should, but because perfect as an absolute is a difficult word to use in any conversation, in this instance I mean that perfect implies without physical or mental disability; don't get me wrong, physical and mental disability, although life-changing, certainly isn't life-ending and all life is precious.

The word disabled is all-encompassing and in many cases, modern medicine has found a way to navigate life for many of those born with a disability. My point here is that the flaws or conditions we pick up along the way tend to happen to us as our life progresses and our stay here goes forward; if you then combine this with the effects that age brings, manifesting as either illness, accidents or disability, then the prospects for a life without physical or mental failings is nigh impossible. If we look at the numbers for society as a whole with regard to the flaws that we are currently discussing, then these numbers tend to increase significantly as we approach the end of our stay.

Obviously, when we talk about flaws, we accept the inevitably of character flaws and the fact that everybody has them, so don't worry, you're not on your own; thankfully though, these can be worked on and either improved or even eradicated.

Character flaws in themselves are bad enough but then there are those of us who have either a mental or physical disability to consider, then the numbers will tell us that these too ramp up before we leave the hotel and tend to accumulate through physical and mental strains that are inevitable if you're staying here.

Some people are mentally and physically stronger than others, but as with anything, even the strongest amongst us has a breaking point and sadly we can discover our own at any time during our stay.

Whether you then consider those mental and physical breakdowns to be flaws or not is the debate here, they are certainly a disability and can prevent a person from living an Un impinged life, or a normal life as our society calls it. I balk at using the word normal, because if I've learnt anything during my own time in the hotel, it is that normal, although it is oft used, doesn't really exist.

To this end and understanding that words are crucial, I have developed a position on the use of the word disabled, feeling that it is a totally inappropriate way to describe a person who has had the misfortune to encounter these mental or physical barriers.

I use the word unable instead of disabled and will clarify my thinking a little later in this chapter, but the reason that I prefer unable, is because each of us has inabilities so the word unable in my mind is a great leveller and therefore doesn't carry the stigma that disabled has come to bring with it.

As I said, words are vital a physically 'disabled' person who not only has to contend with their disability, also has to mentally contend with their issues, this can, as a consequence bring with it mental issues, a double whammy and totally unnecessary.

So using the word unable intentionally dilutes the sense of bleakness that being labelled disabled may have. Disability numbers for the United Kingdom in the most recent survey available as I write, go back to 2018, and for its purposes, it breaks down the numbers for disability by age as follows, there are 13.3 million people considered to be disabled in the United Kingdom of which 7% are children, 18% are working age adults and 44% are of pension age. Thus confirming as we discussed earlier of those flaws that disability brings are more prevalent as we reach the end of our stay, thus the highest number with disabilities is in the category of those of retirement age, who's surprised? I believe that the trick is not to allow those flaws to dictate how you live your life, which can be easier said than done, but you have to take control of your individual situation, whatever that means and therefore attempting to live your life retaining your options, attempting to make life as easy as possible, while still retaining the pleasure it gives you, but never losing your attitude of striving for personal achievement and milestones that make the whole game both challenging and never stop being fun.

I know both age and disability bring new practicalities with them, I'm not naive enough to think otherwise, but I believe that those twin detractors simply mean that as in a hotel, you look to use a disability-friendly room if it suits your purposes, an option that you would never consider in your earlier, fitter years, indeed you would reject it out of hand and understandably so, because in those early days, the flaws have yet to rear their ugly heads.

But if you have disabilities or flaws that necessitate adaptions, then adaptions it must be, therefore a room with a walk in shower, or rails around the room, are helpful to you in making your life easier than it would be if those options didn't exist, you are navigating your stay in the hotel to optimise the happiness it gives you.

I can speak of disability as a flaw with some authority, because in spite of thinking I had enough flaws already, yet another was to be given to me several years ago, who decided I needed it and why they felt I needed it I will never know, but it is said that god gives his toughest battles to his strongest soldiers, so let's go with that.

If I was given the option, I would have happily refused it, but it wasn't an option, I had no say in the matter and as we have already calculated, you never know what life has in store for you. What I would now consider to be a major personal flaw happened to me as I entered my fifties, I have always liked to stay as fit as possible, doing some form of exercise every day of my life, purely for personal fitness, although I would never have considered myself to be obsessive about it! Fitness has always made me feel both a sense of well-being and purpose, in fact, I have reached the conclusion that the gym is one of the very few places in life that you rarely, if ever, have regrets about.

You can go to a bad restaurant and have a dodgy meal, go to a bar and have too many drinks, or go out on a date with the wrong person, all giving you cause for regret, but the gym is one place that I have never come away from thinking, I wish I hadn't gone there today, or feeling worse for going. Yes, I've been tired after a tough session or twinged a muscle or got a bit of cramp, but the masochist in me comes out every time and I always think, what better way to feel knackered than by improving your physical and mental health, I love it.

So let us go back to 2004, when a good friend, Mike Hancox, suggested doing something that was fitness-related but totally out of my comfort zone.

Mike was a decent marathon runner, something that I had never considered, he knew I went to the gym every day and that I was competitive, so he threw down the verbal gauntlet, 'I'm running the New York marathon this year, do you want to join me?' How could I refuse, it was early enough in the year to give me time to train for it!

I was a fair runner, I could do ten miles comfortably, but had never run further than that, so I accepted the challenge, I was running for charity and it would push me to train a little harder and give me a sense of achievement, what's not to love? 'Count me in,' I said to Mike and I started training for my one and only marathon, which was in New York City. I was running for charity, raising money for Weston Spirit, which was the Simon Weston-run charity, to help young, underprivileged people acquire skills and training and get into work.

I did a lot of running that year in the build-up to the event in November, but only once did I run a distance of twenty miles and if somebody had told me at the end of that to run another six miles, giving the marathon distance of twenty-six miles, I couldn't have done it.

However, I had confidence in my ability and desire to achieve the goal, along with an understanding that the atmosphere and the buzz of the event would carry me beyond the twenty-mile post right to the finishing line, so we flew to New York from Manchester on the Friday before the event, which was, as usual on the first Sunday in November, the year 2004. It was an incredible day and I managed to run it in a time of four hours, twenty-one minutes, which was a personal best for me, in fact it was a personal only, so I was incredibly pleased with myself, obviously I was no Mo Farah, I wasn't challenging the winner of the race but neither was I there to make up the numbers, I guarantee I gave it my best shot.

Now, when I look back at running 26.2 miles, I feel proud of my achievement, it was a great thing to do and I am so pleased to have it on my life CV, but that day provided me with a little more than just running the race, through the five boroughs of that great city, enjoying each one in turn, but it was once the event was over and I had time to contemplate what I had just done, I realised that I had learnt a life lesson, I hope that doesn't sound too pretentious, but it taught me something that I will never forget.

When I arrived at the starting line approximately an hour before the race was due to begin, along with the other thirty thousand or so runners, you have a little time to stretch and warm up before the event, but at the same time it is impossible not to study the 'opposition' as you would with any competitive environment, after all, never forget that the marathon is a race, a competition, not only with the rest of the runners, but with yourself, your own physical and mental toughness! As I evaluated the competition, it looked intense, don't get me wrong I was not under any illusion about my own ability and I didn't expect to win the race, but I was there to give it my best shot and so obviously I was checking out those around me, with a cursory glance, assessing their potential and what I thought their chances in relation to my own were. Some I thought I could never beat in a million years, whereas I looked at others and for whatever reason, whether it was the general look of the person as an athlete, muscle definition, their weight in relation to size or even the quality of running kit, led me to think that I had the beating of them over the twenty-six plus mile course.

But running, if you use it as a metaphor for life, doesn't always work out in the way that we expect it to and the marathon had a few surprises in store for me, which as I mentioned, taught me a life lesson which, at no time, whether throughout the build-up to the race or during the race itself, I hadn't expected. The New York marathon takes participants through the five boroughs of New York City, that incredible city and here I was at the starting line on a bright and crisp November morning, it was only once the race had started that I began to notice that around me there were people who looked a lot fitter than I did, they looked like the archetypal marathon runner, but here was I, going past them and by the exact same token, there were those who looked, shall I say, a little dishevelled, a bit chunkier, more ungainly, but these people were going past me.

This theme carried on throughout the race and over the full distance of the course, which reached its conclusion amongst the trees and wildlife in the picturesque setting of the ever-changing, always inviting, at this time of year, beautifully autumnal Central Park, located between the Upper East and Upper West Side of Manhattan.

I had been to New York several times in the past, not least of all, a memorable time I had spent with friends at a fabulous bar in Central Park on my stag night, several years earlier, but never was I so glad to see the park, appearing in the distance, as the finishing line and the end of the course appeared before me, which on the day of the marathon is congested with runners strewn everywhere, relieved to find themselves at the end of a tough challenge. I overtook a few people as I pushed hard and put in a final spurt, towards the finishing line, but I wasn't the only one, because others were doing exactly the same as me and as fast as I thought I was going, people went past me, even at that late stage, all of us with one thing on our minds, the finishing line was in sight, the clock was ticking and our finishing time became everything as our goal was virtually achieved.

The lesson I learnt in these moments was that there were people in front of me that I would never have imagined could ever beat me and there were people behind me, some by a very long way, that I thought I could never have beaten. But isn't that life itself, there are people, enjoying incredible success, that you look at and wonder how they ever got to be in the position that they find themselves in, then there are some people that you look at and know that they are far more capable or have far more talent, to achieve more or do more with their lives than the place in which they currently find themselves!

This was literally the opposite of judging a book by its cover territory, you can look at anybody and judge them by what is before you, but it's impossible to know what lies within, more often than not, you may be correct in your evaluation, you can see a person who dresses slovenly, maybe a little unkempt in appearance and believe them to have a sloppy attitude to anything that they do in life and that could be totally true. However, that very same person could be totally focused and have an incredible attitude in everything they do, they just don't value personal appearance that highly in the great scheme of things and obviously, that doesn't make them right or wrong, it's just the way they are.

Therefore, I believe it to be wise to never underestimate the strength of a person's desire to achieve a stated goal, because you can never truly know. These thoughts have stayed with me throughout my life and I know there are endless books, filling the shelves with positive attitude thoughts and quotes and I used to love them all, I could always find at least one little nugget in the thousands of inane throwaway lines that I would happily plough through.

You can read as many inspirational quotes or recite your favourite PMA book from memory, but there is more to it than that, I believe desire, aspiration, or any worthwhile goal, in order to be achieved, the feeling must come from within, you can read as many Attitude equals Altitude manuals that you can find, but unless you are mentally tough and the goal is real, then it is a futile exercise.

Back to New York and having run the marathon, little did I know it, but my life was about to change forever, although at that time in life I was blissfully unaware of what was coming next and unknowing that my own mental strength and positive attitude would be tested to their limits.

Having completed my one and only marathon, looking at a map of the 26 mile course around that incredible city made me realise the size of the achievement, a realisation that was to give me an immediate sense of pride and what I can now confidently say over twenty years later still gives me a sense of, Go me! During the build-up to the race, training every day with an ultimate goal of running a long distance, this was an extraordinary thing to attempt because there are thousands of people running marathons all over the world every week, so it didn't seem so special that little old me was about to have a go!

However, when I looked back and considered the memories that I had of that whole weekend, the people that we met and the actual run itself, it was then that I realised and appreciated the enormity of the achievement and the task I had completed!

What a great thing to do and today, the memories still linger, but these days I have a more difficult challenge, this is far more difficult than a 26 mile run, it is a challenge that I face and one which is with me 24/7, it is omnipresent, at least for me and as such it is a daily challenge, with defeat not an option.

When I look back, I believe that the marathon and the challenge that the run presents, I believe it has set me up to face my greatest competition, for it was only five years after running over 26 miles that I would find myself unable to run 26 inches.

A couple of years after the marathon, I was skiing in Zell Am See in Austria with friends and having a terrific time. In the winter up in the mountains at the numerous ski resorts, the snow is perfect and enhances an already beautiful landscape with a blanket of white, lying perfectly across a slumbering world until early spring when gradually the blanket disappears and the country wakes to a chorus of birds singing their encouragement to the willing flowers in the perfectly manicured fields surrounding the chocolate box villages. We have been many times to Austria and love every visit, however this time we were skiing with friends and after a morning on the slopes, just before heading off for lunch, our ski guide Wolfie, an acoustic guitar-playing, ageing hippy, said we would meet at a mountain restaurant that had a great reputation for the most fabulous pasta dishes accompanied by a really decent wine list to be followed up with kaiserschmarrn, a fantastic Austrian dessert; if you don't know it, Google it, you can thank me later.

My wife and our friends headed to the restaurant as Wolfie tapped me on the shoulder and said that he would show me a little more of an adventurous route, to get there. I wasn't the greatest skier, but I was a bit kamikaze and could never resist a challenge, so off we went, Wolfie leading with me close behind, it was pretty scary and at one point we went across a very narrow ridge.

I found it more challenging than it needed to be, because my right ski wouldn't hold a straight line and kept veering to the right, it was a little unnerving but we got there in the end, and we arrived to our friends and a cold Warsteiner as we ate on the terrace enjoying the sun and the spectacular mountain views. Lunch was fabulous the pasta was perfect, we drank a bottle of Tignanello which was, as usual superb and as we topped up our suntans, the kaiserschmarrn arrived and along with an espresso and finally a schnapps downed in one to round of lunch, perfection was achieved.

Through the enjoyment of that afternoon and into the après-ski of early evening, I had a little nagging voice in my head, it was telling me that the moment crossing the ridge as being a little weird and although I mentioned it to my wife in passing, I sensed something wasn't quite right, however the hazelnut schnapps was flowing and for the time being I wasn't overly concerned.

Back home in the UK a few months later and I was still enjoying running every day, probably around five or six miles or so, sometimes a little further, combining this with going to the gym, most days and generally trying to stay fit as possible I headed towards my fiftieth year in the hotel.

I felt I was in decent shape, far from perfect, but my attitude was always incredibly positive, I didn't need books or podcasts to motivate me, I was fortunate, because for me, it came from within, don't ask how, it just did.

I never felt unhappy, down, deflated or defeated whatever was going on and fortunately for me I appeared to have an in-built resilience, which I didn't know at that time, but both it and my resolve were about to be tested to their limits.

At this time in our lives, we were living in a small village in Cheshire and the roads around the village, provided many varied routes which were perfect for running around, providing an ever-changing backdrop, I would run daily and really enjoy it.

After I had run through the streets of New York and was now back home again, one crisp winter's afternoon, I was running through the village and for no reason whatsoever, I fell over, not aware of what caused me to go down, but it was more embarrassing than painful and I was able to carry on running, a little weird I thought, but nothing more than that.

Two weeks later, I was back pounding the streets when once again I went over, it appeared that a pattern was forming and the second time it happened, I hurt myself a little more seriously than the first. Several years earlier I had a hip resurface operation, I had arthritis in the joint due to years of running, which necessitated the operation and at first thought that this may once again be causing me a problem, but the hip felt fine and in my own mind I sensed that this wasn't the issue. I found a hip surgeon who was supposed to be the best in the North of England, I had a private consultation, telling him that I sensed my hip wasn't the problem but as I had fallen twice, I wanted his expert opinion on what he thought was going on. He did a couple of innocuous tests, involving me closing my eyes and putting my palms out, I lost my balance ever so slightly and immediately he spoke the words that would change my life forever.

'It's MS,' he said confidently. I'd heard of it and thought I had an idea of what it was, but my scant knowledge was a million miles away from the reality of the condition. I got back into my car and drove home on an approximately fifty-mile drive, calling my wife on the way, giving her the news; she was at work and probably had a similar understanding of MS as I had.

Upon arrival at home, I was straight onto the PC and googled MS, it didn't look good and I was at the start of a new chapter in my life. I didn't know anybody that had MS, so there wasn't anybody that I could call for a bit of advice or simply explain to me what it is, of course I had heard of it, but I have heard of nuclear fusion and I couldn't explain that either. Google was my go-to for an insight into my newly, yet to be diagnosed condition and as I mentioned, it didn't read well and of course, I had to be tested in order to establish whether I had it or not, but I sensed that the guy I had just had a consultation with wasn't a million miles away from an accurate diagnosis. Over the next few months I had tests, examinations and consultations with various NHS professionals in order to establish my condition and after approximately three months I was diagnosed with primary progressive multiple sclerosis.

I won't bore you rigid with it, but basically it is a neurological condition which in my case was and still is with me constantly and the condition would deteriorate, hence it got progressively worse. The only consolation I had was that there was no guarantee at what rate the deterioration occurred and at what speed, so without fully understanding the implications, maybe I could influence the rate and speed of decline. Luckily for me and even though I say it myself, I have an innate mental toughness that was to hold me in good stead for the road ahead and my subsequent positive diagnosis, also the fact that I exercised every day I believe to be a massive plus. The only way of knowing this, is the fact that having met several other people with the same condition I do believe that your attitude, to both physical and mental problems can be influenced by the way you confront them. Of course, I understand that there are different circumstances and illness is subjective, but through it all I have found a positive attitude to be a vital ingredient, conducive to making the unbearable as bearable as possible.

Understanding that we all have flaws, I think the easiest way to look at things is this and I tend to use it to explain that life just isn't simple. We all have strengths and weaknesses and you need to adapt your world to make sure it works for you and plays to your strengths.

If my wife compared herself to Usain Bolt purely in terms of running ability, then Mr Bolt would think she was hopeless compared to his outstanding ability, however, as I can no longer run, then to me, in terms of her ability to run better than I can, my wife to me is Usain Bolt. There is a fabulous quote attributed to Einstein but subsequently it is found that this may not be necessarily true, however it does not devalue the quotation which is this, 'Everybody is a genius. But if you judge a fish by its ability to climb a tree, it will live its whole life believing it is stupid.'.

This quote probably runs perfectly alongside my thought of comparing Usain Bolt to my wife purely based on their running ability. If I compared my wife and Usain based purely on their business acumen and running a successful business, my wife would win that competition by a distance, so it is horses for courses and any other ancient trope we can recall to reinforce our point. Whichever works best for us, I believe that we can successfully use that thought process when evaluating how are flaws negatively affect us and focussing not on the negative but the positive aspects of our lives. As an update on my MS situation nearly ten years later, I have got worse over the last decade but that is only to be expected, I continue to use the gym every day of my life and I fundamentally believe that by doing this, I have and still am slowing the progression of the inevitability of what my condition has in store for me.

But can any of us know what life has in store for us? None of us has the luxury of knowing or the ability to see into the future and if we did, could we guarantee that what we could see would only be those things that please us? There can be a lot of sadness during our stay, so maybe it is best we don't have the privilege of knowing what is to become of us.

Chapter 9
Lost Property

Every hotel has a lost property cupboard; in fact, in the bigger hotels, you may actually discover that they have a lost property room, necessitated by the amount of things that guests lose or misplace. Lost property is the place in which anything that has been lost or left behind by those who are staying or have stayed in the hotel will be kept until it is either reunited with its owner or disposed of by the hotel.

It is a rather obvious parallel, simplistic even, but in this chapter, in common with the rest of this book so far, believing that *Life is a Hotel* and in order for it all to make perfect sense, then along the way we possibly can and in the majority of instances, unavoidably do, lose things that are either precious to us and essential to our happiness, whereas at the other end of the scale, there are those things that we have accumulated during our stay, that are replaceable and therefore inconsequential to us.

There are those things which can have a major effect on our lives, disrupting our stay here or those other things that aren't of great significance and in spite of their loss we are able to carry on regardless. But loss in whichever form can have an impact on us, all depending on how precious we consider the object or thing to be and at what stage of our lives we lose it, which is equally as important as a consideration.

Depending when loss occurs in our lives, when we are young, when we are old, our vulnerability may or may not be heightened and inevitably our ability to handle it will consequentially mean that there will be times when we are in a better or worse condition to handle the loss. Several years ago, I was lucky to see a film called *Lost Property*, a short, animated film, and although the lost property department is an integral part of any hotel, the film helped inspire the title of this chapter.

The film is a love story with its two leading characters on a journey of discovery; what a fascinating journey it is and we have the pleasure of watching it unravel before our eyes. The lost property in question is an office, which is concealed in a collection of hidden rooms throughout the hotel and it is in these rooms in which the couple find remnants of their past; here, the film considers the idea of memory loss and the ageing process, exploring how memories shape who we are and how we move on in our life carrying them with us everywhere we go, ultimately, they are how we are defined.

Although it is a love story, the way the film interprets the fragility of the mind is the key to its powerful message and the way we sail through our lives taking things for granted until we are exposed to that fragility, demonstrating to us how lost we are without it. The film is about hope persistence and devotion, in the face of the dreadful progressive neurological condition Alzheimer's, a disease which effects the brain and is the most common form of dementia.

As the disease becomes a part of life of one of the main characters, the film explores how we learn to live with the destruction that it inevitably causes. It's not an easy watch, but is sensitively constructed, providing a thought provoking piece and covering a taboo topic, that would be easier to ignore, but the film boldly takes it on. Lost Property while looking at the effects of Alzheimer's and how it robs a person of their identity, examines how our memory which is so fragile, yet remains so deeply ingrained in us, that in spite of the disease, our identity remains, doing so in spite of the unforgiving assault upon it.

Bravely, the film looks at how we, and those we love, cope with the disease and how it affects all. The lost property office in the film is a metaphor for the mind, shared memories are tucked away just waiting to be reclaimed, available at any time and on immediate demand, no matter how random they may be. In a world where the minutia of everyday life is documented and available on demand 24/7 it makes you realise the power of memory, recalling dim and distant memories instantly from the most obscure corners of our stay in the hotel, simply reinforcing that we have an incredibly powerful tool at our disposal.

Yet in the real world of the hotel, the actual lost property will invariably have a collection of odd socks, mobile phones, jewellery and umbrellas and many more obscure items all lost or left behind, waiting to be reunited with their erstwhile owners and if they are not, what happens to these items, where do they go, are they even missed? The film *Lost Property* cleverly imagines the hotel's lost property office and compares it to our minds, with all of the items finding themselves there because they have in some way been forgotten about, not unlike our own memories.

Each of the objects will have its own story and its own reason for being there, with its own tale to tell, having a special meaning to the person it once belonged to, although an item may appear to be insignificant, the story that is attached to it may mean the whole world to somebody, the owner. Let's take a look at the words, Lost and Property, although not immediately obvious and indeed most of us who are not looking for greater meaning than that globally accepted two word expression, but it is there, so much so that I find both are equally interesting in their own right.

These two words 'lost property' are so frequently seen together that I am surprised we haven't created a portmanteau for them. A portmanteau has two meanings, it is a large travelling bag, typically made of stiff leather and opening into two equal parts, but it is also a word that blends the sounds and combines the meanings of two words; for example, motel—motor and hotel—or brunch, breakfast and lunch. I am going with the latter and believe that we could we create a portmanteau for lost property. So, I have considered this crucially important issue for a few moments and have created a newly crafted word 'Loperty'; it is a perfect word to describe our old friend, Lost Property, but at this time, only you and I are aware of it, so respecting the newly created Loperty and in an effort to bring it to global prominence, I will persist for the rest of this chapter with the more conventional Lost and Property, simply to avoid confusion.

Most of us make huge assumptions in our lives, and as if to prove the point, it is easily done, but in this instance I believe that the use of the word 'Property' is one of them. If you look at the definition of the word, property means an object that belongs to someone, with belong meaning ownership, but although it may be nine tenths of the law, possession does not always mean ownership. I realise we are dancing on the head of a pin, but the subtleties are so important and when we are looking at a definition for the purposes of this chapter, then the word property suggests an ownership that I believe really doesn't exist, everything is a library book, everything is on temporary loan, now, that may sound a little simplistic, but bear with me.

I recall a fabulous advertising campaign for the prestigious watch brand Patek Phillipe, their average watch costs approximately the same price as a decent family saloon car and yet their advertising which is still running today having been launched originally in 1996, actually refutes the concept of ownership, let's take a look.

'You never actually own a Patek Phillipe, you merely look after it for the next generation,' says the advertising campaign; how incredible, spend £50,000 on something that you never actually own!

But let's consider this a little further, it actually lends itself to my library book theory, do we actually 'own' anything? There are many examples of religious text that lead us to further understand the futility of the proposition of ownership, not an obvious source for affirmation of any theory you may think, but important contributions nonetheless, let me list just a few examples for us to digest.

For we brought nothing into the world and we can take nothing out of it. Timothy

For when he dies he will carry nothing away, his abundance will not follow him down. Psalm 49

Naked came I out of my mother's womb and naked shall I return thither. Job

If you want to be perfect, go, sell your possessions and give to the poor, and you will have treasure in heaven. Then come follow me. Matthew

All of these and many others serve to highlight how temporary our ownership of anything is, including the luxury and privilege that is all a part of our time spent in the hotel. But I believe some of us need to feel ownership of things, possessions, tangibles, evidence of our success, these items represent us, they define us, we surround ourselves with them, they give us security, our comfort blanket if you will. Things that matter to people in their lives are often the physical possessions that they have accumulated during their stay in the hotel, their house, their music or even their dog, these items become the means by which they express who they are or what they have become, an indication of what they aspire to be.

But is there a trade-off, surely there has to be, is our individuality lost at the hands of modern consumerism, do we trade the baubles and trinkets that our modern society deems to be worthwhile and that we should strive for, in exchange for our humanity, are we lesser for collecting these things or do they add value to our existence. Do they enhance us as a person or are we reduced, these are massive questions and there is no definitive answer, they are all subjective and I believe, depending upon your perspective, no answer is wrong.

The problem we have here is that it is so difficult to assess and offer an opinion without sounding sanctimonious or at the very least judgemental, if those things that we accumulate as we enjoy our stay in the hotel define us, then similarly their loss would leave a hole in our world.

We can tolerate the loss of a favourite tie, a piece of jewellery, or the latest mobile phone, these things are replaceable, obviously, their loss may cause a little inconvenience, but not sufficiently for us to change our lives because of their loss.

We can agree that the loss of replaceable items can often cause a ripple to our daily routine, but not sufficient, to dwell on the matter or make life-changing decisions because of them, but what happens to our lives when those things we lose are a little more than just an accoutrement, a loss so massive as to disrupt our world, often forever.

The loss of your wife, husband, partner or a close friend, even a pet, these are irreplaceable and yet in spite of their absence, life goes on, which is often unthinkable that is until it becomes a cruel reality. Once you realise that this absence is permanent, once you have acknowledged the loss, then in that moment, life changes forever, what shall we do with it?

Death of a loved one is possibly the greatest test of human resolve a person can experience during their stay in the hotel, to lose a person who is sharing and has shared a large part of your stay is incredibly difficult and for some it can be too difficult to handle.

There are so many implications of no longer being in the hotel with a friend, loved one or partner and they are all life-changing, from the loss of future dreams and shared aspirations to increased family and household responsibilities.

Your identity as an individual or part of a team of two, inevitably changes forever, we become a different person, on a more practical level, there may be some form of financial loss, there is the possibility of increased loneliness and isolation which may lead to an increased vulnerability and to health problems, wow, it doesn't paint a pretty picture and neither does it provide a great deal to look forward to. Rarely do we stop and think that if we are in a significant relationship, there is a 50/50 chance that you will eventually grieve the loss of your partner. Probably because this is not a pleasant thought, we put it to the backs of our mind, but sadly it is a reality. The loss of a long-term partner can be totally debilitating to the strongest of us, leaving that person feeling entirely alone and incomplete, the sense of feeling that you have lost a vital part of yourself is both painful and disconcerting.

Suddenly, the world is a different place and a whole new range of emotions can wash over you, feelings of loss, guilt and even a loss of identity, through all of this there has to be a healing process which can only happen once you have verbalised your feelings, acknowledged the loss and regroup in order to move forward.

It is believed by some, that what cannot be put into words cannot be addressed, to this end, it is helpful to find a group or an individual who will let you get the words out, to elicit the words that you don't want to say, a space where you can talk about the person, their life as well as their death. What you miss about them, your own feelings of loneliness, sadness or anger, giving you an opportunity to remember and rejoice in their last days, those days that you shared until the end of their life and of your relationship with that person.

There are some incredibly serious consequences of not getting our feelings out and many studies have looked at those suffering grief from the loss of a loved one and how it impinges on their lives. Sadly but possibly inevitably, mortality rates are actually higher amongst those who do not articulate their grief, than those who feel able to get their emotions out. Another incredible observation is that the mortality rates become even higher amongst males who die within a year of the death of their spouse, which is again both sad and even possibly understandable.

Are we really surprised, or is it just one of our societal norms that means that it is more difficult for men to express their emotions, not all men, but certainly a majority, which is far from being a good thing. It is impossible to know what is normal because nothing is normal, so, although you may not feel compelled to do so, it is vital that you create your own time line to make sense of the grief, of the loss, otherwise the future is potentially bleaker than it need be. The mourning period must become a nurturing process as life is rebuilt and reorganised, where the surviving partner feels like half of them is missing, because they are no longer around, then by acknowledging those simple facts and understanding that the future will be very different for them and as their identity inevitably changes, then compassion and understanding are vital. The issue has been that couples can often become a single entity, in any social arrangements, we are planning, we invariably see the two individuals who comprise the couple, but invite them as one.

Indeed, it's not just how we see friends but how they see each other, unintentionally but actually and in many parts of their lives find that they are defining themselves as a couple, I can even think amongst our own friends that If Diane and I are considering the theatre or a meal out, even a holiday, then it's with Chris and Clare, Mike and Jo, Mick and Jayne or Dorcas and Neil, so loss is profound when one of a couple is no longer around.

Every relationship is unique with different dynamics and interaction so it is impossible to generalise too much but if the partner remaining is now a widow or a widower, they find themselves in a role that they neither relish or desire. A role that can be as difficult for them to play as for their friends to embrace, table for three replacing table for four, it even sounds sad. As with any loss or any item that is found in Lost Property it is crucial for our survival and the rest of our stay in the hotel that we learn to live with that loss, which is easier said than done but a coping strategy must be developed. The major difference with a physical item finding itself in the lost property office as opposed to a person is that at some point in the future, the lost item may be reunited with its owner and is no longer lost, that luxury doesn't exist when a partner dies, sadly that loss is forever, or is it.

As we consider in the chapter titled *Where To*, if you believe in an afterlife then maybe you also believe that you can once again be reunited with those you have loved and for those that have that belief then all is not lost and hope can still burn bright.

So let's not prejudice any possibilities of future reunification and instead just agree with one thought that we all must agree on and that is the thought that remains constant throughout this book and moreover in life itself and that is that nobody actually knows. You can argue the case but the facts are undisputed, nobody knows, there are eight billion of us staying in the hotel at the moment and all of those that have stayed here before we arrived and the one common denominator that we all have, is that factually, nobody knows what we are doing here.

Not one bright spark amongst us, past or present, have found a definitive answer to our eternal question of longevity, so opinions rage amongst those searching for a credible answer. Some loss can be a lot easier than others to come to terms with, but you need a strategy to navigate the feelings that loss can bring.

You should never beat yourself up mentally if you lose something that you consider to be precious and of course it is okay to feel upset in the following days or weeks, you have to give yourself time, you will create your own timeline, you will move on when you are ready and that inevitably becomes perfect timing, for you as an individual. If your sense of loss is profound and the item is something that is irreplaceable then the impact can be great, but it is still possible to navigate this feeling of loss, with the right support from those closest to you.

You can consider how your life feels different if you think of it before the loss and how your life is changed afterwards, whatever the outcome, you need to adapt and then you can look for a way to move forward. For most of us, the loss of a material possession is a rare occurrence, we are diligent in our covert protection of them and rarely expose them to the opportunity to become lost, underlining their importance to us and how they validate our lives, our existence and sometimes, their mere presence in our lives ensures peace of mind, comfort and ultimately our mental well-being.

One study by a sociologist considered the effects of loss, this was not a contrived experiment discussing effects of a potential loss, but an actual study, whereby the person making the study sat in a lost and found booth and evaluated real-life cases of people who had experienced loss. The study gave the observer an opportunity to see how individuals deal with a sudden threat to the normal order of their lives and the future expectations, the loss of physical items that became part of the framework for their lives. In the survey, six hundred cases of loss were considered, tracing the loss from the moment of their discovery, which is when they are reported through the rollercoaster of emotional experience, the ups and downs of those people that have suffered the loss.

Those surveyed were in cities such as Brussels, London and Toronto aged from five to eighty and with various occupations, a balanced sample of people.

The top ten items lost were:

Mobile phones
Cameras
Keys
Wallets and purses
Rings and various jewellery items
Bracelets
Sunglasses

Bags
Coats and jackets
Laptops and electronic gadgets

The survey was in-depth and followed up on each of the six hundred cases and found many common themes in people's shared experiences and how each handled their loss. It is found that it is not the actual loss that becomes the issue, but the impact that the item has on their feeling of identity, they are slightly damaged, fractured or even broken.

The study then looks at whether the person experiencing the loss tells others about their loss, sensing that it may reflect on how others view them, how could you, what were you thinking, how could you be so careless? From there it appears important that the loser finds a way to come to terms with the loss and there are only a couple of options if they want to move forward with their lives.

There is one fundamental question that needs to be addressed in order to move on and that is, 'Does its absence pose a threat to how I see myself and my grounding in the material environment enough to react to it or can I go on with life as usual?' Put simply, do I feel such a sense of loss that it is impossible for me to live life as I want to and fulfil those things that I want to achieve or will its absence hinder my goals? Sentimentality of the lost item is important to evaluate in the whole equation but as far back as 1890, William James gave us an incredibly incisive contribution when he opined that losing an object was akin to a reduction of self!

This may sound incredibly deep and not quite relevant to a pair of misplaced socks, but James was a leading philosopher and psychologist at the turn of the nineteenth century, he was a co-founding member of the School of Pragmatism, the school advocating that the meaning of an idea can be sought in its practical effects, that the function of thought is to guide action.

I needed to reread that several times and allow it to sink in and having done so, realise the power of that thought process in striving to look for greater understanding of our time here and therefore incredibly helpful to our cause. William James went on to say, regarding loss, that part of our depression at the loss of possessions is to our feeling that we have a sense of shrinking of our personality, a partial conversion of ourselves to nothingness! That is deep, but putting it a little more simply he is saying that as a whole we are the sum of the things that we accumulate and come to define us and if one of those piece drops off or is lost, then that piece although in isolation it could appear to be inconsequential, it becomes significant in that it is a lost piece of what we are, wow, don't you love this guy?

There are a couple of main ways forward when loss occurs and they can take a little inner strength, you can either, abandon concern for the missing object before proceeding to search for it, but denying that the article is permanently lost and will return when least expected, so it is not lost but simply misplaced, where are my car keys? Alternatively you could throw up your arms and acknowledge that the item is lost and you will never see it again, there is no point wasting time looking for it and it is best to SUMO, Shut Up and Move On, no amount of worry or concern will bring it back! If you acknowledge that the item is lost forever then showing no great concern means that nothing is threateningly absent, its loss will not cause havoc in your world, believing that the item is around the house, hidden temporarily but it will reappear, suppressing any desire to need to search for it immediately until found. Loss is an inevitability in life and to most of us it isn't a big deal, depending on the importance of the article, so having a coping mechanism is vital to being able to move on with our lives when any loss occurs! If you stop looking, you stop finding and only luck will bring a lost item back into your possession, but if an article is found, was it ever lost?

Property is the second part of the well-known expression lost property, or as we now call it, Loperty. In a society in which accumulating property is perceived as something that we strive for, then it is important to define the word property, although it is a word that we use liberally in everyday life.

Property is an object or objects that belong to someone, the dictionary will tell us, but that in itself is a little ambiguous, for in order to know what that actually means, the word belong must also be defined. However, if we look at the dictionary definition of belong we find something like, be the property of, which is unhelpful, as it means we are going around in circles, but I feel we need to persist with identifying what property means and whether ownership of anything is truly absolute, or merely as I sense, is purely temporary. Maybe we don't own anything and that all we have are our memories, which themselves can fade over time due to old age, so what is the answer, in order to combat the loss of memories, do you keep a diary, write a journal or intimately document your successes and failures along the way, on the understanding that they too may vanish unless committed to paper.

To me it does seem a little futile to write volumes full of memories, diarising the minutia of our daily lives, only to end up, in our twilight years with dementia, a time when remembering our own name is a virtual impossibility and the dusty pages of an old diary serve to highlight sadness of irrevocable memories once cherished. As we have discussed earlier, today's kids are photographing every waking moment of their lives, negating the need for writing a journal to navigate the memories, they are creating a degree of permanence society has never known before, so we can only guess at the future impact.

Because this development is so fresh and still in comparative infancy, we have no way of knowing whether the OAPs of the future will recall their memories in their dotage by flicking through the latest device to recall those forgotten moments as the once unthinkable happens and they too near the end of their stay in the hotel. Ownership of property is one thing but until the late 1960s in England and this may seem hard to believe, but a form of ownership of a wife by her husband still existed. Having been established as common law for several centuries and fully functioning until the mid-19th century, Coverture was a legal doctrine which meant that upon marriage, a woman's rights and obligations were subsumed by those of her husband, assuming that legally, at least, a husband and wife were one person.

The rise of the women's rights movement in the mid-19th century meant the world was starting to see a radical change and it saw Coverture being criticised as oppressive and hindering women, which would be difficult to argue with. The oppression and hindrance was stopping women from exercising property rights and also from entering certain professions, but the advent of the women's rights movement saw this influence gradually reducing, so much so that laws were changed or at least were modified, then weakened and ultimately eliminated. As I mentioned earlier, certain aspects of Coverture still existed up to and until the 1960s, these were mainly major financial commitments or obligations, which even then were the domain of the husband. One example of this which seems incredible to believe existed until so recently was property purchase.

It seems absolutely incredible to believe but a female was not allowed to buy a property in her own name even up to the mid-1970s, there were overriding reasons for this and it was not simply a gender issue, the fact that so few women worked full-time or were in regular employment, they could not justify borrowing a significant sum enough to fund a mortgage, but those who could would be able to do so as long as they had a male guarantor! That in itself perpetuated the inequity and it seems impossible for us today, seeing how society has changed, to believe that was the way things worked.

Women's roles in society have changed so much since the 1900s, little by little, with incremental change until the 1960s and 1970s, this was a time when women became a force in both the housing market and the employment market, this meant that society had changed both dramatically and irrevocably, most of us would think it was mainly for the better and although no longer being the property of men, the change meant that women with their indebtedness through work and property and the inevitable dependence by women on men, was now seen to be disappearing forever. Although this country has moved on, which is laudable, I believe that in spite of the huge progress, that there is still extensive work here to do, the rest of the world is catching up with our lead, but in some cases, there remain various countries whether it's due to their cultural or religious reasons and beliefs that result in women still being marginalised in their own countries with treatment which is inferior to men in many aspects of life.

I think the easiest thing to do would be to consider some examples that we currently find are treated as the norm throughout the hotel and observe their impact rather than either criticising them or giving an opinion. Change is the only constant in life, in fact, if you look at man's evolution, change defined as progress has always been with us, although it feels that the pace of change is increasing and increasing rapidly, therefore it is our ability as a society to adapt to change that help us to evolve as both a society and as individuals, thus making us accepting of this place during our stay in the hotel.

Change is evolution and it is evolution that gives me an opportunity to give a brief mention to one of the past residents in the hotel, a resident that, while he was staying here, made an important contribution not only to his own generations understanding of life, but he also left a legacy which gave a certain clarity to future guests and he accomplished all of this, all while he was staying in the hotel. Basically evolution is change, change which happens over generations, change which occurs slowly, but sees life adapt to its surroundings in order for it to survive, these evolutionary processes see certain characteristics becoming either more common or rarer and ultimately dying out, depending on whether the species feels them necessary for it to thrive and sustain itself.

Charles Darwin is a well-known name from our past, indeed, he was a previous guest in the hotel, just like you and I. His book, *On the Origin of Species*, published in November 1859 is a vital work of scientific literature which is considered to be the foundation of evolutionary biology! In short, the book introduced the scientific theory that populations evolve over the course of generations through a process called natural selection, survival of the fittest if you will and when it was published, it generated scientific, philosophical and religious discussion.

In terms of our perspective, he established that as generations before us and after us enjoy our stay here, we adapt our lives to live in the hotel, improving the building, maintaining the grounds and cleaning the swimming pools, or the seas, as we colloquially know them, generally making sure we look after the place as custodians for future guests.

However, currently, there is a generational clash with many of the younger generation and many of those who have been here for a longer time, but are both aware and concerned, this group is clashing with the majority of the older generation.

Both factions are monitoring climate change observing how we as current guests and those previous generations, those who stayed here before us, have and are currently, being irresponsible, how we are letting things deteriorate, allowing the seas to become polluted, global temperatures to rise through our irresponsibility and our abuse of pollutants.

One example of the conflict between generations is carbon emissions, currently being debated throughout the hotel. We as guests have a responsibility to leave the hotel as we would wish to find it and accordingly, there are problems which we have started to address in order to 'save the planet', but if we believe that Darwin was right, then whatever twists and turns the hotel experiences, humanity will navigate them.

The strongest will survive, the weakest will die and this reinvention, the reinterpretation, the new version will move on, suitably able to face the future, whether on a global, societal level, or on an individual basis.

Society is constantly changing and as it does, more often than not, being driven by those who have recently arrived here, comparatively speaking and therefore those who are nearer to checking out for the final time may find it hard to adjust, to the inevitable change that they are seeing all around them.

Sadly, those guests nearing the end of their stay are not a crucial part to the long-term future of the hotel and their departure, although inevitable, becomes convenient, we all become an anachronism and in spite of trying to remain cool, trendy and on message, we find ourselves in a world that is no longer for us, it's no longer our world, we have handed over the baton; it is now in the temporary ownership of the next generation and it is at this time that death becomes a friend.

I realise that is a dreadful conclusion, but that's the way it is, there's nothing you can do, survival of the fittest in a place when you no longer exercise or go to the gym is impossible! Darwin's theory may be wrong or it could be right, either way it is a thought provoking and extremely valuable contribution and we thank him for it!

However, we were discussing the treatment of women in countries that aren't as progressive, or at least as progressive as we like to think we are, so let's take a look around the world at what we can expect.

Throughout the world, the treatment of women is magnified, exposing inconsistencies and seeing them treated as something akin to second-class citizens, if not that extreme then certainly prejudiced, especially when compared to men, these inconsistencies are invariably due to one of two major influences, depending on the country concerned, instrumentally it is either a country's religion or its culture that tends to impose a second-class citizenship on the female of the species in those countries, where they are perceived as the inferior gender.

Woman is the *Nigger of the World*, sang John Lennon, in his 1972 album *Some Time in New York City*, also released as a single; unsurprisingly, its title and subject matter started a controversy.

Incidentally, I could not imagine that song either being written and certainly not released today, however, the song was written due to the fact that Yoko Ono had actually coined the phrase in an interview in 1969 and it was then quoted on the cover of *Nova* magazine, it obviously struck a chord with Lennon and Yoko and the song discussing women's subservience to men and misogyny across all cultures was written.

Probably due to the song's offensive use of a racial epithet and a perceived inappropriate comparison to women's rights and of the struggles of African Americans, it had little airplay and wasn't a commercial success. I have always loved the song ever since I heard it in 1973 when I bought John Lennon's *Some Time in New York* album, even in those days, I could see beyond the use of the N word as being more than gratuitous and thought the message was powerful.

Lennon made a valid contribution to the debate and he said in a TV interview that the word Nigger was intended to mean any oppressed person and not simply a black person as it is used across Afro-Caribbean cultures, where the N word, as it is known, is used amongst those black communities and its use is seen as ironic and taking back control of the word.

The song aside, Lennon had a valid point, bearing in mind this was the early seventies, over 50 years ago, a very different time, but today we find ourselves in a place where the female can still be seen as second-class citizens.

Not everywhere, have we seen incredible progress in women's rights, indeed there are outliers, those countries that haven't caught up with the programme and haven't made in roads to equality, more often than not, for religious or cultural reasons, as I mentioned earlier, so let's have a look at what is going on around the rest of the hotel.

A recent UN Human Rights report, specifically looking at the treatment of women and environments where their treatment was inferior to their male counterparts, told of women being treated as second-class citizens in Iran, the report looked at life in that country and they observed just two of the many issues that concerned them were girls as young as 10 years old being married and also that cases of domestic violence were problematic throughout Iranian society.

Another global study found the women of Nepal and Yemen being treated as second-class citizens in their own countries, highlighting massive inequities in those countries.

There are so many examples of inequality around the world and citing a long list would be futile, as I write we still await the first female president in the United States, although many countries around the world have or have had female leaders in their country, so power isn't inaccessible, it's just a little bit harder to achieve, things that men often take for granted, not all men obviously indeed, should we choose, we could find inequality within the male gender, based primarily I believe on class, education and wealth, which are, when you think about it, effectively all one and the same thing, although wealth can be found anywhere, a person's determination to succeed is not the privilege of the upper class, ambition has no boundaries, I am talking more about opportunities which I do believe present themselves to the chosen few.

You will have noticed that I have ignored the use of skin colour as an easy excuse for failure and let me briefly explain why.

If I went to Pakistan, the parliamentarians would all look culturally similar, the same I would suggest in both Somalia and China, if we cared to look at their parliamentarians, we would discover the same to be true, incredibly it is the oft demonised, but progressive western countries that contrary to those aforementioned examples, encourage and actively promote a diversity and to prove my point I give you Barack Obama.

This topic could be a whole new book, so I would rather not do it the injustice of skimming through it, instead I will simply allow my own thoughts to develop and see where they take me.

In the meantime, we needn't, as a society, beat ourselves up as to the accomplishments of females, we have seen them in space, fighting in elite combat units all over the world and they have taken every category of Nobel prize available, being the leader of a country, an international bank and every other career they have chosen to partake in and as mentioned earlier, excluding those regressive countries where equality is yet to be achieved, to religions were progress is limited purely because of gender, outside of these countries, there are no limits to what either sex can become.

One interesting fact to present itself to us, by the most recent calculations, the highest paid tv stars in the world were Judge Judy, Oprah Winfrey and Ellen DeGeneres, all female, one is an octogenarian, another is a woman of colour and finally, one is a gay woman, virtually covering all the bases, that we are led to believe are marginalised by society and whose progress in their chosen field will be limited.

I sense there is a bigger cloud looming on the horizon and one day we will look back and scoff at the simplicity of the gender debate before it exploded, those halcyon days when it concerned just two genders, we will wonder how we could ever struggle with equality with only a couple of options to consider, yet with, at the last count I read that there were as many as 72 genders, then I sense the debate is only going to intensify and that there will be casualties.

If I had convinced myself that ethnicity merited a whole new book, then gender would need its own library, so in the short term let's look at the things restricting women's progress in the gender binary world.

Religion, surprisingly, but possibly understandably appears to be most resistant to societal progress for the female gender, with women often relegated to a second tier status, incredibly meaning that in some faiths, women being barred from ordination to the church, some religions actually ban women from praying alongside men, or even from stepping foot into a house of worship altogether.

For females in several regions, clothing can be far more restrictive than that demanded for their male counterparts to wear, examples ranging from headwear, to covered arms or long skirts all designed to impact on women and therefore imposing restrictions on their lives.

So property although we can call anything our own, at least temporarily, ownership is a debatable term, due to our own temporary existence on the planet, our own stay in the hotel is a brief one, so maybe custodianship is the best we can expect and then if that is the case, what is the big deal about who owns anything, who something belongs to, its literally a case of, so what?

We know nothing is coming with us when we go, no matter how well secreted it may be about our person, so it seems rather pointless dwelling on what could be, or even, what might have been, although in regard of taking things with you, we need to consider the ancient Egyptians, for they had a very different perspective on things, having developed the concept of the tomb from other cultures which had existed long before they ever did.

They fine-tuned the tomb as a burial chamber, look at the Great Pyramids, them are the most fabulous examples of the genre and they are perhaps the most famous tombs that the ingenuity of mankind has ever created.

The pyramid is a structure with four triangular outer sides reaching a point at the top, there are examples from different cultures around the world, but possibly the most famous advocates of this form of burial were the ancient Egyptians. Fabulous examples of the style have become known as the Three Great Pyramids built in the fourth dynasty for three pharaohs, kings of ancient Egypt—Khufu, Khafre and Menkaure. These three pyramids were more than just monuments to royalty, they contained the mummified bodies of the pharaohs and included alongside them their worldly effects which were thought to protect the dead and also be used by the kings in the afterlife.

The Great Pyramid of Giza was built for Khufu and stands at a height of nearly 500 feet, it is the last of the Seven Wonders of the world still standing. It is estimated that it took 20,000 workers 20 years to construct the pyramid and deep inside it are the king and queen's burial chambers, with extensive hieroglyphics inside detailing Egyptian life and practices of the time.

The pyramids are the most ostentatious of the tombs we have left to us but it is worth us looking at their purpose and what those who stayed her before we arrived, sensed was coming next and whether the wealth and property accumulated during their lifetime would be worth anything to them once they had died.

Basically, a tomb is a house for the dead, which may appear to be counter intuitive, who needs a house to live in when they are no longer alive, but the original purpose was to provide the deceased with a safe place to spend their time, and along with their bodies which had been mummified in order to preserve them, had all of the vital necessities required for a wonderful and fulfilling time in the afterlife.

Briefly, mummification was an fascinating process and its practice gives us an insight into those ancient Egyptians and their beliefs. The mummification process took approximately seventy days and it saw the body being dried out, removing organs and the brain, but leaving the heart in place, believing that it was the centre of a person's being and intelligence.

It was a fundamental belief of the ancient Egyptians that the mummified body was a home for the spirit and if the body was destroyed by it not being preserved or cremated, then that spirit no longer had a home and might be lost, the spirit being essential to enable the person from whom it originated, to enter the afterlife.

So the tomb itself was crucially important as it housed the body that enabled the spirit to do its work and contrary to what many of us believe, its origins were not in ancient Egypt, however they more likely originated from the prehistoric practice, which saw the burying of the deceased in their own homes, although after a time, even this practice was replaced, when during the renaissance period, the graves that we use and have become more common today, so much so that they are in common usage.

As their popularity grew and they became more popular for both the elites and the masses, we saw the introduction of cemeteries, which became a common sight, and their appearance saw the building of tombs die out.

Maybe the Egyptians had it right, with their focus on an eternal life, giving them a certainty of life beyond death, which inevitably made the process of death a little more acceptable and even bearable and who knows whether they were right or wrong and if they are right and eternal life is a thing, then maybe they are they walking amongst us today!

That is the beauty of faith, it is a beautiful thing if you have it, or a case of mental gymnastics if you don't, it is either a belief without evidence or it is a belief based on a perceived degree of understanding, but if you have it, especially in religious terms there is no absolutely no need for unalloyed proof, the faith gives you confidence in your understanding and as nobody has ever come back and told us otherwise then how can non-believers tell those with faith that they are wrong.

The Egyptian pharaohs with tombs laden with the essentials for the afterlife, from the basics, such as a bowl, comb and food, to the extravagances, such as furniture and jewellery, in fact storage space was essential, providing an important part of tomb design, during those times, burial goods were big business and would test the concept of a lifetime guarantee!

The Egyptians even developed the funerary boat, their equivalent of you or I jumping into a taxi when we are leaving the hotel once we have checked out, but these boats took the deceased passenger into the afterlife, sailing down the River Nile, the significance of the boat being that the Egyptians conceived it as the means by which the gods crossed the skies.

Ancient Egypt has left us all a lasting legacy in the hotel, so many aspects of its life from literature, architecture, language and trade, not forgetting their contribution to the development of mathematics, to name but a few of their outstanding contributions they are there for us all to see as incredible work that not only altered their own lives during their stay in the hotel, but also helping to shape our stay and those who will be checking in, longer after we have departed.

Inevitably as with any successful era, Egypt saw its own decline when in approximately 30bc Roman forces took Egypt from Alexander the Great and made it part of the Roman empire, but the Romans changed little as Egypt in its own right had become a successful and strategic location, with trade, architecture and religions all absorbing Greek, Egyptian and subsequently Roman values, it is this melting pot that became a model for many parts of our world and as we progress it is easy to see how fortunate we are to follow them, as our own stay can and has been enhanced by their mere existence.

The Egyptians showed us that property taken into the next life was for them, considered to be a reality and that the constraints of our human existence would help us in the afterlife. In that they are still there, still in their tombs and their worldly goods haven't been taken with them, what, if anything, does this mean?

It could mean that they never actually needed them, because the afterlife is a totally different proposition than our understanding of life in the hotel, it could also mean that they tried to take their items with them but couldn't get them out of the tomb, or it could simply mean that as the pharaoh was dead, there was no afterlife, it has to be one of these three things, but even after generations have stayed in the hotel, we still have absolutely no way of knowing the answer.

A good friend of mine is a funeral director in Darlington, County Durham in the northeast of England, and I have always been intrigued to know what he senses when he is alone with a body, preparing it for the time after death. Does he see an empty shell, being the body before him or does he see a 'being' waiting to move on to the next stage, or the next part of the game, whatever that may be.

There is, of course, no definitive answer and it is all down to the individual and their interpretation of what they see before them, but in answer to my question, he told me this. He never looks at the physical body and sees an empty shell, in fact, having spent time with and being involved in the preparation of many dead bodies, readying them for their last scene, he does find that although he feels there a sense of finality about the process and that in spite the existence of the physical form in front of him, the body of the person may be there, but the person has gone and that they no longer exist.

It is a basic demand of our human existence that our deceased need to be looked after and helped on their journey once they die and dealing with death bodies every single day must create a form of alexithymia where you are detached and take emotion out of your work, so whatever his feelings, my respect for his work is immense, for one day, we will all of us require his talents, whoever and wherever we may be.

None of us is getting out of here alive!

Chapter 10
Changeover Day

In most hotels around the world, especially during the summer and winter seasons, they regularly experience what is known as changeover day, the day that sees the replacement of the cohort of guests who have all completed their stay in the hotel and are replaced by a new group of people.

These hotels also accommodate those who wish to wander in and out at their own discretion, people who live their lives day to day, indeed there is no hard and fast rule for enjoying your stay here, as with any hotel, some will stay longer than others, but the point is that every single person will go through the same experience.

Whenever you arrive or whenever you depart, there is a procedure that everybody goes through, you either vacate your room for the final time prior to your departure, or arrive, check in at reception and enjoy entering your room for the very first time.

Changeover day is the day in our hotel when we see brand-new arrivals checking in, a time which can always be exciting, but sadly there is a payoff for this excitement; in order to accommodate our new guests, we need existing guests to vacate their room, so we have to say goodbye to those who have been staying with us, an incredibly sad time for those guests left behind.

We can look at life on either an individual or a generational level; every individual and every generation will eventually depart and be replaced, so although the hotel itself remains constant, it changes as old guests leave and new guests arrive, think about that for a second, it is a powerful thought and bears truth to the aforementioned Heraclitus line about 'man never stepping into the same river twice', change being the only constant.

As we have already discussed, we don't have a de facto one for one swap in order for the changeover principle to work, thankfully, in order for one new guest to arrive, in the hotel, we don't have to evict an existing guest, we don't need another person to vacate their residency, in fact there is plenty of space in the hotel, however some parts are tremendously overcrowded, while other parts are underpopulated, the limits on a successful management of the hotel is more dependent on resource, such as food, water and energy, so effectively, the growth in population becomes self-regulating, but we would be naive to not acknowledge that there are pressures on all of the planets resources, everything is finite.

The change that happens to our population tends to happen organically and population replacement although we see it is currently on an upward trajectory, there are no imposed limits on global population, although different regimes in countries around the world have been known to impose restrictions.

We shall take a look at those regimes and their impositions a little later, however in the short term, my point here is to draw the parallel that a regular and vital function of every hotel on the planet is a Changeover Day, a function that actually advances my theory—life is a hotel.

I see changeover day as the day when we see the latest arrivals arriving in the hotel, arrive in order to begin their experience and sadly but inevitably, we say farewell to those we have known and maybe even loved.

Even within our own families, the contrast between the happiness of a new arrival in the family and the sadness of the departure of a close friend or relative is stark, but we all experience both at various stages of our stay here in the hotel, we are conditioned to accept the ebb and flow of life and death and see them as the norm, giving us a greater tolerance of the inevitability of bot, especially death, which of the two is more difficult to handle.

The arrival of a newborn baby is a glorious event, it is celebrated in many different ways in very different parts of the planet and it is interesting to look at the way that those different cultures celebrate the arrival of a new born child, an event that you will now understand that I would like to think, was the equivalent of the arrival of a brand-new guest arriving in reception and checking into the hotel for the very first time.

Despite it being such an extraordinary event, the miracle that is childbirth and the frequency with which it happens all over the world every single day of every single year is incredible in itself, I have used the word miracle and indeed some do choose to use that word to describe it, seeing it as a gift from their chosen god, but whatever the truth of it is, it is happening right now, somewhere in some part of the hotel as I write this, and somewhere in the hotel at the very moment that you are reading this.

There are tremendous variations across the planet, throughout the hotel in both beliefs and practices in the build-up to childbirth and then, the actual birth itself, all of which and in their own way contribute to the new baby's life as it goes forward, once it has finally arrived at reception and has checked in to the hotel, focussing initially on the conditions and environment of the birth and then as the child progresses during its earliest years, years which ultimately having a major influence on the development and conditioning of the child and therefore contributing to the adult that they become, the finished product if you will.

It is a rather nice thing to do to look at different customs and cultures and their treatment of the arrival of a new guest in the hotel and the influence that those early days can result in.

Let me briefly interject while this is fresh in my memory, I will come back to the different cultures and customs, I promise you, but I have just been driving through Bradford having been for a Starbucks, the roof on the car was down and the sun was shining, I was stopped at the traffic lights and happily watching the world go by.

What I believed to be was a family was standing together at the crossing; as they crossed and began walking in front of my car, the family, which consisted of a mother, father and their young daughter approximately ten years of age; I am making a lot of assumptions here, but I can only believe the emotions that I was feeling and what I was seeing before my very eyes.

The family looked a little unkempt and their general demeanour suggested to me that they were lacking purpose and I found myself wondering what chances the daughter was going to have in her own life, what were her aspirations and how much influence her parents had on her destiny, I know that sounds incredibly condescending, I know it sounds pompous, even arrogant, but that is not me and is not my intention, actually it is coming from a well-intentioned place, I promise you.

Maybe the parents had a difficult childhood, possibly they had a bad start in their own lives, who knows, certainly not me, but I found myself thinking of the unfairness of it all and of course there will be a lot of children in a far worse position than this girl, those kids who don't know their parents or have parents that are totally disinterested, at least she was with both of her parents which is a massive plus.

Conversely, at the other end of the scale, there will be children who have everything, whatever that oft used phrase has come to mean, we can all say hazard a guess with some confidence of being right, of its meaning in a materialistic and family environment, they would appear to have everything they need and more, they have the lot, but as we all know, there is no secret recipe a perfect life and there are no guarantees, the best you can do is to create an environment that put the odds in your favour.

'Give me the child until he is seven and I will give you the man', a very famous and frequently used quote attributed to Ignatius of Loyola, the founder of the Society of Jesus, a religious order of the Catholic Church whose members were known as Jesuits! Although the quote is attributed to Ignatius, this has been disputed and it is believed that Voltaire mischievously attributed the quote to him.

Many of the world's greatest words are often unattributed or wrongly attributed, but irrespective of who said what and when, the point still stands that once a newborn baby checks in at the reception of the hotel, those first years are crucial to initial development and ultimately become the foundations for the rest of their lives. But if the first seven years are so important and it really is true that the first 2,555 days are crucial to the cognitive and psychological health of the child, then what makes it so? Parenting styles change not only across continents and cultures but also within individual countries, the perceived best practice of parenting and child development theories can become not only antiquated within a generation, but they can also be also disproven.

For example, in the 1940s and 50s, it was believed by paediatricians that it was better to feed babies formula milk as opposed to common consensus today which suggests that breastfeeding is best; breast is best is the chant from those who attend today's prenatal classes at the National Childbirth Trust.

Popular opinion changes rapidly, indeed there can and has been pressure put on new mothers by the current breastfeeding demand, with some mothers unable to fulfil their duty, engendering feelings of guilt that have culminated in catastrophic consequences, but although that is a huge area to discuss and the debate rages, it is not for us to do so here and now.

We are more concerned with Ignatius and his words and do those words still hold credence all of these years later, or are they as redundant as the formula milk? It is difficult to know, but as every first-time parent knows, there is no manual for them to follow when bringing their child up; like many aspects of parenting, the answers aren't black and white, but if you step back and consider it for a moment, it is hard to believe that the first seven years have a finite effect on the child's life, one thing is for sure, those first seven years for the child development of social skills are crucially important, but defining that person for life, that's a bit of a stretch!

By the age of seven, children are putting the pieces together in their own heads, not always getting them in the right order, but that is what parents are for, helping them arrange those pieces, the pieces that will give them a foundation for the rest of their lives, this is a time when their brains are growing rapidly and they are learning how to communicate and interact with the rest of the guests in the hotel—indeed, the rest of the world.

At this stage of their lives, they are starting to make relationships of their own, outside of their primary carers, their mother and father, the major influences on them, having been in their lives from day one.

This is a time when they are starting to look for acceptance among their peers and long-term friendships can be formed in these early days, if you think of your own early days, it is not difficult to think of those friends at infants school, names that you still remember and some who you may still be good friends with years later, it is a wonderful stage of your life and we often think fondly of those early school days.

So these are incredibly powerful times, although as we meander through them, we are often detached from their importance, not realising the role that they have in our personal development and our stay in the hotel, which can be and is heavily influenced during this time.

It is remarkable to see how the world celebrates the daily new arrivals to the hotel in so many very different ways, for example, a new father in England will know that it is tradition to go out with his male friends to the pub, to wet the baby's head, it is quite a basic ritual which involves new dad going out with his mates to a favourite pub where the guys all celebrate by getting drunk.

This may not seem the most imaginative of ways to welcome the latest guest in the hotel, but it is a tradition that has been practiced for many years, believed to have originally come from the baptism of a baby where the baby's head is wet with holy water, but latterly it has seen the liquid change from holy water to alcohol, consumed by the father, behold, another miracle, although it's hardly the wedding at Cana, water into wine anybody?

Dad and his chums are out at the pub, while a physically exhausted mum stays at home, surrounded by nappies; Dad, of course, is out telling the world of the trauma of his newborn child's birth and what he has been through—what a hero!

Around the planet, there are many and varied ways of celebrating a new born baby's arrival and I think it is nice to consider these, because as you would imagine, not only are they diverse, that's a given, but fascinating on their role within the different cultures that they exist within.

Firstly, let us take a look at Japan, where mothers while giving birth try to avoid the use of painkillers, this may sound extreme, however this relates to their religious beliefs, they are Buddhists and as such the belief is that the pain experienced in a natural childbirth makes the mother stronger, toughening her up for performing the role of a mother and preparing her for the intense demands ahead.

The Japanese have long respected this centuries-old belief, although the times are a-changing and the use of epidurals is slowly but surely becoming a little more commonplace in the country. In Japan, the culture dictates that baby's father is rarely allowed to attend the birth of his child, only permitted to do so if he has attended parental classes with the mother-to-be.

After giving birth, the mother will then go to the home of her parents, where she will stay for a month or more, staying in bed for the first twenty-one days of the baby's life when friends and family will drop in to greet the baby with gifts and where they will celebrate by eating a Japanese dish called Osekihan, a meal made up of red rice with red beans. What a fabulous tradition, designed to help both mum and baby at the most important time when both need both support and a little TLC.

Backpacking our way over to Brazil, things are a little different over there; during her pregnancy, the expectant mother is treated like a princess when out in public, moving to the front of any queue and generally wrapped in cottonwool by the whole of society.

Then, once the baby is born, friends and relatives visit mother and baby, bringing small gifts which are reciprocated by the baby with a 'signed' token of thanks to visitors, thanking them for a warm welcome to the hotel and thanking them for bringing a gift.

In Germany, the midwife and her role in the proceedings are held in the highest regard where birthing is concerned; their attendance at any birth is mandatory, whereas the attendance of a doctor is optional; the midwife is queen, or possibly king of all they survey.

There is something quite unusual where Germany is concerned about the new baby and somewhere that they depart from the rest of the hotel; we find the existence of a book of approved baby's names which is held at government offices throughout the country. The purpose of the approval of names is simply in order to ensure that the child is not open to ridicule because of its name, therefore an act that is seen as acting in the best interests of the child, a form of child protection as they check in at reception.

Parents must adhere to the list of approved names, but should the parents wish to use an unusual name then there is an appeal process available, this is where the parents must give an exceptional reason why an unusual or unapproved name should be made, seeking approval for their choice.

I can understand the thinking behind the approved names book, but the world, indeed Germany itself, is a rapidly changing country and as it evolves, with the demographics of the country altering, will this generation be accepting of a country limiting the potential names for their children, which is no doubt well-intentioned, but I sense a little Orwellian.

In 2015, Angela Merkel, the then Chancellor of Germany, uttered the words 'we can do this' as she invited refugees from Syria, Afghanistan and Iraq into her country; almost one million arrived, bringing with them their culture, heritage and children's names.

It will be interesting to see how the latest influx of diversity affects the approved names book in an evolving country; where once Fritz, Maximilian, Sophie and Magda would have been popular, we see Abdul, Jabar and Iman as part of the mix, traditional Middle Eastern names that will inevitably change the country forever, enriching the German culture, introducing a new dimension to the country's development and asking questions of the approved names book, which may not survive the rapid evolution, we will surely see.

There is a lighter side to this of course, inevitably when you try to control any situation, there will always be somebody who tries to push the barriers to see how far they will go, which is not necessarily a bad thing in any situation, given that everything we do is man made and we are all making it up as we go along.

With regards to our old friend, the book of approved names and the authority that administers names, which is called the Standesamt, both funnily and interesting to note are a couple of names that have not been approved by the courts, in spite of there being an extensive list, I think three of these will suffice in order to give us a flavour of the culture, of what is considered to be unacceptable.

One proud parent tried to name their newborn baby Borussia; this was disallowed, considered to be offside, as it has connotations with the German football teams of Monchengladbach and Dortmund, so that was shown the red card. Möwe was another to be disallowed, the name translates in English to seagull and seagulls are seen as a nuisance or pest, which any child given the name would feel as a burdensome epithet.

Finally, we have Pfefferminze or in English, Peppermint, this was denied because it is primarily considered to be a healing spice plant, which in itself is possibly inoffensive, indeed it is rather a positive influence, but still, it was not considered to be acceptable.

I do have a list of names that, although unusual, were allowed, just don't ask me why, so we have, in no particular order of preference, Fanta, Emilie, Extra and the fabulous Pumuckl. So all imagination and creativity is not thwarted in Germany but there are certainly limitations on original thinking.

By the way, Pumuckl is a German cartoon character, a red-haired sprite, popular throughout Europe and known by different names but not really heard of in the United Kingdom; fancy calling your child Pumuckl and getting away with it!

Popping over to the Netherlands, where they have a rather nice welcome for the new arrival once they have been born; during the first week, we find that a nurse will visit the mother's home every day, providing any necessary medical care but also cleaning the apartment, possibly cooking and giving any much needed parenting skills. The nurse also manages the flow of visitors to the house to see the new baby, making sure that mother and child are not overwhelmed, but to welcome those visitors that do make it through the front door, the nurse will make a traditional snack, which is given to visitors to celebrate the birth.

The traditional snack is called Beschuit met muisjes, which means biscuits with mice; what a lovely thought, that is as long as you're not scared of mice.

But hark, there is nothing to be scared of, the mice are actually small pieces of liquorice which have blue and white coating for boys and pink and white for the girls, though the way the gender debate is raging around the western world, how long this tradition can remain this simple is anybody's guess.

That tradition is all well and good as long as we find ourselves in the good old days of binary genders, but these days we recognise at the last count 57 genders and so the future will necessitate a whole spectrum of coloured coatings to cover the traditional liquorice in order to satiate the zeitgeist.

Either that, or non-traditionalists will refuse to acknowledge the binary sweets and ignore the snack, seeing it possibly die out forever, which would be sad but inevitable.

Looking at Turkey, there are no such thing as baby showers or indeed celebrations, until after the baby has been safely delivered, whether it's superstition or not wishing to tempt fate. Mother and baby stay at home for the first twenty days after the birth, with friends dropping in often with a small gift and to share a drink, which is called a Lohusa Serbeti, a traditional sweet drink of water, cinnamon, cloves and sugar, designed to help bring on milk in the new mother.

After twenty days, mother and baby return to visit the friends who brought gifts and give them a single egg delicately wrapped in a handkerchief, designed to be a positive for a healthy baby; candy is also given as a sign to give a good-natured baby.

Also in Turkey, there is the age-old superstition of rubbing flour on baby's hairline and eyebrows, this is supposed to grant the baby a long life; in the words of Tevye, the dairyman in *Fiddler on the Roof,* 'it's a tradition'.

There are many traditions in the hotel, too numerous to mention, but that would necessitate another book and now is neither the time or the place to discuss them, but whatever the traditions around the world, the most important start to the life of our new arrivals, wherever they are born is whether they are brought into a loving environment or not, that is the most basic demand of any newborn baby.

I think that is probably the most crucial of all of the variables that influence a child's life in its early years, we live in a world in which there is such massive inequality, so if we can find any sanctuary that provides a place where there is a totally level playing field and there can be no difference in the quality of provision, then surely the love given to a newborn baby by its parents is so.

It is without question the one thing that is the most important and fundamental need and it is possibly the only thing that costs nothing and that, of course, is love. Wealth and poverty are inevitably two of the eternal factors than can determine the quality of a person's life, along with so many others but it is love that sustains us and makes us thrive, the rest is simply embellishment and detail.

There is such a massive wealth disparity throughout the world, but that does not prohibit or slow the growth of population in spite of these extremes the speed with which the global population is rising is accelerating.

If we go back to the year 1800, the global population was one billion and as we already know, that is if you've been paying attention and keeping up, the current world population is an incredible eight billion.

Technological advancement combined with improvements in global agricultural production, sanitisation and medical advances have all combined to reduce mortality rates, which means people are living longer, causing an exponential growth in the world population.

The irony though is that while population growth in wealthier nations has slowed, it is the poorer nations, countries that are not as wealthy, that population growth is increasing.

On current projections, it is suggested that the population number will peak in the mid-21st century and once that peak has been reached, it starts to decline by the year 2100, however to most if not all of us reading this, we will no longer be in the hotel at that time, having checked out by then, so our personal focus will be on the time that we spend here, but with one eye on our legacy and how we leave the place for future guests.

The most recent estimates of global poverty suggest that currently just over nine per cent of the world's population live in extreme poverty, which sounds dreadful, but in order to understand what that actually means, we need to understand what that actually means, therefore we need to establish what they mean when they talk about extreme poverty.

Who better to consult for a definition than the World Bank, so let's look at how they define it; extreme poverty is defined by a person living on $1.90 a day or less. However, it is not simply a level of income but also what a person in that position can or cannot afford to buy, so the definition then becomes a question of whether a person is in absolute or relative poverty.

Absolute poverty is when a person cannot afford the minimum nutrition, minimum clothing and minimum shelter needs in their own country, whereas relative poverty is earning below fifty per cent of the median income, which is the exact middle income of the polar extremes, the highest and the lowest, in the country that they live in.

This equation takes into consideration the costs of everyday life in the relative country that a person is in, obviously this can highlight massive discrepancies, as being in poverty in one country can be massively different to being in poverty in another, that is due to the economic success of the country, hence relative poverty was created, therefore in a wealthy country, as a number it needs to be put into context, as it will be massively different to the number in a poor country, so both are relevant but more importantly relevant to the country they are in.

As there are 195 recognised countries in the world, from one to one hundred and ninety-five, there is a table of wealth based on GDP, Gross Domestic Product, a macroeconomic measure of economic output of a country.

The list of countries by wealth gives us a top 5:

1. Luxembourg
2. Switzerland
3. Ireland
4. Norway
5. United States

Possibly a surprise to us all that little old Luxembourg is top, but obviously the landlocked country has transformed itself from once being dependent upon the steel industry to today being one of the world's major financial centres, which has driven its wealth.

Although it is top of the list of wealthiest countries in the world, Luxembourg is only the world's 66th largest economy, so obviously the size of the economy hasn't hindered its position; compared to the largest economy in the world, the United States of America, Luxembourg's GDP number is small.

The USA has a GDP of over $220 trillion, whereas Luxembourg's is just over $84 billion, very different indeed, the USA as a nation contributing over 24% of global GDP. These numbers are difficult to comprehend but what they do highlight is the disparity between rich and poor and highlight how your quality of life is determined by the part of the hotel into which you are born.

To elaborate on the point, let's look at the countries at the polar extreme on the list, perusing the names of those countries from top to bottom and thus considering that the top five in the list as being the wealthiest, then we must also take a look at the bottom of the list at those countries which are inevitably the poorest countries by GDP, it makes for uncomfortable reading, meaning it's difficult to put any type of positive spin on their situation, it is only possible to feel for these countries and their people, acknowledge their situation and then do as much as we can to get them out of their situation.

At the very bottom of the list is Central African Republic, which came in last considering it specifically for measuring its fiscal success by its income, using the measure of Gross National Income or GNI. There can be reasons for its poor ranking, but the main reason that we see Central African Republic in its lowly position is possibly down to its long history of colonisation, with the country gaining its independence from France only in 1960 and although independent it has subsequently had many upheavals such as coups, corrupt officials and religious violence.

The GNI of Central African Republic is small, at just $663 per capita, which with a population of just under five million and mineral reserves which include diamonds and metals, its recent past is outrageously turbulent, with corruption in both its government and industry which have sadly combined to have a deeply damaging effect on the country.

The second poorest country on the list is Burundi, neighbouring Tanzania in East Africa, this country was also colonised, only this time by Germany before passing it over to Belgium, after World War 1, doing so by a League of Nations mandate, sounding like a pawn in a rich man's game, the country finally gaining its independence in 1959.

Burundi is a resource poor country, mainly dependent upon agriculture for its income and employment of the population, the country is dependent on aid from foreign donors with over 40% of its income coming from this source.

Sadly, but not surprisingly, the World Happiness Report of 2018 found that Burundians were the unhappiest people on the planet, is anybody surprised.

This could be sneeringly described as poverty porn, but it is not meant to be, I believe it is important to look closely at these numbers which, although I've tried to keep to a minimum in order to highlight the inconsistencies that can occur when your quality of life can and is determined simply by where you are born and where you live on the planet, or more importantly and for our purposes, where you are staying in the hotel.

Poverty and wealth contrast massively and every country will have microcosms of both within their borders and we are all aware of the differences that can occur in our own lives, if we find ourselves at either extreme, whether being born into either, be it because of geographical luck or by design, through our own efforts, by relocating to a place that may provide us with the opportunities, opportunities that were not lent to us by our own original place of birth.

I am sure we can all think of the poor part of town, wherever we live, a place that doesn't have to be of Burundian proportions to prove the point, but sufficient enough to feel blessed, lucky, or successful, you choose your reasons.

We can all gain inspiration should we need it from the fabulous 19th century story of Dick Whittington and his cat, an enduring story based on the real-life Richard Whittington born in the 14th century. Richard came from a wealthy family but as he was the youngest son in his family, he suffered from a bit of legalese called primogeniture, where it is the firstborn child who inherits the family's wealth, instead of the alternative and possibly a little fairer principle of it being divided amongst the surviving family members.

Richard made his own way in life as a cloth trader in London, dealing in luxury fabrics such as silks and velvets, so successful was he that between the years 1392–1394 he sold luxury fabrics and materials worth £3,500 to King Richard the Second, which in today's terms would equate to £1.5 million.

Richard was to become Lord Mayor of London thrice, and he was an incredibly successful businessman, but in the 19th-century pantomime which tells his story, he is depicted as a poor boy who makes his way to London from Gloucester to make his fortune. The story highlights the opportunities life gives to those who decide to leave the place they were born in order to search to make a better life for themselves.

What is fascinating is that there exist tales which are of medieval origin from Germany and Italy as well as a Persian story, we have found, possibly a modern-day parable, all telling similar tales of a poor man searching to make his fortune and succeeding, a global phenomenon indeed, the need for believing that hope exists where there appears to be none.

There is a desire a need for us to know that our fate, at least our financial fate, if not our spiritual fate is not determined on the day we arrive in the hotel, based purely on the place of our birth, we want to know that we have free will and that life is not simply a fait accompli!

While it seems eminently possible that this could be the case, our cards may be marked from day one, however Dick Whittington and those related stories from around the world, all afford us the chance to believe that we can control our own destiny.

It is important to distinguish between money in its raw form and the life that it can provide, you would naively imagine, the more you have the better it gets, hence people are driven by its accumulation, but there is another driver in the search for a good life and that is spirituality.

Spirituality is a fundamental appreciation of life and an awareness that comes from within, irrespective of your financial situation, your lifestyle, or your achievements as an individual, it is a sense that there is more than just the physical world that we all exist in and maybe a feeling of a connection to a higher power, both are fundamental in making sense of it all and possibly helping us to optimise our personal satisfaction from our stay in the hotel!

What appears both incredible and possibly distasteful, depending upon your own thinking is that currently in our world, the eight wealthiest people in the hotel own the same wealth as those who make up the three point seven billion people who make up the poorest half of humanity.

How can this happen, it seems incredible that this sort of disparity exists, but it does, these figures, provided by Oxfam certainly highlight the unfairness of it all, or maybe if not simply unfair, maybe they just highlight the irrationality of it all.

Maybe you can't work it out, maybe it doesn't matter anyway, because in any society, extremes will naturally exist, even if they are not designed to be a part of the structure of society, that's just the way it is, the way it was and the way it always will be.

Maybe it's the price we pay for having free will, exercising our freedom of choice, doing our own thing; compare this to the animal kingdom, where if you look into a farmer's field in spring, every newborn lamb looks like the next, there may be slight differences obviously, if not sheep maybe a flock of pigeons, every single one of them looks like the next, there is no pecking order, but in our human lives, *Vive La Difference*! Those differences cover every aspect of our lives and that includes wealth, all humanity is in there somewhere.

When so much of the global wealth is in the control of so few people, all that we can hope is that the money is in the hands of the 'right' people, those who will have a degree of philanthropy, who want to share their fortune, maybe they have a caring nature and are happy to help out wherever and whenever they can.

Of course, life gives you more options if you have money, but those options only exist in the world that we know, but what about the world that we don't know, because we don't know everything about the hotel.

We are aware that there are many uncontacted tribes around the world, all living a life of total isolation, a life unaware of and unimpacted by our first-world dystopian paradise.

Is it their loss, or are they the lucky ones, let's consider how they are living their lives in the hotel, in spite of it being unconventional by our own standards.

There are uncontacted people in many parts of the world, amongst those we are aware of, we can find them in Brazil, Peru, West Papua and Philippines, to name just a few countries.

We need to know what we mean, when we call them uncontacted people, so let's look at a definition, well the definition of uncontacted people is, communities or groups of indigenous people living without sustained contact to neighbouring communities and the rest of the world.

Sometimes, sporadic contact may occur, but their wish to live in isolation, holds greater importance to these people, where once upon a time we would describe these people as, the Lost Tribes, we no longer use that term and have moved on from what we now consider to be a disparaging epithet, we now give them a more considered and respectful title of, Indigenous People's in Isolation.

Our understanding of their lifestyle has changed and so much so that in 2009 the United Nations introduced guidelines and recommendations on these people and their rights to self-isolation.

Our knowledge of these people as the definition infers, is limited to virtually nothing, that is simply because of the life that they choose, indeed the little we do know comes from the experience we have from neighbouring communities and sadly our own, intrusive aerial footage, which I sense is more than somewhat disrespectful.

While researching these peoples, there was one expression that resonated with me and that was a comment about the Ayoreo people in Paraguay, it was they who described the bulldozers destroying their natural habitat of forest, which happens to be South America's largest forest outside of the Amazon, they saw their habitat being destroyed, watching the bulldozers do their grotesque work, the Ayoreo expletive observing the destruction by the bulldozers and described them as 'Beasts with metal skin', imagery, which I think you will agree, is so powerful.

While the world that we inhabit is more connected than ever, unbelievably, these people manage to exist in the world on their own terms, although often with the help of government policy in their own country, although disappointingly and uninvited, there are regular occurrences of both missionaries and tourists who recklessly have been known to break any local laws that exist to protect these people, ignoring them and choosing to penetrate the uncontacted communities.

It would be fascinating know more about these communities, my own conditioning tells me that there must be a hierarchy of sorts in their unconventional society, whether by the seniority of elders or the strongest or maybe a gender based hierarchy, who knows, their societal values are a mystery to us, they are not contaminated by our thinking but surely parallels must exist in our separate but shared world.

However their societies are structured, it would be fascinating to discover whether they have arrived at similar conclusions to ourselves, have they established societal values comparable to those that we have, there are so many interpretations that can offer alternatives to those that we have established, so to randomly amuse ourselves with one or two would be futile, therefore I will resist the opportunity.

Suffice to say that whenever the inevitable happens, as surely it will, and the first meetings are convened of our parallel worlds, wouldn't you just love to be there and watch as each side reveals the strengths and weaknesses of their ordered societies and reveal the choices that their ancestors have passed down to them.

The birth of a newborn baby in the hotel is celebrated in many and various ways around the world and in those early years, our geographical location can influence the whole experience of the newborn child during their stay, whether from extremities of poverty and wealth, or the cultural values that our place of birth determines to be our norm, meaning that we inevitably accept the restrictions that any culture will place upon us, often not seeing impositions as restrictions, but just accepting them as the way it is.

If we are looking for a point to our stay, the reason we are here, then by evaluating the influences that are placed on our personal lives, we may gain an insight into our purpose, our existence merely a stepping stone to the greater good, a cog in the machine, you can choose your analogy.

That observation is only valuable if you have reached the conclusion that there is a purpose to our time in the hotel, but at this moment in time, I am not sure that I have.

Changeover day in any hotel is an exciting time for all concerned, including the hardworking members of staff who oversee the smooth running of this crucial day. It is a day when old friends leave us and new friends arrive, a time of renewal a time of sadness and a time of excitement, a very busy time when staff often take departing guests to their departure location and also collect new arrivals, often collecting them from the same point that some departing guests have left from, be they airports, railway stations or shipping ports all of which serve as locations for both arrivals and departures, obviously there are a wide variety of methods of transportation, too many to include but all providing that interface between the start and the end of the experience.

The departing guests often leave in the morning while new arrivals often check in later in the day, as the hotel staff refresh the hotel facilities that have been used by the departing cohort.

Of course, not every hotel works on the principle of one or two days being nominated as a changeover day, but many do, it is rare for a complete changeover of guests, departing and arriving on the same days, like life itself, people are leaving and arriving throughout the working week, 24/7 if you will.

The parallel of people leaving and people arriving, from and to the hotel, in my mind reinforces the whole, Life is a Hotel theory, so let us look at the reasons why I feel that this important part of hotel life mirrors our whole experience, topping and tailing our stay.

Inevitably, it is a time of great happiness to see a stream of new faces arriving in reception, each one with it all before them, all with their hopes and dreams of what is to come, there is so much to look forward to, but as we know, to have a positive you must have a negative, for us to know good, we must know bad, so to counter the excitement of new arrivals presenting themselves at reception, we have the upset, the sadness of those to whom we are waving goodbye, those that we have got to know, to feel a bond with and even to love.

When we consider departures from a hotel and in order to reinforce the parallel, if we acknowledge births as the new arrivals then death is inevitably the departures, whereas births are joyous occasions, conversely death would be the polar opposite, more often than not, it is an incredibly sad, even distressing time, not least for the deceased, but also for the friends and families of the person who has died and has checked out of the hotel for the final time.

Death is a time for sadness, but it can also be a time of celebration; 'it's better to have loved and lost than never to have loved at all,' Alfred Lord Tennyson wrote in 1849 in his poem, *In Memoriam*. This is a powerful thought and contributes to the reason for us to celebrate a life well-lived.

Celebration of the life of a recently deceased person is an incredibly diverse experience, there are so many different ways seen throughout the hotel that the occasion is marked indeed there appear to be as many variations for the recently departed as there are ways in which the recently arrived are treated, therefore I believe it is incumbent on us, so much so, that we are obligated to consider how different cultures treat the inevitability of death.

My wife and I arrived in Singapore for the first time in the mid-nineties, we were on holiday and both really looking forward to our first visit to southeast Asia. We were picked up by limousine at the main airport in Singapore, Changi, and were driven through the city centre on our way to the hotel which we were staying in, sadly it wasn't Raffles as that fabulous institution was closed for a full refurbishment, we were right in the centre of town, which in itself is a spectacular experience.

We had been on an overnight flight and were in first class so managed to sleep on the way over and arrived bright eyed and bushy tailed, just in time for the early morning rush hour traffic, which wasn't great, making our journey into the city centre rather slow, we were experiencing Singapore traffic congestion in full swing and enjoying every minute.

As we were sitting in the back of our car, another car went flying past our stationary vehicle, beeping its horn, blasting out loud, vibrant music and waving flags and streamers and generally letting us all know it was on the road and coming through, nothing was stopping it.

I asked Marvin, our driver, who was totally unflustered by the racket, what the fuss was all about; he told me it was a funeral on the way to the cemetery!

Even at that time, nearly thirty years ago, I thought, *wow, that's the way to go, letting the whole planet know that it was all over and you were going, checking out of the hotel for the final time*; I loved it.

Sitting in the back of the limo, my mind wandered, inevitably, thinking of alternatives to the type of funerals that I had known or had ever been to, which wasn't a voluminous number, possibly only grandparents and a long-lost uncle, but being born in Liverpool and brought up in the UK, I only ever remember seeing the sombre occasion that our culture has created as our norm, all reverential and black.

I do agree that there appears to be a sea change, I sense the times are changing a little and people seem a little more confident to express themselves, but change is slow and invariably the black protocol still exists in this country.

Saying that I am aware of a number of new businesses springing up that offer bespoke, themed funerals, whether they are for bikers, rock bands, football teams, boy bands, take your pick, but things are gradually improving and I for one applaud it.

But what else is out there, similar to new arrivals, we have seen how birth is celebrated differently in different countries, they have vastly different takes on departures too, just as we experienced on our visit to Singapore, so let's take a look at the alternatives, the different ways that cultures and religions throughout the hotel handle one of life's few certainties, death.

The more I research and find out the options that are available, then maybe I will find something that I would choose for my own departure, I certainly don't feel that the conventional black tie and black suit reflects the way in which I would want to be remembered, there must be more.

Since I have started writing this book, my thoughts have focused on the whole process of death and I honestly think that checking out of the hotel can be made a far more spectacular occasion than we allow it to be.

Yes, I understand grief; yes, I understand sadness, but through it all, I believe each one of us deserves to have our departure to be shouted from the rooftops.

So much so, that I have come up with a way in which each of us can personalise the whole occasion, even down to the coffin, our final resting place, our passage to the afterlife, our DeLorean DMC 12.

There are so many burial traditions around the world, that they offer a rich seam for us to explore, once we have acknowledged that the death of a loved one is invariably both a sad and difficult occasion and as with all things in life, people can and do react very differently to the event, once people have come to terms with their loss, then necessarily in the aftermath, the planning starts in order to celebrate the life and simultaneously honour the death of the individual, these celebrations are often commensurate with those of and appropriate to the deceased's culture.

There are vastly different rituals around the world, so with changeover day in mind and looking at how people check out of the hotel, let's look at these distinct ceremonies from around the planet, the options that are currently available in the hotel.

Let's go first to Tibet, where the burial of choice amongst Buddhists is the sky burial, which to our western values may appear a little extreme in the treatment of the deceased's body; far from treating it with reverence and TLC as we like to do, it is instead disposed of as if it were just an old tin can that once was full of baked beans but now its contents having been poured into a pan for edification, making the container virtually useless!

To our sensitive ears, this treatment of a human body may sound mercenary, but the thinking behind the process makes total sense and is incredibly virtuous. The belief is that the soul of the deceased is returned towards heaven and to this end, the body is no longer of use, so it is left outside, to the elements, often on a mountaintop to decompose while simultaneously providing food for birds and other animals to devour, stripping the skeleton of its flesh.

Often and in order to help those creatures that desire to feast on the remains, Buddhists may cut the body into smaller pieces, this is a process known as excarnation, which basically means the total removal of flesh and organs from the body, leaving the skeleton free of flesh.

Excarnation is believed to allow the soul to leave the body while embracing the circle of life by giving sustenance to other creatures, the body now being an empty vessel with the remains being disposed of in the most generous way possible.

Looking now at the sky burial, this is keenly practiced amongst the Caucasus nations, which is an area found between the Black Sea and the Caspian Sea, here the body will be allowed to decompose and feed the surrounding wildlife, with tradition dictating that the body shall be left in a hollow tree trunk.

Unsurprisingly, this type of burial is not legal in the UK in spite of there being a Buddhist population here of nearly a quarter of a million, but fear not, in spite of the name, the sky burial will not be coming to a satellite channel near you any time soon.

As a polar opposite to the sky burial, we have a water burial, which is embraced in many Nordic countries; during this process, you will find coffins being laid upon cliff tops, directly facing the sea, awaiting their turn, before finally using the seas as a burial ground.

The bodies can either be set adrift on a 'death ship'; the 'ship' carrying the body is set alight and either allowed to set sail along a river or put out to sea, cast adrift into the ocean, giving it back to the gods, while the water is seen as a place of sanctuary, where the body will be carried to its final resting place.

It is not unusual for a boat to be used to carry the body to its final destination and we can see its use in many cultures; more often than not these tend to be seafaring countries, the romantic notion of a body being cast off on its final journey guided by the randomness of the oceans is in itself poetic; I love the idea.

Some cultures actually use a boat as a container when burying a body, even if that burial occurs on dry land, a recent example of such being unearthed in Suffolk, England, where a twenty-six-foot-long craft had been dragged from the river, a half mile away and lowered into the ground, with the decayed remains inside.

In the Solomon Islands, water burials see the laying of bodies on a reef in order to feed the local inhabitants, primarily these will be the local sharks, but many species will inhabit the reef. Once again, this is a fabulous example of the circle of life, simultaneously feeding the creatures while freeing the body of its earthly duties.

Burials at sea are common practice for military personnel, it is a regular occurrence and can be found in in many cultures, this is a usual practice, in which the deceased are honoured, not only for their service but for their life and love of the waters of the world.

So although it is not a common practice, it is understandable that those individuals or cultures which live in harmony with water see it fulfilling a natural role in a person's concluding act during their stay.

Famadihana is a new one for me, I find it both interesting and maybe a little sinister, because the ritual, which is practiced in Madagascar, is the act of 'dancing with the dead'; it is literally the reopening of tombs every few years and renewing the burial clothes of the bodies, while simultaneously music as dancing proceeds around the tomb, this act, which translates as 'turning of the bones' is believed to speed up decomposition while pushing the spirit of the dead towards the afterlife. That sounds to me like the ultimate in leaving parties, seeing the act as one of prolonging life itself and also as fundamental to the leaving experience, it just becomes an extension to a person's longevity and as normal as taking part in the actions of daily living.

In Zoroastrian beliefs, the body of the deceased is believed to defile everything that it touches and to that end it is therefore treated as though anything that comes near it, or even worse, into contact with it, can be contaminated, so much so that interring or cremating the body is unacceptable as doing so would compromise the purity of earths elements of earth, fire and water.

The body therefore is cleansed, traditionally using bull's urine, as are the tools used to cut the clothes off the body, but once it is naked the tools that were used to cut the clothes are destroyed, such is the perception of the toxicity of the corpse and how noxious it is considered to be.

Once cleaned, the Madagascans then carry the body, they put it at the top of a tower which is known as a, Tower of Peace and there it is left to be devoured by scavenging birds, once it has been cleaned of all flesh, the bones are collected before being put into a central pit, situated in the tower, once collected, it is here that they are burned, this is seen as the concluding and final act of the ritual.

Celebrating the life of the dead can also be an ostentatious affair, this is possibly best exemplified in Varanasi, which is one of the oldest continuously inhabited cities in the world and for Hindus, the most sacred place on the river Ganges!

Varanasi is the place where bodies of the deceased are placed on funeral pyres on the banks of the river, brought there by their families and draped in a simple white shroud, once cremated the ashes are thrown into the Ganges, the most sacred river to Hindus, known as the god Ganga, the river is a lifeline to many Indians who live along its banks through its over fifteen hundred mile journey from the Himalayas to the Bay of Bengal!

By the act of scattering ashes, thrown into the Ganges, the Hindus, who fundamentally believe in reincarnation, believe that the soul is transported directly to heaven and thus avoiding the laborious but necessary process of rebirth or transmigration, reincarnation, which can necessitate going through the process, returning in forms as diverse as a fly or a cow and instead of this, the soul finds moksha, which is a transcendent state, which once achieved, means the cycle of reincarnation is avoided, having achieved moksha, the perfect state for Hindus!

To highlight its' importance to the Hindu faith and how the Ganges completes the circle of life, the words of Swami Vivekananda are crucial to aid our understanding, he said 'My bones are destined to make coral in the Ganga', Vivekananda a driving force in the promotion of Hinduism to be accepted as a world religion spoke those words which summarily define the water burial, the soul gone the bones remain and help to form coral in the Hindus most sacred place.

Many cultures around the world including my own, use cremation as part of the ceremony, but in South Korea they have taken things a little further, they use the ashes and make them into beads, which are made in fabulous colours, Pinks, turquoise, blues or black, these beads are then put into a vase or suitable container and they are treasured, kept safe as a permanent and beautiful reminder of a deceased loved one.

These beads are a recent innovation and we're created out of necessity, because due to a shortage of land used to be used for burials, that necessity, South Korean government put a sixty-year limit on burials and once that time is over, the land is to be reused once again for burials. Ironically and although these beads have only developed through necessity, it is becoming clear that the people of South Korea obviously prefer the beads as a lasting memory and the country has seen the number of the once conventional land using burials reduce to a mere thirty per cent from sixty per cent ten years ago.

Interestingly, seeing a business opportunity, a seemingly shrewd businessperson thought the beads were such a brilliant innovation that they thought they would take it overseas and try the concept elsewhere, so the dead bead business has been launched in the Unites States of America, but interest was sadly lacking and the volume of sales could not sustain the business and it closed.

Finally, let's take a look at the Philippines, an incredibly diverse country, an archipelago in the western Pacific Ocean, consisting of 7,641 islands. Inevitably, when you have over seven thousand islands grouped together under the umbrella of one nation, diversity of thought and culture is refreshing and inevitable, therefore throughout the region there are influences from Spanish, American and Chinese inhabitants along with the indigenous Filipino traditions which have all conspired to give a who's who of death rituals amongst the islands inhabitants.

I will look at three or four examples of this incredible and unusual diversity given to us by the Philippines, not just to provide an insight into the workings of that country, but just so we realise what other options are out there, should we be looking for something a little different in our own lives.

The Tinguian people live in Luzon, which is the largest island in the archipelago; they deserve a book in themselves, but this isn't the time or place, their culture is incredible with a fascinating chronology in its development, but for our purposes, let us look at how they deal with their deceased. Their dead are dressed in fancy clothes, placed in a chair and propped up so they appear to be sitting upright in the chair; indeed, sometimes the deceased has a lit cigarette placed between their lips!

It is their belief in deities and spirits, the greatest of whom is Kadaklan who lives in the sky having created the earth, moon stars and sun, that leads them to believe in a life after death, this life being spent in the ultimate destination which is a place they call Maglawa, and it is in preparation for the journey to Maglawa that the corpse is dressed and readied for the journey, as they sit in their chair dressed up ready to go.

Benguet is a landlocked region in the north of Luzon, the largest island of the Philippines archipelago, but there are subtle cultural differences between the Benguet people and their fellow islanders the Tinguians.

Similar to the Tinguian people, the Benguet people choose to sit the deceased's clothed body in a chair at the entrance to their home, but in this instance they have their feet and hands tied together and they are blindfolded too.

This takes place for eight days, when in the ninth, burial of the body takes place, the body buried, the clothing burnt and thrown into the river, the belief is that the spirit is sent on its way to fulfil its objective Maglawa!

As we discussed earlier, when you have the assembled 7,641 islands in the Philippines archipelago, diversity is almost inevitable this is never more obvious than when looking at the burial rituals of the people of Sagada, who unlike many of their compatriots choose not to sit their deceased in a chair, but instead opt for a practice that is also found in both China and Indonesia, this is the ritual of hanging coffins, not from any random place, but the bodies being hung from cliff tops in an attempt to bring the souls placed inside the coffin, closer to heaven.

Sagada is a mountainous region and the coffins are placed underneath natural overhangs, or on a ledge or even placed inside a convenient hole in the mountainside. The coffins are small and this is because the Sagadan people bury their dead in the foetal position, believing that people should leave the world in the same position as they arrive.

Another fascinating part of the culture is that the coffins are often carved by their occupants during their own lifetime, actually making your own bed and lying in it. Although this is a popular form of burial, it is often reserved for distinguished members of the community, then according to merit, or achievement, we find that the higher hanging the coffin is placed, the more important the member of the community.

There are also cave burials for the rest of the community where bodies placed in coffins are then placed in limestone caves, placed on top of each other, the belief here is that the spirits of the dead are allowed to roam around and protect the living.

The hanging coffins of Sagada have become a tourist attraction and you can even check out reviews on TripAdvisor for advice on bus tours and local hotels and restaurants to visit while your there, as death imitates life perpetuating commerce through their demise and in their absence, who'd have thought it!

Heading south we arrive in Cavite located on the Southern shores of Manila Bay, one of the fastest growing provinces in the Philippines, but in spite of the change that naturally occurs through expansion, tradition remains a high priority, it is here that the deceased will have chosen a hollowed out tree before their death and once deceased they are entombed in it, just the body in the majority of cases, but in a sarcophagus if the deceased happens to be a community leader, luxury.

Oh, and just one more for the road, on our whistlestop tour of the Philippines and its traditional death rituals, we take a glance at the Itneg people of Abra who customarily bury their dead underneath their own houses.

If I remember correctly, the last time I saw that happening was in an episode of *Brookside*, but that was back in the eighties and I think Mandy Jordache and her daughters were from Aigburth, not from Abra, they were certainly from Liverpool, but who knows?

So there we have it, a taste of changeover day and the inevitable departures of those leaving the hotel for the final time, giving us an opportunity to think about the variety that other cultures give us and obviously as we look at different practices from around the world, it stimulates your thinking and takes you out of your own comfort zone, meaning you're not just accepting of what has become the norm in your own country and maybe considering the different options available around the world.

Of course, there are cultural differences that restrict our options in the United Kingdom, so the prospect of my wife throwing my ashes into the beck that flows at the bottom of our garden is remote, however there is a suitably large hollow tree behind the garage that I've got my eyes on.

Briefly but interestingly, each time I fly back to the UK from Majorca, I always look forward to flying over what others may consider to be a rather boring twenty minutes of the two-and-a-half-hour flight and that is the time spent traversing the Pyrenees at thirty thousand feet and four hundred miles per hour, looking down at the vastness and beauty of the landscape, yes remote, but with an eerie peacefulness that suggests to me it would be a perfect final resting place for any of us, our final slumber spent surrounded by the awe of magnificence and permanence.

Yes, I know the logistics of placing a coffin or similar corpse capsule down there would be difficult, it would take a little navigation in order to place the body down there, to a place where due to the inaccessibility of its location, a place where no roads exist, but maybe a hearse copter, or a death drone could be the answer, flying over a convenient accessible-ish location and the bodies parachuted down, once landed, a team on the ground could arrange a suitable location and voila, there you have it, Mountain Memorials has been created, a burial ground created and situated in a place of eternal solemnity.

As you can see, my mind has started wandering and it has been catapulted beyond the Pyrenees into thinking about how we could make things a little more interesting in this country, how can we develop our own ritual of the funeral and the whole funereal experience.

I too am more than likely conditioned by my environment, so initially my thoughts for leaving the hotel are not a million miles from the conventional burial that we are used to in the UK, as I have already mentioned, I have no particular religious beliefs or convictions and my personal understanding of the cremation or burial ceremony is conditioned by what I have seen and those that I have been to.

So here's my idea, I have always loved those very large, often dark brown, Louis Vuitton, trunks, I believe they are called a portmanteau, yes, portmanteau the same word that is used to describe the combining of two words to form one new word as we did with Loperty, in our Lost Property chapter earlier.

You would often see these fabulous pieces of luggage in old black-and-white films, being loaded onto steam trains or cruise ships, the portmanteau was used in the golden days of travel by the wealthy and the famous for carrying their fabulous clothes, accoutrements and travel essentials, when taking a long distance cruise or holiday that would have necessitated a large collection of the owners outfits especially for those worn by the ladies, whose glamorous ball gowns and formal evening wear, would be worn at a glitzy cocktail party, or an elegant reception!

For the gentleman, things are a little more straightforward, invariably requiring only a penguin suit to compliment the extravagance of their partners outfit, never taking the limelight from them.

The portmanteau itself smacked of a long distance journey and in my own minds eye I see a trunk emblazoned with souvenir stickers from exotic locations around the planet, places that catalogue those journeys and places visited and enjoyed by the owner.

So here it is my, fabulous idea, I see a world where the body of the deceased, suitably preserved, obviously, just in case reincarnation is a thing and as we know, nobody knows whether it is or not.

The body is placed inside a beautifully refurbished, or even better a specially made, bespoke portmanteau, internally it will have an extravagant lining of plush velvet, or similar which will neatly cover the interior, an interior which will have compartments for essential items that you may need, mobile phone, radio, any food and drink of choice for sustenance, the possibilities as you see are endless and hark back to those ancient Egyptians who would take some of their treasured possessions into the afterlife.

That's the inside covered, but the outside is also tailormade to the instructions of the imminent inhabitant, so visualise if you will the usually robust exterior being personalised as it is furnished with those souvenir stickers from the favourite places that the occupant has enjoyed spending time in during their stay in the hotel.

We all have our favourite places around the world, locations which fill our heads with those memorable occasions, the great night out, the romantic weekend away, the place you learnt to ski, the resort that you went to each year for twenty years and became an integral part of your life, or the place where you would meet the person who became a friend for life, there are so many examples, too many to cite, but exist they do and the beauty is, that each one that is part of your journey, those places that you have been to and people you have met during your stay in the hotel, they are the ones, it is those fabulous places, it would be those stickers from those places which would adorn your very own personalised trunk, there are thousands of stickers available from all over the planet and they can stimulate a million memories, even helping in their own small way to smooth the grieving process, whether it is you spending your remaining days helping to design your own unique montage, a montage that will decorate your sarcophagus or if not you, your friends and family after your sad demise sat together and recalling times in exotic or even mundane locations that have resonated with you during your stay, the places that you have loved and have played a large or even the smallest part of your story, the life that belonged only to you, shared with a cast of thousands, but ultimately yours.

As we have read, a trunk is not an unusual receptacle for the people of Cavite in the Philippines, though their trunk of choice is a hollowed out tree trunk, yes I also see a trunk as the solution, but I see it being a travel trunk.

Obviously, the trunk is synonymous with long-distance travel and therefore its very essence complements the next part of our journey, a journey to a happy destination, a haven, a heaven a place of sanctuary.

To travel in style on your final journey suitably attired in a prestigious portmanteau, with all of your favourite places adorning the exterior, sounds to me like the perfect way to go.

Chapter 11
Housekeeping

Housekeeping is one of the most important functions in any hotel; without a well-functioning housekeeping department, the grandest or the most bijou hotel would be like a ship without a rudder, they would be functioning but totally without direction.

Housekeeping ensures the cleanliness, maintenance and aesthetic appeal of all rooms and public places within the building, also making sure that the complete estate is as fresh, attractive and as functional as possible to ensure that the daily activities performed in its many diverse locations are able to be enjoyed to their optimum.

Housekeeping is considered to be a behind-the-scenes function, meaning that more often than not, those who work in the department rarely come into contact with the public, being seen and not heard, doing any essential work during those times that they do not impinge on the smooth daily running of the hotel, the original swan on the water if you will, regally gliding across the water but paddling furiously below.

Because their portfolio covers such a large number of services, some of the functions that they perform mean that it is inevitable that some members of the department come into contact with many of the hotel guests during their stay here, instances such as cleaning the bedrooms or public spaces, filling the mini bar, taking away the laundry or providing a turn down service, would all necessitate coming into contact with guests.

The whole department is on standby 24/7 for 365 days a year, think about it, safety, security, privacy, hygiene and sanitation are all fundamental to a sustainable business and indeed a successful hotel.

A more recent development is the awareness of the hotel of its own carbon footprint, the hotel and its overall effect on the environment, taking responsibility for its own obligations to a sustainable future, looking at its very own ecofriendly credentials, with many of the newly arrived guests demanding that the hotel functions in a viable way, for the benefit of not only those guests that are here today, but those arriving tomorrow and in the future.

The climate change agenda is a fairly recent development, but it has rapidly become a global development, it is a new understanding of the way our hotel functions, meaning that all of our lives are changing rapidly making us rethink how we are actually treating this place, the place that we are asking to house not only us of course, those who are currently staying here, but also those future generations, who are yet to arrive.

In 2015 the world community reaffirmed its commitment to sustainable development, the 193 member states through the vehicle of the United Nations pledging to maintain sustained and inclusive economic growth, social inclusion and environmental protection and to do so in both partnership and peace.

This commitment is targeted to 2030 which is rapidly approaching, getting closer by the year, it is based on an understanding that its ambitions are universal, transformative and rights based, an ambitious plan of action for countries, the UN and all other actors. The agenda is a blueprint for eliminating extreme poverty, reducing inequality and protecting the planet.

Instead of being just rhetoric, a talking shop of virtue signalling and good intentions, this is all about taking actions, to improve life for people, sustaining the planet and striving to enhance the prosperity of all people, encouraging us to take transformative steps, bold steps that are needed to shift the world onto a sustainable and resilient path.

There are five core principles in the agreement, all as I say, designed to take everybody forward together and the five principles are as follows:

Universality. All countries irrespective of income levels and development status, to contribute to a comprehensive effort aimed at improving sustainable development. This is applicable in all countries in all contexts and at all times.

Leaving no one behind. The 2030 Agenda seeks to benefit all people and leave nobody behind, doing so by reaching out to all people in need and deprivation, wherever they are, in a manner which targets their specific challenges and vulnerabilities. Doing this generates a demand for local and disaggregated data to analyse outcomes and track progress.

Interconnectedness and indivisibility. The 2030 Agenda rests on the interconnected and indivisible nature of its 17 sustainable development goals

(SDGs), therefore it is crucial that all entities responsible for the implementation of those SDGs treat them in their entirety, instead of using them as a shopping list, picking and choosing the goals that they think are achievable or appeal to them.

Inclusiveness. The 2030 Agenda calls for the participation of all segments of society, irrespective of their race, gender and identity to contribute towards its implementation.

Multi stakeholder partnership. The 2030 Agenda calls for establishing multi stakeholder partnerships for mobilising and sharing knowledge, expertise, technology and financial resources to support the achievement of SDGs in all countries!

They are the five basic aims of the 2030 Agenda, well-intentioned and to all intents and purposes for the greater good, but inevitably as with any organisation or collective, there has to be a leader, whether individual or supranational and that being the case, should we know who or what they are and should we, the people who are paying for the representation should surely have input into the decisions of those representing them.

There is a danger that this type of organisation becomes a little cultish and therefore will not get the buy-in from everybody, which is vital when you are driving a global message.

The ideology which is no doubt admirable has become a little fanatical, with those who don't buy into it one hundred percent being insulted for their views as opposed to being debated with logic and reasoned argument.

Given that there are 193 countries in the United Nations, I sense that because these countries have all signed up to Agenda 2030 then they have individually lost autonomy and are restricted to any actions they may wish to take by restrictions imposed on them by the Agenda 2030.

To a degree, this can even negate the importance of changes in a country's political parties in any those 193 countries, because policy decisions are being made at a far higher level than the simple domestic politics and politicians that used to be responsible for their own countries, with future direction and policy being given by the UN.

The UN really is a fundamental part of our hotel's structure, it has an impact on all of our lives, often doing so while we are blissfully unaware of the decisions that it makes on our behalf. The United Nations was originally established on the 24th of October 1945, after a series of meetings set up to establish the organisation, the original 51 founding members has grown today to its current 193 members, representing almost all of the worlds sovereign states.

Initially, the stated aims of the organisation were to maintain international peace and security, developing friendly relations amongst nations, to achieve international cooperation and being a centre for harmonising the actions of nations.

Don't forget, the formation of the organisation came at a time when World War Two had recently finished and inevitably therefore another of its aims was to prevent future world wars, to this end it has been successful, so much so that by the 1970s the UN budget for economic and social development programmes far outstripped its budget for peacekeeping, the organisation was morphing into an all-encompassing global administrator who saw itself in prime position to take a greater role in the running of our hotel, which considering that 193 out of the world's 195 countries are members, meant it had assumed authority.

Today, world peace is simply one part of the organisation's brief; the UN has further six principle organs:

1. The General Assembly
2. The Security Council
3. The Economic and Social Council
4. The Trusteeship Council
5. The International Court of Justice
6. The UN Secretariat

Each department has incredible responsibility for running its own very specific area of the hotel.

Alongside these important functions, the UN also has several specialised agencies, consisting of funds and programmes doing vital work:

1. The World Bank
2. The World Health Organisation
3. The World Food Programme
4. UNESCO
5. UNICEF

Some you will be aware of and others not so much, but as the world moves forward, I sense that each of these will become more familiar as they take a more active role in all of our lives and each of them hopefully contributing to global societal wellbeing.

When you examine the functions and responsibilities that the UN plays in the housekeeping and running of our hotel, you can see that global society has created a back of house management team to take care of any potential issues that may arise, every base appears to be covered and as we discussed earlier, Agenda 2030 focuses on the way forward for all.

A major part of the 2030 Agenda puts the spotlight on sustainability which has become the focus of the world movement, but we needn't be surprised, because for any hotel worth its salt it is an important part of the business mix and indeed survival and it is to that end that the UN is taking us, but surely it should always have been that way, it is simply that we have been through an era of expediency and flagrant abuse that I sense, if this era is not over then it is rapidly coming to an end.

There have been many reasons for this volte face, for that is how I see it, or if not a total volte face then it is certainly a major change of direction, this is not least of all because of the younger generation, a youth movement, unaccepting of the old ways, a youth movement with its own heroes, figureheads that are leading the assault on old school methods.

Sustainability has become the buzzword for the current generation, however it is a difficult definition to tie down to an absolute interpretation, but if we have to look for one, then it is best interpreted, certainly across the ecofriendly divide, as the capacity to cross the generational impasse to ensure that earths biosphere and human civilisation coexist!

The generational impasse has always existed but I sense we are at a point when it is wider or deeper than ever and maybe that is just an inevitable symptom of progress.

In spite of the impasse and irrespective of which side of it you are on, the focus is ensuring that we all look after the place we live and ensure that the hotel not only remains in great shape, but that we all take responsibility and not only maintain the place but also improve our living space, guaranteeing our own environment and making sure that as custodians we accept our duty and hand it on to future generations in as great shape as we possibly can.

If we are to achieve sustainability, it is going to take a concerted effort, we need global social change, which is difficult to achieve, because people are and become entrenched in their ways, ways which sometimes become anachronistic, they are no longer fit for purpose and need to be changed.

So this means massive change, necessitating radical thinking, which presents a social challenge, involving international and national law as well as urban planning, changing transport systems, managing supply chains differently as well as individual lifestyles all geared to provide us with a form of ethical consumerism, however that is defined.

We have all enjoyed excess to a greater or lesser degree, but inevitably there must be a price to pay for excess and slowly but surely we appear to be realising what that price is, therefore, changes need to happen and quickly, if we are to continue enjoying our stay in the hotel.

New ways of daily living are a must, creating an environment that is conducive to sustainability, re-evaluating the historical economic structures that we have created, focussing on industry, agriculture and architecture, combined with the use of the latest science in order to develop new technologies, such as renewable energy and green technologies.

These new ways of living will bring new opportunities, partially created by the generational change and new generational thinking, it is those new demands that the change will have created, a new industrial revolution if you will, or possibly an industrial revolution lite is needed, with a focus that still serves our insatiable demands for industry, but in a new way, as far away from heavy industry as possible, meaning that is suitable and relevant for the world going forward, greener than it ever was.

But where does the responsibility for change lie, who will drive that change, especially when there are so many vested interests at play and there are still divided opinions on the best way to address change.

Has the debate been won, does every country take responsibility to look after their own part of the world? Because unless we are all pulling in the same direction then just a few well intended groups dotted around the place all doing their own little bit, is futile, simply because it does not stem the inevitable or at least, perceived threat that we face from our abuse of resources and the mess we have created and are creating.

We are currently enjoying, or maybe not enjoying, the emergence of numerous environmental movements across the world, they use non-violent civil disobedience, or at least that is their stated aim, in an effort to compel governments to modify their actions in order to avoid what they believe are the irreversible tipping points in both the climate and ecological systems, tipping points that are bringing us to both social and ecological collapse!

The current climate change and ecological movements are just the latest pressure groups in a long line of special interest groups demanding social, environmental and political change in a world that can sometimes be slow to move and change course, should it be needed.

Every aspect of our lives is a magnet for those with a vested interest, those who are looking for change In their chosen area to be brought about by using pressure in whichever way they deem will be successful for their cause.

Food, environment, culture, animal welfare and abortion are just several examples of areas that are constantly monitored, along with many, many more by special interest groups whose sole purpose is to focus on an agenda that they believe that unless they are monitoring it day to day, that abuses of whichever type may actually occur and those in their minds, their purpose is to stop these happening.

The quality of management of any hotel will determine its success and to this end, the public will vote with their feet, depending on how the management team do their jobs, with the advent of a more proactive clientele, a younger generation who are happy to give their views on every aspect of their stay on any of the review platforms that have emerged during their lifetimes, this process is now so much easier than it ever has been, this generations access to and understanding of the power of social media is at the forefront of every aspect of the debate.

Indeed, at the most recent G20 conference, we have seen different individual domestic governments actually using cool and trendy influencers to help them with getting their message out to their domestic audience and the rest of the world.

On a macro level, we can consider individual governments around the world to be the hotel management teams, in each of those countries and obviously depending on the politics of that country's government, if it exists in a thriving democracy, this means that it can be removed should the public feel that they aren't doing a good job, obviously this isn't relevant to every country, especially those countries where the government is not democratically elected.

The most obvious contender here is China, a country that is a huge global juggernaut and one that is responsible for many of the worlds perceived ills, whether on a human rights or a pollution level, it does however presents its people with a fait accompli, they have no alternative.

The United Nations is an intergovernmental organisation and aims to maintain international peace and security, developing friendly relations amongst its members and to achieve international cooperation, attempting to create a global hotel management, if you will.

The UN was formed in 1945 after World War 2, with the aim of preventing future wars, maintaining international peace and security, protecting human rights and delivering humanitarian aid as well as promoting sustainable development.

All of these things taken individually are a huge job to attempt and if we consider these roles as a collective responsibility, then each is a function of running a successful hotel, all of those things that are needed for the maintenance of a successful business and a smooth running operation.

Having looked a little deeper at the roles fulfilled by the UN, in the absence of any real competition for the position, the big question we have to consider is whether the UN is important or impotent, indeed, is it possible for one organisation to unite the one hundred and ninety-five countries we have on our planet, each one can be seen and must be treated like an individual guest in our hotel, because each country has their individual needs and demands, culture, heritage, politics, so as an organisation with all of its stated aims firmly entrenched, the UN has a difficult if not impossible job in pleasing everybody.

If you consider the hundred an ninety-five nations on the planet, as individual guests of which one hundred and ninety-three are full UN members, the other two, the Vatican City and Palestine are non-members but both are included in UN document observance.

Put simply, the Pope as head of the Vatican City, chooses not to get involved directly in international politics and Palestine is considered to be at war with Israel so will not be allowed full membership until a peaceful solution is found.

So, of the 195 countries in the world, all of them are signed up to the one organisation designed to manage the place as successfully as possible, so from a point of view of good intentions, we couldn't ask for a greater buy-in, the organisation is all-inclusive and every country has representation.

Think of the job of satiating the individual needs of all of those countries, I am sure like me, you have struggled to get consensus on which wine to have with dinner, when dining with friends on a night out, especially if a couple of them like red, others may prefer white and of course there may be a couple who are non-drinkers. That sounds difficult enough to organise, so multiply the situation times twenty and think about trying to get agreement of a single position, or a way forward when trying to corral one hundred and ninety-three opinions at the same time in order to decide a global policy on climate change or a strategy for world peace, it is at these times that global democracy takes its place at the table.

Inevitably, there are criticisms of the UN, most notably by two recent presidents of the USA each observing how difficult it is to find a single solution to any problem, which shouldn't come as a major surprise.

There is a quote which is attributed to George W Bush, 'Free nations will not allow the UN to fade into history as an ineffective, irrelative debating society'; offering support to the UN and acknowledging the difficult job it has. Conversely, Obama said, 'Divisions within the security council continued to hamstring the UN's ability to tackle problems'; he was directly referring to different transgressions that the UN was reluctant to get involved in, but was compelled to. Obama realised that the demands from every vested interest in every decision that the UN became involved with, meant that it was effectively, ineffective, a sclerotic impediment to potential progress as it was tasked with making everybody happy.

There have always been and always will be many calls for reform of the UN since its founding, but very little consensus on how to do so, but reasonably there are only two alternatives for change, giving us two camps for a way forward, you either have some of the critics, those countries wanting the UN to take a more effective role, while other countries preferring a reduced role, a less intrusive position, and simply restricting its role to acting within humanitarian affairs.

The institution has had more than its fair share of controversy since its inception, with accusations of not only inefficiency within the organisation but also of corruption too.

It is a fact that the job is a difficult one to fulfil, the general manager of the hotel, but as long as the UN exists in its current form it is the only solution we have for what is undoubtedly a role that needs to be filled, a case of, in the land of the blind, the one eyed man is king.

The UN has no direct competition for its global role and the only challenges to it comes from those individual countries that make up the individual membership.

It may sound like an old claim, but if the UN is seriously looking to administer the running of the planet, then as a talking shop for each of the individual member countries to come together, it becomes incumbent on each of those countries not only to be responsible for its individual destiny, but for the organisation as a whole.

The demands of the population of any country are understandably not very different wherever you go, you have a population, a variable number of people who all experience the same things, within reason, throughout their lives, put simply they are all born all live and all die, in between they need education, a health service and all of the infrastructure put in place to service the needs of a functioning society, the major difference that can occur is the political interpretation of how all of these things are provided and administered by a government, elected or unelected to whom the people of that country rely on for direction in their individual lives and for the greater good of that country.

That sounds quite straightforward in itself but as we have discovered the individuality of the peoples of the world when represented by a national identity presents itself to have a cultural identity all of its own.

As we have developed our structured societies within the hotel, we have learnt how to develop individual political philosophies in such a way that irrespective of their philosophical values and beliefs, whether political, monarchist or theological, we have managed to find a way that we can establish in each of those countries whichever their chosen path, different ways of looking after and controlling their populations and we find a wide variation of styles in implementing the regime, inevitably because the demands of population are universal, there are many crossovers in implementation, presenting many common characteristics amongst those styles.

It is important to look at those different types in order to see how this hotel is being managed, the positives and negatives of the systems we have established and whether we have inadvertently discovered a perfect system.

The type of government a country has is usually identified by the type of authority that the government has and uses in order to rule the country, the mandate, if its people are allowed to give one, that it has from its people, to assert its authority and run the country.

Whether it's an autocracy, which is where we see power being in the hands of one single person taking sole responsibility for not only the legislation of that country, but the executive and the judiciary and ultimately making government policy.

Secondly, there is an aristocracy, which sees the government powers rested in the hands of a small number of people, we can see them as a privileged ruling class, more often than not a monarchy, where the reigning monarch is seen as nothing more than a figurehead, a cosmetic seat of power representing the country on the global stage, with little or no power.

Thirdly, we have a very common form of hotel management, certainly the most common form in Europe and the one that we live in here in the United Kingdom and that is a democracy, which is a system of government where the citizens of the country exercise their power by voting for the government it deems suitable.

But even this can be diluted and when it is it presents us with two very different types of the same thing, you can either have a direct democracy, this is where the citizens of a country vote on each individual issue or secondly a representative democracy, where citizens elect representatives from amongst themselves, the elected representatives meet in order to represent the views of the majority and the rights of the minority are protected by limits placed on the government and certain individual rights enjoyed by everybody.

It is often considered that the direct democracy is the purer example of the two, but there are few examples of a successful country practicing this form of government within the hotel, the most internationally renowned and successful practitioner of the form is of course Switzerland, which is known equally for its form of government as its folding army knives, yodelling or fabulous chocolate, the country is held in high regard throughout the world as a beautiful, successful, peace loving country, so it is worth taking a brief look at a country often considered to be getting many of the big calls right on the way to manage their internal affairs.

Swiss neutrality is a staple of the country's foreign policy, meaning it will not get in armed or political conflicts between other states, a policy designed to guarantee external security and to promote peace.

The country has a diverse culture and international community, with four official languages, it is a jewel in the heart of Europe renowned for its natural beauty a paradise for hikers or winter sport enthusiasts, incredible flora and fauna, with a natural environment that is protected, the country has lower greenhouse gas emissions than many of the OECD countries, it has a robust recycling system and has pledged to be climate neutral by 2050.

There is so much to like about the Swiss way of life, but inevitably, nothing is perfect and so to that end, let's take a look at criticisms or at least perceived criticisms of the direct democracy model and if not criticisms of the model, then certainly the way that Switzerland choose to implement it which, because of the nature of the Swiss people, is obviously specific to them and their culture.

The criticisms as such are as follows, firstly, Switzerland is such an incredibly expensive country to live in, which if you've ever been to the country, you will know is true for the casual tourist, it is pricey place to spend a few days, absolutely beautiful but expensive.

Maybe, as if to complement the extravagance of the place, is the fact that it is virtually always near the top of the list of the best places in the world in which to live, it is currently in fifth position in that particular table.

Another criticism is that while it is easy to appreciate both the organisation and pragmatism of Swiss society, it is notoriously difficult for outsiders to feel welcomed into its bosom, the sense is that the people are polite, yet quite reserved, in the workplace surnames are used unless invited to use a Christian name by the owner.

As if to reinforce the rigidity of Swiss society, the newly arrived resident can feel like something of an interloper, this is manifested by the recent report citing that 62% of expats living in the country felt it difficult to make Swiss friends, the average across the world is 36% so there is a noticeable difference and it is believed that most Swiss people prefer to stick to their close circle of friends and because they are great respecters of personal privacy, it could be a long time before a newly arrived person is invited into an existing bunch of friends.

Swiss culture is notoriously slow to change, woman's rights, same sex marriage, the gender pay gap and LGBTQ+ rights have taken longer to achieve in Switzerland than its progressive European neighbours, the slow implementation of these cool and trendy values, of moving with a changing world, is seen as a reluctance for a country that we would consider to have traditional values, not to be guilt tripped by its neighbours and subtly forced to change their way of life.

The slow change, those ancient traditions and the stuffed-shirted-ness of the Swiss people could be a symptom of direct democracy or it could simply be a symptom of being Swiss, it is hard to know or come up with a definitive answer.

As Switzerland is such an outlier amongst its European neighbours and as we are looking at housekeeping, I thought it a good idea to analyse a country that implements direct democracy as a way to manage the hotel.

The alternative to direct democracy as we know is representative democracy, which as I mentioned earlier is a far more common example of the democracy genre, so let's have a look at what it offers to the would be hotel proprietor.

I live in a representative democracy and therefore I am as indoctrinated into believing that it is as fabulous form of government as I would be if I were living under the communist regime of China, but as a form of hotel management let's have a look at what the direct democracy offers to its guests.

Quite simply representative democracy is the system where elected persons represent a group of persons known as their electorate and those elected people sit in a parliament and make decisions on behalf of their electorate without consultation on every voting decision they make.

Interestingly and possibly unsurprisingly, the first time that a representative democracy appeared in the hotel was during the times of the fabulous Roman Republic, it was this early Roman model of government that I sense inspired many political thinkers, so much so that modern democracies imitate the Roman model, with supreme power resting with the people, their elected representatives and their nominated leader, how incisive were the Romans and the society they created, they really were ahead of the curve.

Watching a representative democracy work close up is easy, I live in one, it is easy to see both the positive and negative sides of the structure, but as usual, when you are too close to something, to anything, it is difficult to be objective about it.

So it is important to research independent views in order to gain an understanding of the benefits of a representative democracy.

Most importantly, I would suggest is the fact that the people have a say in their representation and ultimately their government, which has to be a crucial part of the equation, meaning that the people have a voice and if their chosen representative isn't up to the task or not successfully representing those views then the people will speak and they have the opportunity to change their elected member.

Decision making is simplified as the whole of the country doesn't have to be canvassed in order to reach a decision, their elected representative reducing this potentially time consuming process and this allows the country to function more smoothly, making it an efficient form of government.

Obviously, there are negatives too, mainly that the votes of the elected representative once in parliament doesn't always reflect the will of the people, indeed it is impossible to represent the views of 100% of them, which is both understandable because it is indeed flawed, because a single person representing their constituents wishes cannot satisfy every opinion in that constituency and the representative is not bound by law to represent the majority thinking of their constituents.

Unless there is a fixed term limit to the representatives tenure, then it can be difficult to oust a sitting representative if his electorate become dissatisfied with their performance.

Finally, there is a sense that the system can invite corruption, with candidates misrepresenting their real views simply to attain power and once in office the representative can then lend their votes to any willing buyer.

In conclusion, a representative democracy should result in government created by the people for the people, but for that to function perfectly, it takes the voter to have freedom to express their wishes to their representatives and the willingness of the representative to act accordingly!

Not as common as the representative democracy, we have the republic where the governing of a country is considered to be a public matter, with all offices of state voted for directly and all people share in the ruling of the country.

The most obvious thing about the republic is that it doesn't have a monarch and in the absence of such the head of the country is a president.

We can take a cursory glance at the USA to see how a modern republic works, there is a lot to admire but a republic also has its faults, reinforcing the point that when looking for the perfect way to run the hotel, you could borrow parts from each of the options we have created.

The positives of the republic are geared to society, its structure and the infrastructure that it provides for the benefit of a smooth running of the society, it is felt that as it provides the opportunity for citizens to participate in government that a sense of publicly beneficial civic virtues develop within that community, this leads to a society that values honesty, decency, responsibility and patriotism, which when focused correctly can really benefit that society.

The republic tends to be a many layered system of government, with administration and responsibility for the functioning of the country having possibly too many decision makers in the system, yes, offering checks and balances, but these multi layers could actually be the Achilles heel of the system.

Political decisions become weaker when power is dispersed through many levels, such as executives, courts and legislatures, instead of acting in unison they tend to operate with self-interest, conflicting with each other rather than assisting each other, inhibiting progress.

All in all, a decent option when considering hotel management but there is one further option to consider, which is federalism. Federalism is a system in which on democratic principles, power is shared between national and regional governments, which combine with each other to create the federation.

So at the hub there is the main national government which is elected democratically with the regional or provincial governments which are also democratically elected, between them sharing the job of administering the hotel and the way it runs.

The balance of power is different amongst those countries that prefer a federalist government, with either the central government or the regional governments holding the majority of power.

Interestingly, the EU could be seen as the ultimate federal state, with powers sitting with the European Union but also the individual countries within the federation being empowered to run with a degree of independence.

You will have your own thoughts on whether the EU is a good or bad thing, but knowing how the model works will inform your opinion, you could see it as either empowering for countries or restrictive as it takes away controls, individuality or borders.

It is a difficult conversation and we have seen in the UK how political, indeed how toxic the debate can become and in our search for the definitive version of running the hotel, federalism certainly has something to offer.

We can dilute the types of government analysis a little further, simply to explore other systems out there and not limit our understanding to what we already know, yes I do realise that this book wasn't meant to be about governments of the world, but in order to realise the strength of the parallel of our stay here being just like a stay in a hotel, it is nice to acknowledge that the hotel has a management structure that is designed to look after the guests, a management team as temporary as the guests themselves, but continuous and evolving.

Therefore, let's take a look beyond those most common types of government and consider the socioeconomic structures and ideologies used by countries and how their government works within the structure, a structure that they use in order to maintain social cohesion, their countries identity, its culture and a stay in the hotel that works for the people in their care.

There are a number of socioeconomic structures but the most commonly used are capitalism, communism and socialism, and I think by briefly outlining each of the three, that we get an insight into managing the hotel or in this case the countries that have chosen each one, as a viable proposition!

Capitalism is the financial system that we are living with currently, in our western democracies, it is a system where the trade and industry of the country is in the hands of private ownership operating simply with the purpose of making a profit, the success or otherwise of the individual business is determined by supply and demand and that simple equation will determine the success of the business concerned, but the essential feature is the desire and need to be profitable for survival.

We have many examples of successful businesses within our own country, businesses that have traded successfully for many years and have evolved through great change in technology, product development and legislation which all contribute to threaten the success of any business, unless it remains suitably flexible to adapt to any change that comes its way.

The changing nature of the world and the way the world is becoming a globalised entity means that the hotel is becoming more monolithic than it ever has been, which can present advantages, such as economy of scale to any business, but the individual demands change from country to country, thus presenting a downside to the capitalist dream.

A byproduct of a successful business is employment of others and thus helping society to thrive, so it is for the good of society that capitalists exist.

Communism however is a totally different proposition to capitalism, in fact it is the polar opposite, it is a far left socio, political and economic ideology acting within the socialist movement, with a goal of establishing a communist society.

Basically, that means a society which is centred around common ownership of the means of production of everything, therefore everybody in that society shares in every part of that society, allocating products to every member of that society, through commune or the communist party, with production being for actual use and not simply for profit.

In a communist society, there is an absence of private property, social class and the state as an institution. The economy itself is a planned economy which directs the production and distribution of goods and services, with each person contributing to and benefiting from that economy by their ability to contribute and their needs from it, what's not to like?

However, there are pros and cons, on the positive side there are several benefits to this system, with everybody getting the same chance of a successful life, nobody is inheriting property or wealth, therefore they have the opportunity to be successful purely based on their own talents.

Almost everybody is employed, which is a positive for mental wellbeing and for reducing crime rates and as the system asks each to contribute to the society as they are able, no role in society has greater value than another, reinforcing the idea of true human equality.

Almost everybody is educated, for within a structure that has the aim of improving that society then education becomes a vital tool for advancement, just about everyone in a communist society is offered the opportunity to seek out an advanced degree.

Finally, another major positive of the communist society is that both agriculture and manufacturing have an emphasis on their ability to make a huge contribution to society.

As well as contributing to the GDP of the country, more importantly than this is the fact that they provide for the people's needs while using the fewest resources, building up the infrastructure for these sectors means that innovation in other areas is encouraged as there is no need for higher yields and cheaper products to stay competitive!

Those things all sound really positive, so what, if any are the negatives, as with most things, whether positive or negative they are subjective but let's look at the perceived flaws.

Firstly, the government owns everything, whether it is property, businesses and production means, the free market is eliminated from society, there are no laws of supply and demand to set prices for consumers to pay and because of this, planners lose the information necessary for the production cycle.

Because there is no feedback, there can be a tendency to either underproduce or overproduce products because it is ill informed about customer sentiment.

Secondly, there is no freedom of speech in a typical communist country, when individual needs are forsaken for the good of society as a whole, the demands of an individual can suffer.

By suppressing the individual, those in power can retain it, so freedom of the press is sacrificed too, which is not particularly healthy.

In the words of a well-known advocate of the communist model, Karl Marx, 'Censorship is a tool that the powerful use to oppress the powerless'; in spite of this, Marx was a fan!

Diversity isn't encouraged or indeed desirable, that is simply because, when individual needs mean that society needs to be more flexible in order to accommodate different cultural demands then diversity cannot be encouraged as it will be seen as nothing more than a disruptor.

Efficiency and productivity very often suffer as there is little motivation to stretch, because effectively there is no consequence of doing so, either positive or negative.

There is no need for entrepreneurs because the production cycle operates irrespective of their absence or existence, as long as it is fulfilling domestic demands, then that is sufficient, which is rather stifling for any potential innovation or aspirational communist youth.

There are strict rules in place governing the structure of the classless society, the same amount of finding is given to each sector, there is no hierarchy of importance, farmers and administrative workers receiving the same, which can cause problems in certain societal segments whose work may or may not be more demanding!

Another negative view to consider is the lack of opposition to the communist government, there is no other opinion, no counter position to challenge the government narrative.

The goal of a communist government is to hold onto power by any means necessary, as the government controls all levers of society, they can distribute propaganda through the media, which it obviously controls, measuring the performance of any controls they have put in place and cracking down on any dissent, that is if any dissenters dare to raise their objections.

People are asked to survive on the bare minimum in communist countries and saving money is not allowed, any surplus income you may earn is taken off you once you've reached your allowable limit and it is then redistributed, society is everything and individuality is unimportant, you are a cog in the machine, it is the machine that is important, not the cog.

In conclusion, I think the idea of community ownership, working for the mutual benefit of others and having control over the outcomes that can be possible in life means that it is possible for the model to outperform capitalism.

The only problem here is that if those in positions of power go rogue and are untrustworthy, it is impossible to change them, this is a major flaw.

The advantages and disadvantages of communism show us that it can be a dangerous form of government because it is inflexible, it has an invasive implementation process, which may provide individual benefits, but can harm more than it helps, lacking compassion for the individual needs.

Finally, we look at socialism, which although it is the final one of the three types of socio economic system for us to consider, this one is the most popular amongst those currently available for our consideration.

Socialism is a system in which workers democratically and socially own the means of production, public services are commonly, collectively and state owned, with the likes of education and healthcare being prime examples.

In our world, socialism has become the antithesis of capitalism and it is those two concepts that have become the most common, with many socialists seeing socialism as state capitalism an assertion that could be true and if so, it could be considered to be a hybrid of the two systems. Socialism has many perceived positives from the reduction of relative poverty, due to a welfare state and a basic minimum income for those who are unable to work, through illness, and those who are unemployed, maintaining a basic standard of living.

Free healthcare, which of course isn't free, but is provided free at the point of need to whoever needs it. As I say, it isn't free because it needs paying for, but not as a direct cost to the individual needing it, but the cost is absorbed by the many, that is socialism in a nutshell.

By improving a nation's health, there is an indirect contribution to the country's productivity and in the longer term, higher economic growth and a more cohesive society.

The cohesion brought about by the nation's health and an equality of opportunity and reduced inequality, if people feel they have a fair stake in society, it creates harmony and employees more committed to the success of the business.

Because socialism chases not simply a profit, but a common good and social cohesion, advocates will tell you that casualties of the capitalist dream can fall by the wayside in a survival of the fittest regime, which is the antithesis of a socialists dream.

Companies are run for the benefit in the public interest and not for the interests of shareholders, industries such as power or railways have externalities which are ignored in privately owned companies whereas public ownership allows those industries to plan for long-term investment, low prices for consumers and improved safety, which are forsaken to a degree when annual profit is the goal!

So they are the positives, but let's take a look at the negatives as we must, which basically are geared to one fundamental flaw, being a lack of incentive or motivation for those inclined to with to do so.

Whether that lack of motivation comes from a progressively increasing tax rate, which negates an individual's ambition, or indeed from too high tax rates, which may force successful individuals to take their businesses to countries that are offering reduced tax bills.

The welfare state too can cause disincentives, if it is too generous, it can become a reason not to work, it was designed to be a safety net and not a hammock, but if benefits for individuals are seen as being sufficient then for some people they may choose not to work, reducing the workforce and thus harming individual ambition.

Unions tend to flourish in a socialist country and socialist policies are geared towards strengthening them, which can lead to an us and them environment and inevitably to labour market antagonism, leading to strikes and an unproductive society.

There are other failings but as I pointed out initially, all are geared to a dumbing down of striving, positive attitude, or naked ambition, when all of your needs are catered for it can certainly dull the desire to work harder and appear attractive to unambitious people, which has to be a major flaw.

In every culture, there will always be lazy people, always be those who are happy to leave it to others to get on with creating a more successful world, it depends on your personal view on whether this should have a consequence or not as to your personal politics.

So basically, these are the most common types of regimes that we have developed over centuries that are designed to enable us to manage the hotel, politics and the political world is omnipresent throughout the hotel, from individual countries to global decisions.

George Orwell said, 'In our age, there is no such thing as keeping out of politics, all issues are political issues and politics itself is a mass of lies, evasions, folly and schizophrenia.'

Those words always hold true and it is because politics is such a fertile and attractive arena for people to be involved in, that it attracts so many people to it, at all levels, whether by joining a political party and standing for election or by either forming or joining one of the many groups of special interest activists around the world, currently we are experiencing a plethora of climate change activist groups, protesting at every opportunity and attempting to influence politicians sufficiently to alter the course of human life, convinced that they are doing good, they are hoping to extend our stay here by their actions.

Irrespective of whether you believe in their cause, their desire to influence the future by their actions and unity must be respected and shows what is possible, when you focus and apply yourself.

It is believed to be the American journalist, Paul Begala, who quoted, 'Politics as show business for ugly people', with the narcissism of politicians being worse than that of celebrities of both stage and screen.

Maybe it is the scent of power that drives them, but then it was the well-respected Henry Kissinger, the German-born American politician and diplomat, who described 'power as the ultimate aphrodisiac'; apparently, he was known for seduction and as a ladies man. Henry put his incredible success down to the lofty positions he held in the geopolitical world, hence when asked he offered the immortal line, which will resonate with generations both past and future.

With the advent of television combined with the current trends incredible growth of Twitter, now called X, YouTube, Instagram, and TikTok, politicians have become media personalities, they are celebrities in their own world, indeed they have transitioned from simply being political to becoming media stars, in the UK we have even just experienced a failed government health minister coming third on a TV reality show.

I think back to a major participant in the political pond, Karl Marx who amongst many things was a German political theorist who had an enormous influence on the global intellectual, economic and political history.

His critical theories about society, economics and politics were so perceptive that his name has become synonymous with social theory, indeed Marxism has become a global school of thought, with variations available globally.

The point here is that one resident although he was only a guest, just like you and I, similarly enjoying a stay as temporary as the rest of us, can have such an impact on the place while they are here, Marx was truly impressive in what he achieved.

When you realise how hard life is when actually living it day to day, it makes it even more incredible that somebody can have such an impact while having such a relatively brief stay, well-done to him, but he is only one of many individuals who deserve our respect for the way they have used their brief stay in the hotel and have made such a tremendous impact!

In terms of housekeeping we must realise that some guests are more demanding than others and it is the function of a good housekeeping department to keep all of the residents of the hotel happy, irrespective of their individual demands and the foibles of us all as individuals.

So how can we determine whether or not our demands are being met, it is important for us to establish whether housekeeping are doing their job and believe it or not, there is a way to establish the point, so in order to do so, we have our old favourite, the United Nations to thank for work that they have done and that is their esteemed World Happiness Report.

The World Happiness Report is an attempt to survey all of the individual nations of the world and trying to establish their levels of happiness based on their own lives, with the report in which it correlates various categories of quality of life factors that give them a 'league table' of happiness. Each report is available to be downloaded from the World Happiness Report website.

The first report was published just over ten years ago in 2012 and for contributors and respondents, the Cantril Ladder system of measuring happiness is used. The Cantril Ladder is an interesting system being a system where the user imagines a conventional ladder with the rungs numbered from zero at the bottom to ten at the top, with the top of the ladder being how you would envisage your best possible life would be and the bottom corresponds to how you imagine the unthinkable, being your worst possible life would be.

The user then fills in the questionnaire applying the number between ten and zero which they feel represents how they feel currently and where they stand on the imaginary ladder and it is this that is known as the Cantril Ladder. This then leads to the Cantril Ladder future, which is the step the user either feels, hopes, or indeed wishes that they will be standing on, five years from now.

Whether the Cantril Ladder is of value or not, or even whether we consider that the report gives us a true indication of the happiness levels throughout the hotel, that is not the point, it is indicative of happiness, such that we understand its meaning to be and it is that measure that provides us with an insight into the parts of our hotel that are providing its residents with both a happy and enjoyable stay?

The UN are doing a good job in striving to look at how we are enjoying our stay, whether we are getting as much out of the experience as possible especially when comparing ourselves to those other guests who are staying in different parts of the hotel, who are going through exactly the same process as ourselves.

Of course, it is impossible to have a definitive answer with this kind of thing, because people's expectations and experiences can be so different, even when two people are staying in exactly the same place, whether it's the same country or even the same hotel or maybe even the same restaurant, people can have the same experience but interpret them differently.

You probably know as well as I do, that you and I could go out for a meal to the same restaurant, you may have a fabulous time whereas I could come away disappointed, but in this case and as a guide to the way the population of a country feels, the Cantril Ladder is currently the best guide that we have.

The most recent report was completed in 2021 and bear in mind that this survey was carried out during the Covid pandemic so naturally people's levels of enthusiasm for anything will have been tempered by the global effects of Coronavirus, people had been living a new normal life for over 12 months and therefore the results may be a bit skewed.

However, the pandemic was a global issue and therefore it effected every country, so from that point of view it does make it could be a great leveller, but irrespective of those circumstances, it still makes for interesting reading.

The 2021 World Happiness report couldn't ignore its effects and so it set its aims at looking at the effects of Covid 19 and how the people of the world, that's you and me, the guests currently staying in the hotel, have fared, focussing on the effects of Covid on the structure and quality of people's lives and to then evaluate how governments around the world had dealt with the pandemic, inevitably each country had autonomy for its response to Coronavirus and so the responses were very different, and having considered responses it looked at why some countries handled the pandemic better than others.

People are inevitably drawn to see where their own country appears in the rankings contained in the report, but not just that, they are also intrigued to know if there is a pattern and if so, what the secret of life is in those countries that are ranked at the top of the ladder.

The survey is consistent in the questions it asks each of the contributors in each country in order to achieve a report that is not skewed in any way by either unfair or loaded questions, which could be designed to achieve a desired result.

Since inception to its most recent incarnation, the report which is now in its ninth year is starting to establish certain factors, certain consistencies that appear to make for a happy life as long as certain criteria are met, these are identified as environmental drivers and it is these that determine happiness levels, a throwback, if you will, to Maslow's Hierarchy of Needs!

The latest report showed us that the same in common with earlier years, the same environmental drivers as previous years had driven the happiness of people this year, wherever they may be. So let us take a closer look at those drivers of human happiness, possibly unsurprisingly they are health, which is fundamental to life, trust and more importantly, being able to trust and depend on others, generosity, whether personal or from others, not necessarily financially, but also of time, giving your time to help others can be equally as important as any financial contribution can ever be, somebody to count on when needed, that could possibly a partner, but family are crucially important too, income is probably self-explanatory and finally freedom, which can be interpreted in many ways.

People continued to feel happier when they had good health, sufficient money and someone to count on and whenever needed, they experienced both trust and generosity from others, it combined to mean that seductive cocktail gave them the freedom to make life decisions, safe in the knowledge that they would be unimpaired by negative demands that could disturb their happiness.

What is incredible is that the Nordic nations that appear to be the happiest places on Earth and the happiest parts of the hotel that we are all staying in.

The glory goes to Finland for the fourth consecutive year that country appears in pole position as the happiest place to live in the world, closely followed by Denmark, Switzerland, Iceland and then the Netherlands!

So is it possible to discover what it is that makes fabulous Finland such a great place to be and indeed if it is that good, shouldn't we all move there to enjoy our own version of the 1946 Frank Capra classic, *It's a Wonderful Life*, where we could all optimise our enjoyment of staying in the hotel and if we did all up-sticks and head to Finland, would the Nordic heaven, become a Nordic hell and overnight would it become the worst place to live, due to overcrowding.

Who knows, but certainly when a country is consistently held in such high regard by its people then they must be doing something right, so let's take a closer look at the paradise that is Finland.

The Nordic country has a relatively small population of just five and a half million people, with the Finns considered to have one of the happiest lifestyles in the world, to that end and to confirm this, the population has voted accordingly.

The Finnish lifestyle consists of a massive connection with nature, mainly due to the landscape of the country, one that the Finns enjoy to the maximum, taking every opportunity to embrace it.

A close connection with nature is in itself thought to be vital for mental wellbeing, but combine this with easy access to the great outdoors, then life is good, enabling this lifestyle is the fact that ninety per cent of the country is covered in either forest or water, providing an idyllic environment to both live and raise a family.

The Finnish people contributing to the report, submitting their opinions have also asserted their implicit trust in their own government, which is a parliamentary government and a republic, trusting them to help them not just in the good times, but significantly their trust during a global pandemic strengthened, expecting their political masters to do their best for them and manage the country through what was a global crisis.

Having given them close scrutiny, it would appear that when looking at the crime numbers in Finland that levels of crimes are low, especially when compared to major comparative economies of the world, but I honestly believe that therein lies the real issue.

I couldn't imagine the mafia or South American drug cartels setting up in downtown Helsinki, because quite simply, the population size of the country wouldn't justify the criminal business model setting up there.

So maybe the places that the Happiness Report highlights as great and happy places to live are that way because of location and population size. Is it fair to have the same expectations of a city the size of London with a population of nine million and compare it to a country the size of the idyll that is Finland? I would suggest not. The Happiness Report no doubt serves a purpose but surely for objective truth, it is nothing more than whimsical.

As luck would have it, a good friend of mine, David, moved to Finland several years ago to live with his two young sons and Finnish wife; moving there from Chester, which is a famous 'Roman' city in the northwest of the United Kingdom, with a population of approximately 100,000. David and his family left Chester to live in a small Finnish town called Savonlinna, found in the southeast of Finland, with a population of approximately 35,000 people.

So who is better placed to ask about life in fabulous Finland than a man who has moved to the place that is the happiest place to live in the whole of the hotel.

I thought it would be interesting to get David's feelings of his new homeland in comparison to the country he had left behind and how his new life compared to the one that he had once had and that he had enjoyed, here in the UK and whether the Happiness Report resonated with him.

I discussed this with David and it was interesting to hear what he had to say and how he felt his new life with his family, his wife and boys aged seven and ten years of age, compared to what he had known in the UK both as a child, going through the English schooling system and then as a grown man, watching his own children growing up in a different country and able to compare the experiences.

Childhood is especially precious, preparing you for the life ahead and therefore watching his own children grow up in a part of the hotel that was thought to be the happiest place in the world was surely an investment in their futures.

David told me that the main difference he had found between the UK and Finland was that the work-life balance in that country is encouraged to be evaluated on an individual basis, encouraging people to take personal responsibility, meaning that it is equally important for mental wellbeing and physical wellbeing and to focus on those things as your life outside work is just as important as it is inside work.

Maintaining a healthy work-life balance is as beneficial for the individual as it is for their relationships, both with the company as well as their friends and family.

Companies that gain a reputation for work-life balance gain an excellent reputation and an attractive proposition as an employer, which is beneficial when you consider the difficulty many businesses have in recruitment and retention of good staff.

The Oxford Economic Forum suggest it takes 28 weeks and at least £30,000 to recruit and bring a new employee up to speed, whereas if your employees are happy, the investment in their wellbeing justifies any time invested in their lives.

Money is not seen as the most important driver of a person's life, but a happy balanced life with quality time being equally as important in the equation as success in their career.

I think we have all seen since the Covid lockdowns that people across the world aren't in any sort of rush to go back to their old work practices, we are now finding that working from home is seen as the new normal, certainly by employees and a four day week is not controversial, these things are changing working patterns and employee expectations forever, which is fine, as long as productivity and ultimately the business does not suffer.

So work-life balance is a huge factor that my friend David has noticed as being a major difference between the two countries, since arriving in Finland, having enjoyed those halcyon days spent in Chester growing up and starting his working life, but wait, there is even more to his new homeland to applaud and admire.

Finland and its people have an appreciation for their human rights, the things that we consider as fundamental freedoms that everybody is entitled to, these rights are many and varied, ranging from and including freedom of speech, freedom of movement, equality for men, women and transgender people, there are also constitutional rights to consider as they too are important, detailing the government's role in our lives, what authority they have and what they can and cannot expect of us as citizens.

With rights come responsibilities and there is a trade-off in what you expect your government to do for you, then they can expect a civil society where its citizens expect to play their part.

Let's take a brief look at how David and his family spend their downtime; the social side of their lives is very different in Finland, starting with the fact that most families, including David a family, have a sauna as a part of their home, you could possibly see it as the equivalent of a home swimming pool in Australia, but along with the sauna, many people also have a summer cottage, often in a rural or outback type location, in the middle of nowhere, here their time is spent, either chilling or enjoying a more rural, what sounds like an idyllic, hunting, shooting, fishing, back to nature type existence.

In the summer, it is not unusual for the country to shut down for a full four weeks, while the population recharges itself, it is during this break, that the population spends time enjoying life maybe going away to their country retreat, that's if they are fortunate enough to have one and it is during this time that the people gain a sense of wellness, possibly even a togetherness, reinforcing their family values, as they take time out just before heading into their usually harsh climate in the winter months, a time in which the country and its weather conditions can become quite severe in extreme locations as the winter blanket falls and a snow covered country, although aesthetically pleasing, indeed beautiful to look at, can also become a logistical nightmare, causing problems for many people in the country.

Incredibly, during those four weeks of the summer shut down, it is calculated that approximately ninety per cent of the country takes the same four weeks period off at the same time, enhancing the feeling of togetherness that is a vital contributing factor to their happiness.

I imagine the other ten per cent are working within the industries that keep the country ticking over during this period, no doubt they will too get a break when appropriate.

Crime is low in Finland and as if to reflect this, bicycle theft is the most common crime against households and individuals, the low crime numbers may be a consequence of only water buckets and hot coals from saunas to purloin, fortunately for the Finns, violent crime is low as are domestic and commercial burglaries.

Maybe it is because pay differentials throughout the country aren't huge, therefore the gap between those earning the most and those earning the least is narrower than in most comparative countries.

Wages across the country are high, but then again taxes also are relatively high and while unemployment is low across the country, indeed to retain the low unemployment numbers the government provides incentive schemes for companies to retrain employees, refreshingly with these schemes age is no barrier to the retraining of employees, inevitably this gives both hope and purpose to those who may be feeling that a premature retirement is being thrust upon them by their age, or even by technology.

As with most western countries immigration is currently a big issue and will no doubt become a an even bigger issue, as the decade progresses, currently there are an estimated 89 million, refugees, asylum seekers, economic migrants or just displaced people on the move currently within the hotel, people looking to change their rooms, because they are unhappy with the room they are using at the moment.

89 million is a large number and of course the people on the move are looking to relocate to somewhere better, somewhere where they can take advantage of all that is available to them in order to optimise their stay here and no doubt, they want to contribute to a society that values them and will allow them to contribute to, so why wouldn't a migrant go straight to, the country that finds itself at the top of the happiness table.

Immigration is a big issue in Finland or as big as it can be in a country that has what we would consider to be a relatively small population of five and a half million people, however, in line with its values, those who do want to do so are encouraged to emigrate to Finland.

Unsurprisingly, the new arrivals are welcomed with open arms, however unlike many other countries, these people are encouraged to integrate fully into the country and with its people, this is done by providing language training and also with cultural integration schemes which are perceived as beneficial to both immigrant and indigenous people and seen as vital by the Finnish government, more a case of the country being one that is multiracial and not just multicultural, there is a subtle difference.

Multiracial means that the country welcomes people from any country as long as they wish to help Finland and to that end new arrivals will be helped by the Finnish people, a perfect symbiotic relationship, with both parties benefiting.

Multiculturalism is a nice idea and probably works well in EPCOT, the theme park in Florida, but in the real world it can cause problems when people want to leave their country of origin but bring with them the culture and the values of the country they are leaving behind.

This can inhibit integration into their new host country and cause problems not only for those who have recently arrived, but for those they are asking to welcome them, whose own culture becomes diluted by people happy to be there but not wanting to integrate.

Immigration controlled and suitably integrated can be a huge benefit to any country and the example of Finland and how it is choosing to take advantage of the benefits are there for all to see.

In common with many countries in the west, birth rates are reducing and people are living longer meaning that the country has an ageing population this realisation has led them to encouraging immigration, stressing the benefits to both parties, obviously to the country which needs people to keep the economy going and to those moving there, to enjoy a better life.

Interestingly, Finland also indulges its people and has a celebratory day, which is a flag day for patriots, indeed the people are encouraged to fly the flag, of course this is not compulsory, which will inevitably appease naysayers and non-patriots, but for those who feel pride in their nation and its people, they are allowed to indulge their patriotism and although the people are not overly nationalistic and certainly cannot be accused of xenophobia, possibly satiated by the flag day and the appreciation that their country is understandably proud of its global standing.

Speaking to David, it is transparently about this aspect of life in Finland, it is obvious that he is totally happy in his newly adopted home, describing it as his forever home, having relocated from one really nice location in a beautiful part of the hotel, Chester, to the fabulous Finland; yes, there are things that he misses, the obvious times spent with friends, family are possibly the hardest part of the trade-off, there is of course the great British pub, his love for going to watch his favourite football team, the incomparable Chester FC, but beyond that there is not a great deal more.

That is either a sad reflection on the country that he has left behind or a really positive interpretation of the country that he has moved to, but whichever way you want to look at it, here is a friend that has found happiness in the hotel, which is surely the ultimate achievement as we are all here looking to enjoy our brief stay as much as possible.

So if we look at something as nice as the example that David has given us, it is apparent that finding happiness is totally possible, in this case, if you have a love of or desire for that back to nature and intrinsically quiet lifestyle that nature provides, then this applies to you, you too could live the dream.

If we've learnt anything during our stay in the hotel, it is that people are very different, David's new lifestyle wouldn't be for everybody, some people may have been envious of the life he had in Chester, we are all looking for a different experience, looking for different outcomes.

I would suggest that many of us, indeed possibly the majority of us, are not even thinking about, the experience that we are all currently going through, instead the majority are plodding on, taking it all for granted and not considering or even looking for an alternative, even if that alternative may provide a total change of life and a happier experience.

Change can be difficult, we get into comfort zones in our lives and it is a lot easier to do nothing rather than to make a decision but it is import to remember that by its very nature, change allows us to move forward in life to grow as people experiencing new and exciting things.

Change is not a placebo, you can make mistakes, because not all change is for the better, but once you have accepted that change will move you forward, then if you make a mistake initially and your first choice is not the right one, then your mindset is sufficient enough to change again until you find contentment.

It brings opportunities to improve your life as we have witnessed with my friend David, who has improved his own life and that of his family. Yes, it was a tough decision to leave Chester, taking his boys out of school, leaving his job and leaving friends and family behind, for a new life with no guarantees; fortunately, it has worked out well, but you have to work at it too.

My overriding thought is that we are all going through the process, all experiencing our turn, all having our very own stay in the hotel, which as we know doesn't last forever, so why wouldn't you push the boundaries, do those things that stretch you, do the things that take you out of your comfort zone and taking you, well, to who knows where?

In a sense it was partly this thought process that inspired me to get involved, to do something that I have only ever given scant consideration to, before finally sitting down and doing something about it and to start writing this book.

I always had those niggling thoughts in my mind, like many of us do, things like, what is it all about, what is the point, if any and if there is a point, do we have licence to make the most of our stay, where do we do it, who with and what are the consequences of those choices that we make.

In isolation, each of these are massive questions, however I am surprised that more intellectual brains than mine have still not worked it out, still not come up with the answers to those questions, is it really that difficult, the answers must be out there, that's if there is an answer, or maybe there isn't.

In fact, even that simple question is a fabulous one to contemplate, it is either, there is a reason we are all here and we haven't discovered the reason yet, or there is no reason for our existence and our search for answers is futile.

Wow, there are two answers to one of the biggest questions we will ever consider!

Now this may sound ridiculous, but last weekend I actually said to my wife that if I was locked in a dark room for six months, focussing one hundred per cent on the point of it all, the meaning of life, that I, yes silly old me, I would make progress and come up with an acceptable theory, a theory fully thought through, developed and valid, maybe not right, but definitely a contribution to our greater understanding.

By the way, even if it isn't right, who can tell me it isn't, because nobody knows, so my thoughts are as valid as anybody else's!

One of the big problems that we have is that we are all too busy getting on with the chores of daily life, the minutiae of the daily grind, which prohibits us from having the luxury to indulge our whimsical philosophical theories and so, we don't.

Because we don't, I would think that we are all the worse of for it, we've let the experts get on with the deep thinking and philosophy for centuries and apart from some great ideas and giving us some really powerful rules for a life well-lived, that's it, they haven't provided us with any definitive answers and I for one, personally want more than that.

As I have always maintained, there are currently over eight billion of us on the planet, all of us staying in the hotel and as there is no definitive answer, each of us has the guarantee that whatever we believe to be true, whether shared with others as part of a religious collective or influenced by a cultural understanding, or it's just what we believe, each of our convictions is equally valid as the next person, because nobody actually knows!

Chapter 12
Have You Signed the Guestbook?

Whenever you stay at a hotel, any hotel, the only way you have to acknowledge that you have ever been there, especially for the benefit of those people who are staying in the same hotel after you have been there, is to sign the guestbook. The book is usually located somewhere in or near the reception and guests staying in the hotel are encouraged to leave a comment on their stay.

You can choose to leave a witty comment about how much you've enjoyed your stay or leave what you consider to be even a little sage advice for those who will be following in your footsteps; the comments could be incisive and may be valuable to those who come after you, comments can be as mundane as 'don't sit at the table near the window in the dining room' or 'watch out for those steps near the bar at the end of the night'; neither of which are of major importance, but small observations that will assist the reader during their stay; the reader can either choose to use or ignore the advice and maybe even pass it on themselves at the end of their stay.

Previous guests who have stayed in the hotel before our arrival have an incredible influence on our own lives, they have created a pathway for us to walk on, a pathway that makes our own stay that much easier and in many cases, possibly a little more pleasant.

Can you imagine the chaos for all concerned if each generation was starting from scratch? What an incredible thought that is, it would necessitate the whole process being started with every new cohort, all responsible for ploughing a new furrow, but fortunately for everybody, that isn't the way it works; instead, it is more of a relay race with the baton being passed from generation to generation.

If life really is a hotel, then we are all just temporary residents, here for a relatively short time, guests who are here to enjoy their stay of varying lengths of time, and not one of us, irrespective of our wealth, status or exemplary behaviour, will stay forever, nothing is ours and we don't take anything with us when we go, so understanding all of that, the only thing that we have and can guarantee is our legacy, manifested by what we say and do during our stay and in turn whatever memories we leave for those who will be staying here next, or long after we have departed and checked out at reception.

Memories of our own stay here are both temporary and more probably irrelevant to those next guests arriving after we have checked out, obviously if it is our own family, the memories are more important and can linger a little longer, In my own case I remember my mother and father, in fact I am lucky enough to have both of my parents still alive, although sometimes calling myself lucky to have them both here is a bit of a stretch, they have their moments, when they are absolutely infuriating, but seriously, I'm only joking mum and dad if you're reading this.

My personal memories go back a little further, I can just about remember my grandfather, who died when I was a ten-year-old and of course, my grandmother, who I got to know a little better and sadly died when I was eighteen years old, but beyond that it is difficult to recall those, earlier generations, even those related to me by blood.

Those earlier generations whose existence wasn't as easily recorded for posterity as it is today, photography as an example would have been in its infancy and visual moving recordings were virtually non-existent, so prohibiting the passing on of memories of those who stayed here before us.

Interestingly, the advent of new technology and the current penchant that society has for recording every waking moment is changing the way we live our daily lives. This may change the way we remember both this, the current generation and all future generations that follow, we will certainly have a more intimate view of their daily existence which I feel is in many ways a very good thing, as we will have access to remember those earlier guests, people who are related to us and people without whom, we wouldn't even be here, enjoying our own stay.

What is important to consider and more often than not is something that goes unsaid, is that those generations that were staying here before our own arrival, have made our lives easier by developing and improving our ways of living, inventing those things that we today take for granted, light, heat, cars, money and right up to today where it is this generation that is rapidly developing new technology, which as we improve and innovate further and ultimately will pass on to future guests who will no doubt make things even better and interestingly will never be aware of a world where the things that they take for granted, never existed.

I think it is important to acknowledge that not every development is a positive one; whichever field it is in, mistakes will be made, whether technological, mechanical, physical or lifestyle and the world is littered with ideas that have considered to be positive and yet when we look back today with 20–20 hindsight, we are amazed that they ever made it past the idea stage.

We can look at some mistakes that our society has managed to make and see how, those we would consider to be intelligent people, across all continents of the world, make extreme errors of judgement that have effected millions of guests in the hotel and in many cases have cost them their lives, most obviously amongst those mistakes are wars, tragic events seeing different nations and different ideologies fight amongst themselves.

As an example, during World War 1, over fifteen million people lost their lives and subsequently in World War 2, with more effective weaponry and improved technology, over seventy million lives were lost; these are just two examples in recent history of wars that now appear both senseless, needless and utterly futile, maybe we as a society we can learn from these events.

We in Europe do formally remember these events and Armistice Day, which occurred on the eleventh hour of the eleventh day of the eleventh month of 1918, and brought an end to World War 1; we remember those lost lives in World War 1 across Europe at the same time each year and the time of eleven am on the eleventh of the eleventh is known as Remembrance Day and those who died in the line of duty are remembered with the words, *Lest we Forget*, resonating and informing our determination not to make the same mistakes again.

Sadly, there are still regional wars across the world, even as I write there is war in Ukraine, there is fighting in Palestine and around the world there are civil wars, seeing opposing factions within one country wrestling each other for power, as we repeat the mistakes of the past.

So maybe we haven't learnt the lessons from the aberrations of earlier generations, but surely the birth of the United Nations in 1945 with 192 members is certainly an asset in stopping future wars and through international cooperation then it will preserve world peace, let us hope.

Wars have been a blight on the world since time began, but there are things of lesser importance that we have knowingly signed up to that highlight major mistakes across the world, some have had long lasting and irreversible consequences, some are not mistakes but simply stepping stones, necessary to improvement and part of the developmental process, so before we move on, let's look at a couple of examples of what I mean.

This first example is a particularly sensitive one, but highlights that mistakes can be made with every good intention but whether through poor research or lack of good advice it can present a catastrophe that would affect the lives of thousands of individuals and change the potential of their time in the hotel forever.

In the late fifties and early sixties, there was a drug marketed around forty-six countries to be used by women who were pregnant. Sadly, this drug, Thalidomide, was used inappropriately and created what became known as the biggest manmade medical disaster ever, with between ten and twenty thousand babies being born worldwide with a range of severe deformities.

Thalidomide was introduced in 1953 as a tranquilliser, a medication for tension, anxiety and morning sickness, all side-effects of pregnancy but it had never been tested on pregnant women. Initially, it was deemed safe for an expectant mother to take, but concerns were noted after a disturbing prevalence of birth defects and the product was withdrawn in Europe in 1961.

If I talk specifically about the experience of the product in the United Kingdom, the drug was licensed in 1958 and withdrawn in 1961, and ever so sadly, two thousand babies were affected by the drug, babies being born with defects to greater or lesser degrees, but defects nonetheless!

Approximately half of those two thousand thalidomide babies born in the UK died within a few months of their birth and 466 survived until 2010; a financial compensation agreement was reached with the victims and their families, with the makers of the drug paying £28 million.

In Spain, Germany, Canada and many other countries, a similar process occurred with victims receiving compensation, but by this time the damage had been done and does money ever make up for the consequences and lifelong effects of taking a freely available, licensed drug?

This is an example of society getting it badly wrong and then using the only course of action it has available to correct its mistake, that being the law courts and a financial solution in an attempt to help the victims.

Thalidomide was a huge mistake and there are several other examples of high-profile mistakes in the medical world, but let us look at less important mistakes which are often seen as developmental errors or maybe progress, which are of far less impact and importance, they are ultimately seen not necessarily as mistakes, but instead they are seen as stepping stones towards ongoing development, a prime example of this is the technology sector.

Talking of playlists gives me an excellent example of technological progress and many of you reading this may have found yourself in exactly the same position as me, from being that 14-year-old to today and navigating my favourite band Santana through every incarnation of their music, allow me to expand a little and you may find yourself nodding along.

Santana came into my life when I was aged sixteen, a time when I was lucky enough to have a Saturday job in Lennons, which was a supermarket chain on Merseyside, that has sadly ceased to exist and totally disappeared from the high street. I met Kevin, a lad a couple of years older than me and a full-time member of staff who would talk endlessly about music and bands, one of which happened to be the American band formed in 1966 by the incredible Mexican-born guitarist, Carlos Santana. At that time, I had never heard of either Carlos or his band, they weren't really a pop band and like most lads of my age, anything outside of Slade, Mud, TRex or Chicory Tip never existed for me at that time.

Kev leant me an LP from his own extensive collection, it was an album by Santana called *Borboletta,* and that was it, I was a fan and from that point forward, Carlos and his band were part of my life forever.

I used to love going to record shops and would spend many hours flicking through the same LPs that I had flicked through three days earlier, Reading sleeve notes and biographies of band members and other useless information, the minutiae of the genre that served, for the rest of my adult life only to make me an expert on seventies and eighties music, which will be fascinating to some who totally get it and a total turn off to the majority, who don't!

Flicking through the albums I was fascinated to discover that Borboletta was Santana sixth album, so having acquired it, I proceeded to purchase the rest of Carlos's back catalogue, starting with Abraxas because I loved the cover, check it out if you've never seen it, this was followed by purchase of the eponymous first album and I was on my way to being a fully signed up Santana aficionado buying every Long Playing record they ever produced and would produce in the future, I have them all.

Everything was good and I would play my LPs daily, but I was about to discover that my albums were just the first stepping stone in my album collection.

I had avoided buying my album collection on pre-recorded cassette, as I preferred the aesthetic and feel of the album to the inferior small plastic box and miniature sleeve notes offered by the cassette and if truth be told, I didn't think the cassette would catch on, but how wrong could one man be?

I had a cassette recorder which I used to play cassettes on and also to make my own recordings, more often than not from Top of the Pops, every Thursday evening, recording it directly from the TV, that is once I had set the microphone up, which was perched on a pile of books as near to the TV as possible while simultaneously attempting to stop Boo-Boo, the family budgie, from tweeting during my favourite songs as I recorded them, there is nothing worse than hearing the fabulous Blockbuster by the Sweet, a pop classic, but not when the chorus is accompanied by a five-year-old budgerigar.

I also used the cassette recorder to secretly record my nana every time she came to look after me when my mum and dad went out. That was me, thinking I was at the cutting edge of technology with my Sharp tape recorder, whereas my nana couldn't quite believe that I could record her mumblings as she dozed in the chair, much to my amusement.

The portable cassette recorder that I had was quite cumbersome, but in spite of this I would often take it with me when we went out for a run in the car to North Wales with mum and dad on a Sunday morning, sadly it drained the batteries quicker than a Tesla stuck on the M25 in the middle of winter, so listening to my favourite songs was limited to the battery life of the cassette player, but its portability meant that it was still with me wherever I went.

This however was about to change forever as the Sony Walkman was launched in the global market in 1979, yet another stepping stone on our way to the place that we find ourselves today. The Walkman was incredible, it was the ultra-portable cassette player, which if you were of a certain age, it was about to revolutionise your life, simultaneously it was about to give youth culture a kick in the pants too and enable the kids to take their music, which many of them considered it to be a major part of their identity, everywhere they went and to listen on their headphones as they went about their daily business, whether it was going to the shops, spending time with their mates, I'm not sure that chilling had quite been formally invented at that time, or even taking it on a plane and on holiday to foreign climes!

So that was it, I was convinced the cassette was here forever. I proceeded to replicate my collection of Santana albums and many other LPs that I had in my collection, others that I had bought on vinyl and would cherish forever, but now I could take my Walkman and my albums on cassette everywhere and my favourites to play for my own pleasure or possibly to share with friends, listening through one ear of my headphones!

It wasn't just me, the Walkman was to become an icon of eighties cool, culturally its effect was incredible, one magazine opined, 'the world changed' on the day the Walkman was released.

The Walkman was not only to change people's relationship with music as it did for me, but it also altered the way we saw the emergence of new technology, in this case the nature of the product meant that we were listening to our own choices and moving away from radio stations playing their choices for us, deciding for us what they wanted us to hear!

The Walkman saw the emergence of headphones being worn in public, which nowadays sounds unbelievable given their proliferation in today's society, although their shape and style has changed dramatically, they are still functionally the same product.

The Walkman enjoyed global success, and similar to the Hoover in the vacuum cleaner world and Sellotape in scotch tape land, the name Walkman became generic for any model of personal portable cassette player.

Just as a matter of interest, there is a word to describe the use of a trademarked name which, because of its popularity or its innovation, becomes the generic name for the total market range of products—genericization. But we know that in spite of its global success, the Walkman was simply a stepping stone and in spite of global sales of cassettes overtaking the sales of vinyl records throughout the world, 1991 saw the global sales of cassettes being overtaken by compact discs.

I had just about replicated my vinyl album collection on cassette and here we have another incarnation of the same product, unsurprisingly and I remember this vividly, I was not for change, thinking that compact discs would never take off, I insisted on buying any newly released albums on cassette, but once again, I was to be proven wrong.

Compact discs first came to my attention in 1981. I was watching *Tomorrow's World* on TV on a Thursday evening, because it preceded *Top of the Pops* and although *Tomorrow's World* could be a little dry, it could be a great watch. This episode was, not unusually, quite prescient as the presenter played a copy of the Bee Gees album, *Lying Eyes on Compact Disc*, this was the first ever public playing of a CD; after all, the programme was called *Tomorrow's World*, not *Today's World*, the innovation was reproduction quality and portability, but surely they wouldn't be available for many years? It was a matter of months before record shops started selling them, but I still wasn't convinced. I was resisting the inevitable, we were watching progress in action, we were part of it, but I was akin to one of the Luddites, although, unlike the Luddites I never went around smashing up CD players, reluctant to accept their inexorable rise.

So, alongside my now warehoused record collection, I stacked hundreds of cassettes which were now doomed to a life spent competing with my albums for the descending dust, while I proceeded to replicate my existing LP and cassette album collection with CDs of the self-same albums. A Sony Discman, the offspring and successor of the Sony Walkman, was purchased and I was off again, music on the go with a superior sound offered by the compact disc—life was good.

I think my dad took my Walkman to a car boot sale, there was still a market for them, especially as CDs were in their infancy and there were many like me who resisted, at least temporarily, change and were happy to stroll through the streets with their Walkman on their hip!

I didn't get involved in mini discs or laser discs, two stepping stones that appeared, to me at least, to take progress sideways and not necessarily forward; however, I am sure that some of you will have got involved and they are currently taking up space in the attic, cellar or garage. It's time that we brought ourselves right up to date, like the rest of the planet, I carry all of my music around with me everywhere I go on what has become the ubiquitous smartphone.

What a fantastic creation and what's not to love, something that fits into the palm of your hand and contains every piece of music that you could ever want to hear and if there is an old favourite that you mentally misplace, there are ways to rediscover and reignite your passion for every ancient jewel that's fallen down the back of your mental sofa.

Have we reached the other side, have the stepping stones served their purpose, I sense not, I believe the smart phone will be remembered with sentimental, romantic, fondness by future guests in the hotel, long after we have checked out, seeing them as just another stepping stone to who knows where.

But it is not for us to attempt to see into the future, we are merely here to observe and opine, we are here to justify our view that life is a hotel and what has brought us to this conclusion.

Never forget, since I checked in, progress was from the Long Playing record to the smart phone, but there were a few stepping stones prior to the LP, so we have to acknowledge them in our overall evaluation.

So we can all agree that generations pass the baton on and new generations can learn from the mistakes of the past, but what about individuals, let us look at how individuals can impact during their time here, however brief their stay and for whatever reason they are known.

It never ceases to amaze me that there are some individual guests whose stay in the hotel is for as brief a period of time as we ourselves are here, yet they have such an impact on the world as to change it forever and as change happens we once again reference one of our old chums, Heraclitus, 'The only constant in life is change'.

The one constant since the beginning of time may be change; however, for many people the fear of change is a constant too, since time immemorial humans have liked routine and the stability and predictability that it brings, it gives us a sense of control that we can choose the direction of our lives and for many people that is a good and necessary thing.

It is possible for fear of change to become an irrational fear, anticipating change as a negative, not a positive, catastrophising that the future can only deteriorate if unnecessary change is brought about, which as I say, is irrational, because nobody knows for sure what change can bring, but it is that irrational fear which makes it a phobia, one such phobia is metathesiophobia—the irrational fear that due to constant change, you have no control over your life.

Metathesiophobes tend to live in the past, they are unwilling and unable to progress and this then can lead them to a feeling of depression, a mental illness which can directly impact both their personal and professional lives, affecting not only their relationships, but their work and inevitably their career.

Sadly, the reality for us all, not just for the metathesiophobe, is that change is necessary, it perpetuates our personal development and strengthens relationships, which sustain the inevitable need for progress for our quality of life and ultimately our stay in the hotel, if change doesn't happen, we stand still and if we are standing still, we are going backwards, as others will pass us as they move on in their lives.

That may seem to be a huge generalisation, but due to conditioning, partly to a natural resistance and also due to a lack of awareness, we are all to a greater or lesser degree burdened with the values that we collect as our stay in the hotel progresses.

I always swore in my youth that I would never miss an episode of *Top of the Pops*, but life changes and now, pop music and the charts are quite irrelevant as an important part of my life; yes, of course, music is still important to me, but pop itself and today's charts, not so much. Whereas to the newer arrivals in the hotel, pop music helps define and shape them as individuals, not only musically, but also societally, it is a bond amongst their peers, these are the songs that will come to define their generation and be a part of their lives forever.

Pop stars today are happy to indulge themselves by sanctimoniously telling us of their green credentials or opining on the gender debate and inevitably, because they are icons to the kids, their views will influence the young minds that love them for their music and their lifestyle.

It may seem a rather fatuous analogy, using pop music to highlight the point, but once you no longer have an interest in something, then your views on it are similarly entrenched in a time in which you were, you love your era, your generation. You will hear a dad tell his teenage son that music was better in his day, while splendidly unaware of what today's music has to offer, so how can dad know, he has zero interest in today's music; therefore, dad unknowingly is well on his way to becoming a dinosaur!

To those that arrive after us, they know of nothing else, so they don't see change, all that they see is all that they know, it's their normal. But as we know, evolution is incremental by the second, or any other man made constructed time frame, that you may care to choose.

Never forget, we have given the world time as a measure of our lives, but this is our invention, the physical planet is totally unaware of the clock, or of what we have created in order to satiate our need for rationality or order.

Although time is a construct of our own making, change is inevitable and happens over time and it coincides with our own decline, sadly we experience a natural and irresistible physical decline, which in spite of us challenging it, we can only ever delay the decay and cannot defeat it.

Because change is a necessity, we are individually merely a temporary obstruction to its progress, as it advances, it brings with it our own demise, which as I say is inevitable because nature must have her way.

Our health and fitness, become casualties, but slowly, as life and the world evolves, changing minimally but incrementally by the day, however that change becomes seismic when it is generational and as our generation declines, our individual natural timespan concludes and we are allowed to check out of the hotel just in time and hopefully with our dignity intact.

The more I write this book about life being a hotel, the more I find myself applying my own time to actually thinking about the way life works; and believe me, once you start writing a book, it becomes all-consuming, your days and nights are constantly in book mode, thinking about what's been written and thinking deeply about what is to come; any moment could be the most inopportune moment when you may stumble over thoughts that could initially be just a simple throwaway line, but that thought, that one line starts to germinate, gaining a life of its own and ultimately the idea can begin to encapsulate your thinking. The more you dwell and start to do further research to back up your assertions, it is at that time that unbelievably, but wonderfully, I discover that it's not just me, but other guests, those that arrived a long time before I checked in, have had similar thoughts to my own.

Once again, let me say that if we were given the time in our lives and with a greater insight, I do believe that it would be totally possible to discover our purpose and an answer to the one big question, to which there is currently no answer—What is it all about?

As if to reinforce this, while simultaneously giving you a recent example of this happening to me is in regard to my thoughts about the dinosaur and its extinction, although the dinosaur and its extinction are not necessarily due to the creature becoming redundant or an anachronism in its environment; indeed, if it wasn't for the Chicxulub Impactor, we could debate whether the dinosaur would still be roaming amongst us, maybe in a slightly different form, but having evolved to accommodate a changing world.

After all, animals live everywhere on earth, whether in those places that have incredibly high temperatures, or conversely, in the places that are extremely cold, some places have a lot of water and plants, whereas others have little water and few plants, one fabulous example of this is Antarctica which is aesthetically a naturally beautiful place, with more than 99% of the region covered in ice, yet in spite of the hostile environment, there are plants growing there—lichens, algae and moss—animals live there and thrive.

We find animals dependent on the sea for their diet and nutrition, alternatively there are migratory creatures, inevitably mainly birds, who have the ability to leave one continent when winter arrives, for another warmer climate, returning when it becomes more hospitable, but the point is, that life finds a way, it adapts through necessity, survival is everything.

Psalm 90:10 says, 'The years of our lives are threescore years and ten and if by reason if they may be fourscore years, yet is their strength, labour and sorrow, for it is soon cut off and we fly away.'

The scripture isn't suggesting that god has put a limit on our lifespan but giving a fair average and taking into consideration of the numerous and very relevant factors that affect our stay here, we are given approximately seventy years, or maybe eighty/ninety if you're lucky and fortune conspires to give you a little extra time, but nobody will be going much beyond that, so if you've got things to do, then this is how long you've got to do them, it's up to you to fit it all in and please don't say you weren't warned and you ran out of time.

This psalm cleverly tells us that the imminent arrival of death is constant, which in your younger years, I don't believe that you are even conscious of death being an option, you are invincible, whereas in your latter years, you are far more aware of your own mortality.

For me, the parallel with the hotel is an obvious one and it equates to checking into the hotel where, on day one, you have absolutely no thoughts of checking out or even how long you have got left, whereas as you approach the end of your stay, you are aware of having two or three days left and inevitably how much time you have to fit it all in, or not, as the case may be.

Of course, there are no guarantees, but if we use the three score years ten as a handy guide, this means that you can justifiably calculate the number of years that you have to do those things that remain on the bucket list.

If we research a little further into this area of the Bible, we discover that it tells us that an individual life is regarded as being over after a very short period of time, regardless of a person's years spent on earth, death comes soon and from the perspective of history, our stay here is virtually irrelevant when looking at how long we get to stay, compared to the timeline of the planet.

These Bible extracts acknowledge that life is about seventy to eighty years, they will be full of toil and trouble and then it's over. In my opinion, it is those years that take us into our ultimate decline, in which we become the dinosaur and unfortunately for us, just like the dinosaur we become extinct, not as a race but as an individual.

Once we have gone, then life moves on we remain unknown to the vast majority, we are forgotten by most but remembered by a few, the revolving door of the hotel sees new guests arriving daily as new guests arrive and others come to the end of their stay.

The question is, how do we quantify whether we have had as enjoyable a stay as possible, could we have done more, could we have achieved greater success, seen more of the planet, got to know more people, met different people, been something that we weren't, or have we become exactly what we are.

It has always struck me as quite bizarre that in any situation that we find ourselves surrounded by other people, whether it be a shopping mall, a restaurant, an airport or indeed any crowded space, that we as people, individuals who are all going through the same experience as those that surround us at that time, whether it's those people who are standing next to us or the people that we can see, we invariably find ourselves limiting our direct contact, those people that we talk to, to as few as one other person in that space and possibly, depending upon your personal circumstances, you may speak to nobody at all.

How does that happen, individuals all going through the same things but choosing only to share our experiences with very few people, it is crazy and possibly sad.

If we acknowledge that the spoken language may be a potential barrier to communication, although it's not insurmountable, why don't we speak to everybody that we come into contact with, because to a greater or lesser degree we are all going through exactly the same things as each other, every single day that we spend here in the hotel.

Back to the Bible, the end of Psalm 90:10 talks of 'life being filled with labour and sorrow, soon cut off and then we fly away'. The psalm is telling us that our lives are relatively short, they are not filled with sunny days and smiles, but labour and sorrow, so why not absorb every opportunity to speak to as many of the other guests as possible, you never know where those conversations may lead to, yes of course we all have free will and some people may choose to live our lives in that way, but my point is that the majority of us do not live their lives in that way.

Just take a step back and observe how, like an army of ants busily getting on with their role in the colony, we walk past each other, ignoring those people in our personal space, indeed the ant colony is a fascinating hierarchy, displaying its own well established societal values, its own evolutionary path is a remarkable tale of a well-crafted and perfectly functioning society.

Our own reluctance to mix with our fellow guests can be observed everywhere from the shopping centre to the cinema, to the beach, where unless we are with the handful of people that we may have gone there with, for some reason, we limit our social mixing to the group we are with.

In spite of having nearly everything in common with all of those that we see, those other people that are staying in the hotel at the same time as we are, we limit ourselves to investing in relatively few close relationships with other people.

Shouldn't we speak to everybody, sharing experiences, learning new ideas, whether they be good or bad, ultimately making our stay as fulfilling as possible. Which begs the question, what makes our stay a good one, what is it that makes a life well-lived and if that question is ever to be answered, is it to ourselves, contemplating our own satisfaction, or is it to a higher power?

These questions along with thousands of others are all similarly fashioned are striving to understand our purpose as an individual or part of a collective, as part of a family and I've always been fascinated with those who have been here before me and have obviously been as consumed as I am about the meaning of it all and have summarised what they have learnt in a witty, pithy but memorable phrase.

As you would imagine, there is a whole catalogue to choose from, so I will opt to look at what I would suggest to be 'persons of interest', people who have lived a life that's full and travelled each and every highway; one such person that falls into that category is the fabulous Mae West. 'You only live once, but if you do it right, once is enough!' Mae was ahead of her time as the Hollywood actress, born in 1893 and stayed as a guest in the hotel for 87 years, was known for her sexually liberated views, bawdy double entendres and sexual independence, in a time when women didn't do those sorts of things or have those opinions.

Mae is not considered to be a philosophical icon or a great thinker of her age, so you may consider her to be an unusual choice to source a quote from but I think you will agree that her words are profound and as you get older you come to realise it is all a part of the process. Mae signed the guestbook in her own inimitable style, she won't be forgotten any time soon and I sense even future generations will look back at her stay here and smile.

As I say, there are millions of others that I could have quoted, all with different levels of achievements and all making a different type of contribution during their stay, the one common denominator is there desire to express their feelings and make their own individual, often incisive contribution.

Another of my personal favourites is from the American adventurer, writer and generally indefinable Jack London, he is the type of person who doesn't have global renown, but he certainly let us know that he was here and that he stayed in the hotel, you can safely say that Jack signed the guestbook.

It was the inimitable Jack London that, shortly before his death in 1916, who said, 'I would rather be ashes than dust, I would rather that my spark should burn out in a brilliant blaze than it should be stifled by dry rot. I would rather be a superb meteor, every atom of me in magnificent glow, than a sleepy and permanent planet. The proper function of man is to live not to exist, I shall not waste my days in trying to prolong them, I shall use my time.'

London checked out of the hotel after a stay of forty brief years which were action-packed; the man was a dreamer, a visionary, which can be a lethal combination in either the right or wrong hands.

There are millions of previous guests we could quote for their incisive views on what they believe it's all about, but for every one who has left a legacy that we have the privilege of hearing, there are thousands more that we will never know. But even those people, the voiceless, they are acknowledged in the incredible 'Elegy written in a country churchyard' by Thomas Gray.

An elegy is a poem of serious reflection and typically a lament for the dead, so don't expect anything uplifting and fun, but the words and thoughts that they inspire are incredible; in this instance, I will offer only a few of those priceless words from the elegy in order to provide an appreciation of Gray and his observation that there are so many who don't get anywhere near to signing the guestbook, but in spite of that, they still have a fulfilling existence.

Gray's 'Elegy written in a country churchyard' is quite a long piece and I believe it offers support to my point that there are and always have been thousands of guests who simply enjoy their stay in the hotel and then leave, without a fanfare or a rendition of Chopin's *March Funebre* upon their departure.

The guests who are polite to the staff, respectful of the rules of the hotel, on time for breakfast, never late for dinner and pay their bill before departure, leaving the shampoo, soap and hairdryer in the room as they pack to leave—decent, lovely people—you may even be that person.

However, back to Gray, and his words taken from the elegy encapsulate perfectly the lives of the silent guests, those that stay here without notice to the majority, they are known to close friends and family, but without national or international acclaim, feeling the need for neither.

Gray wrote beautifully, observing the numerous graves in this particular churchyard, filled with those who have led unremarkable but fulfilling lives, a churchyard that would be replicated a thousand times over throughout the country, throughout the world.

Full many a flower is born to blush unseen and waste its sweetness on the desert air…

I love that line and the way that it speaks to those who haven't necessarily signed the guestbook in order to be known by everybody, but still had an enjoyable stay amongst family and close friends and those whom they loved and who loved them in return.

There are many fabulous literary contributions to those guests who have stayed unknown in the hotel, it is fertile ground and I could have filled this book with incongruous contributions from the work of others, but that is not the purpose of this book.

What Gray and his literary chums manage to do is to expose our thinking to the importance of every guest, guests who, although we do not know them by name, they have still contributed to the stay of those other guests, no matter how tangentially, to those whose stay has coincided with their own.

Every generation is a collective, a cohort of guests that are here at the same time, as we ourselves are part of the current cohort. Some generations have Elvis, others have Rudolph Valentino, maybe Eva Peron or Obama, they are people who are just another guest in the hotel at the same time as they are, but guests that stand out from the rest, for many and varied reasons, not always for their fame but also for their infamy.

Each generation has more than one flagbearer to identify it, whether they be political, philosophical, theatrical or musical, but these people are generational talents and when you step back from lauding their achievements, they, just like you and I are here for three score years and ten and trying to make the best of it.

From a distance we may applaud their success, but do not be deceived, because like you and I they too will struggle with the minutia of daily life that is necessarily part of all of us and everything we go through.

There are many ways that we celebrate the passing of those we have not known but have contributed to or in many cases defended us during our own stay here and one of the most poignant that has become common throughout the world is the tomb of the Unknown Soldier.

Through the ages, one of the dreadful consequences of warfare has been that large numbers of unidentified soldiers, historically very often men, who have paid the ultimate price for their country or for the freedom of others, by giving their own lives fighting for the cause.

Casualties of war has given us the consequence of those brave souls who have lost their lives, the unidentified remains of soldiers, especially those found on the battlefield, unidentified due to poor record keeping, or the dreadful injuries that weapons can inflict on a body, or simply the haste in which the bodies were to be buried, whether it is for decency or dignity or simply to ultimately mark the burial site.

In Arlington, the national cemetery in the USA has a permanent, Tomb of the Unknown Soldier, this neoclassical, white marble sarcophagus stands atop a hill, overlooking Washington DC and has done since 1921.

The tomb provides a final resting place for one of America's World War One service members, obviously an unknown soldier, who represents the large number of the men lost fighting on behalf of their nation in that theatre, the tomb has also added further unknown soldiers from later conflicts added in both 1958 and 1984.

The tomb itself ultimately serves as a focal point for those who wish to pay tribute to those who have paid the ultimate sacrifice and given their lives for their country, soldiers killed in action, but not just that, it is more, the site also serves to provide a space where those who wish to reflect on war and its effects and ultimately the futility of war can sit, contemplate and consider.

The eerie silence of Arlington makes it a perfect place to consider our own mortality and that of those now departed, the many contradictions offered by war. It is a place charged with powerful emotion and its magnificence demands respect and appreciation.

Many countries around the world have these monuments and they often have an inscription engraved into them, similarly fashioned around the same thought, usually beautiful words crafted for such a memorial…*Known but to god*. Now, that is a beautiful sentiment and as the soldier is unknown, these words are powerful in their simplicity, the only concern I have is that in order to fully appreciate their sentiment, the reader needs to have a belief in god in order for them to resonate.

However, let's not look for negatives and just acknowledge that in every country with an army or fighting force, the Unknown Soldier is vital in that it acknowledges the necessity of the country to rely on those people, it needs them, those people prepared to die for that country, in order to satiate the country's appetites to fight.

The monument itself symbolises sacrifice, indeed the anonymity of the entombed soldier is the key to the symbolism of the piece, because it could actually be the tomb of any person that died in service of the nation and it is because of this that it represents all who have died in service for the nation are symbolised and thus respected.

The whole point of discussing the tomb of the Unknown Soldier is to highlight a point that although the guestbook exists, not everybody signs it or makes their mark on the world during their stay.

One fascinating guest to have stayed in the hotel from 1889 to 1977, a full eighty-eight years, was Charlie Chaplin, an actor, writer, composer and film director to name just a few of the crafts that English-born Charlie mastered.

A child from a humble background, his father was never around and so it was left to his mother to bring him up, he was sent to work as a child to the workhouse before his ninth birthday, when at the age of fourteen his mother was committed to a mental asylum, a childhood can't come much tougher than that.

Yet Charlie sought solace in acting, both of his parents had been in the music hall and so this was a natural escape he took to the stage and at the age of nineteen, he was a part of the renowned Fred Karno acting company and he went to America, which proved to be both an incredible career move and a gift to the world!

This was a seminal time in the history and gave the world, in the words of Chaplin's biographer, David Robison, 'the most dramatic of all the rags to riches stories ever told', and if you read the story, it's hard to disagree with him.

Quite unrelated to me writing this book, a good friend of mine, Nancy Carlisle, who happens to be a big fan of Charlie Chaplin, showed me some of the actor's thoughts which he had written during his stay in the hotel.

He tells of his tough upbringing and the success that he had made of his life, Charlie chose to leave a written legacy, he gave us four statements, which are all worth reading so I will put them here for your perusal:

1. Nothing is forever in this world, not even our problems.
2. I love walking in the rain because nobody can see my tears.
3. The most lost day in life is the day we don't laugh.
4. The six best doctors in the world are the sun, rest, exercise, diet, self-respect and friends.

Stick to them at all stages of your life and enjoy a healthy life …
If you see the moon, you will see the beauty of god …
If you see the sun, you will see the power of god …
If you see a mirror, you will see gods best creation. So believe it …
We are all tourists, God is our travel agent who has already identified our routes
bookings and destinations… Trust him and enjoy life.
Life is a journey. Therefore live today!
Tomorrow may not be.

I love the whole piece of *Four Thoughts*, obviously Charlie was a religious man and his beliefs appear to have influenced his thoughts, yet in spite of that and not to say he's right or wrong, I absolutely love the travel agent analogy, of course I do, it's adding weight to my own thoughts.

I love the idea that similarly to myself, Charlie has had various experiences in his life and he has looked to interpret those experiences in a way that we can all understand and that make sense to him and hopefully to others, seeking inspiration from his thoughts! The beauty is that nobody can say that Charlie is either right or wrong, it is what he feels and believes, his code for a successful life, a life lived well and one that is accessible to everybody, from the richest to the poorest, his own success and riches did not isolate his thoughts to his own privilege, they appear to give him a comfort blanket or incubate him from most people's realities of living life one day at a time.

His *Four Thoughts* allow virtually anybody to adopt Chaplin's understanding, from diet to spirituality, and if those ideas resonate, then you are free to run with them. Similarly, I am offering my perspective and therefore laud Chaplin for considering our lives, their purpose and a way of living, I would encourage everybody to have an opinion, safe in the knowledge that nobody can definitively be told they are right or wrong.

It is interesting to me that Charlie considers both physical and mental wellness in his *Four Thoughts*, because inevitably they are both part of a greater whole and depend on each other for a good life. Mental awareness has become an increasingly important part of life as times have moved on and society now realises its importance at every stage of our lives, from childhood through to old age, there are many potential flash points in our lives, from both societal pressures and those pressures we put on ourselves, however they manifest themselves.

What is incredible is that the words of Chaplin were written in a time when they wouldn't have been as fashionable as they are today, so he was ahead of his time and very brave to opine in this way. You don't have to agree with every word, but they certainly offer a platform for debate and demand closer analysis.

The line of god being our travel agent is a nice line and reads well as a throwaway comment, but I sense that Charlie felt it was worth a lot more than that. It takes both a belief in god, but also that god has planned our lives for us; it is written, he has 'already identified our routes, bookings and destinations, trust him and enjoy life'. I find this a little more difficult to comprehend as it means that our lives are pre planned and we have no influence over our life, our free will and fate don't exist.

According to free will, a person is responsible for their own actions, therefore not all behaviour is pre-determined.

The question is do you believe in fate or destiny, which in itself is a massive question and another of those questions that can determine the way you live your life, they are fundamentally at opposite ends of the spectrum and yet both deserve analysis, so let's consider both options and how they apply to the Four Thoughts.

Fate is the development and actuality of events that happen outside of a person's control, that can be considered to be predetermined possibly but not necessarily, by a supernatural power, we can debate supernatural powers at a later time, but let's go with their existence for now.

Traditionally, fate can be described as forces outside of your control that make things happen, an example of this could be, being late for work and missing your bus, so you get the next and it is on that next bus that you meet the man, woman or gender fluid person that you eventually marry, share a civil partnership, or spend the rest of your stay in the hotel with.

Fate is the force, principle or power that has predetermined the events that led to the meeting on the bus, it was meant to be, a done deal, not open to revision.

Traditional understanding of why fate exists tells us that as a power or agency that predetermines and orders the course of events, it does so much so that the course is unavoidable and in fact inevitable. This concept is based on a belief that there is a fixed natural order to the universe and in some interpretations the cosmos!

As an alternative to fate, we have destiny, which is a slightly different proposition to fate in that, fate is concerned with life in the present, where every decision an individual has made has led them to their present situation, whereas destiny is a look into the future, where a person's actions will not affect their future.

Destiny is a term specifically used in relation to the outcome of events, it is concerned with those events, how they have worked themselves out and the inevitability of every outcome, however good or bad it may be.

That same sense of ultimate destination, a fait accompli if you will, actions were inevitably all leading to that point in the future, they are simply a result of destiny and how it controls the way in which things finally work out.

This brings me to the belief system which is known as Fatalism, a part of a group of philosophical beliefs that the outcome of future events are inevitable and, to that end, resistance is futile.

Human beings are powerless to do anything other than what they do, there is no opportunity for free will in this scenario, more a case of, it was meant to be.

This is all interesting from a perspective of Charlie Chaplin and his Four Thoughts, where Charlie seems to believe that there is a theological fatalism.

Theological fatalism is a belief that an omniscient god exists and that they—he or she—have foreknowledge of future events and because of this, it means that free will doesn't exist.

I think it is interesting to establish Chaplin's understanding of how life works, in order to validate his four statements and to that end it gives us an insight into the way he lived his life. I sense Charlie felt that those hard lessons he learnt as a child were simply readying him for his inevitable future success, shaping the man and giving him an appreciation of life that never knew privilege, but found success in spite of his hardship and possibly because of it, we must allow Charlie to define himself, to understand what he has learnt and to pass on his thoughts for future guests.

There is an alternative to his fatalist understanding of the world and it is the antithesis of fatalism and that philosophical position is called free will. Free will is where each person has the ultimate control over their actions and therefore their own destiny, it is having the opportunity to choose between different courses of possible action, unimpeded. Free will is linked to the concepts of moral responsibility, praise, guilt and sin and other judgements which apply only to actions that are freely chosen.

Whether free will exists has provided some of the longest running debates in the spheres of philosophy and religion, this however all boils down to just one burning question, which is whether we have control over our actions or not.

Everything else is rather irrelevant; if you can answer that question with certainty, you will have made a contribution to one of the most difficult questions that we have.

There are many nuanced interpretations of free will including compatibilists and those that believe in determinism, I don't want to get bogged down in one very specific area, but do feel that because some people, some previous and existing guests in the hotel live their lives by these codes and for that reason they are worth further investigation, sadly for you and I, just not in this book.

For what it's worth, I believe free will exists but it exists only within the constraints of what we are born in to, what do I mean by that you may ask, well I believe that those opportunities that we have in our lives are limited from the moment that we are born, initially by the constraints of where we are born, which part of the country or the world can offer vastly different outcomes and then we are limited by who our parents are and their understanding of life and these are just two amongst the many influencing factors that limit our potential.

In his book, *The Audacity of Hope*, Obama said, 'Values are rooted in a basic optimism about life and a faith in free will', while discussing living in the USA and the American dream! Effectively, given his own story, Obama was advocating for free will in an America that has allowed him as a black man, to be as successful and he is and therefore encouraging everybody in his country to follow in his footsteps and follow their own individual dreams.

This can lead us straight into a nurture versus nature discussion, which in itself is taking us a step further away from the hotel and the time that we spend discussing it, but I believe that because it effects everybody that stays in the hotel then it is worth having a brief look at this very specific discussion.

Nature versus nurture is the debate whether human behaviour is determined by a person's environment, such as parenting, location and lifestyle or by the persons genes. The alliterative expression Nature, Nurture has been around since Victorian times, when a very clever man called Francis Galton discussed the influence of heredity and social environment on social advancement, motivated to do so by his half-cousin, Charles Darwin, who had written his own book, *On the Origin of Species*. The concept is quite straightforward to understand whether you believe it is your upbringing or the talents you're born with that determine your success in life, so I will look at the two extremes of each position, in order to make the point.

The views that humans develop all of their traits from nurture was a deeply held belief of a great English philosopher, we have come across previously in this book, so we go back to 1690 when John Locke used the expression 'tabula rasa' which means blank slate and suggests literally that, each human is a blank slate, that society, upbringing and all of those influences that we understand, can impact on the blank slate and shape it to produce the person.

At the other extreme, we have heritability which is an understanding that it is genetics that determine a person's life, which I would personally feel, that although there must be an influence from a person's genes, it would be difficult for me to throw myself behind it as an absolute, also if it were an absolute, this could become a little more of a political view in that it could lead to advocating for the extreme, which is a belief in and seeing the development of eugenics.

If I were to be pushed to decide between the two, I would think that it is inevitable that both have a contribution but it is difficult to know where the dividing line is between an inherited ability and an acquired trait lies, if at all it ever does.

How's that for sitting on the fence?

Thinking about these influences from the perspective of the hotel and what it is that determines your success, enjoyment or indeed the quality of your stay, all can again be seen as vital ingredients that have parallels with the thoughts of the great thinkers and philosophers, believe it or not, I appear not to be the first person to think these things.

If you think about any person on the planet who is born into a life, where either nature or nurture determine the quality of that life then surely as we discussed earlier, there are huge variations between for example the chances of a person born in either the poorest country or the richest country on the planet and the opportunities that those two extremely different environments present and irrespective of that persons genetics, I've got to believe that the life opportuniliges are far more limited in one than in the other, the opportunities in a wealthy country are surely going to be preferable to those in the poorest country, ultimately this must have a huge effect on the quality of your stay in the hotel.

Of course, there will be people in poorer countries who will make a magnificent success of their lives and inevitably there will be people in wealthier countries, who in spite of having every opportunity, they still don't manage to enjoy their time here and don't make the most of their stay.

Whether those two scenarios are as a result of nurture or nature, who can be sure, whether it is fate or free will, we do not know, but as with everything we discuss, your opinion is as valid as any previous or current guest, here in the hotel!

Let me just interrupt my flow there for a few brief moments, because as I am writing about nature and nurture, quite coincidentally, my wife and I were at the Alhambra theatre in Bradford yesterday, for the matinee performance of the Willy Russell musical, *Blood Brothers*.

I do love the theatre, but yesterday was the first time I have seen this show and if I had gone to the extreme of having arranged a special viewing or a private performance of the show, to be used as further research and evidence that the nurture-nature debate is valid and would further my understanding and the writing of this chapter, then I could not have seen *Blood Brothers* at a more opportune moment.

In spite of my wife already having seen it a couple of times, she hadn't really sold it to me, so when the afternoon came around to jump in the car and drive to Bradford to see it, I wasn't really that bothered about going or not, but I did and as I say, how wrong was I?

The story is set in Liverpool in the 1960s and tells the story of twin boys separated at birth, with one staying with his birth mother living a relatively underprivileged life, while the other twin, Edward, is brought up by the wealthy employer of the mother, for whom the boys' mother cleans house.

We follow their lives as they grow up, when at age seven they accidentally meet and become friends, ultimately becoming Blood Brothers. The story continues as they go through teenage years and then into their working lives,

Mickey the child considered to be underprivileged has a menial job, but is then made redundant, while Edward the wealthy son flourishes, as he enjoys his pampered private education, followed naturally by his time spent making new friends at university.

The story concludes with a series of events that lead to both boys dying on the same day at the same time by gunshot, coincidental and possibly improbable, but making for an incredibly powerful final scene.

It is a roller coaster of a ride through turbulent times, which finishes for both in exactly the same way, but the moral of the story is how two people born of the same mother and the same father, but presented with different opportunities in life, can ultimately have very different outcomes.

So does *Blood Brothers* reinforce the nature-nurture theory or doesn't debunk it? I would suggest that it tells us that Willy Russell believes that it is nurture that is the trait that defines a person's path in life, but then he reminds us just how temporary the nature of our stay in the hotel is, whichever stage of your stay in the hotel you are at, however well or however badly it is going, it can all be brought to a premature ending at any time.

For me, it is difficult to accept that statement. I believe it begs the question of whether the end is premature or not, because there are no guarantees in life of your longevity, your length of stay here, there are just massive assumptions on our part.

Yes, we hope to be able to enjoy the allotted three score years and ten, or even better, four score years, but it's not a given, some people amongst us aren't staying in the hotel for a fortnight, some of us are here for a long weekend and that's just the way it is, so death isn't premature, it is sadly for the owner of that life, death is not premature it is simply mature and even though through tragedy or accident, it has just reached a natural conclusion.

Having immensely enjoyed watching *Blood Brothers*, it is pure coincidence that last night, I was back at the theatre, only this time it was an evening with Sir Michael Parkinson, the erstwhile Saturday night BBC chat show host who, at the time of writing this book, is on a nationwide tour discussing his extensive career in television, the show saw Michael on stage with his son, Michael Junior, taking the role of interviewer as he discusses in what is a very cleverly scripted interview, interspersed with relevant clips of Dad's interviews from the archives of the Parkinson chat show, to provide an entertaining and insightful evening.

The format works superbly well, and the in-depth discussion provides the audience with an peep into Michael's feelings and ultimately his personal observations of his guests and his reflections on both his own and their lives and achievements.

For those who don't know, Parkinson was a staple of British Saturday night television from 1971 right through to the next century, Parky has he was affectionately known to the audience, finally hanging his microphone up in 2007, his longevity a symptom of his enduring charm, professionalism and skill as an interviewer which saw him interview the biggest names that stayed in the hotel during those years.

Parkinson was the British Johnny Carson, David Letterman or Jay Leno, but the late-night chat show where, in many cases, the host had become as well-known as his guests, a procession of the great and the good, from all walks of life, from film stars, to sportsmen and politicians or anybody that had the good or ill fortune to find themselves in the public eye at any given moment, the appetite to find out more about these people has become insatiable, latterly spawning a generation of magazines analysing the minutia of these, 'celebrities' lives.

But Parky was the British version of the genre, a likeable man, whose sympathetic manner could elicit the most delicate of stories from his guests and as I mentioned, he had the biggest names on the world stage before him, having an intimate one to one conversation with his victims, for that is what they ultimately were, televised to his national and sometimes international audience, guests who had a story to tell or remarkable achievements to be lauded, Parky had them all and it was his own career that was being celebrated on his current tour.

The format of the evening reinforced Parkinson's success as an interviewer, with highlights from his voluminous back catalogue of shows, interspersed with personal anecdotes, his own observations and stories of those stars that he has met throughout the years, in many cases, people that he had got to know and had become friends, but all of those big names that he had interviewed throughout his lengthy time spent on TV.

I have already acknowledged that he has met some of the most important characters who have stayed in the hotel during both the 20th and 21st centuries and it was insightful to listen to his story's and revisit those famous names and their characters.

Listening to those reflections throughout the evening, it reinforced my understanding that your life is limited to those characters who are staying in the hotel at the same time as you are and though this may not appear to be specifically limiting, or putting major restrictions on your own life choices, it certainly limits your possibilities or outcomes.

I desperately wanted to hear from Sir Michael whether he felt there was a common theme that led his guests, from their chosen field, sport, politics, the arts, to achieve their success, what was it that was driving them to attain their individual success, is there a single factor, a common denominator that pushes them to go above and beyond that, which the majority of us are prepared to sacrifice for success, because inevitably there is a price to pay, otherwise, everybody would be a superstar and patently, we are not.

From Jacob Bronowski to Billy Connolly and in between, a cast of thousands, there was a brilliant diverse range of 'celebrities' and generally, a collection of individuals who were acknowledged as being both successful in their chosen field and sufficiently intelligent to interpret their success through the art of conversation.

Cannily, Parkinson always left it to his audience to draw their own conclusions from each of his guests, he managed to navigate a straight line of impartiality.

I wanted Parky to give me an insight into what he felt it was that those who were enjoying a fabulous career appeared to have come through, in order to achieve success, was it an incredibly tough start, had they experienced adversity and stayed strong, coming through it all and were successful in spite of or possibly because of their back story.

I could be way off beam but I sense that there must be something that these people have in common and if ever somebody was fortunate enough to get a sense of whether there is or there isn't, then Michael was the man to listen to.

At the end of what was a very enjoyable evening with Parkinson, I knew so much more about the people he had met and those that he had willingly let slip that he felt great affection for, but I don't believe I had heard the answer that I was desperately waiting to hear, so maybe there isn't one, maybe it really is as simple as the story of our old friend Charlie Chaplain, lending support to the idea that it is incredible poverty that can push a person out of their uncomfortable zone and make a success of their lives.

My recent *Blood Brothers* and Michael Parkinson experiences may have thrown a little light onto this chapter, offering as they have, different perspectives on signing the guestbook but if we go back to where we left off before recounting those two highly entertaining interludes.

Is it free will or fate, could it be nature or nurture, I am sure that you will have an opinion on both, but lend me your eyes and consider this, it is a third option, one that I believe is another more specific area that we need to consider in order for us to fully understand and appreciate our stay in the hotel and it is something that I obliquely referred to earlier in this chapter and without sounding to arrogant or indeed pompous, this is a theory all of my own!

I believe that our lives can be determined to a degree by the people who are alive at the same time as we are here, the people who are guests in the hotel while we are here.

Surely and incontrovertibly, it is those guests and those alone who can share our experience and to that degree they can influence us, so let's consider the potential outcomes, the possibilities that our fellow guests can have.

I certainly know this has happened to me, but have you ever found yourself staying in a hotel and really enjoying your time there, however, either when you arrive, or probably worse, half way through your stay, another guest arrives, along with their equally irritating ensemble, to shatter the peace and calm of your stay.

Either they are too loud, self-obsessed, inconsiderate, ill-mannered or simply just too garish for you to ever consider being in their company, let alone spending time with them, or worse strike up a friendship, but here they are, they are there at the same time as you, in the bars or the restaurants, on the terrace, by the pool, invading your stay with their presence or irritatingly hearing their inane ramblings to a poor unsuspecting member of staff as you sit behind a broadsheet newspaper savouring the dying embers of the day on a sun lounger, watching the sun take your lead and make a sharp exit behind the nearest horizon.

These people are sharing your time, this is yours, but sadly it is theirs too, you are sharing your experience in the hotel, simply as an accident of birth and you both find them here, staying in the hotel at the same time as you, they surely that must effect your stay in the hotel, if you take this thought to its extreme, then inevitably if I were to be staying in a hotel full of Manchester United fans then me as a Liverpool supporter wouldn't really enjoy the experience, or consider checking in to a hotel only to find out they were hosting a Star Trek convention and the whole place had been taken over by Trekkies dressed as Kirk or Spock milling around, in every nook and cranny of the hotel.

It may be fun if you love the 60's television creation of Gene Roddenberry, sadly I don't and for me to be sharing space with the aficionados would be unbearable. Now those may be extreme examples, but these scenarios are meant to highlight the point that fellow guests will inevitably influence your stay here.

In fact, to add a little balance, let us imagine the hotel was full of Liverpool fans, all loving the same football team that I do, then surely my stay would be far more pleasant, with less opportunity for confrontation and friendships and relationships far easier to build, with all of us sharing a common interest if not a passion.

That is another extreme position which in reality would never really happen, unless Liverpool fans were all staying together in a hotel before the final of a major tournament, which isn't too unrealistic, but real life is always more balanced than that, with a mixture of people and a spectrum of interests, personalities and emotions from love to hate and everything in between.

If we go back to 1889, when the English football league started, fans of Preston North End would have been in their element; they were English champions, winning both the inaugural season and the following season, their fans could not be happier, so if you were staying in the hotel at that time, as a Preston North End fan, your stay here was a beautiful thing, but if we fast-forward to today, Preston North End find themselves in the second tier of English football, loyal fans of the club will still follow the team, but their highs won't be as high and their lows will be a little lower, compared to the halcyon days of 1889 and 1890.

My own team Liverpool didn't exist in that first season of the league, so if I had been staying in the hotel at that time, I would either have supported Everton, the only team representing the city of Liverpool, or I may have had no interest in football.

The point is that your time in the hotel is conditional on the rest of the guests who are staying here at the same time as yourself. The analogy of football teams applies to every aspect of life, politics for instance has given us war mongers and peacemakers, music has given us chamber music and rock, the arts have given us Picasso and Rothko all at different times in the evolution of the hotel and all very different offerings that limit your options to optimise your experience.

Realising that my options are limited to those who have been staying here at the same time as I am, I consider myself to be fortunate that Carlos Santana was staying in the hotel at the same time as me and that Liverpool football club have been champions of Europe six times so far during my own stay, but things could be so very different.

I am reflecting on the thought that we are each of us individuals who have a bespoke experience, but our individuality is determined not simply by our own existence at a moment in time, but the existence of those here during our stay.

As a final thought on this, not only can we enjoy the company of those that we are sharing the hotel with, but we can also choose to enjoy the music, films or writing of those who were here a long time before we have checked in, whereas we have no way to access those who are due to arrive long after we have checked out.

A simple example of this is the work of actor, Will Hay, an English comedian born in 1888 and died in 1949. I remember vividly as a child watching his films with my dad, fabulous black-and-white films, where we saw Will play an ageing schoolmaster, complete with mortar board, cape and cane, the type of film that I watch now and see how life and the country have changed so much, we are in a different time if not a different place, but Will is a person who stayed in the hotel and had left, long before I turned up, yet here I am, one of his biggest fans.

We can look at the talents of those who preceded our stay in the various mediums that we have available to us and although Will Hay is a favourite of mine, think of the voluminous work of the millions that stayed before us, providing us with incredible insights into their stay and the legacy they have left behind, I love it.

Of course, you are not totally happy to be in the hotel at the same time as every other person who is staying here, in fact you can actually dislike some people, irrationally so in many cases, in fact, you can find yourself disliking people that you don't even know, which has happened to me.

I went through a phase in my own life where I was absolutely bored rigid of seeing Pauline Quirk, the cockney actress and celebrity, on television constantly; she had a spell in which she seemed to appear on every TV panel show, game show, reading the news, she was everywhere and although I didn't know her and have never met her, I couldn't stand her.

Pauline irritated me for no obvious reason and don't forget, this was in the days of four TV channels and no internet, so now that there is more access to media, your options for viewing are far more plentiful, so the opportunities to shop around are many, even so some latter day attention seekers can be spread so thinly across all media and those characters in spite of their protestations and desperation for privacy, you can read, hear or watch them anywhere and everywhere.

I have got over my dislike for Pauline Quirk, probably because she is not getting much TV work these days, but I sense that my Quirkphobia may be replaced by another irrational dislike of some over exposed 'personalities'; could Harry and Meghan replace Pauline Quirk? We will see.

Chapter 13
Let's Look at the Photos!

In my own lifetime, the holiday snap has evolved beyond all recognition; even the term snap is now an anachronistic phrase that most Gen Z kids wouldn't understand if you dropped it into a conversation with them when discussing your holiday photos.

I was born in 1960 and my earliest recollections were of taking pictures or my dad taking pictures on an instamatic camera, once or maybe twice a year if we were lucky, but this annual event of amateur photography has now morphed into an era where the photo opportunity seems to present itself on a moment by moment basis, today nothing is off-limits, every single aspect of life is fair game to be immortalised forever on the mobile phone or tablet de jour.

My first holiday abroad was in 1972, with my mum and dad, to San Antonio, Ibiza, which in those days was a very different place than it is today. We were flying on the defunct Cambrian Airways from Liverpool's Speke airport to Ibiza airport, my grandmother and aunties came to wave us off at Liverpool airport, it was as if we would never see them again, I look back and laugh now, but this was cutting-edge travel in those days and excitement levels were high.

Granted it was a BAC 1–11 we were flying on, but to us it may as well have been Apollo 11, the first space flight to land man on the moon. I look at the photographs now and they are fabulous, would you believe that my dad, who was approximately 35 years old at the time, flew to Ibiza in a three-piece suit, a collar and tie and this was in August, temperatures were at their highest, he must have been absolutely sweltering but he never mentioned it.

Even to this day, I can remember feeling the heat of the Spanish sunshine as we disembarked from the aeroplane using the rear door, remembering how hot it felt and the prospect of spending two weeks in this tropical paradise, which seemed like a lifetime—excited isn't a big enough word!

As we disembarked from the plane, there was a local photographer on hand who took our pictures as we climbed down the steps, what we didn't know at the time was the photos could be collected two weeks later when we, the conquering heroes, returned to the airport for our return flight home.

When out fortnight was up and we arrived at the airport for our return flight, the photographs were strewn across a table, near to our departure gate, in no particular order, necessitating passengers to look through the pile before discovering a picture of themselves about to set foot onto Spanish soil, many for the first time; did the great explorer Sebastian Cabot know such excitement as new lands of the Caribbean beckoned his imminent arrival and he discovered their existence?

The photo-sifting provided much hilarity for all on our flight, laughing at those surprised faces, unaware of the welcome committee at the bottom of our aeroplane's steps, a committee desperately anticipating the arrival of more lily-white faces from colder English climes.

Old hands knew what to expect, they were here last year and knew the photographer lay in wait and suitably they responded to the camera's intrusion by giving a catalogue model pose at the top of the steps, whereas first-timers like ourselves looked a little dishevelled, having been contorted by three hours in a tiny aeroplane seat and feeling the blast of Spanish heat for the very first time as the doors opened and we set foot in Espana.

In Ibiza, we were staying at the Hotel Riviera on the opposite side of the bay to the main town of San Antonio, a small fishing village; of course, there were bars and nightclubs, but nothing to the extent that we see there today. Ibiza is now a magnet for the euro trendies and coolest kids on the planet, but in those days there was a naive charm about the place, it was still an authentic Spanish fishing port, unspoiled by the commercialisation now and those memories will stay with me forever.

Two weeks before the holiday and the suitcases would be brought out of the loft and dusted down, mum and dad shared a big case, while my excitement at the prospect of my first flight followed by a two-week holiday abroad was only heightened by being given my own suitcase and I had licence to decide which clothes from my rather limited collection would be chosen and paraded before the European jet-set.

I'm sure my mum was casting a beady eye on everything that I packed to ensure that I had suitable attire for the trip, but at the time, I honestly believed that I had full responsibility for my outfits and was entrusted to oversee the contents of the case.

As I write this, I can still remember my favourite trousers, a red, blue and white pair of striped jeans, I thought they were fantastic and would have slept in them if I had been allowed to. I still have a fabulous photograph of mum and me standing on a beach in San Antonio, wearing the ubiquitous jeans, just in case I am ever called upon to prove their existence.

As well as packing the cases ahead of the trip, there were other holiday rituals which were a regular part of the build-up, with each act being as keenly anticipated as the next, a well-ordered, regimented procession which all led to the main event.

I will give you an insight into the build-up which culminated in my favourite chore, and that was a trip to Boots the chemist. You may think, hardly the shop of dreams for a twelve-year-old boy from Liverpool, but to me, it signalled the start of the adventure, as Columbus would have visited the ship's chandlers to load up the Santa Maria, Roald Amundsen getting supplies in order to lead an expedition to the North Pole or Henry Morton Stanley stocking up with goods and equipment before embarking on his search for the vanished Dr David Livingstone.

To me, Boots was all of these things, for it was here that my vital supplies for the trip were purchased, including my personal favourite, the rolls of film for the camera. Yes, of course, there was the obligatory new flannel, a new bar of soap, Factor 100 suntan lotion, and the four rolls of film for our Kodak instamatic camera.

Boots had a fantastic system with their camera film rolls, each box contained the cartridge, the 24-photo roll of film which was inserted into the camera and the essential prepaid envelope, addressed to Boots film developers, somewhere in Nottingham if I remember correctly; this was posted the moment we arrived back from our holiday and had unpacked our suitcases. The developers would then process the pictures within a matter of days, which was a relatively speedy service; however fast it was, it still couldn't assuage our impatience which was a constant, until the moment they were sent back to us.

Believe it or not, the photographs when sent back to us were in colour, which, although it seems hard to believe now, was a fairly recent development in the world of photography and inevitably this brand-new innovation only added to our excitement.

When you consider that the title of this chapter is *Let's Look at the Photos*, the way the medium has changed, even in my own lifetime, is absolutely remarkable. Photographs have become an increasingly important part of our lives since the invention of the camera, from its earliest inception as the Camera Obscura to its development in the early 1800s and through a meandering list of scientists and technicians who researched and improved the product bringing us to a place that would allow George Eastman to form the Kodak company in 1892 and a family business that for those staying in the hotel at the time, became synonymous, virtually globally, with photography for several generations.

Kodak developed a memorable strap line, which was 'A Kodak Moment', which came into common parlance for any moment that was to be photographed and kept for posterity, this was both excellent marketing, but also it created an international brand awareness, guaranteeing financial success and an excellent business model.

To a lesser degree but equally as successful in the United Kingdom, I can remember the Kodak success story being replicated by one other camera company, here I am talking about success in my own lifetime and this was the Olympus camera company and their Trip camera, which, when I was in my teens, had a generation of people of all ages going around asking anybody that was holding a camera, if they were David Bailey.

Bailey was an iconic British photographer, widely known for his fashion photography and his crucial role in shaping the image of the Swinging Sixties and cleverly, Olympus signed him up to front their Trip campaign, which was in itself a shrewd move by the camera company as this was not really a time of the now ubiquitous celebrity endorsement and if they were ever seen, they were certainly not to the levels that we are used to today.

Bailey's own looks and his cool and trendy image combined with a great product meant for overwhelming success for both the camera and Bailey, whose name became synonymous with photography in the eighties, no matter who manufactured the camera.

In spite of the absence of multimedia channels, Bailey still managed to help shape the aspirations for an emerging youth culture ad because of his input. Bailey, now in his eighties, is alive and well as I write and has become a successful sculptor and artist, still exhibiting his work; that sounds to me like a perfectly satisfactory stay in the hotel.

But back to Kodak and their impact on life, for it was that company along with others who brought the simple camera into the homes of us all, with an affordable piece of equipment that would allow us to record our lives and allow us to keep those memories for posterity.

A physical record of our stay in the hotel could now be kept in albums of photographs and could illicit the fondest memories at the mere turn of a page.

So our trip to Boots to collect four rolls of camera film prior to departure meant that our holiday would stay with us forever, not simply in our memories, but with photographs which enabled us to regale friends and family who had dutifully come to wave us off on our maiden flight.

Although we had been surprised at being photographed as soon as we had landed and walked down the steps of our aircraft, from that point on, our camera never left us; wherever we went for the next two weeks, the hotel, the beach, restaurants we visited, the mock bullfight where my dad was in the ring waiting for the 'bull' to arrive and, of course, the obligatory barbecue night.

Photographs at any and every opportunity and once the holiday was over and we returned home, I could not wait to put each roll of film in their prepaid envelope and post them to Boots immediately!

Then we waited in eager anticipation of the postman with his early morning delivery, this was a time when the post was delivered in both morning and afternoon, so if the photographs hadn't arrived in the morning, before I went to school, then they could possibly arrive at approximately 2 pm, while I was actually in school; it meant that as soon as the school bell rang, I would get to the bike sheds and race home on my Raleigh Olympus racing bike in order to see if they had arrived in the second post.

The three of us were equally excited at the prospect of revisiting our Spanish memories as soon as the people at Boots had done their work and developed our recollections. I would be on guard duty until the delivery day finally arrived. I could see Brian, our postman, coming up the path with four rather large colourful envelopes in his hand; to him it was simply another delivery, one of hundreds he would make during his normal day, but to me he was holding my life in his hands, certainly my past, but Brian was totally unaware as he proceeded with less urgency than my impatience demanded.

All four envelopes arriving at once was magical, considering the numbers of photographs that Boots would be processing, especially during the busy summer months of August and September which I imagined would have been their busiest, but thankfully, they all arrived and that meant an evening for the three of us to look forward to, sharing and recalling our memories once more.

The television was switched off, we all sat together in the living room and carefully put the envelopes full of photographs in sequential order and then for the next three hours sat absorbed, scrutinising every photograph.

The very first picture was the obligatory close-up of clouds taken above the Liverpool skies from the aircraft window; don't forget this was our first flight, so seeing clouds close up was mind-blowing. I was twelve, don't forget.

From the Liverpool clouds to those sun-kissed days, the Mediterranean nights, and two weeks' worth of incredible memories, I vividly remember laughing at the photograph that had me and half of mum, my dad was a rubbish photographer, then there was the random picture that none of us had a clue what was it supposed to be, more often than not it was my own failed attempt at an arty Spanish sunset.

For the next week, we would look at those pictures every day at different times and remember what a fantastic time we had; in retrospect I pity those unfortunate family members who we visited at the weekend to repeat the recounting of our family holiday, each picture explained in minute detail, how they had the patience to sit through it, why did we put them through it, I'm not sure, but they indulged us and sat nodding and laughing at all the right places.

Those simpler days seem a million miles from what this current generation have access to today. If my grandmother or grandfather came back to the hotel today, they wouldn't have a clue what was going on, with the changes in technology, societal values and norms changing by the week and people in general having a totally different perspective on life.

Society has eternal demands, giving us those underlying societal values such as truth, honesty and decency which will be a constant part of many people's lives, but the hotel that your grandparents stayed in was totally different to the hotel that their descendants live in today; inevitably, the same will happen to this generation, even though we have no idea what the future holds, we can rest assured that change is inevitable, often manifesting as progress, but many times appearing as an imposter.

This lends itself to my theory that we all become dinosaurs in the end, each one of us destined to become an irrelevance during our own lifetime.

As if to prove my point, I was speaking to a friend a couple of days ago; he has two daughters at university and both girls are politically and socially aware and their values are totally in tune with the zeitgeist, but to them, their father's values are miles apart from their own.

The girls see themselves as young progressives, but the irony is that they are part of a generation that is as contradictory as having Greta Thunberg at one end of the spectrum and Kylie Jenner at the polar extreme, representing all colours, creeds and genders, from opulence and greed to minimalism and need, they are all in there somewhere.

Although at the time of writing, if it's a gauge to go by, Kylie has twenty times more followers than Greta, so who knows where the future lies.

What this generation do know is that their time in the hotel will be shared along with billions of others people, all guests staying here, there are currently eight billion as well as these two female 'celebrities' who will continue to influence theirs and society's direction for as long as they are allowed to, which I sense will be longer than is sensible for either the influencers or the influenced.

Back to my friend and his girls at university, as their father he will, of course, attempt to give parental guidance, but there will come a time, that is if it hasn't already happened in this family, where the stabilisers have come off the bike and the two girls now see lovable old stuck-in-his-ways dad as the dinosaur of the family. This is part of the process and although it seems implausible, they too will become dinosaurs to their progeny, should they choose to have any, and if they choose not to have children, then society itself will sit in judgment.

They too will be a product of their generation and its thinking, which will become as dated as every preceding generation. John, their father, was trendy in his day, but now, he's just the old man with opinions as anachronistic as he would be and would look if he went clubbing with them to Ibiza!

I realise this may sound a little insensitive, but I used to believe that I would never become my parents, that I would never stop watching *Top of the Pops* every week, I'd always get New Musical Express… I was never getting old, or certainly my mindset was that of the eternal youth, but like everybody else, you do; in the same way that the majority of eighteen-year-olds don't buy DIY Monthly, a magazine for the aficionado of home improvements; similarly, the vast majority of middle-aged men don't buy Punk Rock Weekly, or whatever the current popular music magazine is.

That is because, for the majority of middle-aged blokes, their music is created by those who they shared the hotel with in their earlier years, their own youth and those musicians tend to stay with you until you check out of the hotel, even if they have checked out before you. It would be difficult to take advice on your stay in the hotel, if you have already been there for over a week and somebody that only arrived in the hotel yesterday started giving you advice on finding your way around, it doesn't tend to work that way.

It was Chicxulub Impactor hitting the earth 66 million years ago that signalled the end of the dinosaur, the creature having been around for the previous 230 million years, had the Chicxulub not happened, had it missed the earth completely, would the dinosaur still be with us?

The Chicxulub Impactor was an accident, but if it was going to happen, it could have happened anywhere in the world, depending on the spinning of the world and where it was when the Impactor hit, which happened to be in the Yucatan peninsula in Mexico, leaving a crater that measures an incredible ninety-three miles wide and twelve miles deep; its devastating impact saw not only a tsunami, but ash and dust clouds so dense and pungent that they could have shaded the earth from sunlight for the following ten years!

It was these effects along with an earthquake measuring twelve on the Mercalli or Richter scale and it was this combination that created a horrible, hostile environment, along with a cooling planet, which led to the mass extinction of a myriad of species, believed to be approximately seventy-five per cent of those that inhabited the planet at that time; unfortunately, their number included the dinosaurs.

The likes of Chicxulub is hopefully never to be seen again, not just for us staying in the hotel now and in the future, but for all of the other life that we hold dear, whether it be flora, fauna and wildlife. So the dinosaurs did die out, becoming extinct, but they encountered more than their share of bad luck in doing so. If the Chicxulub Impactor had entered earth's atmosphere ten minutes earlier or ten minutes later then the hotel today would be a very different place.

The Chicxulub landed in the shallow waters of Mexico's Yucatan peninsula, but moments either side of contact would have meant the Impactor plunging into the deep waters of the Pacific or Atlantic Ocean, which would have absorbed much more of the impact, limiting the expulsion of sulphur-rich sediments that choked the earth's atmosphere for the months and years ahead.

Should that momentary change have occurred, obviously there would still have been a catastrophe and there would no doubt still be an extinction of certain species, although we know not which, we can only speculate.

Let us imagine that this slightly altered timeline for a moment, that Sliding Doors juncture when the planet wasn't in that exact place at that exact time, a time which was fortuitous for some, but not for the many. If the earth's rotation was at a different point, would the dinosaur or its descendants still be with us, would the landscape be different and what would the impact of a dinosaur legacy being a part of our lives be on man, would humans and dinosaurs have evolved together and found a way of living together?

Some scientists believe that dinosaurs were already heading towards extinction as the earth was cooling and the climate was not going to be suitable for them, the catastrophe that was Chicxulub simply speeded up the process.

Chicxulub was not the only massive change the hotel was experiencing 66 million years ago; a couple of hundred years later, the earth experienced the Deccan Traps; this could be perceived as the hotel having an issue with its waterworks and in desperate need for a good plumber.

The Deccan Traps happened relatively soon after Chicxulub and I think it would be amazing if there was no correlation between the two. The Impactor went deep into the earth's crust and there must have been some internal movement below the earth's surface. It makes you think how different our lives could be, even today, had the damage been to a greater or lesser degree, either of which would change the course of history.

The Deccan Traps are in India and represent one of the largest volcanic features on earth, approximately two thousand metres thick and cover an area of 200,000 square miles, but originally when active, they were approximately 600,000 square miles, with lava flows covering over 1.5 million square miles, which is half the size of India.

Once again, volcanic gases and sulphur dioxide being released meant that the climate at that time began to change and actually started cooling by an estimated two degrees Celsius. Of the two, it was Chicxulub that affected the greatest change, due to the dust cloud it created and the duration of that cloud, but combined, both events speeded up the extinction of species and plants; as a result of these events, the hotel was changed forever.

This series of events and the direction the hotel took was irreversible and brought about the demise of the dinosaur. Individually, we are all destined to go the same way as the dinosaur, because obviously, we as humans will continue to function within society until we ultimately die, but our relevance to society diminishes as we age; our influence is reduced within the territory that we roam and spend our lives.

As a footnote to this dinosaur discussion, I would like to let you know about a little thing I discovered while doing my extensive research for this book. I was unaware of the name for the earth's landmass before it began to break up into continents 175 million years ago, a supercontinent known by the name of Pangea.

I was aware of it as a brand name and the Pangea that I know of is a retailer in the northwest of England, from whom I purchased a life-sized hippopotamus for the garden, made out of reclaimed metals and built in Africa. Our family hippopotamus, which we affectionately call Bruno, was for the first time that we became aware of Pangea, when they had a fabulous display of their range of life-sized animal pieces of garden art on display along the quayside.

Little did I know what Pangea actually meant when I started doing business with the company, but now that I do know, the name feels rather appropriate. What if Pangea hadn't split into continents but had remained intact? The world, in fact, the hotel would be a totally different place than we now know.

If the world was one landmass, the landscape would be unrecognisable; instead of living on this island that we call home, we would be living next door to our neighbours in Canada, Australia as we know it would have a winter climate and with all of us living in one country, would we all get along better or would things be so much worse because regions get very protective of their own region?

One thing that has always baffled me is how come there are so many languages in the hotel, not only are they voluminous in number, but they are all so incredibly different and even use different characters. I understand that even in my own country, there are different dialects and accents, which bring with them their own distinctive words and expressions, some that will in many cases make no sense to people, even those in the same country.

My own language of English is derived from a language called Old English, which is better known as Anglo-Saxon and a variety known as West Germanic, although today, English includes words from many languages. When the Normans conquered England in 1066 as a result of the Norman Conquests, they brought with them their Norman language; from this the Anglo-Norman vocabulary was created with many shared or at least similar words in both the French and English languages.

The English language has also assimilated words from many other foreign languages, Latin and Greek are major contributors as is Spanish. There is an interesting development of organic change currently happening in America as the southwestern United States sees a change in its demographic as many Latin Americans head north to cross the border and live in the United States.

The influence of the Latino languages, mixing with the drawl of these Southern border states, is creating a vibrant culture from which the existing language is a beneficiary.

Here in the United Kingdom, we regularly use words originating in Denmark, Sweden, Arabia and Russia, words which are easily spotted when you think about them. As with the Latin Americans crossing into North America, when British people travelled overseas in the days of the empire, not only did they influence the language of the countries they went to, they also brought words back with them. We are grateful to the Indian sub-continent giving us many fabulous contributions, which have enriched our own language.

Words such as pyjamas, bandanna, dungarees and my own favourite, bungalow, all used in our British language as a result of them being brought back from the sub-continent. Interestingly, having researched my favourite import from the language of the subcontinent, bungalow, a word which entered the English language in the late 17th century, was brought here by those British people living in India and were housed in a single-story *bangla*, which is a Hindu word, and used to describe a house, whose design was in a Bengal style, so the single-story house in the United Kingdom eventually became a bungalow—fascinating.

It was the ancient Sanskrit students who gave us the earliest research into etymology, because those intellectual ancient Indians considered both sound and speech to be sacred, so much so that through their interest in the study of language was born, taking us through ancient Greco-Roman, to medieval and into the modern era, to bring us right up to date.

Language is as fluid as the Ganges and it changes over generations, with each generation bringing its buzzwords to the table, providing additions to the existing vocabulary, words that their generation has spawned, the language of youth can be a little arcane to those who have no use for these emerging words and phrases, but once they are adopted by the current generation, their creators slowly begin a petrifaction process and become one of the vital ingredients that see something that was once cool, become totally uncool.

It is the language of a generation, along with their clothes, their music and technology, those temporary fads, that are onetime seen as being trendy for as long as they are current, but the essential qualifications on the CV of any aspiring dinosaur, once that generation starts to burn out and become less influential, with its power in decline as, a new emerging generation is waiting in the wings to take control.

So, if Pangea had remained as one, we may have had one global language, a global culture of global foods and global thinking, but we know the reality of what happened and we have five continents all very different from each other and all with their own individual identities.

So, the dinosaur was always destined for extinction, that's life in the hotel, nobody gets to stay here forever, each generation will have its own time, its own lifespan and the younger generation will then repeat the same process as the generation before them, which means that my friend's daughters will become dinosaurs too, which to them, at this moment in time, seems unthinkable, as they are both too young to appreciate this, but those of us who have been here for a little bit longer and are nearer to the end of our stay…we know the way it works.

The dinosaur wasn't able to use a camera, so maybe that's the link, their demise was sad although inevitable as ultimately the camera will be, which has adapted to change and now its function is found within the greater leap in technology that is the mobile phone which has become ubiquitous amongst this current generation as well as with some forever young Baby Boomers, trying desperately to keep up with Gen Z'ers everywhere.

The Gen Z kids are those born anywhere between the years in the mid-90s to the early 2010s. These people have never known a time when the mobile phone didn't exist and therefore their lives are contained within that small piece of metal and plastic and it is as integral to their very existence as the air that they breathe.

Those days of waiting for the family photographs being returned by postie from Boots are as distant a memory as the black-and-white world that those photographs reflected. But surely there is a trade-off for having every waking moment of your life documented with a photo, a tweet, an Instagram post, or the latest viral TikTok video.

A person exposing their life to constant scrutiny must inevitably lose something and maybe we will only understand the true implications of this 24/7 access all areas of people's lives in ten or twenty years' time, when the fallout has occurred, we start to see emerging trends, certainly the cracks will be appearing and these crash test dummies, being used to trial the permanent intrusion that the mobile phone provides, starts showing.

Showing us not just the benefits of the technological wizardry, but also its faults; there will, of course, be positives, but I maintain that there will also be negatives, long-term effects such as mental health or changes in relationships which I feel must be effected and so they will inevitably become societal issues.

From my point of view, I think the scariest prospect of a fully documented stay in the hotel is that the Gen Z'ers who are the guinea pigs, the pioneers on behalf of future guests in what is effectively a social experiment, start to fulfil their potential as a generation and mature, it is only then that we will fully appreciate the change that they have been subject to.

Of course, I have a mobile phone myself and occasionally post on Facebook or tweet or X as we now know it, but I don't use Instagram or Tik Tok, but don't forget, I am old enough to remember when Friends Reunited was cool and trendy, so I'm still ahead of the curve; not.

But there will be many people of my age and older who do use TikTok or its latest incarnation and I applaud them, they will see the latest viral dancing dog video long before I do and that may make them feel good and that's the point, its freedom of choice. Inevitably, apps will come and go and trends will change as time goes on, but the primary users of the latest technology are the kids who are possibly easier to manipulate than their parents who haven't really got a clue whether they should be using Tik Tok or Clip Clop.

The old expression, 'If youth knew, if age could', springs to mind, a very old French expression originally created by Henri Estienne or alternatively a quote by Sigmund Freud, depending on who you care to believe; however, I have employed extensive research and a definitive answer is hard to establish, as opinion appears to be divided on the originator of the expression. However it is not the origin that is the issue here, I would prefer to focus on the profundity of the quotation and the more I think about it, the more I believe that this quote is a perfect complement to my belief that life is like a hotel.

'If youth knew' simply represents those arriving in the hotel and enjoying their first few days getting to know the place, where to eat or drink, the nicest bars in the village, the people to avoid or those to spend time with and so on, it's the steepest of learning curves which every single person who is fortunate enough to check in at reception in order to stay in the hotel, has to navigate.

'If age could' is fairly self-explanatory from my point of view; as you grow to have an understanding of what is good, what is bad, what you enjoy and what you don't, you tend to have made your mistakes, you realise that you don't have that much time left to do all of those things that you want to do or spend the time with those you have grown to love spending time with, sharing your stay with.

Importantly and unavoidably, as your stay in the hotel progresses, you will change, you as a person, not simply the physical differences that ageing presents us all with, but your values can become very different to those that they once were, your priorities change, you also begin to realise that it won't last forever, for it is those circumstances around you that are beyond your control or influence that alter your perspective.

When you arrive in high spirits for a skiing trip, literally and metaphorically in my case, you think of the glorious prospects of a week that is full, of snow, schnapps and apfel strudel, it is all in front of you, like the moment you jump off the ski lift and stand at the top of a neatly manicured piste, it is all in front of you, waiting for you to make your own mark on the mountain, descending gracefully, or tumbling like a nervous beginner.

It could be your first time at a new resort or reuniting with some old acquaintances in a favourite hotel up in the mountains, you're with friends, each of whom is looking forward to a fabulous holiday, but on the first day, a bad fall takes one of your party out and an accidental broken leg means that one of your party has to spend the rest of the trip sat in the hotel during the day, while everybody else has a blast on the slopes, followed by some decent apres-ski!

Life can change that quickly; in a moment of time, you have to be able to reassess your situation and move forward.

When you first arrive in any resort, it's all in front of you, the fun lies in finding those things that you enjoy, the experiences that make it all so exciting and it is a time when as well as having moments of self-discovery, we start to build relationships with fellow guests, but it's not all as hedonistic as it sounds, in spite of many of us, including myself, having those sybaritic tendencies and making it all as much fun as possible, we may also find ourselves looking for purpose, a reason for being, having those 'why are we all here' thoughts, which can see us searching for like-minded people or others who share our way of thinking, whether it is similar beliefs or understanding of life, whether these are religious, political or even supporting a football team, but relationships for the majority of us can form a fundamental part of our existence.

I have always found that when you are up in the mountains there is a heightened sense of your insignificance, surrounded by the majesty of the landscape, the mountains exhibit magnificence and a beauty, offering awe inspiring surroundings that expose your insignificance, which can inspire those like-minded souls to examine their existence and question their purpose.

Relationships can be both positive and negative, people can let you down, even those closest to you, it is impossible to know what another person is truly thinking at any time about anything, even a person with whom you share your life, your selective inner thoughts and intimate moments, you can never truly know what another person is thinking and it is for that reason, that ultimately, we are alone in the hotel, with our own thoughts.

In spite of this lottery, we all manage to become invested in other people's lives, simply by being in the hotel, you have parents and possibly siblings and maybe grandparents and an extended family all people who are related to you by blood and so have an interest in your life, it is these bonds that provide us with strength and support during our stay.

Outside of our families, we then build other relationships with those previously unknown to us, people that we are attracted to for many and various reasons; interestingly and with a nod to these relationships, Harper Lee opined in *To Kill a Mockingbird*, 'you can choose your friends but you sho' can't choose your family, an' they're still kin to you no matter whether you acknowledge 'em or not and it makes you look right silly when you don't.' Lee wrote this in her 1960 classic of modern American literature, a story loosely based on Lee's observations of her family, neighbours and friends during 1936, when an event that happened in her home state of Alabama, even though she was only ten years of age; she manages to recall its impact on both herself and the society that she was being raised in.

The novel tackles the issues of rape and racial inequality, but it does so with a distinct warmth and humour, in spite of the gravity of the subject matter, it introduces us to the character, Atticus Finch, our hero, who has subsequently become known for his morals and integrity.

For you pop fans reading this and purely as an aside because I would be interested in this myself, *To Kill a Mockingbird* introduces us to another character, giving us a band name that became part of 90's pop culture.

In the book, we are introduced to Arthur 'Boo' Radley, a reclusive character, a mysterious neighbour who is gossiped about and dismissed because of his secretive life and apparently the character's name was remembered by the members of the band, the Boo Radleys, as a character from a book they had read during their schooldays and considered it to be a sufficiently cool name and so the band was named.

But enough of that, we are getting away from the point about close relationships, the ones that we build outside of our families, indeed for most of us we actually find a lifetime partner and with that lifetime partner family is created, so our choice of partner is crucial, not only for ourselves during our stay in the hotel, but its influence in the future of our extended families.

Obviously, some lifetime partnerships don't actually last a lifetime as divorce rates rise, but that doesn't mean that our appetite for long-term relationships is diminished, most of us still feel a need for a life partner, whether it is a husband or wife, or a suitable alternative, so much so we practice long-term relationships with girlfriends and boyfriends from our teenage years, readying ourselves for the demands of living with another person, preparing us for adulthood and maybe marriage, often getting it wrong, sometimes getting it right, but all preparing us for the real thing.

But can we ever truly know another person? You can know their opinions, their beliefs or their understanding of the world and what they really want from life, what they need and how far they will go to satisfy those desires, some people will go to extreme measures and never communicate their ambition, those are thoughts remain private.

We can only ever know and trust are own thoughts and feelings and even those can change at a moment's notice, we plough our own furrow throughout our time here.

I have always found it a fascinating thought that even though we may have made a lifetime commitment to another person or have spent the majority of our lives with them, can we ever fully know or understand what they believe or think? What is somebody else thinking, is it possible to become so close to another person that you know there intimate thoughts?

As much as some people believe that they know the most secretive thoughts of their partners, I somehow doubt it and find it hard to believe that it is possible and that is in spite of my wife and I spending twenty happy years together and being married for over thirty years.

By the way, that was a joke.

You could be perceive my observation as a comment in my own confidence in our relationship, but I think it's a little more than that, I believe we know each other incredibly well and know our preferences for music, food, holiday destinations, but I'm looking for more than those things.

When I talk about knowing a person, I mean about knowing their private thoughts and due to their very nature, those thoughts are unknowable, whether it's important or not, I'm not sure, but I feel it is vital to acknowledge our time in the hotel is spent independently of others.

This may not matter too much in the early part of our stay, when life is carefree and your relationships are primarily with your family, who invariably have your interests at heart, but as our time here extends from the metaphorical end of week one and into week two, these thoughts become more important to us as our lives progress and relationships take on a new importance a different dimension.

Those people we become attached to in the early years become more than just fellow guests during our stay, it is these people that we look to for support and guidance, while we are here.

Of course, there are also many people who navigate their stay independent of the influence of other people, in as far as it is possible, not needing to rely on others but instead, trusting themselves for every aspect of their stay.

This situation can have happened by design, where an individual is happy in their own company, conversely others can find themselves alone because of the death of a partner and decide that their love was too all-consuming and to meet another person and share the remainder of their lives with them would devalue their previous relationship, or indeed thinking it would not be fair to commit to another person as they as individuals with their own stay too consider, deserve better.

But in my experience, we have spent the first few days in the hotel subconsciously building relationships that we will eventually come to rely on in future, whether they are in our business or our private lives, though inevitably there will be a handful of people we meet during our stay that also become lifelong friends.

How many times have you taken the names and numbers of people that you have spent a fabulous five or six days with while on holiday, fully intending to meet up once you get home to relive those momentous times, but rarely doing so, you're back in the real world, where the daily you lives, the person that has all of the pressures that life brings and none of the freedoms that allow you to be you when removed from them temporarily.

That then poses the difficult question, which is the real you, the one on holiday, or the one at home, or maybe we are all chameleons? However, it can also be incredibly positive and I can think of at least five couples that we have met while being abroad, in various countries, that have become friends and remain so until this day, definitely enriching our own lives, which we have hopefully reciprocated.

Indeed, because of my own fascination for the world of hotels and how I believe that their totality is a metaphor for life itself, I can think of several people who I consider to be good friends who work in the industry and are currently in such diverse places as the beautiful mountains of Austria, the sophistication of Madrid and on to the effortless cool of West Palm Beach in Florida.

We have photographed ourselves in all of these locations and far from sending them off to Boots and waiting for the postman to bring them back to us, we have belied our impending dinosaur status and both my wife and I carry our mobile phones everywhere. Snapping along at the most opportune of moments and although my wife is not immune to the occasional selfie, to this very day, I have never taken one.

This chapter was intended to look at the way the chronicling of our lives, our stay in the hotel, was changing forever from a personal perspective, I can remember my early days of photographs being taken at life-changing events or major milestones, to the current fetishisation of the photo opportunity, presenting itself with every passing minute.

Inevitably, the youth of today will have a price to pay for their permanent exposure to the lens but I sense that I will have checked out of the hotel long before those consequences become fully known. Let us not forget, the Victorians loved to photograph their lives, being tracked by the camera, so much so that they even photographed their dead, which was an incredible development of the genre, but inevitable, as death is as much a part of life as birth.

After-death portraits were a big thing for the Victorians, a time when child mortality rates were incredibly high and in those days a photograph in death was all a family may have to remember a child, who had no opportunity to make their mark in the world and all that was left to honour their memory was a photograph.

Our stay in the hotel will be immortalised by those snapshots of our lives, at least while they still mean something to somebody.

Chapter 14
Would You Go There Again?

This is the one question that is asked by those to whom we recount our time spent on holiday or in any hotel, if you think about it, how many times do you share tales of your holidays with friends, only to be asked whether you would go there again, which of course is important, because people are always open to a recommendation, to being told by another person, especially a person whose opinion they value, what they consider to be either a good or a bad, place to visit, knowing where or where not to go, these are always nice things to bear in mind, more so when coming from a trusted source.

In my opinion and although we know some people will think differently, this hotel experience that we are all going through is literally a once in a lifetime opportunity to take it all in, loving the good, tolerating the bad, taking the rough with the smooth or the highs with the lows.

The Yin and Yang of life is a philosophical theory given to us by the Chinese, which describes the concept of how forces that appear to be opposite or contrary are actually complimentary, interconnected and interrelated to each other. That may sound counterintuitive but actually when you analyse it, the concept is a good one.

We have to back up a little in order to see where Yin and Yang originated and to do this we need to look briefly at Chinese creationist theory.

This may sound a little heavy, but trust me, it's not, because Chinese creation theory differs from religious beliefs, those ideologies which have a single creator, the Chinese symbolic narratives are about the origins of the universe, earth and life not believing in a deity, or a creator, in fact there are a number of contradictory theories, but fundamentally they do not rely on a god!

Traditionally, the understanding is that the world was created on Chinese New Year, the animals, the people and many deities were created during the fifteen day period that it took to complete the creative cycle.

There are many deities to choose from so I will look at just one, in order to give us an insight into the wonderful world of Chinese creation theory, so let's take a brief look.

There are so many characters in the creation myth, of which Pangu is one of the most popular, the theory goes like this, basically the earth was created from an exploding egg, a cosmic egg, which contained Yin and Yang, and it was Pangu inside the egg as the supreme being or Taiji who created the world.

Now, that is all quite complicated but there is a point to this and it is to establish Yin and Yang and their relevance to time spent in the hotel, indeed of the many Chinese creation theories available, Yin and Yang have made the giant leap from eastern to western culture and many of us will be aware of Yin and Yang and what the expression has come to mean.

In two clearly defined periods of 18,000 years, the first was for the cosmic egg to ferment and the second to start creating the earth. As the second 18,000 years elapsed, Pangu breathed, his breath became the wind, mist and clouds, his left eye the sun and his right eye the moon and so forth, you can see where this is heading.

Yin and Yang are the earth and the sky and it is Pangu who keeps them apart as he allows them to grow, but also shaping the world chiselling valleys and stacking up mountains all accomplished using his understanding of Yin and Yang and the inescapable principle of duality in all things.

Duality, or dualism, is a belief which can be either spiritual or indeed moral and the belief is that two fundamental concepts exist, often opposing each other, literally black and white or good and evil, but that is probably too simplistic.

I don't want to make this book too challenging and I don't want to get distracted by my fundamental theory of life being a hotel, which I could easily do by being distracted and looking at the many beliefs that will offer an alternative point of view. There are so many and I can throw a few names at you such as Manichaeism, Zoroastrianism, Marcionism and Wicca.

These four religions offer a belief that more than one god is at work in creating the hotel, some believe that, if there are two gods, one of them is good and one is bad, whereas, some believe that the two gods are equally powerful and complimentary, some implying harmony, some rivalry.

In life and for us individually, in order for us to know what good is, we must also know what is bad and although various religions and cultures may interpret the simplicity of Yin and Yang and give it a more technical explanation, as your stay in the hotel progresses you realise that life in its simplest form is a two sided coin.

They say that grief is the price we pay for love and for every positive in the hotel we must always be aware that there is a negative, we are lucky if we can always be on the right side of the equation, but it is rare for any person to cruise through their life unchallenged by those two imposters, success and failure.

We can always look back over our own lives and of course for everybody fortunate enough to have the opportunity to stay in the hotel, there are things that they would do differently if they were given the opportunity to do it all again.

But it doesn't work that way, you get your chance to play the game, for that is what it appears to me to be and however you play it, the decisions that you make at the time that you make them are for the right reasons, you hope that the decisions that you make will give you as an individual or for you and your family, the best possible outcome, otherwise you wouldn't choose that course of action.

We can all look back with 20/20 hindsight when things have turned out badly, but I don't believe anybody consciously makes bad choices.

But let us say that you did get the chance to do it all again, for me there is no doubt that those things, those situations that you would change would then present their own set of new circumstances that will inevitably also need addressing, of which some will be positive and some will be negative, there are always decisions to be made, some minor, some major, but all life-changing in their own way and although you may strive for perfection, we know that nobody has a perfect life.

It takes time to learn the unwritten rules of life, but I do believe that they exist, there are some rules which will apply to us individually, while some will apply to us as a part of society so as this is a look at our stay in the hotel I thought it may be an idea to look at several of those things that I have learnt during my own stay.

As I said, not all of them will apply to you as an individual, in fact it depends how far you are into your own stay in the hotel when you are reading this whether they are relevant to you or not.

As you get older, you don't necessarily get wiser, but time is a great healer and the longer you stay, the more opportunities you have to perfect your act and not keep making the same mistakes. Alexander Pope told us that, 'to err is human, but to forgive is divine'; we all make mistakes, so forgive yourself the occasional faux pas or error of judgement and as we know, perfection comes from imperfection.

You as an individual are always the result of what has happened to you during your stay, the good as well as the bad, the positives and negatives all makeup what is you, and to change any of them would result in you being a different person.

There is no point dwelling on the past, whatever it was, it has gone forever, whether it was incredible or unbearable, there is nothing that you can do to effect the past, you only have today.

If you hang on to those days gone by because of mistakes that you have made, or regrets that you may have, then ultimately this is destructive and can only damage you and your future, there is nothing you can do to wipe the slate clean.

If you live in the past because in those days, you were more successful, happier, younger, fitter, whatever it was, just say thanks for the memories and move on, remaining grateful that you had those times, because not everybody will.

I have come to realise that there is no optimum time in life, but there are certainly different stages of your stay, the excitement of your first day in any hotel, countered by the sadness of your last day.

Every day that you wake up is a fresh start, a clean slate, a blank canvas, take your pick, but whichever you choose, it is up to you and you alone to make the best of it, making it what you want it to be, you set the limits, sometimes it can be tough, really tough, but if you have the ability to keep your enthusiasm going then that is vital.

Fortunately for me, and quite bizarrely, in spite of any adversity that I have experienced, I have always managed to remain positive constantly. I have come to believe that this strength comes from within, it is an ability to handle the difficulties that life throws at you, me and everybody.

I don't suggest that I have some inner strength that no other person has, but I have a resilience that enables me to make the best of a situation, even when it isn't great, to highlight the point I will often say to my wife, who can catastrophise any situation, that I could have a party in a telephone box, which means that in any situation I could make it work and have a ball!

To a greater or lesser degree, we all have to confront difficulties during our stay and they need facing, it is easy to personalise things, to think that it is only you struggling with the day-to-day travails that can make our stay here far from pleasant, if indeed not a battle!

One of my favourite quotes, attributed to both Winston Churchill and Abraham Lincoln, is, 'Success is going from failure to failure without losing your enthusiasm.'

I'm not suggesting my life is a procession of failures by any means, but what I always am and always have been is positive or in this case always enthusiastic. I'm not sure where it comes from, without being disrespectful to my own parents, as lovely as they are, they aren't particularly positive people, yet I am a very positive person and fortunately for me that attitude never dissipates.

Life does go by very quickly, which doesn't always resonate when you are younger, if you are in you first few days in the hotel, your last day seems like it's a long way away and of course, relatively it is, you have plenty of time to do all of those things that you intend to do, you can put some things on the back burner, you have got lots of time to fit it all in, everything you want to do, but then, as your last few days come into sight you suddenly realise how much there is left to do, those things that you want to do, but have yet to realise.

My point here is that there is always time for new experiences, it doesn't really matter which stage of life you are at; currently, Madrid has been our latest and it has been good to us. So what is the best way to handle your stay, do you plan every waking moment in the minutest of detail, or do you let fate take its course, believing that our destiny is not in our own hands, allowing you to sit back, relax and see what happens?

Whatever you decide to do, whichever way you approach your stay, you are right, there is no science to life, there isn't a definitive answer, there is your own way, it is a bespoke approach determined by you and what you believe to be right.

What always amazes me is that although there are over eight billion of us all going through the same things every day, with varying degrees of success and failure, we never know whether it could have been a lot better, or indeed a lot worse.

Can you imagine if there is an opportunity sometime in the future, once we've checked out to sit in a darkened room, reviewing our stay, with a film or a slideshow, or whatever the latest technology offers, showing us once more, all that's happened during our time here, the highs the lows, the good and the bad, the greatest hits and the biggest misses, do we get to watch it all again, in a speeded up version of what we have been through, the laughter and tears, cringing at the naivety of youth or maybe pride in our legacy, is somebody recording it all for us to see once we have checked out?

Is there any accountability at the end of our stay, do we settle up by paying the metaphorical bill as we check out at reception, it could be a physical or indeed a mental transaction and if there is, then what is the price to be paid and who to?

These are massive questions for those of us who remain unconvinced by everything that religion has to offer, yes of course all religions tend to offer some sort of insight, but as for a definitive code to live your life by, every day that you are here, for me personally, none of the religions, at least those that I am aware of, provide me with the answers that I feel that I need in order to make sense of it all!

If, like me, you don't have faith, that doesn't negate the need for some answers, questions still need answering, questions like, what has it all been for, because as with the rest of the guests, currently staying here, nobody actually knows and really some of us don't care?

At least if you do have a religion, then you are given some of the answers, should you choose to believe them, for this is where religions actually come into their own, a one stop shop for answers to the big questions.

Religions provide the answers to those who need them and in doing so, they provide comfort and support to those staying in the hotel and needing a tour guide to show them around the place.

Having any religion can give those people who are currently staying in the hotel a purpose in life, especially amongst those who feel socially disconnected and needing something more than relationships with other people to inform the quality of their stay.

Relationships with family, friendships with close friends are still a vital part of their stay, but some people are looking for a little more meaning than birthday parties and weekends spent sharing times with fellow guests, what is the point, is this it or is there more and this is where religion steps in.

Religion can provide an explanation of the origins of our world, creation and man's existence, so for that reason you no longer have to keep searching for answers to those big questions, your holiday representative in the hotel will do that for you, you have your tour guide here to help with your stay, to provide the answers that life presents.

Absolving you from looking for answers and allowing you to search for a happy life, lived within the constraints of your religion of choice. It's all about creation, the origins of the hotel and to this end, there are many works which discuss the creation and ultimately, when reading through masses of contributions, it boils down to two types of people, those that think it must have been created by a god, we call them theists, or those that believe that nature determines what we have and everything in our world comes from nature and we call them naturalists.

In the world of the theist, what I have often found is, there is more than likely to be a smugness that comes with their religion, that naturalists simply don't enjoy, because they have nothing, apart from their own self-belief, their own understanding of things to hang onto, but the problem for theists is that in spite of their faith, they don't know if what they believe is true, so probably best not to be too inquisitive or questioning.

Religion and faith are superior to the alternatives in that they attempt to provide the answers to those big unanswered questions of life, in doing so that then provides us with a couple of alternatives, we should either applaud our friends who have religion, for their confidence in their belief, their faith in whichever god they have chosen to fully commit to, that enables them to wander around the hotel with the supreme confidence of knowing the purpose of their stay.

Conversely, we may ridicule them for their delusion, the total arrogance in believing that it is them and only them and their religious cohorts that knows the inside story of what is going on and what happens next, could to most non-believers appear at the least, delusional.

Those that are religious, no matter which god they are committed to, are all on a metaphorical all-inclusive stay, everything is taken care of, other than the day-to-day machinations of their time as an individual in the hotel, there is absolutely nothing else for them to concern themselves about, it has all been done for them, by millions of previous guests, who have had those self-same beliefs and felt a common purpose and a shared understanding of what it's all about.

Whereas those without religion are staying on a room-only basis, meaning that for the majority of their stay, they are left to their own devices, contending with their own thoughts, sailing their ship alone as they navigate the waters of life.

Making sense of life as it comes at them without the crutch that a religion offers, instead accepting the randomness of their stay for exactly what it is, a cacophony of circumstances that will baffle the most intellectual naturalist.

Room-only is exactly as it says, it is as basic as it gets; you get your eight hours a night to sleep, but the other two-thirds of the day, you are left to your own devices, whether it's for sustenance, food, or your physical and mental wellbeing.

With just over 30% of the world's population choosing Christianity as their religion of choice, and representing the largest single following of any one single religion in the hotel today, these people all believing, to a greater or lesser degree, that they have the definitive understanding of life itself, which of course is totally acceptable, because people can believe anything they choose to, just as long as they are not putting demands on the rest of us, compelling others to chime with their beliefs and modifying our existence, our stay in the hotel, to fit in with theirs.

Yes, 30% of the world's population is a big number, but it is still a minority, so we must never allow people who do believe and have religious conviction to coerce, however subtly or unsubtly those of us who don't have their conviction or commitment to their ideology, expecting other people to adhere to their beliefs and comply with their demands.

There are other religions for us to look at, we have Islam, Hinduism and Buddhism along with several other belief systems, which also have large if slightly smaller numbers globally of followers than Christianity, all of which believe that they too have the insight to the way the world works and indeed what it's all about, but whatever their interpretation of life, invariably they all demand that true adherence to their faith means that they expect followers to live their lives during their stay in the hotel, by the demands of the faith, by their rules.

I have no issue with anybody having a belief or a faith in anything, because nobody knows definitively what is going on, then how can anybody be told they are wrong in their belief.

That being true, what has always struck me as rather contradictory is the fact that they can't all be right, simply because these religions are so diverse, yes, with many similarities and crossover thoughts and agreements but also having different interpretations in their understanding of life, with a range of opinions so diverse, that the probability of them all being right appears to me at least as being impossible.

The third largest demographic in belief systems, if we can call the third ranking largest group such, because it is the antithesis of a belief system, but with 16%, the third largest group of people in the hotel is irreligious, meaning they have no religious beliefs at all, either a total absence of belief or an indifference to it. There has been a substantial growth in the number of those with no religion in recent years, so much so they have been labelled 'nones' but once again, even in the field of nones, we find nones by degree, none is not as absolute as it sounds.

This is another area that I feel has been hijacked and intellectualised by interested parties, keen to segregate and desperate for an identity matched only by religious zealots who are keen to tell us all about their beliefs and how it is they that know what the rest of us don't, it is they who have the gift of insight.

There is a smorgasbord of delights on offer to the nonbeliever, you can be anything from, a secular humanist, an atheist, agnostic, ignosticist, secularist and on and on it goes, with many others all competing for the title of non-believer.

The field is as complex as religion itself, with the minutest point of difference being enough to necessitate the formation of another group of badge wearing deniers.

I don't feel the need personally to have to declare the minutiae of my thought process in order to establish the intangibles of what I don't believe, I think the statement is self-explanatory but of course, the existence of the vast number of sub groups does stimulate conversation.

Going back to the prospect of having a film show, played to us once we have checked out, a place that is yet to be formally discovered a cinema in the sky, a huge multiplex filled with the recently departed, all sitting there with a bucket of popcorn and a giant Diet Coke, waiting to watch the rerun of their lives.

If we were given this opportunity, in a place, somewhere, who knows where, identified by us where we will do a review of the compilation of our time spent in the hotel, a Greatest Hits if you will, then wouldn't that be fascinating.

Maybe we don't leave it to others and we do our own review, as we approach reception for the final time, this is a time in our lives when we often have time on our hands and maybe this is our opportunity to contemplate our salad days, those distant times when we were young and inexperienced, the days that invariably are bathed in sunlight and stars as our memories are recalled.

It is good that we tend to remember the nice bits, think of those special times, the friends we've made the places that we have been to that will always remain special to us, some of those memories will be tinged with sadness too, the people we miss, those who have checked out prematurely or expectedly, but who we would still want to be here, helping us to enjoy our own stay.

This process will happen to each of us in turn and it is only as we near the end of our stay that we start our personal reflections, yes our memories are triggered by an event or an occasion every day of our lives, but your collection of lifetime memories become more powerful as checking out becomes a reality, it is those early years that are spent capturing the memories that we ultimately come to reflect upon.

If there is no ultimate review of our time in the hotel, no scrutinising of our bill as we check out at reception for the final time, apart that is from our own reminiscences, then without some form of accountability, that for me literally begs the question, what has been the point?

Is our stay simply inconsequential, no after-match analysis, no enquiry, no price to pay, no score given, it's just a bit of fun, saint or sinner, it doesn't matter, because the outcome is irrelevant?

There are and have been so many guests, both those who are here today and the billions who have stayed here in the past, that the turnover of guests would make it logistically difficult, at least for us human folk, to comprehend the management of the outcomes.

But imagine if it were to be managed by a superior being with super powers then that could make the whole proposition possible, that would make more sense, but obviously nobody knows.

The point I'm trying to get to is this, through all of life's dramas, the fun, the sadness, the disappointment, the thrills, the pride, the pain, every emotion that this rollercoaster throws at us during our stay, so what, yes it might be fun, sure we will all experience happiness and sadness and ultimately death, that's great, but what is the point?

Would the world be any different if you or I had never stayed in the hotel, for us individually we would be none the wiser because we never existed, we never got to take our turn, to play the game and as a consequence the influence that our existence has on those around us while we are her would disappear and to that degree this would alter the course of those people's lives, nobody would be any the wiser of course, but different they would be.

The thought is fascinating, what could have been, but again, so what? Their existence is as irrelevant as our own and so yes, their lives would be different but ultimately, so what? What are we doing here, why is procreation so important, that's if it is and if it is, then to what end, why are we all playing this game, we are doing it without knowing whether there is any consequence whatsoever of our staying here, or if not an actual consequence then at least a reckoning at the end of it all and so with this being the case it is hard for any of us to know with any degree of certainty what the point of it all has been.

As Christmas approaches and I near the end of writing this book, I find myself looking forward to something that has become a Christmas tradition in our house. We have grown to love Christmas films, we have several favourites— *Christmas with the Kranks*, *National Lampoon Christmas Vacation* and *Dinner for One* and many others, including one which would be fabulous at any time of the year, *It's a Wonderful Life*.

The 1946 American Christmas drama fantasy film, directed by Frank Capra, is based on Philip Van Doreen Stern's short story, *The Greatest Gift*, and with loose ties to the Charles Dickens' classic, *A Christmas Carol*. The plot of the film is to give us an insight into the life of our hero, George Bailey, who through his business dealings finds himself contemplating suicide, but George is assigned an angel named Clarence, whose job it is to look after George.

We see the relationships that he has created from his early childhood, where we see him saving his brother's life, sadly to his own detriment, as he loses the ability to hear in one ear, to his business clients, people that he has helped in buying their homes, often first-time buyers, he has helped in his banking business, then on to his own family, his wife his children and all of those people that his own being, his own existence has influenced and continues to influence.

The point at which we see George contemplating suicide is systematically exposed by Clarence as a selfish act and of course George has not thought to consider how his death would inevitably effect those other lives.

The film is about our interconnectedness and how our lives and our relationships intertwine, giving us a type of Jenga dependency on each other, where the pulling of one of the pieces has an effect on all of the others in the stack, whether they are at the very top of the stack or the adjacent brick.

But more than this, George's brother, a World War 2 hero, is alive because George has saved him, thus enabling his brother Harry to save lives and become a war hero. If it wasn't for George, his brother wouldn't be alive and neither would those lives his brother saved in the war.

The knock-on effects of one person's life is there for all of us to see and more often than not, never consider until it is explained to us. The real lesson of *It's a Wonderful Life* is that in spite of great ambition and striving for achievement in life, it is the thin layers that we build up day to day that go rather unnoticed and can seem irrelevant at the time, but it is these that combine to create us as an individual.

A filo pastry effect, if you will, which if you had just one single layer of filo pastry for consumption, it would go virtually unnoticed, however the layering of many slices to form one beautiful taste of indulgence, which, when it is done well, makes for an absolute gastronomic delight.

Love for our friends and family, the decency that we offer to those people around us, not necessarily doing great things, but possibly more importantly doing those small things in a nice way, these are the moments that we carry with us, not only during our stay in the hotel, but maybe beyond, we simply don't know.

To our knowledge, we haven't had any returning guests to stay again in this fabulous hotel and if you think about it, because it is such a brilliant place to stay, surely there must have been at least one person who wouldn't mind coming back for another visit, have another stay in the hotel and do it all again.

Maybe returning guests do walk amongst us and a condition of their second visit is that they mustn't tell any other person that they have been here before and if they do, they forfeit the rest of their stay and are withdrawn immediately and this accounts for sudden death syndrome!

I feel a conspiracy theory coming on!

We do know that some people are convinced they've been here before and there is a cottage industry in past life regression, a process that takes its victim, sorry client, through hypnosis, back to the last time they were last here, staying in the hotel, living as another person in a different era, but this has been discredited as either delusion or wilful malpractice by the practitioner and those convinced they are regressing, but once again, who knows?

But when you think about and consider those millions, no billions of previous guests all milling around somewhere looking for another resting place, where are they now, what are they doing, who are they with, the questions are endless and it just because nobody knows the answer, but that doesn't mean that there isn't an answer.

I am always amazed that the combined wisdom and intellect of our forefathers and the geniuses we currently have staying here, that we are no further ahead in our understanding of our purpose.

It still fascinates me today and even more so as I have written this book, my interest is sparked even further than the moment that I first set out to write it, I suppose it is obvious, but the more I've researched the more my interest is piqued.

When the whole *Life is a Hotel* thing started, all that I had was a desperate need to understand what life, death and everything in between was all about and in my own mind, I had worked out that the whole process was simply replicated by the experience of staying in a hotel.

Check in, stay a while and then check out, meet a few of the other guests who were staying at the same time as you are, wave some people off who were leaving, welcome new faces as they arrived at reception and finally say your own goodbyes as you check out for the final time, I'm sure that you've got the idea by now.

But as I read further and began to think a lot deeper, researching the elements of the understanding that I felt was developing and attempting to create a more coherent theory, the more I started believing that I was possibly on to something.

As I write this part of the book, we find ourselves in the Christmas-New Year period of the year, a time when various media outlets review the year and remind us of those 'celebrities' who have died this year; I cannot help but feel that although with each and every life that expires, not just those celebrities that we have created, but every single person who leaves, there is inevitably great sadness amongst both family and friends of the person concerned; although they are no longer with us, those people have simply checked out of the hotel and their stay is over.

But don't forget, in the majority of cases those checking out of the hotel will have checked in long before most of us who still remain and so therefore, although it is sad, it is just the natural order of things; the earlier you check in, the earlier you check out and nobody is here forever.

Where to and what happens next, I think we have concluded, that none of us know the answer to those points, but without doubt, those people have left, never to return, but of course, life goes on and to the majority of the eight billion of us still here, having never met, heard of or even been aware of the existence of our fellow guests who have just departed, our own lives carry on as if nothing had happened and nothing as a consequence of their departure will change life for us.

There can be individuals in your next village, the nearest country or on the other side of the world, a person as unknown to you, as you are to them, whose existence is of absolutely no consequence to you or indeed the rest of the world, a person who will live life under the radar, famous for absolutely nothing, but just getting on with living their lives as anonymously as if they never existed.

But they do exist, they exist in the world of celebrity and superstar, the Yin and Yang of the guest list.

No world audience for these people, they neither have global acclaim, nor seek it, except from those inevitable interactions that do occur in their lives of glorious mundanity, existing only within their own families, groups and community of friends.

Their often small repetitive daily interactions with a close bunch of people, friends and acquaintances whose existences all have an interdependency, helping them to coexist in a world of anonymity, but this is sufficient, they do not desire a brash existence, lurching from drama to drama, causing havoc and leaving a trail of destruction wherever they go.

So what is the point of those people's lives, would the world be any different if they had never been born, if they had never checked in in the first place.

The anonymity of their existence could be and is countered by the great achievers amongst us, those people who are staying here at the moment, making significant ripples throughout the hotel and so by using the term, great achievement I don't necessarily mean great success, I mean great notoriety because there are also those who can make a huge impact for nefarious reasons, currently Vladimir Putin is known across the world, but not necessarily for the right reasons or for good.

Whatever your thoughts, the discussion here is about those who are making an impact on the place during their stay, good or bad and the impact that they make. Currently, we have guests including Elon Musk and Jeff Bezos, just two examples of many who are currently making a major difference to the way the hotel is being run. The great inventors, Alexander Graham Bell, Leonardo da Vinci or Archimedes, people who were responsible for inventing the telephone, the helicopter and the cog, respectively; their contributions to the world have been immense and have altered the way we live our lives.

But the question then must be, would their inventions have come to fruition and been invented by another person if those three had never been born, or if they as individuals hadn't discovered or developed them, we will never know, but more importantly, in that they have had such a major impact during their stay, do their achievements make their lives far more important than those of us who haven't made big changes to the society that we live in.

The contributions of those three examples have helped the rest of the world and the people staying here in a major way, whereas those of us who haven't made a single significant difference and have simply existed, has there been any point?

What a conundrum, great success no doubt and life-changing, but is that sufficient to declare that they are more important or better people than millions of others, surely that is impossible to answer.

It's a Wonderful Life seems to tell us that every life is important, even though the person concerned may feel that their contribution doesn't deserve merit and maybe that is the point, we all have a part to play.

If I remember correctly, it was in Shakespeare's fabulous play, *As You Like It*, that Jaques tells us, orating the words of the Bard, that the world is a stage and that there are seven stages to a man's life, often referred to as the Seven Ages of Man. But Shakespeare, who was without doubt as clever an original thinker as we have ever seen staying in the hotel, was a babe in arms when Richard Edwards, in his play *Damon and Pythias*, wrote the lines, 'Pythagoras said that this world was like a stage, whereon many play their parts, the lookers-on, the sage.'

But can any thought be original, as I sit here writing about life being a hotel, is there another person in the outback in Australia or possibly a bar in Helsinki thinking the exact same thing as me and contemplating committing their thoughts to paper?

There are eight billion people in the world, staying in the hotel today, so it seems virtually impossible to think that any thought is or indeed can be original and all we can say is that whenever one person becomes the first to declare their thinking, to the rest of us in the hotel, then that becomes the original thought.

No doubt one area that is, by its nature, constantly innovative, if not constantly evolving is technology, it is full of original thinking, it is a sector that demands creativity and originality, pushing the boundaries of its thinking, desperately seeking innovation and always will, that is its very nature, but conversely there are other areas of our lives where our future thinking is conditioned to a degree by our historical thinking and our historical great thinkers and I would suggest that philosophy is one of those areas and any groundbreaking thinking will only be born out of major societal change, so progress is possibly glacial.

Therefore, it is worth considering Shakespeare's words as our current definitive and his explanation of the Seven Ages of Man as they absolutely add value to my own thoughts.

All the world's a stage,
And all the men and women are merely players,
They have their exits and their entrances,
And one man in his time plays many parts,
His acts being seven ages.
At first the infant, mewling and puking in the nurses arms.
Then the whining schoolboy, with his satchel and shiny morning face,
Creeping like snail, unwillingly to school.
And then the lover, sighing like furnace, with a woeful ballad
Made to his mistress eyebrow.
Then a soldier, full of strange oaths and bearded like the pard,
Jealous in honour, sudden and quick in quarrel,
Seeking the bubble reputation, even in the cannons mouth.
And then the justice, in fair round belly with good capon lined,
With eyes severe and beard of formal cut,
Full of wise saws and modern instances;
And so he plays his part.
The sixth age shifts into the lean and slippered pantaloon,
With spectacles on nose and pouch on side:
His youthful hose, well saved, a world too wide for his shrunk skank, and his big manly voice.
Turning again towards childish treble, pipes and whistles in his sound.
Last scene of all, that ends this strange eventful history,
Is second childishness and mere oblivion,
Sans teeth, sans eyes, sans taste, sans everything.

When you consider that *As You Like It* was published in 1599, it is obvious that although the world has changed dramatically in the following four hundred plus years, that nothing has really changed. The language may be a little different, but the same principles and values apply, although we may believe that we have changed the world and improved it dramatically over that period of time, unfortunately for us, life hasn't really changed at all, especially as man goes through his life stages.

I find it really interesting that Shakespeare is looking to analyse life, not for its meaning or our purpose here, if we have one, but the generality of it all, suggesting we all go through those same stages of progression, irrespective of our circumstances.

Since I embarked on my own epic journey and started writing this book, I wouldn't be so arrogant or even deluded as to believe that I could find a purpose for our being here, but I certainly feel that this has been an exercise that has certainly clarified my thinking and certainly to a greater degree it has helped my understanding of what it's all about.

No, I don't have a definitive answer, you wouldn't expect me to, I'm not that clever, but I have come to terms with the checking in, spending time and checking out theory, with a side order of is this it or do we go somewhere once we've checked out! That seems to make a lot of sense to me and in order to satiate my theory, I have looked at the aspects of life that I believe are consistent with my hotel comparison and thus, far from dissuading me that my theory doesn't hold water, it has reinforced in my own mind that I have stumbled across a unique but coherent understanding.

Am I any further ahead from when I started writing over two years ago, I believe that I am, I certainly feel that when time is spent, not necessarily in isolation, but certainly with focus and without distraction, doing nothing but considering our purpose in the hotel, then that focus can pay dividends.

So much so that I am amazed that greater minds than mine have not made greater progress in our understanding of what it's all about, that is because, if you consider the number of great thinkers that we have had staying here as guests and the technology that we have at our disposal today, then surely we it can only be a matter of time until clarity emerges, until we experience our Eureka moment.

Eureka is an interesting word and the assumption is that we all know its meaning and origin, but for those who don't know or aren't sure of the origin of the expression, Eureka moment, it is derived from our old friend, Archimedes, the ancient Greek scholar, who upon stepping into his bath, realised that the water level rose and therefore the water volume displaced equalled the volume of the parts of his body that were submerged, thus meaning that the volume of any object, no matter how irregular the volume, could be accurately measured, which was a huge development in mathematics and so excited was Archimedes by his discovery that he shouted "Eureka! Eureka!" and jumped out of his bath, running naked through the streets of Syracuse. The Eureka moment was born and is now commonly used when anybody makes a discovery or invention, literally meaning 'I have found'.

But alas, no, neither I nor any other guest, past or present, has yet been able to shout Eureka when searching for questions concerning the meaning of life, what are we doing here, or similar, but there could be a reason for that and that may lie in the idea that some already claim to have the answers, granted without a shred of evidence, with only apocryphal stories to back up their claim.

So have the answers been hijacked by religion, by scientists and an assembled collection of naysayers, dare anybody come up with the actual truth, if they discovered it, because it would shatter the truly held beliefs of many people, if the answer lay outside current religious or scientific theories, understanding and convictions.

Is the world ready for a new branch of science or religion that discovers the meaning of life and after millions of years of our hotel's existence and the advent of guests having temporary residence but not knowing why, can you imagine if there was a definitive answer and it was provable?

Let's take a moment to imagine a scenario where the truth about our purpose and existence were finally discovered and proven beyond doubt to be definitive and assuming that the discovery was unrelated to any of the worlds current great religions or cultural beliefs, none of the established accepted explanations of our purpose, or our reason for being here proved to be valid, but there was instead a brand-new and original but provable theory, can you imagine the reactions of all of those followers holding the totally acceptable legitimate beliefs by the values that we currently hold to be true.

Can you imagine any person with firmly held cultural or religious beliefs who would accept refutation of their faith when presented with these newly discovered 'facts' or are their beliefs, their cultures and religions so ingrained in and a part of our societal values, that they negate the prospect of any new truths being discovered now or in the future?

Does the existence of any religion preclude research into the meaning of life from being successful in its findings, are religions so entrenched as part of our society or a part of the establishment that to question their fallibility would be verging on treasonous, irrespective of whether their existence is based in fact and we have seen how hostile the followers of many faiths when non-believers dare to challenge their values.

Alternatively, can you imagine if it was discovered that just one of the world's great religions turned out to be right, imagine the unrest amongst the followers of those other religions that were not the truth, the global unrest would be unmanageable, there would be global turmoil anarchy and revolution, with people refusing to accept that their religion was not, 'the one'.

That leads me to consider that scientists may well have actually discovered the meaning of life, discovering that it has absolutely nothing to do with any of the world's religion but instead it is purely a scientific process, one by which, having discovered the truth, we now understand our purpose, but they cannot release their findings, believing that mass hysteria would ensue if the world's religions and other scientific theories were debunked and so, not to throw the world into turmoil, they choose to say nothing and allow the existing providers of both religion and conspiracy theory to carry on in splendid ignorance and preach their beliefs!

We have seen through the advent of social media that, we no longer need experts, facts can be subjected to ridicule as mere opinions and reporting of news even by the most trusted media institutions is now seen through the lens of their own declared bias or leanings, impartiality seems to have disappeared and sourcing your information from a source without an agenda is difficult.

Fake news, although having no fixed definition, has over the last five years become the default line used by people who are both unknown or well-known which they liberally apply to anything that is not favourable to their personal perspective, or a story that has managed to find its way into their echo chamber!

The rise of social media, Facebook, TikTok and Twitter, now known as X, have for example seen a dramatic rise in opinions being given a public platform, not only to a national audience in whichever part of the hotel you live in, but anybody with the inclination can now have their views being given on an international platform, available globally, to virtually anybody, where they are published instantaneously and in real time.

The potential is incredible and possibly frightening if in the wrong hands or with malicious intent. Because of their success, we find that there are new platforms appearing by the year and as I write this the latest one to appear is called GETTR.

GETTR was officially launched on 4th July 2021 and it appears to be making a real push into the media platform sector from the turn of the new year in 2022, with January seeing my awareness of the brand being reinforced daily and advertised everywhere.

As we see the sustainability of established platforms and the coming and going of the newer ones, can you imagine if this technology had been available to the ancient Greeks, the early Christians, or the first Islamic scholars, to me that is a powerful thought.

The platforms would have given them the power to push their message, instantly to a global audience, no longer any need for missionary workers to travel the world, pushing their message, instead the gospel could be spread at the push of a button.

If they felt there was competition or alternatives were threatening them or challenging their beliefs, they could ban them from their platforms or their timeline, creating an echo chamber.

Whether they are religions, cults or even cultures, that are pushing their message, what other actors would also have access to the technology and wishing to sending their own messages, advocating for their beliefs, from individuals in their attic bedroom to the globalists, all of these voices competing for the same space.

We have seen how global politics has changed necessarily because of the tremendous advances in technology and inevitably that has enabled savvy politicians who, realising the power that they have at their fingertips by the effective use of social media and its persuasive, efficient use in campaigning in recent years with both information and indeed disinformation thrown into the mix for good measure, so much so it has become difficult to know what is factual and what is fabrication.

Interestingly, the advent of AI has complicated matters even more, as now we can see the most skilled manipulators using it to create actual video footage of people appearing in situations or saying words that they have never uttered in places they have never been to.

This begs the question, how do we know who to trust, or do we inevitably find that we are living our lives in our own echo chamber, only surrounding ourselves with those opinions that chime with those that we hold, believe to be true, or least of all that we agree with.

This is known as confirmation bias, in which our search for information, whether it comes from the media we choose to watch or listen to, echoes or repeats our own opinions back to us, reinforcing our commitment to them. Even the social circles and friends that we mix with agree with us every one of our beliefs and opinions are often accepted without challenge and if there are contradictory opinions, we choose to ignore them or even ridicule them, calling them fake news and even going as far as to believe any ambiguous evidence or opinions that chime with our own beliefs, in order to validate our thinking.

This is why critical thinking skills are so important and yet so many people come to ignore them, indeed, critical thinking would be a major help in our attempt to look for a meaning of life, so what is critical thinking?

Basically, it is the intellectually disciplined process of analysing and evaluating, based on observation, experience, reflection and information from impartial sources and having done so, you should be in a position to form a judgment. The process will obviously differ slightly from person to person, but there are basics that need to be adhered to:

- Analysing arguments
- Discovering the facts
- Challenging your prejudices
- Draw conclusions

They are the basics on which to build your argument and irrespective of the subject matter, the use of them should enable the user to reach an informed opinion, whatever the subject matter!

The problem is that these days, many of those in the current younger generation are ill-equipped to reach a position that is based on impartial information, whether it's a debate about gender, race or climate change, that is because there is currently only one narrative available for kids.

Irrespective of your position on any debate, being part of a generation experiencing a form of groupthink cannot be healthy and we can see how this effects those younger generations, because they are not used to having their thinking challenged and then when they do encounter a contradictory opinion to their own, the Gen X or Gen Z kids, who are being and have been brought up in today's education system, compounded simultaneously with manipulated media messages offering one dimensional arguments, means that they struggle to understand that a different position exists to anything that they hold to be true and it is for this reason that they are given the epithet, Snowflake!

This may sound a little unfair, if not downright insulting, but to the generations that preceded the current crop of youngsters, generations who have had far tougher upbringings in a society that wasn't as progressive and having an upbringing that is not as cosseted as that of today's youth, they see the lack of mental strength to be a weakness that will serve them poorly as their lives progress.

There is no doubt that we are in the foothills of this technology and the communication skills it offers us and unquestionably, its impact will continue to develop and grow until it is replaced by a superior form of communication at some time in the future and who knows when that is and what it will bring. Can you imagine how different the hotel would be if the great thinkers and innovators of earlier civilisations had today's technology at their fingertips, but unfortunately that's not the way it works, our stay here doesn't work like that.

We are all a product of our generation, of the people and the facilities at our disposal in the hotel during our stay here, whereas on an individual level, we are each of us limited by our own levels of experience, our own understanding of the world and the way that we believe that it works and obviously we are limited by our own ambition, or lack of it.

My own favourite hotel on the planet is the Klosterbrau in Seefeld, Austria, and over the years, we have stayed there several times. When we first started going to the Klosterbrau, the hotel didn't have a gym, which is a facility that I like to use every day, whether at home or on holiday, so although I loved the hotel, I didn't use the gym, but as it was a skiing holiday, that wasn't a deal-breaker and didn't stop me loving everything about the hotel.

However, today, over 25 years later, it has a fabulous fully equipped gym, which will add to the enjoyment of those guests currently staying and those who will be staying in the future, giving them options and even greater enjoyment from their stay, that those staying 25 years ago didn't have.

I realise that the gym in the hotel does not stand comparison with say, Aristotle having a laptop, but you get the point, your stay has subliminal limitations, that while we are here we are thankfully unaware of, so we work with what we've got, but as society moves on we realise that progress inevitably brings a change in societal thinking and as a world, as a hotel, we evolve.

I mentioned earlier that I had run the New York marathon and in doing so, there is something that I have learnt by taking part and it has stayed with me ever since, indeed I have found that for me it has become an absolute truth and a metaphor for life.

The New York marathon is always run on the first Sunday in November and on the beautiful, bright, crisp, sunny autumn morning that I was taking part, I found myself lining up with approximately fifty thousand other runners at the start of the marathon, inevitably there was a little bit of waiting time, which is understandable when you are trying to organise the start of an event with over fifty thousand competitors, all arriving at the starting line of the event approximately one hour before the actual start time of the race, your time is spent finding your starting position, doing some thorough warming up exercises and stretches, warming your muscles up in preparation for the race and readying yourself for your runaround the five boroughs of that fantastic city.

Once you get to your allotted starting point, having got your preparation done and feeling as ready as possible, you have the opportunity to look at those other competitors around you that you are in competition with.

If, like me, you are a fun runner and not a professional, you are in the marathon but you are not there to win it, you are there to finish the course, which is still a massive achievement in its own right, and secondly you are there to finish in your fastest time possible.

The marathon is as much of a mental achievement as a physical one, that is a given, but there is a lot more to it than that and it is at the start of the race, just before the clock strikes ten and the race begins and you start running, it was there that I learnt this incredible lesson.

Inevitably you look around at the other competitors lining up against you, nodding and smiling, knowing exactly what they are thinking and about to go through and it was at this time that I noticed that some of those competitors around me looked a lot fitter than I did, or others had the latest technology, whether it was the lightweight, breathable clothing or a pair of fabulous new, 'Go Faster' trainers and it is there that you gauge your competition in the most basic way of all and that is as simple as whether you will finish ahead of those around you or not, after all it is a race and therefore competitive.

I vividly remember that alongside me, there were some people who looked as though they'd been wearing the same running shoes since Philippides ran from Marathon to Athens in 490bc and here they were, wearing them one more time for today's race. There were other competitors wearing a worn-out t-shirt with I Love Donny Osmond on or T Rex Rule…you get the idea, it wasn't the latest gear.

However they looked, whether it be fabulous and a sporting superstar or an attitude of, I just couldn't care less how I look, it was difficult not to evaluate them and how you feel you will run compared to them, I suppose that will be the natural competitor in me, which isn't necessarily a bad thing, I was here to do my best.

But the revelation for me came at the end of the race, once I had crossed the finishing line after running around New York, through its five boroughs for four hours and twenty-one minutes and ending up in Central Park, having started on Staten Island.

It was here that I learnt what I consider even to this day to be, for me at least a major life lesson and it was this; as I sat on the pavement in Central Park, with my finishers medal hanging proudly around my neck, I watched as hundreds of runners crossed the line after me, while simultaneously observed many others, happy, smiling runners milling around having conquered New York in a better time than mine, I realised that those I had seen at the start of the race, some looking like the elite athlete Mo Farah, others looking like Mo Slater on Eastenders were now once again gathering around me.

Looking at them, I realised that there were those people who had finished in front of me that I thought could never beat me and yet there were some people who finished behind me that I thought I would never beat and for me, that is life itself, encapsulated in one moment. It is impossible to prejudge because an extension of prejudge is prejudice and you can never tell the mental toughness of others, simply by looking at them.

As I considered my impressions of the moment, I went on to realise that you can also combine that thought with the fact that at the start of the event, everybody looks good, that's the easy bit, it's the finish that's important and by the end of a gruelling run, you tend to look a little dishevelled, obviously some of us can look a lot worse than others, but it is easy to look cool before the action begins, it's how you handle everything that's thrown at you that counts.

If life is a race and we are all competing with each other then it is both impossible and never a good idea to pre judge another person, as I mentioned, from pre judge we get prejudice and that is never a good place to start you can never know the mental toughness or resilience of another person what lies within and often physical appearances are no guide and the idiom 'appearances can be deceiving' tells you all you need to know.

In those early days in the hotel, when you're in your late teens to early twenties, a time when your life is just starting for real, you find yourself, unknowingly in a time when the decisions that you make determine the direction your life takes, everything is ahead of you, you invariably look and feel fabulous and in terms of being a physical specimen you aren't going to look and feel much better in your whole life, these are great days, as good as it gets.

But inevitably there are trade-offs, you may still live with your parents, you may be in a small starter home, you're more likely to be chief bottle washer, than chief executive of a company and therefore your pay won't be incredible, but because most of your peers will in most cases find themselves in a similar situation, then it tends to be all rather irrelevant and life is good.

But as you cruise through your teens and twenties into your thirties, and metaphorically come towards the end of the first week of your stay in the hotel and you look forward eagerly to the metaphorical weekend, it is by this time your life will have started taking a more defined path as things become a little more serious and your hotel bar bill starts to increase.

As you enter the second week of your stay, you now know your way around the place, you know which is your favourite table in the restaurant, you know those places in town that you like to go to and those acquaintances that you made in the first few days of your stay are now on even friendlier terms.

This is a pivotal part of your stay in the hotel and now it is those new arrivals or those in their first couple of days will look at you and see you as one of the old hands, maybe even counselling you for advice on the hotel, getting around the place, what's good, what's bad.

It is also at this stage that you will notice that there are some people, maybe friends or family who have come to the end of or are nearing the end of their stay and you will know of or know personally, some people who have left altogether, people who have checked out.

What is incredible is that those checking in today, will be totally unaware of those who have recently checked out or those who have been fortunate enough to have stayed in the hotel before them, not through any fault of their own, but that's the way it works in any hotel.

When you check in, your room will have been cleaned and everything will be looking like new, even if the night before there had been a party in your room held by those who were staying there, celebrating their last night and going out with a bang, but life moves on at a rapid pace.

Unless you had attended the party, you would never know that there had been one the night before, the place is ready for the latest arrivals to make the most of their stay, the stage is set, ready for the new people, once again it becomes a new world to be enjoyed, given to those fortunate enough to have the opportunity to stay here.

As the second week progresses, your friendships grow even stronger, you are becoming more comfortable in your environment, you feel that you know the way the place works, those things that in the first few days appeared to be complex and confusing are now, quite simple and easier to understand, you have come to know some of the staff on first-name terms, but by the same token, there are some of them that you don't particularly like and therefore choose to avoid them, that could be because you don't like something about them, it could be their attitude, their manner or something about their personal preferences that you don't agree with.

Nobody appeals to everybody, nobody is universally loved or despised, whoever they are, I am sure, the Queen, the Pope and Mother Theresa all have their detractors, in spite of their attempts to live a decent life.

It can often the institution that they represent and not the person themselves that can be an issue for some people, but my point is, that universality is impossible to achieve and it doesn't matter whatever the percentage of naysayers is, there will always be one.

We are all very different and those people that I have become friendly with during my own stay are not necessarily the same people that you may be friendly with, we all have different settings for who we do and do not like, what type of person you are and are not attracted to, we are not all the same and let's be thankful for that.

Although you can generalise to a degree about the common traits of different nationalities and cultures, but the cultures and nationalities are ultimately made up of individuals who all aspire to different things and have different demands and expectations from their lives and it is this that makes our own stay in the hotel so fascinating.

It allows you to meet people who are like minded and then sharing our stay with them and in many cases choosing to commit to them and sharing our lives and our stay with them.

Currently, approximately two-thirds of those staying in the hotel are married or cohabiting so a majority of those staying in the hotel are choosing to spend their time with another person and finding a partner for life can be a fabulous thing, however if you compare us to animals, this is quite a rare thing, with only three to five per cent of mammals partnering for life whereas it is believed that an estimated ninety per cent of birds species partner up for life.

But the times are a-changing and as our society changes and now we look beyond the once conventional man and wife, we currently embrace a plethora of relationship types and therefore a friend for life outside of a conventional marriage arrangement can be as integral to a happy life as taking a walk up the aisle with a husband or wife!

Given that not everybody will be fortunate enough to meet the love of their life in the traditional sense, but they have a special friendship with another person then those friendships must be validated and put on a par with any other relationship.

During your stay, you will have soulmates, life partners and even confidantes, and there are subtle differences between each of these; a soulmate doesn't have to be a romantic lover, they are people that will either walk along side or lead you in a direction in your life that you feel that you need to go in and they will also be around at pivotal times, but not necessarily forever, nothing is forever, moreover they will come and go as you need them, helping you to learn life lessons, being there as and when you need them. It is for this reason that we acknowledge their importance to us as we ignoble them with soulmate status.

A confidante is typically a close friend or relative, a person with whom we share everything with, but again not necessarily a bed. During our stay, we get different things from different people in our lives, we need friends and confidantes, even if it's just in order to complain to them about our romantic partners.

When we look at our interactions and relationships with other people, we can see that as well as us having relationships with people who provide for our own very different needs, we ourselves come to mean different things to different people, as individuals we are complex, we may find that we have love for others apart from our life partner, which is possible, it can also be vital for our own well-being and similarly to the well-being of those that we share the emotion, the love with.

You can expand your definition of a life partner to include those people who are very close to you that you feel a love for, those wonderful people who are the only ones that can make you feel a certain way and that can serve to make you as an individual, feel fulfilled, however fulfilment manifests itself for you as an individual.

The relationships that we make while staying here become vital to us, they are an integral part of our stay, without them we are alone, unable to share the experience that life is giving us and their presence helps us to fulfil ourselves.

But is alone a bad thing, does an existence in which we are splendidly isolated have a point, do we need to share the ups and downs, the good and bad with others in order to get us through, are relationships part of our reason for being, or a total irrelevance?

Even if we have many friendships, love and relationships, ultimately we are just us, we are all responsible for ourselves, there is no science, nobody is right, nobody is wrong, you do what you need to get you through.

While we are talking about our relationship with others, please allow me to briefly interrupt this section of the book, simply because as we sit here in January 2022, I have today attended the funeral of a friend. She had spent seventy years in the hotel and left her husband, daughters and grandchildren to continue their stay without her, she has checked out before they have, leaving a great deal of sadness behind for her family who are very close and her many friends who were in attendance.

Lovely words were spoken by a lady who had never met my friend, we were played a couple of pop songs on loop as well as her brave daughters reciting poems that they had chosen. One of the songs chosen was *Three Times a Lady*, the Commodore's track from the late seventies, which before introducing the celebrant felt compelled to tell us that she, the celebrant, was a big Lionel Richie fan, good for you I thought, but I doubt anybody is interested, which may sound harsh, but I felt it was an unnecessary contribution to the service.

Maybe to prove the point, earlier in the service we had been treated to *Only You* by the Flying Pickets. I sensed the celebrant wasn't a big Flying Pickets fan as she chose not to comment on the family's choice of that particular classic, if she had been a fan of the band or that particular song I'm sure we'd have known about it.

I was left at the end of the ceremony feeling a little emptier than when I arrived and that wasn't simply because I had said goodbye to a friend, but the celebration of her life, I felt was inadequate, she deserved greater appreciation and thanks, more than the underwhelming thirty minutes that we were treated to, hurrying out at the end of our allotted time as the guests for the next ceremony waited patiently outside to celebrate their recently, dearly departed!

Is that it, a couple of pop songs, two deep and meaningful poems and friends and family go for a few drinks at a local pub and feast on sandwiches, chips and a few salad leaves. It all felt rather unsatisfactory for a life well-lived and a good friend checking out of the hotel for the final time, although I don't know what I expected, I felt that there should be more.

It made me think briefly of my own departure and ideally with a little thought and preparation, surely anything is possible, indeed certainly an event that it would be a pleasure to attend, a little more personal, I want a stand-up comedian at mine please, I told my wife, but I don't think she was taking me seriously!

But who does that, who spends hours planning for the eventuality when it is the last thing in the world you want to talk about, you don't want to speed the process up by any means and by either entering into discussions with close friends or family you are normalising death, which isn't an attractive proposition in anybody's book.

Even though checking out comes to us all, it is not until we are into the last few days of our stay, when we may have relevant conversations with those who are close to us, family or good friends, when we may have some input into the decisions about our own departure, or in some cases the task is left to others to plan the event having when the deceased has not discussed their wishes with anybody, leaving the reality of planning their departure for others to determine, which is very hit and miss.

There are so many constituent parts to the day, your favourite music, readings from the great works, the type of service, the friends and family who you want to be in attendance to say farewell, what type of food, the venue, in fact all of those things that if we think about it in advance, we have the opportunity to make a valuable input into and hopefully make the whole process a little easier, certainly I believe with meticulous planning it will be more fulfilling, if not for the deceased, certainly for those there to share the experience.

But the question of leaving is eclipsed by a bigger question, for those who believe that there is more to come and that is, would you go there again, which with our limited understanding of the possibilities or the options available to us and due to our total lack of knowledge of what it's all been about, for those that believe that there is something next, our options appear to boil down to either, a return to the people we have known and loved, or a brand-new existence, uncontaminated by our previous stay.

It could be better, it could be worse, but it would be different, an opportunity, unknowingly granted to have another go, to do it all again.

However, can you imagine if there was a third option and we actually got to do it all again, fully aware that we had been here before, if you were given the chance, would you want to take it and if you did, what would you do differently the second time around?

Maybe there are those amongst of us that are cognisant of the fact that they have been here before and are more than happy to tell us that they are, whether we choose to believe them or not is a different question! But we need to put the thought out there, it is their truth so is important to acknowledge such.

Whether true or not is irrelevant, the overriding thought must be, if you could do it all again, would you and the next question must then be, if you were given the opportunity, what if anything, would you do differently!

This takes me back to the wonderful song, *The Way We Were*, a fabulous song written by Alan Bergman, Marilyn Bergman and Marvin Hamlisch, best known for the original version sung impeccably by Barbara Streisand and first seen in the film of the same name. The song actually references the thought process of doing it all again and I think as a piece of prose the words are worth absorbing, obviously if you have access to Barbara belting it out, have a listen, but if not and purely because I like them so much and also because they are relevant to this part of the book, I will give you an opportunity to absorb their beauty, they are as follows and possibly they may even be a little thought provoking, which is what we are all about!

The Way We Were

Memories light the corners of my mind,
Misty water coloured memories of the way we were.
Scattered pictures of the smiles we left behind,
Smiles we gave to one another, for the way we were.

Can it be that it was all so simple then,
Or has time rewritten every line,
If we had the chance to do it all again, tell me would we, could we.

Memories may be beautiful and yet,
What's too painful to remember,
We simply choose to forget,

So it's the laughter we will remember,
Whenever we remember, the way we were

The way we were.

I love those words, powerfully describing how memories are with us throughout our lives, some cherished, some are not and we choose to forget them, others may need a little recall from those distant days, but eclipsing these well written and beautifully observed lines is the indulging and controversial thought that if we had the chance to do it all again and if we did, would we or could we, how marvellous.

Those words say it all for me and posing the question that encapsulates the chapter makes it even more special.

If I consider the thought of doing it all again, I can recall at least a couple of occasions in my life that I haven't necessarily made the right choices, countered by the times I feel that I have made the right decisions, would you want the chance to do it all again, I sense there would be a price to pay and surely you would know what to expect something that cannot happen if you only get one chance.

I rode on the Big One in Blackpool, a rollercoaster which when it was first unveiled in 1994 was the leading white knuckle ride in the country and I had the pleasure of going on it in that year.

It was new, it was massive and it was a thrill and I loved every minute, literally the highs, which were very high and the stomach churning lows of the three minute ride, it was breathtaking and I wouldn't have missed it.

A couple of years later, I was in Blackpool once more, with friends, who had never been on the Big One, so I took the opportunity to go on it again and although I enjoyed it, I didn't find it as exhilarating the second time, I knew what to expect, where the highs and lows were.

It is everything about the element of surprise and never knowing where the excitement and the thrills would come that makes doing it just once makes it so special and maybe that is why we only have one chance at life.

Familiarity they say breeds contempt and that can lead to complacency which can set in as we adjust ourselves and our expectations, fully aware of when to expect the thrills, which will not and cannot be quite as thrilling the second time around.

As if to reinforce the point, I recall a time in several years ago, spent with my wife in Paris, we visited the Eiffel Tower and I may have mentioned, I am not the best with heights and as we ascended the Tower we came to the first viewing platform, which I now know is 187 feet high, this was enough for me, but I looked above and saw the top of the tower in the distance and knew that in order to embrace the experience and get the most out of I, that against my better judgement I had to get there, in spite of my reservations.

The second platform is 377 feet high; once again, I felt that this was sufficient for me, I'll wait here I thought to myself, the views of Paris were spectacular but no, I had to go on and eventually stood at the top on the third and highest accessible platform which is at 906 feet!

It was a fabulous experience and I wouldn't have missed it for the world, the views, the atmosphere and a well-deserved glass of Rosé champagne at the top as we surveyed the streets below, we found ourselves doing the same thing as every other tourist and looking for our hotel in the splendour of the beauty of the city below.

As we descended, we stopped once again at the first platform, which as I mentioned earlier is a mere 187 feet high, even I felt totally at ease, having experienced the magnificence of the top, to be back on the once daunting first platform was child's play!

Life can play those games with your mind, teasing you with what is and what isn't achievable and sometimes it can make you feel vulnerable, or others allowing you to feel invincible, with the potential should you so choose it to be all conquering, it is weird how it is our own inhibitions or irrational fears can stop us from doing the things we are inspired by.

So the chance of doing it all again really could be an attractive proposition, to iron out the mistakes, do it better, do the things you never got the chance to do, there could be many attractive reasons to have another chance, but possibly the reason that we only get one stay in the hotel is that having done it once, the highs and lows, the expected and unexpected would surely contradict the purpose of our stay.

To face the challenges as they present themselves and to take it all in our stride, embracing the experience as it happens, if you know what to expect at every turn, you can anticipate the challenges, then surely it takes the fun out of the experience. So choose your favourite—YOLO, Carpe Diem, Seize the Day—your options are numerous but all pointing to us having one ride on the Big One.

Chapter 15
I'll Settle the Bill!

Well, here we are, back to reception, I have tried my best to explain to you the parallels that I believe provide an excellent case for a stay in a hotel being a metaphor for life and our brief time spent here on the planet, the place that we all call home during our short stay here.

This may not come as a great surprise, but as I have written this book, spending my time researching, I have become even more convinced that my theory is at worst plausible and at best, absolutely perfect and the best thing is, who amongst us can tell me that I am wrong, because as we know, there isn't a person staying in the hotel currently or who has been here as a previous guest who can tell me that I am wrong.

From the very first chapter, considering the size of our hotel within the galaxy and the prevailing conditions that allow us to exist and function within our solar system, we are but a single grain of sand on a beach, yet with heat, sunlight, vegetation, water, fresh air and so much more all conspiring to work perfectly and in harmony, allowing us to have the lives that we are so fortunate to have.

Moreover, if we understand the science, that there is only one hotel, we are all staying in a small family-run business, not part of a chain or one of the large hotel groups that we have all heard of—Holiday Inn, Four Seasons or Radisson—this is a one-off, we are staying at one in a chain of one.

When I think about it, that does not even sound plausible, when you look at the size of the galaxy, yes I know it is impossible for us to visualise its size because it is too big for us to comprehend, but given the enormity, do you think it seems possible that in all of the physical space that the galaxy consumes, is it feasible that there is only one planet just like our own, with life, human, and plant, with animal, deserts and oceans and everything else that makes this place what it is, do you think that we are staying at the only habitable hotel available, because to me it sounds unbelievable to believe that to be true.

If there is more than one hotel, then that begs the question, that if we are simply just one hotel of many in the group, we are a part of a chain of hotels dotted throughout the galaxy, at many various locations, with different inhabitants, living totally different lives, maybe more than once, then who knows what is out there, will we ever know and if one day we do discover our neighbours, will they have discovered the meaning of life and have total understanding of what it's all about and the point to our existence.

When we analyse the hotel itself and the experiences of those of us currently staying here experiences that are bespoke, which can be incredibly different for all of us and there are many contributing factors for this, however when you actually look at the different outcomes possible for our guests it becomes clear that depending on which part of the hotel you are staying in, whether you are enjoying outrageous opulence or suffering extreme poverty, both of which coexist amongst us, in spite of us all staying in the same place at the same time, we see that the reality can be either brutal or beautiful and because as individuals we are more often than not, too busy simply getting on with our own lives, wrapped up in solving our own particular issues, doing the hard yards every day, then it is often difficult to consider the plight of others.

Some do consider the plight of others every day of their lives and we have successfully created many charities and aid organisations around the world which give relief, aid and assistance to the numerous causes with which they may have a special interest in.

We must applaud these people, their work is beyond admirable and effectively it is work, that if it wasn't done by these good people, possibly wouldn't be done at all, they are often standing in place of and doing work that governments are not doing, in many cases they are stopping people falling through the cracks.

So, our society has given us opportunities for those who feel compelled to do good things during their stay in the hotel with those guests that are staying at the same time, who aren't fortunate enough to have access to or have accumulated the riches, however those riches manifest themselves, that others have managed to accumulate and that have helped to make their stay more enjoyable.

To those of us living in Europe and to the majority of the rest of the world, there are those obvious indicators of wealth, power and status that although not necessarily recognised as a sign of success in all corners of the world, certainly resonate in our part of the hotel.

If you see somebody driving a Ferrari, carrying a Hermes handbag or wearing a pair of Gucci loafers, all expensive examples of products available to those who have sufficient funds available to purchase them and with labels designed to impress the passer by, but if I wore my Gucci loafers in the Pitcairn Islands or drove my Ferrari on Easter Island would anybody give me anything more than a cursory glance and wonder why I didn't have the appropriate footwear or transport.

I would stick out like a sore thumb even to the point of being the subject of ridicule, a figure of fun, and understandably so.

But those doing good works around the hotel aren't concerned with Ferraris, Versace or Louis Vuitton, they are simply helping those who can't afford or don't have access to the basic demands of life, those things that many of us feel are absolutely basic needs, which are, to many guests, not simply basic needs, instead they are luxuries, so therefore as I said we should laud these people who give their time, their lives.

Charity worker and charity user could actually be described as the perfect symbiotic relationship, because both parties benefit greatly from the relationship, the charity worker has the most incredible feeling of doing good, while the recipient is getting those things vital to aid their survival.

Due to its very nature, it is incredibly difficult to address one hundred per cent of the problem, especially when the problem or problems can be spread to all parts of the planet, so the situation then becomes more of a matter of handling it by degree.

Although fortunately for us living here in the United Kingdom we are considered to be a wealthy country, in the great scheme of things, yet in spite of the fact, there is still poverty here, indeed in order to dilute the impact of the word, we change the language and call several aspects of the problem relative poverty, relative meaning that in comparison to their fellow countrymen.

Some people in this country are underprivileged, so in relation to those people who are doing well, some people aren't doing so good, however if you compared the relative poor in the United Kingdom to those people living in

Burundi who are considered to be the relative poor, then bizarrely those in the United Kingdom would actually be considered wealthy.

I understand it's not a race to the bottom, but underprivileged people in the United Kingdom, when compared to those in extreme poverty in poorer countries, look comparatively wealthy. Which isn't necessarily great for us as a country, but it is incredibly sad for those who find themselves living in poverty in other countries, but we must not look at the reality because it is all a part of being here.

First-world problems is an expression that you will have heard before, it is frequently used ironically but it also used to express a feeling of gratitude that the problems being experienced by the person enunciating the expression are nothing compared to those poor souls in less fortunate circumstances.

It is a self-deprecating term, which indicates that the user understands that there are more pressing problems around the world than forgetting to put their mobile phone on charge, or getting their triple choc, mocha chai latte and realising that it simply isn't hot enough, of course people are allowed to have concern about their own problems, but there are bigger more consequential problems at stake in every part of the hotel 24/7.

In order to look at striving towards perfection, I have worked out that there are three areas of prominence in our lives that need to be acknowledged which together make up a very simplistic formula for a happy life, enabling the individual an enjoyable stay in the hotel.

These three areas won't come as a surprise to anybody but by actually identifying them as three crucial factors, then we can focus on those three things and maybe being conscious of their importance, we can try to ensure that we as individuals are as strong as possible in each area.

Fortunately, we have influence over all three, but as with many things in our world, there is another dimension to the causes of our outcomes in life, we usually call it luck, maybe fortune, accident or fate, you can take your pick, it's up to you how you identify it but there is certainly a factor that has a role in all of our lives, something that, is just simply out of our control, but which plays a part in everything that happens to us.

So, if we discount the role that fate or luck plays in the short term, then we are left with the mix that I believe are the basic ingredients for a successful life, however that manifests itself. In my mind, those three areas are health, wealth and relationships as staples of a pleasant stay, if you can achieve or somehow enjoy the good fortune to be content with your lot in these three areas, then I believe that life should be a blast.

In no particular order, let's look at health and it is clear that good health is a prerequisite to an enjoyable stay, seeing as ultimately it will more often than not be bad health that brings our stay in the hotel to an end, maybe even prematurely.

It is quite possible to still be a guest in the hotel while having medical conditions, even complicated conditions which may impinge on the quality of your experience, indeed some people are still here in spite of their health prohibiting them from enjoying their stay to the maximum, this possibly means that the sufferer may not be having as enjoyable stay as possible, but at least they are here and ultimately life is all we have!

I have met people who, although they are still here, still checked in to the hotel, are sadly finding themselves metaphorically in the last few days of their stay, possibly the final few hours of their time in the hotel, if you consider their age and potential longevity and understanding that nobody lives forever, then sadly it won't be long before they check out for good and for these people but life isn't as much fun as it once was, or indeed it can be and that is simply because their bad health won't allow it to be so.

This is another moment of our time here that resonates with me as yet another part of the hotel analogy, if you think about it, understanding that everybody checks out in the end and the inevitability that this time in our lives presents us with.

Because it is this moment, when we have finally packed our bags, you head down to reception to settle the bill and you have finally checked out of your room and as you look through the itemised bill, with one eye on your suitcases, you grab a seat in reception, waiting for your taxi or other transportation to arrive, sitting there with your cases and memories surrounding you.

As you sit there with time on your hands, you find yourself observing things around you, some of which you might not have seen or been aware of throughout your stay, however you watch as new people are checking in, you see them going through the same emotions that you did as you checked in all that time ago, marvelling at the surroundings, full of excited anticipation and smiling at every new face that they make eye contact with, going through the same feelings and emotions that so many have done before them.

As well as new arrivals checking in, there are other guests milling around, possibly going out for the day, others are rushing into breakfast, late to rise after a heavy night out and not wanting to miss the 11am closing time. There are others who are going into the village for the very first time, they have the rest of their stay ahead, lying in front of them with everything to look forward to and anticipating it all with youthful relish.

You sit there in the middle of all of this commotion surrounded by your luggage and everything that you hold dear, your life is temporarily in your baggage, reception has suddenly become your safe space and therefore you are reluctant to move from your new base, hesitant to venture outside of the hotel.

Not simply because you have seen everything that you wanted to see that lies beyond those revolving doors, you know what's outside, you have been to the restaurants, you've had the coffees, the beers, the burgers and fries and your appetite is satiated, you are full, both physically and mentally, you have done all that you wanted to do and those things that you haven't done are now and will remain eternally just an unfulfilled, distant ambition that doesn't burn as strongly as it once did.

You sit in a reception which at one time was a welcoming experience, once upon a time it was filled with faces old and new mingling to create a cocktail of excited anticipation of days ahead, but sadly now it has become a form of purgatory, many of the old familiar faces who had shared earlier days with you have long checked out and now you find yourself in an intermediate state between leaving you room and getting into the taxi to leave once and for all, it is a state of impotence which is not a particularly pleasant situation in which to find yourself.

You no longer feel in control of your destiny, you are more vulnerable than you have ever felt, and it sucks.

I did warn you that my thoughts on these three crucial pillars weren't revolutionary, but they are vital, so it will come as no surprise to hear that wealth is the second panel of my triptych, which again is not an earth-shattering conclusion and in itself is fairly self-explanatory, we know that money is a man made construct with coins and notes having no value in their own right, but that isn't the point, it is what you can obtain with those coins and notes that give it a value, money is simply a medium of exchange but let us ignore forget the technicalities because they become irrelevant if you have either too little or more than enough of the stuff.

Of course, there are many people who sit happily in the middle, having neither too much or too little but just enough, sufficient for their needs during the time spent in the hotel. That equation is not an easy one, because for many reasons it is difficult to know how much we will need throughout our stay here and therefore the handling of your money is one of the toughest challenges we will have while we are here, learning how to budget and manage our money in order to give our lives stability and from stability comes mental well-being, which as mental health awareness has grown in our society, we are more conscious of the importance of giving ourselves as stress free an environment as possible, enabling us to thrive.

Money, or certainly a lack of it, can contribute to our stress levels, so as long as we are fortunate enough to be working and enjoying sufficient income in order to service our lifestyle, then we can manage to navigate the slalom course of life.

Increased difficulty comes with those who have too little and with a shortage of cash there are inevitable consequences, primarily the quality, the fun, the enjoyment and ultimately your mental wellbeing during your stay becomes a casualty and inevitably suffers.

But who shoulders the responsibility; where do you put the onus for a person, who once they have been given the gift of life, the opportunity to stay in the hotel, who or what determines how much or little they should have?

The word 'society' comes from the Latin word 'societas', meaning fellowship, alliance or association and it is a hugely complex collection of social structures and we see different interpretations of its meaning being enacted throughout the hotel.

So the question remains, does society have a responsibility to its members, when there are some of us who have everything they need and more, while others have absolutely nothing.

Inequality is so difficult to accept but to me this is all a part of the mystery of it all, how can some have too much while others have nothing, if this world was created by an all seeing god, why would they dream of contrasting such opulence with extreme poverty, what warped mind could get a kick out of that, or am I guilty of being too simplistic, maybe I am not quite getting the point, all because of my own very limited understanding of reality, or maybe all I am guilty of is actually over thinking it and it's all just random, there is no construct, it's not manufactured, it's all just a stroke of luck that we all happen to be here, just as were those who were here before us were and those who will check in after our own brief stay and anything that happens to us during our stay is as random as our arrival at reception in the first place.

If we accept that life is precious and without exception, those given the opportunity are all privileged to have the chance to fulfil our dreams, it seems incredible to me that some of those amongst us will have restrictions placed on us, some from the start of our stay, handicaps, physical or mental put on their chances of making their lives anything but fabulous.

Yes, we are all here staying in the hotel at the same time, but while some are staying in the presidential suite, there are others paying their way by washing dishes in the kitchens.

It is the disparity between the extremes that makes me believe that there is a more complex answer to my question than even I have the ability to comprehend.

That's not because I am a bit dim, but because there are influences on a person's life that are happening, long before they are conceived, the die is cast before they actually check in for their stay.

Can you imagine being born into privilege, your ancestors had fought to own land in the country in which you live and now generations later, you arrive, born into that family, a family that now enjoys incredible wealth, trappings of the most sumptuous quality, the best that life has to offer!

Surely the game is over, there is no need to strive for success, you are already successful without lifting a finger, or maybe being born into these circumstances, which appear to be all that on the face of it to be all that anybody could ever want, only serve to invalidate your personal struggle, your purpose and make your whole existence rather impotent, futile.

Yes, you have the good fortune, that is if it actually is good fortune, to never have to work, but what becomes of you, what about your self-determination, your aspirations, are your desires blunted, your dreams thwarted?

Conversely, those who are born into either poverty or a life without those finer things, the opportunity for you to make a personal success of your life is presented to you from day one, even though at that time you are blissfully unaware of your opportunity.

It is such a conundrum, is life about making the most of your talents and optimising the whole experience through your own efforts, or is it about enjoying the fruits of the labour and efforts of others, providing you with everything you will ever need during your stay in the hotel.

If either of those two situations are true, then what happens to those who are disabled, whether it be physically or mentally, are they independently responsible for their own success and if not, then who is responsible for either their success or indeed failure, then again, if they are handicapped from the outset and destined not to achieve, but in spite of the barriers to success, they manage to build a successful life, then maybe there is an increased degree of satisfaction that they feel at making it all work in spite of their difficulties and surely that makes the achievement even greater?

But then what is success, how is it measured, surely it should only ever be judged and be relative to your starting point in life, which reminds me of the brilliant analogy often used in the USA, about being born on third base.

It was originally Barry Switzer, a successful college and NFL football coach, while he was giving an interview in 1986, said, 'Some people are born on third base and go through life thinking they hit a triple!'

I love that quote and it addresses perfectly the thought of success being relative, considering whether a child born into wealth, with all of the benefits and opportunities that such privilege brings with it, whether it is the inevitable public school education or a parent's network of friends and business connections all helping the golden child along the way and helping them to achieve great things, however I sense that any success achieved by such a fortunate child would be nowhere near as magnificent as a child from a working class, one parent family achieving or enjoying a successful career!

Maybe the comparison is unfair, but these questions are so difficult to answer, I do believe that simply by being aware of the disparity and conscious of the reality that they present, then our time in the hotel and awareness of the situations of others may in some way enable us to help to contribute to improving the lives of others and by having a greater appreciation of what others go through and ultimately making it much more enjoyable, then we all benefit.

The third canvas of the triptych, or the third leg of the stool, needed to enable you to have a very pleasant stay is relationships. Relationships can be complicated and I believe that the most satisfying relationships in life are those which are built on a foundation of love, which may initially sound a bit wet, but I genuinely believe it to be true and given that we are all flawed to a greater or lesser degree, then in order for that love to survive what can be the sternest of tests needs to be unconditional, which calls for compromise.

Of course, there are limits at the extremes but to love another person seems to me to be the greatest gift available to us and if it is reciprocated then I believe that you have won life's lottery.

Friendships too are vitally important and frequently the word love can be inserted to describe the closest of friendships, but friendship at any level can be vital for our sanity, for our survival.

But it is those relationships that we build where love is something that bonds us to the other person that I believe are the third of those three vital ingredients that combine to make our stay in the hotel as decent as possible, but never taking anything for granted, complacency is pernicious and can destroy the most perfect of worlds.

Love is one of, if not the most, profound emotions known to us as human beings; of course, there are many kinds of love, but many of us find the ultimate expression of love with a compatible partner.

I do believe that for those who find love with another and discover that they are able to experience one of the deepest and most meaningful aspects of life, theirs is a complete sense of deep fulfilment and I say that as somebody entering their forty third year with another person, yes we've had ups and downs, highs and lows, but through everything the sense of commitment I feel for another person, is on a level comparable only with the regard in which I hold myself, in fact I think I may prefer my wife to myself some days.

You can only ever look at this issue from your own perspective, as we have discussed, you can never truly know what another person is thinking, so take it from me, I do believe I have found love and feel incredibly lucky to have done so, whether I am loved in return, I have no way of truly knowing.

Of course, this crazy little thing called love is not for everybody and whether it is by choice or by accident true love for some is never found and even though I declare myself to be in love, who is it amongst us that can be arrogant enough to declare that they either know or understand what it is that finding true love means?

We know it is impossible to put ourselves into the head of another person and to then know unfailingly that our love for another is truly reciprocated, so that being the case, is it that important, does it really matter?

Maybe as long as you love another, then that is all that is needed, reciprocation is merely a pleasant bonus, but for us to know what it means to love another is as much as we can expect and we should content ourselves with that.

So, I have concluded that it is these three things, three simple things, not unattainable, not beyond the wit of most of us, that I believe are vital for a pleasant stay in the hotel.

However, I do believe that there isn't one of us who is lucky enough to have all three and even those who do, then there isn't one single person that has all three to their optimum, indeed what is more likely and even then, you would have to be incredibly lucky, then you may get to enjoy them all, but that is only by degree.

I have come to believe that if I am right and these do happen to be the three criteria that we can judge a perfect life by, then because nobody ticks every box to its limit, therefore nobody has a perfect life and that must lead us to question if such a thing as perfection, at least in this instance exists and if it does, is it at all possible, I for one do not believe that perfection exists and it is therefore unattainable.

Yes, you will get moments of perfection, the perfect dinner, a day at the beach, a day spent with the love of your life, when everything goes right, these are slivers of perfection, they exist to provide us with an insight into what is possible and it is this promissory note that keeps us going, keeps us hanging in there, when sometimes it would be so easy to simply walk away, unable to battle the unbeatable odds.

Of course, we may choose to look at others and envy them for their wealth, their relationships or maybe their fitness levels, but that in itself is futile and yet, for some unknown reason there appears to be a trade-off, one that we never see and only know it exists, because we know that perfection doesn't exist.

Not one person gets to optimise their stay by having a perfect life, however their perfect lives may look to you and I from the outside, but we can only see their lives from a distance, they make look splendid, but we are all flawed, because life is complicated and naturally that means that all of our lives are difficult.

Acknowledging that, as unpalatable as it may be, then another question inevitably presents itself, and therefore the question that must be asked and is this, do you believe that there is a best time to be alive, not an era or a passage of time, but for us individually, is there a certain age that we go through, a time when things couldn't get any better, when we feel that this as good as it is going to get and if we could, would we put the metaphorical brakes on and by doing so, we would remain at that age at least temporarily and love every moment or even better remain at that age forever, if you could, if it were possible, would you choose to do so?

Would you, in the words of that beautiful Alphaville classic from 1984, remain forever young?

We know it doesn't work that way and thankfully so, but imagine if it were possible and you could take, if not a permanent break, then at least a time out were you could remain at a certain point for another year, another month, the time is irrelevant, it is the principle that I am interested in.

The question is, is there an optimum time to be in the hotel, is it when you first arrive with it all before you, is it halfway through your stay when you have worked out your favourite places, the best restaurants and people you have grown close to, or is it in the last few days of your stay, when you can sit back and take it all in, spending your days watching those young fools make exactly the same mistakes that you did.

Of course, your favourite time wouldn't necessarily be the favourite time of everybody around you, what may be great for you may be intolerable for those you are sharing any moment with.

Assuming that you could take a time out, then I am sure what would determine any individuals choice of a time to linger in their lives would be dependent upon your experience at that time, so therefore the answer would be different for each of us individually, we would each choose a different time to be our favourite.

I was a student in my early twenties and went to Newcastle-upon-Tyne, which for me personally was a fabulous time of my life, not necessarily just for the education that I received, but as much for the people I met there and the jolly japes that made it such an incredible, carefree time of my life.

But even at that time, I learnt a lesson which I believe is relevant to this point, because after a really unbeatable, fun first year, so distracted was I by the après education, that unsurprisingly to my year tutor, I failed miserably when taking my first-year exams. I was inevitably disappointed, so I decided over that summer to get my head down and to have another go and do the first year all over again.

This turned out not to be the best decision that I have ever made, in so much as, the only thing that repeated year made me realise, was that further education just wasn't for me, at least not at that time in my life.

I loved the idea of being a student, but just without the study, which isn't the best way to approach an institution designed to improve your life chances by giving you the qualifications to do so. Fortunately for me, I was lucky enough to have had a fabulous two years in Newcastle, indeed it was at the end of my first year that I met my wife of over thirty years there, so maybe that was why I was there and to that end, it was perfect.

My first year was pure pleasure and was spent amongst my fellow freshers, unusually though, my second year was also spent with another group of freshers, as I was retaking my first year one more time, my fellow travellers for this year were people for whom this was their first year, while I of course I was in my second year at the campus!

While the friends I had made as a first year were into their second year in Newcastle and the second year of their courses, I was doing it all again.

My fellow students were doing all of those things that I had done twelve months earlier, joining different societies, discovering the same bars and all that Newcastle had to offer. I tried my best not to prejudice the novelty of their experience by chiming in with my opinions at every turn, offering my views on what they were doing, blurting out to them what I thought were the great clubs and bars to go to, which societies were the most fun to join and so much more, I was neither dissuading or persuading them to come to the places that I knew and loved, instead allowing them to make the inevitable mistakes that I and every other student makes during their student days.

Those of you who have ever been fortunate enough to have experienced student life will know how fabulous the social side of a student's existence can be, I believe that the world of campus can ultimately form as much as fifty per cent of your education, while the course that you are on makes up the other fifty percent, in my case and I'm not advocating this as a conscious choice, the socialising and lifestyle elements made up one hundred percent of the experience, and those two years that I spent attending random lectures and visiting the library only to sober up and catch up with last night's gossip, they were of minimal help in my personal development.

Although I still hung out with my friends from the first year, I also had friends in my second first year, but they were at different stages of their Newcastle experience and it was difficult to flutter between the two, because quite unintentionally, each cohort develops its own identity, its own leaders and superstars, its heroes and villains, it has its own culture, it is in the process of creating its own history and as an individual you can lose your own identity if you are not part of either group.

I had become a social butterfly, exiled from my friends from my first year and not a fully committed member of my second first year, it was a strange experience and I'm not sure whether it enhanced my time spent in Newcastle, but it was certainly a bespoke experience and it was mine.

I had two great years, but many of you will know that most courses are three-year courses, so my only completing two years probably gives you an insight into my student life. At the end of my second first year, I once again failed my exams, I wasn't as completely distracted in my second year and I did try harder at applying myself to the demands of education, but for whatever reason, it didn't work out, I wasn't up to the task, the honeymoon was over, it was time to get to work!

I had gone up to Newcastle to learn, so when I look back at the experience, what had it taught me? It probably taught me that you can outstay your welcome, it is possible to have too much of a good thing and as we have learnt, nothing very good or very bad lasts forever, so reluctantly and with a tear in my eye, I waved a fond farewell to Newcastle, singing the Bob Hope classic, 'Thanks for the memories', as I took the last train out of Newcastle Central Station and headed to Liverpool Lime Street.

My point is that when you do things for the second time and you are cognitive of what to expect, then it just isn't as much fun, it can't be, the thrills aren't as thrilling, the highs slightly lower and the lows slightly higher.

So the question still remains, is there an optimum age to be or a time in your life to enjoy, the sybaritic existence of the student takes some beating, but who would want to be a student forever? Going to the student bar on a mobility scooter can be a great laugh, as long as you are doing it as an ironic prank, but doing it because it is your only way to get there, isn't a great look!

As with every stage in life, all that you are doing is simply preparing for the next step, the next incarnation of you, whatever that may be; of course, you are always you, but as we know we change daily, not just physically and mentally, but also emotionally, the not stepping into the same river twice analogy really is a powerful observation!

This is all part of the process of the stay, for those fortunate enough to check in, enjoy their stay and ultimately check out, we are given the opportunity to become ourselves, it is up to us what we do with the opportunity.

The antithesis of the folly of youth would be old age, a time of life when invariably, yet unavoidably we experience the worst that life has to offer, a time when we start to feel our aches and pains and illness tends to linger, with greater impact, reshaping our lives and changing our expectations as we enter the final few days of our stay in this hotel, this can also be an extremely sad time as randomly, with all of the accuracy that the national lottery draw offers, those friends that have shared our time in the hotel, begin, one by one to pack their cases, leave their rooms for the final time and hand their keys in at reception, never to be seen again, no longer sharing a drink at the bar or a friendly chat in a favourite restaurant, or even bumping into them in the village and mundanely observing the quality of that day's weather!

Who amongst us would choose this as the time of life to be the one in which we would remain forever, when there are far better options available to us to choose from.

But maybe that is the point, it's all part of the game, you go through each of the stages in turn, some good, some bad, you don't get to choose your favourite time and keep on doing it, that wouldn't be fair because there are others waiting to take their turn, awaiting their opportunity to check in and to do those things that you are and have been doing.

It's a marathon, a twenty-six-mile race, so you don't stop running at twenty miles in the marathon and declare that you've finished, you carry on to the finishing line, yes you're still running along quite nicely and you may be struggling or even starting to feel in pain, you start to consider that if you have to go any further, it will feel worse.

So you don't give in, you keep going maybe at a slower pace because you have to, but you are determined to get there, so you run for the remaining six miles determined to finish the course and once completed, you can bask in the glory of the achievement, of reaching the finishing line, getting to the end where you meet others who know what it takes, who have all been through exactly the same as you, inevitably you share the feeling, the overwhelming emotion with others, who like you have achieved something really special.

When you consider any visit that you have ever made to a hotel, throughout the whole experience, do you find that there is a best time to be there? We are presented with a full range of options maybe it is the moment when you arrive, this is a time when the rest of your stay lies in front of you, you are looking forward to making new friends, discovering new places and new adventures or maybe it is it when you have been staying there for a few days, enjoying your time there, you have got to know the staff, you have made several acquaintances around the place, it's a time when you feel comfortable, you feel that you know your way around the hotel and those places surrounding it that you like to visit or stop by, having a drink, or a little food, or simply to sit peacefully and to contemplate your existence.

Or just maybe, it could be as you enter the last couple of days of your stay, a time when you are possibly looking forward to getting home or wherever you are headed next, you feel that you have done all of the things you want to, your enthusiasm for discovery is not as it was in those early days, you have become a little tired of the same menus, the same faces around the place, you may be missing some of those who have left before you, those fellow guests that you got to know well and who have now checked out, meaning that the whole experience, has become an existence and it was those other faces that helped to make it all so special and without them, although you are surrounded by a sea of new faces, it just isn't the same.

Sometimes, depending on how good or bad the whole stay has been, you simply can't wait to get out of the place and any alternative, no matter where it is, or how unpalatable it may appear could be considered to be a good alternative.

As with most of our lives, that part that we choose to label, the best time of our lives isn't necessarily the same stage of our life for each of us, it is subjective, for instance, they could be those wonderful years of our youth, when life is carefree or contrasted by those rewarding years in your middle age when you have established your career and possibly have a family, but for nearly all of us, it is usually when we feel that things are so good in our lives, so good that we never want them to end, yet sadly and in many cases, we find that many times, those times have ended and it is only when we look back, it is when they've gone that we have an appreciation for what we had.

'Live every day like it's your last, because one day you will be right', has been attributed to many, from Ray Charles to Benny Hill. Whoever originated the phrase is irrelevant, but what it does is to send a powerful message to us all, with one instruction and that is to do it all, to do it all and not slow up, make sure you extract the optimum from every waking moment, because one day it will all be over.

I have already considered in the earlier chapter, *Look at the View from the Balcony*, how your attitude to your stay here can determine its quality and I do believe that my own attitude to life is unconditional, I don't like negativity, avoiding it personally at all costs and disliking it immensely in other people and I am certainly a glass half full type of person, there are indeed people who are glass half empty, we know who they are, but worse than that, I've actually met some people who haven't even got a glass.

We know only too well how your environmental conditions such as, whichever part of the world you are born, whether your parents are committed to bringing you up with values, whether your family is rich or poor, there are many factors that influence your own stay in the hotel and therefore inform your quality of life, as I mentioned when we have looked at its effects earlier, but in spite of any negative influences, no matter how destructive, I maintain, certainly from my own perspective that you have personal responsibility, everything comes from within, the onus it is on you, it is your own attitude that determines and informs how pleasant your stay is.

How often have you heard a friend say, 'I stayed there, but I never enjoyed it'? Well, unless there was something fundamentally catastrophic about the stay, then wherever you find yourself, you have a responsibility to yourself and those with you to optimise the enjoyment of your stay and those who choose to moan about it reflects more on themselves as an individual, it tells us more about them as people than anything else.

When this is applied to our time staying in this hotel, it tells me that some of us will not have a great life and that is partially because of their own attitude to the whole experience and in putting it into context, when applied in the strictest terms of this book, they have stayed in the hotel and wouldn't recommend it and given the opportunity, they probably wouldn't stay there again.

This is as individual as the lives of the more than eight billion people currently staying here, most will have enjoyed the stay and would come back, if they were to be given the opportunity, but inevitably, there will be those of us who haven't enjoyed it for whatever reason, dare I suggest that it is possibly one of the triptych of either money, health or relationships that have been lacking in their lives, one of the three has been so disappointing or even disastrous that it has put them off for life, or even the afterlife and they are glad to see the end of it all.

The point is that not every single person who has stayed in the hotel will have either had or will be having a great time and if we can have the ability to be cognoscente of this at all times, then doing unto others as we would have them do unto us would become our daily mantra.

In spite of our own busy lives, we should try to consider the lives of those we come into contact with daily and maybe make allowances for those who may be struggling and need a little compassion or understanding.

Of course, we don't always know when a fellow guest is struggling, there can be obvious outward signs, but these are not a given, people can hide the signs of personal struggle and pride can be a stubborn master, yet kindness and decency, which cost nothing, can be worth a fortune.

Which floor are you on is an often heard expression, especially after checking into a hotel when you are spending time there with friends, because more often than not, the floor that you room is on, a room which is allocated randomly at reception as you check in, but can give an immediate indication of, potentially at least, how much more enjoyable your stay will be and inevitably this could make an impact on your time here.

Obviously, it totally depends upon you as a person, but for me it is better if you are able to define your environment and it's not a case of allowing your environment to define you, which I think applies not only depending on your allocated room, as in this instance, but similarly as a constant way of leading your life, it is you that defines you, nothing else defines you, whether it's temporary living accommodation, clothes, or even a relationship, you control you and the opportunity to define ourselves is the greatest and toughest test of all, but it can also be the most rewarding.

By its very nature, the allocation of rooms is a random experience and could find you either looking over the bins at the back of the hotel or the romantic moonlit bay at the front, given the choice of those two options, the vast majority, if not all of us would choose the bay view and for obvious reasons, not least of those is that the ever-changing bay view would give us a feeling of well-being that would inevitably improve our stay, whereas the bins view would simply afford us a view of the cleaners and kitchen porters bringing that days rubbish to be out for collection.

Of course, we don't spend all of our days in our room, never venturing beyond our door, but we spend sufficient time in there, days and nights, it is our personal sanctuary during our stay, it is our safe space and anything that enhances the sense of wellbeing it provides, the better for us and those we share it with.

But the point of this chapter is far more than simply a clever play on words, which obviously I think it is, after all it is a book, but also the point is, as we have already established, nothing or nobody is perfect and that each of us are flawed and our flaws as well as impacting on our own lives more often than not in a negative way, but we need also to acknowledge that our flaws, instead of perceiving them and accepting the inevitability of them as a negative characteristic then we can take control and instead, we can decide to see them as a positive, something to build on, part of the road to self-improvement and then instead of a drain, they can then serve to give us purpose in life.

Initially, we need to identify our flaws and once we have and we have accepted them as such, then we can go about looking for a little bit of self-improvement and in the process making ourselves better people, the nice thing is that any success, any personal development will give us a sense of accomplishment and any achievement that we make in our lives is to be celebrated.

Flaws are for everyone, nobody is perfect, a flaw is a weakness and any weakness needs strengthening, changing it from a weakness to a strength, it is how you handle these foibles that can give us a purpose in life, on the understanding that we are all flawed, which means that every single one of us is simply a work in progress.

Lost property is an essential function of every hotel but more importantly for our purposes, loss of anything is relevant to everybody's life in the hotel, there is an inevitability of every persons stay in the hotel and that is loss and merely depending of what is lost, then the impact can range from immaterial and insignificant to life-changing and in between we have every emotion contained within those two extremes.

At one end of the scale are those small things, things that we lose along the way, from a set of cuff links or a tie left behind after a raucous wedding party, to the total antithesis of the loss of a person and even more importantly the people who are sharing our stay with us in the hotel.

It was this chapter that saw the creation of my own portmanteau, the newly created Loperty, a word that can now be used the world over, which combines both lost and property to provide a unique word for the ubiquitous hotel service; whether Loperty permeates our global language as an accepted unification to give lost property its own unique descriptor, we shall see and in the great scheme of things is rather irrelevant, but can you imagine if it did?

The loss of those sentient beings that share our stay can range from our parents, relatives and close friends and acquaintances, right through and in no particular order to the animals that we call our pets.

In fact, I am aware of some people who actually and possibly understandably prefer their pets to people, now that could be a reflection on some of the people that they know, but in many cases I can only agree with them.

Relationships with animals can be some of the most beautiful that any human can experience during their stay in the hotel, different yes, but equally as rewarding and it is because of the strength of the bonds that we build with them, that the loss of a household pet can cause staggering grief indeed sometimes the loss of a pet can be as crushing as that of a human, but the whole point of loss is how we navigate the inevitability of it.

Unfortunately, loss is inexorable during our stay here and it is how we come through that loss that makes the remainder of our stay bearable, or in some cases unbearable. Indeed, I have friends, one specifically that I am reminded of, who has never quite got over the loss of their partner and it appears to me as an outsider to be making the rest of their stay here in the hotel virtually unbearable.

Outwardly, more often than not, they present a brave face to the rest of the world, which at times I have seen crack and it is this which gives me a belief that internally the grief remains as intense as it always has, so much so that their own being collapses as memories are recalled such was the intensity of the relationship and all that relationship brought with it and now, without that other person, their life becomes virtually intolerable.

There are no easy answers, the answers such as they are, come from within and yet this simple statement is the key to our personal satisfaction of our time in the hotel.

We arrive alone and we leave alone and everything that happens to us during our stay is guided by our free will, our freedom but with responsibility acknowledging the rules of the society in which we live.

Then we had a look at changeover day, which I believe is yet another function of every single hotel on the planet, and eponymously it does the hard work for us, defining for us as individuals a time of change, whether it's arriving in the hotel for the first time or leaving it for good, a process which every single one of us has to go through, be they king or pauper, thereby giving to us an opportunity to face one of the few universal events in life.

Change is one of those few things to be such, it is omnipresent and fortunately it is permanent, it is happening second by the second and it is forever, a fundamental to our existence.

In every hotel, changeover day is every day, we see people arriving and departing every day of the week, for me the function of changeover mirrors life itself, whether it is seeing those people being born every day as the latest guests to check in at reception, the new arrivals in the hotel or it is those unfortunate people who are dying, as they check out of the hotel for the last time, both occurring every single second of every single day.

The excitement of the newly arrived and the sadness surrounding departures are a fundamental part of every hotel's daily life, but without this constant flow of arrivals and departures the hotel wouldn't exist, like the world our society thrives on constant renewal, and constant renewal inevitably leads to change, to evolution, progress and improvement, however, whenever and in which way that manifests itself and of course all change is not good, it is not always for the better. The excitement of those arriving at the hotel is a shared experience, mainly amongst those who are checking in at reception for the very first time and this excitement can be found on any maternity ward of your local hospital every day of the week, where new arrivals are greeted with incredible happiness and unbounded joy.

While at the other end of the scale, those who are leaving, checking out of the hotel having had sufficient time during their stay to build up friendships with fellow guests, those people whose stay has coincided with the departing guest and it is these relationships that inevitably make for tremendous sadness when anybody checks out for the last time.

This chapter and the significance of its role in our world is fundamental to this book and in the comparison of life to a hotel, I cannot underestimate how the welcoming of new arrivals and the long goodbyes of departing friends are as crucial to our existence as to the running of any hotel you care to visit.

I have fallen in love with this chapter, I feel that it has helped to shape my own thinking because life changes day to day, second to second and as part of this process, sometimes there are quantum leaps, which have the ability to change the dynamics of our lives forever.

It is important to acknowledge that change happens by the second, but equally as important to realise that time is a man made construct and although it is a fundamental of our time here, it may actually be a total irrelevance.

We may have made up our own rules and foolishly be deluding ourselves that we have worked it all out, but have we? We are all aging gradually and with each passing minute, we change, not noticeably and not even demonstrably but it is happening and there is absolutely nothing that we can do about it.

Fortunately for us, every other person around us changes too, progressing at exactly the same rate as ourselves, which is a phenomenal thing when you actually sit down and take the time to consider this process, like a mudslide it is a thing of pure natural beauty, nothing gets in its way and it has an energy of its own.

This change is mirrored in the life of the hotel, where daily, as new guests arrive and others who have come to the end of their stay are departing the hotel, the process is organic, it is a defining part of the process and is documented as the living parts of the hotel, the life blood of its existence, us the guests, change by the day and necessarily the hotel evolves.

To me, this appears to be of such fundamental importance, that even as I write this, I believe further study of daily change could necessitate a book of its own, but currently it is merely a chapter in this book and therefore it simply helps to complete the picture as a part of my own thinking.

Housekeeping is another of those major functions of every hotel, more often than not having its very own autonomous department in most hotels and as such it is one that allows me to draw the parallel of the running of the hotel on a day-to-day basis with our own lives, paying particular attention to the basic but vital considerations that we all need to make, both consciously and subconsciously every day of our lives in order to be a member of society, or for our purposes a guest during our stay.

We abide by the rules of the hotel and adhere to its restrictions, enjoying the facilities that the establishment has to offer and behaving as any decent guest would do, in order to optimise our own enjoyment and that of fellow guests.

Our actions, however insignificant they may be, all have reactions and we all have personal responsibility to be an upstanding member of our society, because after all, we are all just guests staying in the hotel temporarily.

Yes, we have freedom of choice allowing for self-expression, allowing us to choose as an individual to express ourselves freely, which thankfully in the western culture that I live, we are allowed to have freedom of expression but that freedom comes with responsibilities, to act within those societal norms, but those norms change and as we see, as the norms change so society changes, which is often described as progress, but indeed this is not always the case.

What these changes mean is that both you and I inevitably become dinosaurs, or as I prefer to say, we become dodos. The dodo, the ill-fated bird, became extinct because it was unable to adapt to its changing environment, whereas the dinosaur became extinct through a catastrophic act of nature, a subtle difference I agree, and though both examples resulted in extinction for their victims, their ways of contemplating their ultimate disappearance offers a couple of different lessons for us all to consider.

If we take a look at just one current example of change manifesting as progress, when I was 16 and about to go into the sixth form at school, everybody in the cohort, considered themselves to be either a male or female and outwardly at least, everybody was straight, now I am not naive enough to believe that they were, of course they weren't, of course gays and lesbians existed within the group and rightly so, they are as much a part of society as any random heterosexual, however if we contrast that with the current experience of one of our friends' 16-year-old daughter who is at a grammar school in West Yorkshire and in her group of six form chums she has four friends who are in the process of transitioning, two of whom who are gay and four lesbians, six are non-binary and one identifies as a toadstool!

There is an appetite for individuals to express their sexuality, with a freedom to identify as they choose, all vastly different from my school days and we are encouraged to embrace their freedom of expression and indulge their lifestyle in choices.

Inevitably, the two genders that I grew up believing to be the ultimate definition of sexual expression are currently being replaced by between sixty and eighty genders depending on your view, and the day of the week, no doubt there will be more as the boundaries get pushed even further and what today appears to be incredible to my inner dinosaur will in the future appear to be mainstream, because as we know, change is the only constant.

Currently in the hotel, we have the Green Agenda which is yet is another movement that is taking society in a different direction, seeing climate activists, along with numerous political pressure groups effecting not only the daily lives of citizens but impacting the decisions of governments across the world and putting pressure on them, challenging their insistence on exploration for fossil fuels, such as oil and coal, demanding the increased usage of renewable energy, directly effecting transportation both public and private and even changing the way we farm both crops and livestock, we are in the early comparatively early stages of these movements therefore we will await to discover what the new norms will become and how they change direction for society.

As you read this book, obviously depending on your age, let's say that if you're anywhere over thirty-five, and taking the emotional aspect out of the conversation, can you imagine their bewilderment if your grandparents came back to the hotel for a week? They wouldn't have a clue what was going on!

The hotel and the accepted norms that they left behind as they checked out would be far different from the accepted norms of the hotel today, the one that they would be checking back into for a return visit. The changes are too many to mention but they range from something as basic as indoor toilets instead of the back yard, to computers to mobile phones to fast food delivery at home, or maybe sexuality and gender issues, to electric cars, their heads would be spinning.

But this will happen to all of us, we are all just a product of our generation, we drive change in our formative years and then satiate ourselves that we have created a better place, but then new guests arrive and feel that they can improve the place and so pick up the gauntlet that we have carelessly dropped, allowing them to have their opportunity to bring the change they feel that is needed.

Not all change is good, of course, we know this, because in order to achieve change, there are mistakes made along the way and we know already that nothing is perfect, because perfect is as impossible to define as impossible is to achieve, because in any situation, just like people themselves, their individual demands are so varied that to fully satisfy each person is impossible and therefore not achievable.

Housekeeping in the hotel provides an environment that enables us to enjoy our stay, but we as guests also have a duty to our fellow guests, current and future, to treat the place with respect.

Most hotels have a guestbook which gives the guest an opportunity to comment on their stay, indeed a couple of hotels that I have been to have made a big thing of the guestbook, displaying it in the reception and inviting the guests from around the world to write down their country of origin and a suitable comment, usually complimentary about their time spent in the hotel.

I remember staying at a hotel in the centre of Amsterdam a couple of years ago and the week before we were staying there, the pop star Rihanna had stayed there while playing a concert at the Amsterdam Arena. She had taken time to sign the super-size guestbook, which was in a glass case in the entrance hall, effectively telling the world, 'hey, this is a great place to stay and is enjoyed by superstars and A-listers!'

The guestbook is always signed at the end of your stay, just as the whole experience comes to an end, memories are fresh and emotions are high, enhancing any feelings that you may have had during your stay.

Our legacy in life is sometimes written but more often than not it is in the memories that are still here, those we have left behind, those who have enjoyed us being a part of their stay, but once those memories fade, replaced by new ones and those people who, just like a full guestbook, are replaced by a brand-new guestbook, the old one is taken away and left on a dusty shelf, maybe in lost property, wherever it may reside it is unlikely to be seen or heard of ever again, because it is a record of a fixed passage of time, relevant mostly to those guests that have stayed during that glorious period.

Apart from our memories, we can look back at the photographs and reminisce, sharing those moments with friends, but ultimately that's all we have, what we were, what we've done and what we had. The stark reality of it all is that we've stayed in the hotel and soon it will be someone else's turn. As significant or as insignificant as we were ultimately becomes an irrelevance, nobody gets bonus points or extra time in the hotel for the good work that they may have done or indeed conversely nobody gets penalised for bad deeds done during their stay.

As I get older, I have a growing sense that karma, the principle of cause and effect exists or if it doesn't exist fully as we have come to understand it, then the principle certainly has a grain of truth in it.

The thought that good actions and good intent positively influence the future of an individual whereas bad actions and bad intent, negatively impact the life of the doer, makes sense, but does it justify its own theory, can't we just say you reap what you sow?

If you think about it logically then believing that somebody who constantly does bad things will ultimately run out of luck, whereas someone who is constantly decent and does good things will more often than not attract good.

We can intellectualise that by calling it karma, but maybe it's just luck, but then, if you believe that good luck exists, you also have to believe that bad luck exists and although you would welcome good luck all day long, you would shun bad luck, whenever that imposter would dare to show itself!

Photographs flicked through remind us of our glory days, the highs and sometimes the lows, a way to trigger memories that we may have left behind, but precious nonetheless, but life has moved on the days of physical photographs that we used to hold and keep at the back of a drawer, gone forever, replaced by new technology, where now we have our memories of mind numbing mediocrity recorded hourly and carried with us wherever we go.

This is progress, instead of isolated highlights recording those very special moments, the kids of today will now become their own documentary makers, with themselves as the subject, it can't be long before a human dash cam becomes an inevitability, recording every waking moment, the footage is voluminous, but when do we sit down to review the accumulated archive, the great body of work, a time to watch ourselves having a great time, or doing something significant and if we do, is this recorded for posterity too.

This fixation with ourselves is a narcissist's dream, with the tech giants more than happy to indulge us, as it creates opportunities for an endless procession of advertisers desperate to push the product, as marketeers expand into this new space.

Surely this era of societal development can only be as temporary as the hula hoop, the rah-rah skirt or the Walkman and the dinosaurs of this generation will be extinct before you can say Chicxulub Impactor.

Then there is the question that I would ask any friends returning from a long trip or a stay in a hotel, in this case and in this hotel, if at the end of your stay it would be incredible to be given the option to do it all again, but this time knowing what was good and what was bad, indulging yourself in the pleasures and avoiding the things that cause pain.

I don't doubt that if we were given the opportunity to do so, nearly all of us would grab the opportunity to do it all again, not just because we were unsure of knowing what a future of not doing it all again would hold, is there an alternative?

If we did get to do it all again, could we right the wrongs or simply enjoy it all one more time? Sadly, I don't believe this option exists, we are never given the opportunity to rinse and repeat but what do I know! You will have your own ideas and as we know, they are valid as those of Aristotle, Plato or your next-door neighbour, because factually nobody knows, nobody can tell you with any certainty that you are right or wrong.

What we do know is that both you and I are lucky enough to be staying in the hotel today; yes, we may be at different stages of our stay and all we can do is enjoy it all and realise that one day we will both be gone, we will have checked out and somebody else will be staying in our rooms, doing the same things that we have done and both you and I will be long forgotten.

I sincerely hope that you enjoy the rest of your stay, tick off those bucket list items that you still have to do, enjoy times with your family and friends and, after all of that, I will see you with your suitcases in reception.